Slavery and Sacred Texts

In the decades before the Civil War, Americans appealed to the nation's sacred religious and legal texts – the Bible and the Constitution – to address the slavery crisis. The ensuing political debates over slavery deepened interpreters' emphasis on historical readings of the sacred texts, and in turn, these readings began to highlight the unbridgeable historical distances that separated nineteenth-century Americans from biblical and founding pasts. While many Americans continued to adhere to a belief in the Bible's timeless teachings and the Constitution's enduring principles, some antislavery readers, including Theodore Parker, Frederick Douglass, and Abraham Lincoln, used historical distance to reinterpret and use the sacred texts as antislavery documents. By using the debate over American slavery as a case study, Jordan T. Watkins traces the development of historical consciousness in antebellum America, showing how a growing emphasis on historical readings of the Bible and the Constitution gave rise to a sense of historical distance.

Jordan T. Watkins is Assistant Professor of Church History and Doctrine at Brigham Young University. Previously, he was a coeditor at The Joseph Smith Papers Project.

Cambridge Historical Studies in American Law and Society

Recognizing legal history's growing importance and influence, the goal of this series is to chart legal history's continuing development by publishing innovative scholarship across the discipline's broadening range of perspectives and subjects. It encourages empirically creative works that take legal history into unexplored subject areas, or that fundamentally revise our thinking about familiar topics; it also encourages methodologically innovative works that bring new disciplinary perspectives and techniques to the historical analysis of legal subjects.

Series Editor
Christopher Tomlins, *University of California, Berkeley*

Previously published in the series:

Ashley T. Rubin, *The Deviant Prison: Philadelphia's Eastern State Penitentiary and the Origins of America's Modern Penal System, 1829–1913*
Nate Holdren, *Injury Impoverished: Workplace Accidents, Capitalism, and Law in the Progressive Era*
Catherine Wells, *Oliver Wendell Holmes: A Willing Servant to an Unknown God*
Michael F. Conlin, *The Constitutional Origins of the American Civil War*
Angela Fernandez, *Pierson v. Post, The Hunt for the Fox: Law and Professionalization in American Legal Culture*
Justin Desautels-Stein, *The Jurisprudence of Style: A Structuralist History of American Pragmatism and Liberal Legal Thought*
William Kuby, *Conjugal Misconduct: Defying Marriage Law in the Twentieth-Century United States*
Rebecca E. Zietlow, *The Forgotten Emancipator: James Mitchell Ashley and the Ideological Origins of Reconstruction*
Robert Daniel Rubin, *Judicial Review and American Conservatism: Christianity, Public Education, and the Federal Courts in the Reagan Era*
Matthew Crow, *Thomas Jefferson, Legal History, and the Art of Recollection*
Oren Bracha, *Owning Ideas: The Intellectual Origins of American Intellectual Property, 1790–1909*
Anne Twitty, *Before Dred Scott: Slavery and Legal Culture in the American Confluence, 1787–1857*
Leia Castañeda Anastacio, *The Foundations of the Modern Philippine State: Imperial Rule and the American Constitutional Tradition in the Philippine Islands, 1898–1935*
Robert Deal, *The Law of the Whale Hunt: Dispute Resolution, Property Law, and American Whalers, 1780–1880*

Sandra F. Vanburkleo, *Gender Remade: Citizenship, Suffrage, and Public Power in the New Northwest, 1879–1912*
Reuel Schiller, *Forging Rivals: Race, Class, Law, and the Collapse of Postwar Liberalism*
Ely Aaronson, *From Slave Abuse to Hate Crime: The Criminalization of Racial Violence in American History*
Stuart Chinn, *Recalibrating Reform: The Limits of Political Change*
Ajay K. Mehrotra, *Making the Modern American Fiscal State*
Yvonne Pitts, *Family, Law, and Inheritance in America: A Social and Legal History of Nineteenth-Century Kentucky*
David M. Rabban, *Law's History*
Kunal M. Parker, *Common Law, History, and Democracy in America, 1790–1900*
Steven Wilf, *Law's Imagined Republic*
James D. Schmidt, *Industrial Violence and the Legal Origins of Child Labor*
Rebecca M. McLennan, *The Crisis of Imprisonment: Protest, Politics, and the Making of the American Penal State, 1776–1941*
Tony A. Freyer, *Antitrust and Global Capitalism, 1930–2004*
Davison Douglas, *Jim Crow Moves North*
Andrew Wender Cohen, *The Racketeer's Progress*
Michael Willrich, City of Courts,*Socializing Justice in Progressive Era Chicago*
Barbara Young Welke, *Recasting American Liberty: Gender, Law and the Railroad Revolution, 1865–1920*
Michael Vorenberg, *Final Freedom: The Civil War, the Abolition of Slavery, and the Thirteenth Amendment*
Robert J. Steinfeld, *Coercion, Contract, and Free Labor in the Nineteenth Century*
David M. Rabban, *Free Speech in Its Forgotten Years*
Jenny Wahl, *The Bondsman's Burden: An Economic Analysis of the Common Law of Southern Slavery*
Michael Grossberg, *A Judgment for Solomon: The d'Hauteville Case and Legal Experience in the Antebellum South*

Slavery and Sacred Texts

The Bible, the Constitution, and Historical Consciousness in Antebellum America

JORDAN T. WATKINS

Brigham Young University, Utah

CAMBRIDGE
UNIVERSITY PRESS

University Printing House, Cambridge CB2 8BS, United Kingdom

One Liberty Plaza, 20th Floor, New York, NY 10006, USA

477 Williamstown Road, Port Melbourne, VIC 3207, Australia

314–321, 3rd Floor, Plot 3, Splendor Forum, Jasola District Centre, New Delhi – 110025, India

79 Anson Road, #06–04/06, Singapore 079906

Cambridge University Press is part of the University of Cambridge.

It furthers the University's mission by disseminating knowledge in the pursuit of education, learning, and research at the highest international levels of excellence.

www.cambridge.org
Information on this title: www.cambridge.org/9781108478144
DOI: 10.1017/9781108784344

© Jordan T. Watkins 2021

This publication is in copyright. Subject to statutory exception and to the provisions of relevant collective licensing agreements, no reproduction of any part may take place without the written permission of Cambridge University Press.

First published 2021

A catalogue record for this publication is available from the British Library.

ISBN 978-1-108-47814-4 Hardback

Cambridge University Press has no responsibility for the persistence or accuracy of URLs for external or third-party internet websites referred to in this publication and does not guarantee that any content on such websites is, or will remain, accurate or appropriate.

To Micah,
not because you'd care to read it,
but because I love you so much.

Contents

Acknowledgments	*page* x
Prologue	xiv
Introduction	1
1 "Recourse Must Be Had to the History of Those Times"	28
2 "The Ground Will Shake"	69
3 "Texts ... Designed for Local and Temporary Use"	109
4 "The Further We Recede from the Birth of the Constitution"	134
5 "The Culture of Cotton Has Healed Its Deadly Wound"	183
6 "Times Now Are Not as They Were"	229
7 "We Have to Do Not ... with the Past, but the Living Present"	262
8 A "Modern Crispus Attucks"	300
Conclusion	329
Epilogue	345
Index	356

Acknowledgments

Ralph Waldo Emerson wrote that "our knowledge is the amassed thought and experience of innumerable minds."[1] In crafting this book, I relied on the insights and assistance of countless individuals. But there are people that I can count and names that I must mention. This book started as a dissertation written under the supervision of David Holland at the University of Nevada, Las Vegas (UNLV). David, more than anyone else, challenged me to think carefully about the historical developments and ideas examined in this book. I thank him for his encouragement throughout the lengthy process of completing my dissertation and revising it for publication. For more than a decade, David has provided me with timely and timeless counsel. I am grateful for his expansive idea of what it means to be an advisor. I am a better scholar and a better person for knowing him.

I am also indebted to the rest of my dissertation committee. Elizabeth Nelson pushed me in ways no other professor did. Her penchant for incisive critique is only matched by her capacity for abiding care. Colin Loader's close reading helped me clarify my terms, and Gregory Brown's broad suggestions directed me to carefully consider the project's historiographical significance. As an outside reader, Anne Stevens offered a fresh perspective and displayed great patience as my dissertation evolved.

Other faculty members at UNLV provided consistent intellectual stimulation and practical academic direction. Andy Kirk is among the

---

[1] Ralph Waldo Emerson, "Quotation and Originality," in *The Complete Works of Ralph Waldo Emerson*, ed. Edward Waldo Emerson, 12 vols., Centenary Edition (Boston, 1903–4), 8:200.

most supportive mentors I have had. His advice will serve me well throughout my career. I had the privilege of working with two wonderfully attentive department chairs, David Wrobel and David Tanenhaus. They backed up their supportive words with supportive acts. William Bauer, Gregory Hise, Michelle Tusan, and Andrew Bell also served as excellent professorial guides.

My scholarly creditors include those I worked with at Claremont Graduate University. I dreaded attending Robert Dawidoff's Wednesday class in my first semester of graduate school – I never had a more exacting professor in the classroom. And yet, in that first class, and in subsequent semesters, I developed a great affinity for Robert's idiosyncratic approach. Janet Farrell Brodie, whose guidance was crucial during the period in which I grew most as a graduate student, graciously acted as the second reader for my thesis. Richard Bushman served as my thesis advisor. Aside from David Holland, Richard has been the single most influential force in my academic career. His early and enduring support gave me great confidence. Richard's approach to the past, like his approach to people, inspires imitation. I could not be prouder of my academic lineage.

A number of other colleagues have made this book possible. Margo Minardi, who read an early draft of the manuscript and various iterations of new chapters, guided me in preparing the manuscript for publication. John Turner, Eran Shalev, and Matt Mason also read all or portions of the manuscript and provided invaluable feedback. Along with these excellent scholars, Spencer Fluhman, Dean Grodzins, and John Stauffer offered insight on this project and inspired me with the confidence to pursue publication. Throughout the process of revising my dissertation for publication as a book, David Golding and Ben Park gave me substantive feedback and sustaining encouragement in both writing and conversation. Summer Cherland also provided me with helpful suggestions in the late stages of writing and revising.

This project has spanned multiple jobs, including a beautiful two years at the Joseph Smith Papers Project (JSPP), at which I enjoyed the friendship of close colleagues, including members of the famed "walking group." As this book project reached maturation, I relied on two members of that group – Mason Allred and Christopher Blythe – for predictably incisive suggestions. Since 2018, I have benefited from a supportive department and inspiring colleagues at Brigham Young University (BYU). There are many individuals, at both the JSPP and at BYU, who have made my short professional career a wonderfully enriching experience.

I am also indebted to many archivists. I am especially grateful to the staff at the following institutions: the Massachusetts Historical Society (especially Conrad Wright and Kate Viens); the American Antiquarian Society (especially Paul Erickson); the Boston Athenæum (especially Mary Warnement); the Virginia Historical Society (especially Frances Pollard); the Boston Public Library (especially Kim Reynolds and Shawn Casey); the Watkinson Library (especially Henry Arneth); and the Historical & Special Collections Department at the Harvard Law School Library (especially Karen Beck and Jane Kelly). I also received helpful assistance from the staffs at Harvard's Houghton Library and the Library of Congress. These kind and knowledgeable people helped me locate sources that concretized my abstract thoughts.

In different ways, three editors paved the way for this publication. Dick Holway at the University of Virginia Press graciously informed me how to navigate the process of proposing a project for publication. Suzy Bills and the staff of the Faculty Publishing Service at BYU combed through the manuscript, correcting errors and asking useful questions that helped me sharpen my writing and arguments. Chris Tomlins at Cambridge University Press (CUP) walked me through the process of readying this, my first book, for publication. Chris was as kind as he was informative. Rachel Blaifeder, Cecelia Cancellaro, and others at CUP also shepherded this book toward its completion.

This book was born from loss. In 2012, Micah, my youngest sister, took her life. That blow, which left me reeling, came weeks before I was scheduled to take my qualifying exams. Not knowing what to do, I reached out to David Holland, who provided comforting words and freed me from the guilt of having to spend any time worrying about school. After a week of deep mourning, I made the difficult decision to return to UNLV, in part to distract myself from thoughts that had left me spiraling. A fellow student and friend, Nick Pellegrino, who read every word of my dissertation and provided helpful feedback on later iterations, dove into exam preparation with me. During this time, other friends reached out in ways that allowed me to move forward. I will never forget their efforts to mourn with me and provide a measure of relief.

Alongside the help from these and "innumerable minds," the support that has mattered most is that which I have most taken for granted – that of my family. The love of siblings, in-laws, nieces, and nephews sustained me throughout my graduate school experience and beyond. Their love sustains me still. Above all else, the encouragement and affection of my parents, to whom I owe a massive debt that they know I can never repay, gave me the strength to write this book. Finally, my wife, Madi, deserves special recognition. While this project is older than our relationship, time is not a proper measure of her support. She understands me better than anyone and somehow still loves me. Thank you.

Prologue

Black Lives Matter. One of the most enduring meanings of this phrase is that our laws, institutions, and policies lay bare the awful fact that in American society black lives have less value than white lives. Much of this meaning depends upon an understanding of how the past – including black enslavement and its afterlives – has shaped and continues to shape the present. As historian Joseph Ellis noted, "while all problems in American society have a history, none of them is as incomprehensible, when viewed myopically or ahistorically, as our racial dilemma."[1] In 1857, Chief Justice Roger B. Taney asserted that blacks were not citizens based on what he described as a founding-era axiom: the view that blacks "had no rights which the white man was bound to respect."[2] The Fourteenth Amendment struck down the *Dred Scott* decision, but it did not expunge the racist ideas that had shaped America's institutions, nor did it keep white Americans from inventing new means of reinforcing the social and economic gap between blacks and whites.[3] Certainly writer James Baldwin had much of this – and much else, no doubt – in mind when he wrote that "the great force of history comes from the fact that we carry it within us, are unconsciously controlled by it in many ways, and history is literally *present* in all that we do."[4] As a whole, Americans have

---

[1] Joseph J. Ellis, *American Dialogue: The Founders and Us* (New York, 2018), 50.
[2] *Dred Scott* v. *Sandford*, 60 U.S. (19 Howard) 393, 408 (1857).
[3] On these developments, see, for example, Heather Cox Richardson, *How the South Won the Civil War: Oligarchy, Democracy, and the Continuing Fight for the Soul of America* (New York, 2020).
[4] "Other Essays: The White Man's Guilt," in *James Baldwin: Collected Essays* (New York, 1998), 723, emphasis in original.

failed to come to terms with the ways in which the past has unconsciously controlled us, in part, perhaps, because we have been too busy using the past to try to control our present.

Roger Taney's infamous statement in *Dred Scott* was part of his attempt to use the past to control the present. In his decision he noted, "It is difficult at this day to realize the state of public opinion in relation to that unfortunate race which prevailed ... at the time of the Declaration of Independence and when the Constitution of the United States was framed and adopted." In pointing out the challenge before him, Taney acknowledged historical distance, or the perception of a temporal gap between past and present. He then set about solving the historical challenge he had raised. He explained that by the late 1800s blacks "had for more than a century before been regarded as beings of an inferior order, and altogether unfit to associate with the white race either in social or political relations, and so far inferior that they had no rights which the white man was bound to respect, and that the negro might justly and lawfully be reduced to slavery for his benefit." Taney described this opinion as "fixed and universal in the civilized portion of the white race."[5] The chief justice was not simply providing a historical account; he was lecturing his contemporaries, especially antislavery individuals and groups who clamored for change, on the clear relevance of the past's status quo in the present. In hopes of addressing the undesirable abolitionist agitation and resolving the crisis over southern slavery, Taney acknowledged and then set aside historical distance to recover and apply straightforward original meanings from the founding-era past. These meanings relegated blacks to the status of noncitizens in his nineteenth-century present.

Like Taney, Americans continue to appeal to the founding era in an effort to control the present.[6] Faced with unwanted change, many groups aver allegiance to static truths from the founding past. In a recent example, the Tea Party movement aligned itself with revolutionary tradition and promoted a kind of popular originalist appeal.[7] Capitalizing on this development, political commentator Glenn Beck insists that founding-era documents, including the Federalist Papers,

---

[5] *Scott v. Sandford*, 408.

[6] On the history of such uses, the beginnings of which are coeval with the founding itself, see David Sehat, *The Jefferson Rule: How the Founding Fathers Became Infallible and Our Politics Inflexible* (New York, 2015).

[7] See Jill Lepore, *The Whites of Their Eyes: The Tea Party's Revolution and the Battle over American History* (Princeton, NJ, 2007).

contain eternal truths "that apply to today's world just as much as they did in the eighteenth century."[8] To combat claims that the Papers are "outdated and irrelevant," Beck offers a twenty-first-century "translation" of the Papers even as he also urges readers to be cautious of those "who want to speak in place of those documents."[9] Such efforts to recover – and revise – founding-era texts with timeless meanings recall the antebellum appeals of Taney and others who often set aside historical distance in using founding-era words and deeds to combat unwanted developments. As seen by Taney's decision, such appeals can have far-reaching legal, social, and political implications.

Donald Trump's slogan "Make America Great Again" seems to speak to people's deep-seated desire to cast off alleged national regression; some want to restore the United States to a pristine past that never existed. This slogan, which Bill Clinton also used, originated with Ronald Reagan in the 1980s, the same decade in which some conservatives embraced jurisprudential originalism to combat the judicial activism of the 1960s. Prior to this, constitutional interpreters had used originalist arguments, but it had not been since the slavery debates of the 1840s and 1850s – detailed in Chapters 4 through 7 herein – that readers had so earnestly worked to wrest original intent from the Constitution. Late twentieth-century debates over whether or not one could discern consensus among the framers shifted originalists' focus from original intent to original meaning. Historian Daniel Rodgers suggests that these originalists from the 1980s did not desire to return to the founding past; they wanted instead to escape the complexities of history and the limitations of time.[10] This effort to lay claim to an ideal past in order to transcend history's constraints rests on a facile distinction between contemporary politics (seen as temporary and corrosive) and founding-era principles (seen as timeless and redeeming). As this book shows, participants on all sides of the antebellum debates over slavery, including Taney, worked with similar assumptions. In the face of unwanted change, they, too, tried to silence and banish historical distance.

---

[8] Glenn Beck, *The Original Argument: The Federalists' Case for the Constitution, Adapted for the 21st Century* (New York, 2011), xxvi. See also *Glenn Beck's Common Sense: The Case against an Out-of-Control Government, Inspired by Thomas Paine* (New York, 2009); and Glenn Beck and Kevin Balfe, *Being George Washington: The Indispensable Man, As You've Never Seen Him* (New York, 2011).

[9] Beck, *Original Argument*, xxxi.

[10] Daniel T. Rodgers, *Age of Fracture* (Cambridge, MA, 2011), 241.

While some twenty-first-century Americans work to restore mythic pasts by applying sacred historical texts to contemporary problems, many of their critics dismiss these attempts as either ahistorical political presentism, by which appellants force a false uniformity on complicated founding figures, or as naïve appeals to obsolete artifacts.[11] Of course, such critics cannot help but use the past for their own purposes as well; however, in doing so, they approach historical distance differently. For example, in legal scholar Louis Michael Seidman's 2012 *New York Times* op-ed, provocatively titled "Let's Give Up on the Constitution," Seidman harnessed historical distance by condemning his contemporaries' obedience to "a group of white propertied men who have been dead for two centuries, knew nothing of our present situation ... and thought it was fine to own slaves."[12] While many anxious respondents chastised Seidman – some claimed that Madison had far more to teach us "than his modern critics" – others agreed with him.[13] New York's Steven Berkowitz bemoaned "how 'bizarre' adherence to the Constitution has become."[14] And Lois Taylor of Connecticut wrote, "Finally! Someone with the courage to stop genuflecting before the Constitution!"[15] But Seidman, of course, was not the first American critic of the Constitution.[16]

Like Beck's founding-era appeals, Seidman's historically oriented critique of the Constitution has antebellum parallels. For example, abolitionist William Lloyd Garrison appealed to the Revolution to challenge his contemporaries' allegiance to the nation's legal creed. These critiques not only demonstrate the founding era's persistent allure even among the Constitution's most strident critics but also reveal the enduringly complex nature of American historical awareness. Throughout US history, the fractured experience of American political

---

[11] See, for example, Daniel A. Farber and Suzanna Sherry, *Desperately Seeking Certainty: The Misguided Quest for Constitutional Foundations* (Chicago, 2002); and Michael Austin, *That's Not What They Meant! Reclaiming the Founding Fathers from America's Right Wing* (Amherst, NY, 2012).

[12] Louis Michael Seidman, "Let's Give Up on the Constitution," *New York Times*, December 31, 2012.

[13] Richard A. Epstein, "Our Obsolete Constitution?" *Defining Ideas*, January 8, 2013.

[14] Steven Berkowitz, letter to the editor, *New York Times*, January 3, 2013.

[15] Lois Taylor, letter to the editor, *New York Times*, January 3, 2013.

[16] In a book published less than a month after his op-ed appeared in print, Seidman himself traced the origins of similarly minded critiques back to the founding era. Louis Michael Seidman, *On Constitutional Disobedience* (New York, 2012). Some recent critiques include Sanford Levinson's call for a new constitutional convention. Sanford Levinson, *Our Undemocratic Constitution: Where the Constitution Goes Wrong (and How We the People Can Correct It)* (New York, 2006).

culture has generated varying historical sensibilities. Political debates about sacred texts, in particular, have cultivated layered historical thinking, from shallow to deep.

And yet, while these varied approaches to the past persist, the contours of our historical consciousness have changed; our period is characterized by greater self and societal historical awareness. Some Americans still ignore or discard historical distance, particularly in political debates surrounding a favored past like the founding era or a sacred text like the Constitution. However, their conscious or unconscious disregard of historical distance occurs in an intellectual and political environment in which many of their contemporaries readily call out their reasoning as ahistorical or anachronistic. This signals a reversal of sorts: although many antebellum Americans viewed readings that used historical distance as heretical (even though they rarely, if ever, recognized or described the use of distance as the problem), many in our time see the failure to take distance into account as dangerous, especially in readings of sacred texts from favored pasts. This reversal began to emerge in the antebellum era.

Antebellum thinkers' attention to historical distance stemmed from the debates over slavery's constitutionality, which encouraged a new awareness of historical change and a growing recognition of the temporal separation historical change created. The challenge of calling on a historical text to answer a current crisis began to indicate to some that historical differences set off their present from a favored past, making the founding era more foreign than familiar. In particular, many antislavery agitators began to recognize the existence of a temporal divide between the late eighteenth century and the mid-nineteenth century and to acknowledge that such a divide undercut traditional approaches to the Constitution.

While some antislavery forces joined Garrison in dismissing the Constitution as outdated, others interpreted it based on claims about the framers' own expectations of abolition. In other words, instead of damning a proslavery Constitution, these abolitionists used historical distance to argue for new antislavery readings. All of this drew more attention to temporal distance. And even when figures like Taney tried to set aside distance, their interpretations made its presence undeniable. Thus, as founding-era appeals cultivated an awareness of historical distance, this distance encouraged rather than hindered innovative efforts to interpret the Constitution. This book details the ways in which the interpretive debates over slavery inspired arguments that gave rise to an emerging sense of historical distance and shows how that awareness inspired innovative readings of sacred texts.

Antebellum constitutional debates over slavery followed from and overlapped with similar debates about the Bible, another sacred text, and the much more distant era from which it emerged. Although the founding era has a singular place in the nation's imagination today, the biblical past has garnered at least as much attention; Americans have consistently turned to modern translations of ancient Hebrew and Greek texts to address momentous moral, social, and political issues. During the first half of the nineteenth century, many Americans believed the national crisis over the southern institution – along with many of the other salient issues of the day – should be resolved through a proper interpretation of the Bible.

Anticipating later developments in the constitutional realm, the biblical debate over slavery cultivated a sense of historical distance. In this debate as well, participants recognized and then set aside that distance. For example, in 1850, the eminent biblical scholar Moses Stuart used historical context to distinguish Mosaic servitude from southern slavery and to argue – as many antislavery writers did – that both Mosaic law and Christ's dispensation in the New Testament had started the process of ending slavery as a practice and institution. At the same time, however, he then disregarded the very distance his reading revealed by translating an ancient endorsement of servitude into a modern injunction to obey the Fugitive Slave Law.

Even though readers such as Stuart ignored the sense of distance that their historical readings produced, those readings nonetheless made the temporal gap between favored pasts and present times hard to ignore. Like Taney, who tried to rescue timeless truths from the founding era, Stuart attempted to unmoor universal principles from biblical contexts. Influenced, in part, by the historical lessons of European biblical criticism that had begun to spread across the Atlantic, these readings brought new attention to the vast historical differences between past and present. In the resulting intellectual environment, some antislavery readers voiced a Garrisonian-like willingness to dismiss the once enlivening but increasingly lifeless Bible. Others, however, highlighted distance not to reject the Bible but instead to find in its pages evidence that the first Christians had planted antislavery seeds meant to flower in later eras – and to insist that era had arrived. These distinct antislavery readings of the Bible, which foreshadowed similar developments in the constitutional debates, accelerated a growing awareness of the historical distance separating Americans from their favored pasts.

That sense of distance has increased in the twenty-first century, becoming more widespread even as many Americans continue to use the Bible as a central source of moral guidance. A 2018 survey commissioned by the American Bible Society suggested that the majority of American adults view the Bible as sacred and that more than half believe it to be inspired and inerrant. The survey also indicated that about forty percent of American adults agree that the Bible has too little influence in our society and the same number strongly agree that it contains all the information needed to conduct lives of meaning and purpose. From one vantage point, these numbers attest to the ancient book's staying power in modern times. However, when viewed from a historical perspective, the numbers indicate that the Bible no longer orients Americans as it once did.[17] The online query "Is the Bible still relevant?" yields a multitude of defensive articles, perhaps indicating that twenty-first-century Christians are more anxious about its status than were their antebellum predecessors.

As in constitutional interpretation, the fractured nature of our political culture continues to yield biblical readings that exhibit varieties of historical thinking. In this arena, too, unwanted change often shapes the effort to reclaim past truths. For instance, in a series of recent books political commentator Dennis Prager aims to address what he sees as our societal ills by helping "make the Bible America's book once again."[18] Prager, a conservative Jew, insists that the ten "commandments are as relevant today as when they were given over three thousand years ago."[19] While answering contemporary concerns, Prager also applies the commandments to the issue of slavery, arguing that "kidnapping people and selling them into slavery, as was done to Africans and others throughout history, is forbidden by the Eighth Commandment."[20] Furthermore, Prager explains that biblical slavery was usually a form of indentured servitude and suggests that the laws governing the institution were "more humane than laws that prevailed until the abolition of slavery in the West thousands of years later."[21] This reading echoes those of

---

[17] Barna Group, *State of the Bible 2018: Bible Engagement Segmentation* (Philadelphia, 2018), 17–22.
[18] Dennis Prager, "I'm Back. Here's Where I've Been," *National Review*, January 9, 2018.
[19] Dennis Prager, *The Ten Commandments: Still the Best Moral Code* (Washington, DC, 2015), xvii–xviii.
[20] Dennis Prager, *The Rational Bible: Exodus; God, Slavery, and Freedom* (Washington, DC, 2018), 265.
[21] Ibid., 281.

antislavery interpreters who emphasized the differences between Mosaic servitude and southern slavery.

Prager also offers another idea with antebellum roots in suggesting that the Pentateuch's approach to abolishing all forms of slavery was evolutionary rather than revolutionary. He explains, "Given how entrenched [slavery] was in every human society, had the Torah banned every form of slavery, it is quite likely many Israelites would have simply opted out of the Torah system entirely." To support this reasoning, Prager provides an analogy: "had the founders of the United States banned slavery at the outset – something many of them wished to do – there would never have been a United States of America."[22] Prager's interpretation is reminiscent of some antebellum readings of the Bible, including Moses Stuart's careful contextual reading, which highlighted historical differences and then set them aside to instruct his contemporaries on proper moral and political behavior.

Though similar antislavery readings of the Old Testament can be found among nineteenth- and twenty-first-century Americans, a sense of historical distance more fully shapes current American engagement – and disengagement – with the Bible. Whereas historical distance made the sin of slavery objectionable to some in the antebellum era, Americans now hold as axiomatic the idea that slavery is immoral. Consequently, whereas Stuart used the Mosaic example to instruct his contemporaries to obey the Fugitive Slave Law, Prager's reading suggests that the Pentateuch did not sanction the South's peculiar institution. Even as historical distance informs Prager's reading of the Bible, historical distance also has shaped the intellectual environment to which he is responding. For example, the same sense of distance that has helped make slavery's sin axiomatic has also made the Bible's relevance less obvious to modern Americans, many of whom disregard biblical interpretation as unimportant in ways that would have scandalized antebellum Americans.

A growing attention to historical distance from the biblical past can also be seen in a reordering of the nation's sacred texts: the Constitution, rather than the Bible, functions as the supreme text in American culture. The aforementioned 2018 survey published by the American Bible Society suggests that a majority of Americans "believe the U.S. Constitution itself is more important [than the Bible] for the moral fabric of our country."[23] While this development has antebellum origins, debate in the pre–Civil War era about biblical meaning held the nation's interest in a way that it

[22] Ibid., 280. [23] Barna Group, *State of the Bible*, 20.

no longer does. And so, when individuals in our era, such as Prager, earnestly plea for Americans to return to the principles outlined in a set of ancient texts, more Americans than ever before simply ignore the pleas – if they are aware of the conversation at all. That apathy depends, in part at least, on a widespread awareness of the profound temporal distinctions that divide the past and its prerogatives from the present and its needs.

While these realities make it clear that we approach the past from within an intellectual environment that is characterized by a greater overall awareness of historical change and distance, that environment has roots in the antebellum past. This book, then, provides a historical perspective from which to investigate how Americans confront their most favored pasts and sacred texts in light of historical awareness. Or, to put it differently, it shows that the intellectual roots of the call to read the Bible and the Constitution in light of historical distance and change stretch backward into antebellum soil. Our contemporary modes of historical thought were forged in antebellum fires.

While much more could be said about the ways in which the historical thinking of the past anticipated and diverges from the historical thinking of the present, this book tells a different story. This story is not about antebellum types and modern antitypes. Instead, it narrates how the biblical and constitutional debates over slavery in the decades before the Civil War gave rise to a new sense of historical distance in America. The chapters that follow show that antebellum Americans first began to sense temporal dislocation from their favored pasts in their debates over slavery. As they attempted to construct interpretive bridges to the biblical pasts and the founding era, their efforts began to suggest that the temporal gap between past and present might be unbridgeable. The interpretive debates over the peculiar institution gave rise to a new awareness of historical difference and change, and then historical distance itself became an interpretive problem. In short, slavery roused the American republic to historical consciousness.

Introduction

On June 26, 1857, in a speech given in Springfield, Illinois, Abraham Lincoln crafted a historical narrative of the American founding that countered the one that Chief Justice Roger B. Taney had used in *Dred Scott v. Sandford*. In his Supreme Court decision, given three months prior to Lincoln's address, the chief justice had admitted that if "the general words" of the preamble to the Declaration of Independence "were used in a similar instrument at this day," they would be understood to "embrace the whole human family."[1] Taney had dismissed that observation as irrelevant and, as Lincoln explained, had insisted that the declaration's authors "did not intend to include negroes."[2] Challenging Taney's assumption "that the public estimate of the black man is more favorable *now* than it was in the days of the Revolution," Lincoln argued that "in those days, our Declaration ... was ... thought to include all," while in 1857, the declaration was set aside "to aid in making the bondage of the negro universal and eternal."[3] The Kentucky-born lawyer conceded that the founders "did not mean to assert ... that all were then actually enjoying that equality" but that they "meant simply to declare the *right*, so that the *enforcement* of it might follow as fast as circumstances should permit."[4] Otherwise, Lincoln explained, if the founders had created the declaration as a temporary measure rather than a rights-bearing writ meant "for future use," then the "doings of that day had no reference to

---

[1] *Scott v. Sandford*, 410.
[2] Abraham Lincoln, "Speech at Springfield, Illinois, June 26, 1857," in *The Collected Works of Abraham Lincoln*, ed. Roy P. Basler, Marion Dolores Pratt, and Lloyd A. Dunlap (New Brunswick, NJ, 1953–55), 2:405 (hereafter cited as *CWAL*).
[3] Ibid., 2:403–04, emphasis in original.   [4] Ibid., 2:406, emphasis in original.

the present" and served only as "an interesting memorial of the dead past."[5]

The premonition of a dead revolutionary past never loomed larger than in the late 1850s, when Americans relied on founding texts to resolve the crisis over slavery, and, in turn, the crisis over slavery became a crisis of historicity.[6] A number of abolitionists already regarded the US Constitution as a relic of a bygone era, and now Taney's reading threatened to turn even the timeless Declaration into a historical curio. Debates about the meaning of these founding texts signaled a growing awareness of the discreteness of the founding era. Even Lincoln's response drew attention to the distinct nature of the period to which he appealed. In noting the founders' expedient approach to slavery and their anticipation of liberty's spread, his account acknowledged slavery's strong presence in the revolutionary era. At the same time, Lincoln's narrative identified a historical change the founders had not anticipated: the proslavery betrayal of their abolitionist expectations. Indeed, Lincoln and Taney concurred on this crucial point: times had changed. But while Taney dismissed historical change to recover a static meaning that left blacks without citizenship and its attendant rights, Lincoln used change to insist on an evolving meaning open to future possibilities about blacks' status and situation.

Figures on all sides of the slavery controversy valued context and change differently. But in their efforts to either reject or privilege the interpretive importance of these temporal valences – context and change – participants ultimately underscored the historical differences that divided their own time from the founding era. As Americans confronted the question of whether slavery was still morally acceptable – and did so in a culture shaped by sacred texts, mythic pasts, and a conflicted present – they awoke to a new awareness of temporal distance (i.e., the sense of differences in context and culture between historical periods).[7] Debates about what antislavery writers called "the peculiar institution" were at the heart of this awakening.

---

[5] Ibid., 2:406–07.
[6] I use the terms *revolutionary past* and *founding era* to refer to the period Lincoln and many other Americans appealed to in calling on founders and founding documents. This period includes the time between the writing of the Declaration of Independence and the ratification and initial implementation of the Constitution.
[7] *Historical awareness* and *historical consciousness* are scholarly terms of art that require some finessing. I most often use them to signify a growing sense that historical changes created historical distance between past and present eras, and, more specifically, between biblical and revolutionary times and nineteenth-century America.

Introduction

These debates centered on interpreting two of the most beloved texts in nineteenth-century America: the United States Constitution and the Bible. In the first few decades of the nation's existence, most Christian Americans continued to read the Bible as an ageless text with universal appeal; Abraham, Moses, and Paul spoke across vast chasms of time, and Americans listened. In the same period, the Constitution, alongside the Declaration of Independence, took on a similar status as a text without temporal constraints.[8] It became a kind of legal Bible in the new republic. Americans seamlessly applied James Madison's words to the pressing political issues of the day. Reading such texts in this way made the biblical and founding eras seem like familiar places to visit rather than distinct historical periods to study. The existence of sacred texts (i.e., unique registers of universal instruction) from favored pasts (i.e., golden ages imagined as sharing a fluid relationship with the current era) kept Americans from gaining a clear sense that historical differences and contingencies distinguished past periods from each other and from the present.

And yet, it was precisely the existence of sacred texts from favored pasts that created the possibility of profound confrontations with history. Paradoxically, the potential for recognizing historical distance is greatest when pasts that are assumed to have cultural and ideological affinities with the present receive sustained attention. Awareness of a past's pastness (i.e., its temporal distinctness in terms of human experiences, attitudes, and mentalities) requires that it first become a useful past. Indeed, a past's potential historicization rests on its presentness (i.e., its apparent affinity with the present in terms of human experiences, attitudes, and mentalities). As individuals and groups appeal to a familiar era's figures, texts, and ideas to address present social, cultural, and political issues, that era becomes a prime candidate for historicization. And so, although the enduring textual basis of both the biblical and the revolutionary pasts made these eras most favored, the very endurance of those texts also set the scene for their sustained historical investigation, which threatened to historicize them and expose their inherent archaism. And the characterization of those pasts as archaic suggested that no historical era could claim to transcend time.

---

[8] On the sacralization of the Declaration of Independence in the antebellum era, see Pauline Maier, *American Scripture: Making the Declaration of Independence* (New York, 1997), 154–208.

In antebellum America, slavery, more than anything else, induced those confrontations. Beginning in the 1830s, the issue of slavery broadened a shift to reading the Bible as a historical text – rather than an ageless and universal one – by fueling biblical interpreters' growing emphasis on historical context. This shift set the scene for a public drama about historical readings of the Constitution, which played out as the political crisis over slavery took center stage in the 1840s and 1850s. In some cases, the biblical and constitutional debates were actually bound up with each other, as demonstrated in the writings of individuals such as Theodore Parker and Moses Stuart. This overlap was not always explicit, but, as I seek to demonstrate, the historical nature of the biblical debates conditioned some constitutional interpreters to accept historical readings as normative; the language and methods used among biblical interpreters prepared the way for constitutional interpreters to use similar language and methods. In short, the process of making the Bible historical by bringing greater attention to its distinct historical contexts set the stage for the Constitution's own quick historicization.

Throughout the historicization process, the articulation and rearticulation of historical readings began to expose the archaism of America's most sacred texts and the discrete nature of its most hallowed historical epochs. As Americans began to confront history in new ways, many discovered that their favored pasts were not golden ages to reclaim but troubled eras with universal promises to fulfill. Revered texts from these pasts taught specific truths that had not yet been realized. As Americans reclaimed permanent principles from transient times, they historicized their favored pasts, which signaled that all eras, including the present, bore the marks of time. Unlike anything before, the slavery debates roused Americans to the complexities of historical change and forced them to confront favored pasts as temporally distinct, discrete, and, above all, distant.

The term *historical distance* signifies temporal dislocation and dissonance between historical periods. I use it to refer to more than the simple fact that the passing *of time* creates chronological separation between points *in time*; in my usage, *historical distance* refers to crucial distinctions in human experience across discrete historical eras. In this sense, historical distance corresponds to the social distance that sociologists observe between peoples living in close geographical proximity and the cultural distance anthropologists observe between contemporaries living in different geographic spaces. Individuals with no sociological or anthropological training also notice social and cultural differences; travelers encounter them at every turn. It is with this idea in mind that historians often invoke novelist L. P. Hartley's famous line, "The past is a foreign country."[9]

Temporal differences include material, political, religious, linguistic, legal, domestic, and intellectual distinctions. These differences are largely the products of human-driven changes that range from technological advancement, such as the invention of the railroad and the Internet, to philosophical development, such as the emergence of romanticism and postmodernism. In the era of globalization, social and cultural distances are often taken for granted – though frequently politicized and misunderstood in their particulars. But the fact of historical distance is not as readily apparent, hence, historians' frequent use of the novelist's phrase.[10]

In this book, I demonstrate antebellum Americans' growing realization that historical changes created temporal distances from their favored biblical and founding eras. The *fact* of historical distance is, of course, distinct from an *awareness* of that distance, which emerges with the recognition that irrevocable changes separate one period from another and that people from different eras inhabited fundamentally different worlds. The most profound awareness of historical distance results when individuals and groups begin to recognize that unbridgeable historical divisions and irreversible historical changes separate them from their most familiar pasts – periods populated by people believed to hold views similar to their own. Seeing such a past not as a familiar reflection of the present but instead as a distinctly other era can be disorienting. It is the shock of realizing that those pasts that feel closest, those that seem most worthy and capable of recovery, are deeply different and perhaps best left behind, that pushes the process of historicization most violently forward. This book outlines the processes by which antebellum Americans began to perceive distance from their most favored pasts: the biblical and founding eras.

I suggest that the best gauge of such awareness – though certainly not the only possible measure – is the extent to which historical distance induced novel readings of sacred texts. During the first half of the nineteenth century, lessons from biblical criticism and the demise of the founding generation encouraged a new emphasis on contextual readings of the Bible and the Constitution, respectively. An intellectual framework emerged that encouraged and even demanded that interpreters of these

---

[9] L. P. Hartley, *The Go-Between* (London, 1953; New York, 2002), 17.
[10] See, for example, David Lowenthal, *The Past is a Foreign Country* (New York, 1985).

documents consider context and change. This shift produced readings and narratives that revealed historical difference and distance.

Interpretive debates over slavery, in particular, fueled this development, forcing new kinds of confrontations with history and threatening to unsettle the once-fluid relationship between Americans' nineteenth-century present and their favored pasts. Constrained to consider anew this relationship, some readers downplayed the interpretive importance of historical distance, but others, such as Lincoln, used it to provide new readings of the nation's sacred religious and legal texts. Even as such readings indicated distance from the past, the distance did not render it dead. Instead, it provided new vantage points from which to explore favored pasts and sacred texts. In short, historical distance emerged as a powerful force for interpretive change in antebellum America.

The term *historical distance* has become shorthand for the now-derided idea that the passing of time grants detached historians the objective perspective to properly understand the past. In his book *On Historical Distance*, Mark Salber Phillips troubles this narrow historicist view, which assumes that historical distance, once recognized, can be bridged. Instead, Phillips tracks the persistence of distance as a capacious concept. Not unlike Hayden White's approach in *Metahistory*, Phillips investigates the relationship between historical representations and aesthetics, epistemology, and ideology.[11] In doing so, he depicts the historian's quest for historical understanding as one of a number of mediations with the past, each of which reveals perceptions of distance that range from alienation to familiarization.[12] In this way, Phillips historicizes the concept of historical distance.

During the first half of the nineteenth century, just as *historical distance* began to appear with greater frequency, the historicist usage of the term gained traction alongside other uses. Some English writers used it to denote cultural differences among peoples existing in the same era. For example, poet Richard Monckton Milnes used *historical distance* as a synonym for the different mindsets he observed between what he described as advanced and uncivilized societies. Writing as a traveler and sounding like a historicist, he noted that

---

[11] Hayden White, *Metahistory: The Historical Imagination in Nineteenth-Century Europe* (Baltimore, 1975).
[12] Mark Salber Phillips, *On Historical Distance* (New Haven, 2013).

in forming historical judgments of modern events and persons it is often a severe necessity to transfer our thoughts and calculations from the smooth and solid temper of an advanced form of society into that of one, where all the relations of life are as different as if the distance of the one from the other, in space and time, were the very wildest.[13]

Milnes's observation captured the historicist argument that began to emerge in this period, when writers on both sides of the Atlantic asserted that historical distance inspired "dispassionate judgment" among those examining the foreign past.[14]

Alongside these new historicist uses, writers used the term *historical distance* to signify different historical understandings. Some used it either to indicate that certain topics and events became unfamiliar over time or, in contrast, to suggest that time rendered historical places and writings greater "than they really are."[15] During the same period, a few writers used the term to signify more than the time between two dates.[16] Charles Pelham Mulvany even distinguished between what he described as "distance in time" and "historical distance" to explain how changes in circumstances created a temporal gap that went beyond time's mere passing.[17]

While the main characters in my book did not often use the term *historical distance*, they did use language that reflected a growing sense that temporal changes had created temporal distinctions. Once antebellum interpreters perceived the distance, most of them assumed it could be bridged, and some explicitly argued that proper historical investigation would accomplish the task. While I track such historicist ideas, I focus more on how Americans first began to sense distance from the past, showing how their views of the past moved from familiar to foreign, while

---

[13] Richard Monckton Milnes, *Memorials of a Tour in Some Parts of Greece: Chiefly Poetical* (London, 1834), 65.

[14] "The Late Emperor of Russia," *Putnam's Magazine* 5 (June 1855): 589. See also Thomas Hancock, *The Peculium; An Endeavor to Throw Light on Some of the Causes of the Decline of the Society of Friends* (London, 1859), 71.

[15] James Jennings, letter to the editor, *The Monthly Magazine* (September 1812), 104; Thomas Noon Talfourd, "Lord Eldon and Lord Stowell," in *Critical and Miscellaneous Writings of T. Noon Talfourd* (Boston, 1854); Charles Knight, "Albany W. Fonblanque," in *The English Cyclopædia: A New Dictionary of Universal Knowledge* (London, 1856), 2:941; George William Curtis, *The Wanderer in Syria* (London, 1852), 163; Charles Bathurst, *Remarks on the Differences in Shakespeare's Versification in Difference Periods of His Life and on the Like Points of Difference in Poetry Generally* (London, 1857), 85.

[16] *The Works of the Late Rev. Joseph Milner* (London, 1810), 8:474.

[17] C[harles] P[elham] M[ulvany], "The Living Secret," *The College Magazine* 1 (March 1858): 378.

also noting the persistence of positions that resisted that move. More specifically, I detail the ways in which debates over slavery indicated distance from the favored and familiar biblical and founding eras. The sense of distance unsettled the relationship between those pasts and the present and challenged the relevance of their sacred texts, even as their perception of distance also encouraged readers to reinterpret these texts for continued use. This book seeks to historicize the kind of historical distance experienced as estrangement and to show how it became a useful tool for some American interpreters.

The process by which biblical and constitutional debates over slavery uniquely spread a sense of historical distance was contingent and gradual. As noted earlier, Americans' growing perception of such distance depended on the usefulness of founding texts and pasts. The most profound awareness of historical distance results when individuals and groups recognize that unbridgeable historical divisions and irreversible historical changes separate them from even the most favored pasts. The potential for sensing historical distance is diminished with regard to neglected or unfamiliar pasts. Many antebellum Euro-Americans likely assumed distance from ancient Asia and Africa, but Euro-Americans' minimal attention to such pasts made their idea of distance from those pasts just that: an assumption rather than a realization. While depicting a past in a negative light, as in the case of the so-called Dark Ages, could generate a sense of change and distance, that recognition was mitigated by simultaneous appeals to "pure" pasts or golden ages, like the classical period and Puritan New England. Even when these pasts lost some of their usefulness, other favored pasts, including primitive Christianity and the American founding, replaced them and thus reduced the chance that Americans would feel any meaningful sense of alienation from history.

The classical and colonial periods competed with the biblical and revolutionary pasts for Americans' favor. In the first decades of the nineteenth century, Americans' approaches to the classical past highlighted historical differences from ancient civilizations; they began to find greater use in ancient Greece as an antidote to, rather than Rome as a mirror of, their current political context. Historical criticism also contributed to the estrangement of the classical period. In the 1820s, American classicists such as Edward Everett used contextual explication to address issues raised about the authorship of the *Iliad* and the *Odyssey*. These developments, which created a sense of historical distance, began to challenge the prominent place of the classical world in American culture and higher education.[18] If the pastness of the classical era made Americans anxious, such anxiety would have been alleviated by the usefulness of another ancient era: the favored biblical past.

Generations of Christians had imbued the Bible with a religious significance that made it less susceptible to demotion. In a way, the time separating the sacred biblical past – Americans often viewed distinct ancient eras in the aggregate – from the antebellum present ensured its persistence as Americans' most important historical point of reference. And yet, when scholars began to shed light on the various biblical pasts – when they dug up differences in culture and geography and language – the vast temporal distance between biblical and modern times seemed to widen rather than contract.

Antebellum Americans also appealed to recent colonial times. The colonial experience was vital to the new republic's political instruction, though often refracted through the lens of the Revolutionary War. Puritans became protorevolutionaries and antislavery advocates in the era's histories, until further historical research challenged such representations. For example, one respondent to Moses Stuart's *Conscience and the Constitution* (1850) established slavery's clear presence in New England's past and excused its existence with an appeal to the temporal setting.[19] Similarly, in response to the first volume of John G. Palfrey's hagiographic *History of New England* (1859), fellow Harvard alumnus Francis Bowen informed Palfrey that the Puritans "were mortal men; they made blunders, they shared the errors of their times."[20] Such explanations could expose historical distance between a presumably progressive present and the Puritan past, and this distance worked against efforts to draw lessons from that earlier era.

Narratives signaling distance also had implications for the founding past. Depicting the gradual development of democratic principles toward epochal revolution, either as fulfillment of or departure from the period of Puritan settlement, designated the American Revolution as the historical starting point in the national drama.[21] At once, antebellum Americans viewed the founding era as the culmination of historical development and

---

[18] Caroline Winterer, *The Culture of Classicism: Ancient Greece and Rome in American Intellectual Life, 1780–1910* (Baltimore, 2002).
[19] Amicus, *Slavery Among the Puritans. A Letter to the Rev. Moses Stuart* (Boston, 1850).
[20] Francis Bowen to John G. Palfrey, 30 January 1858, Palfrey Family Papers, MS Am 1704, Houghton Library, Harvard University (hereafter Houghton).
[21] Eileen K. Cheng, *The Plain and Noble Garb of Truth: Nationalism and Impartiality in American Historical Writing, 1784–1860* (Athens, GA, 2008), 153–207.

as a past with permanent relevance. The potential for historicizing this past had been present from the founding moment, when the framers crafted national documents meant to endure – compasses that their descendants would use even after the framers had passed. The establishment of the founding moment as an exceptional point of historical departure – a contingent but rapid post-founding development – promised to place intense scrutiny on this fixed point in time. Such scrutiny held great potential to draw attention to historical distance when later generations looked back for instruction.

Some sources of American legal reasoning did not demand such attention. In the new republic, the use of common law, which emphasized the accumulation of legal wisdom stretching back into Britain's past, valued historical development. While some Democrats dismissed common law as a product of the "Dark Ages," Whigs argued that because of its foundation in custom, common law could be adapted to changing circumstances even as it checked arbitrary judicial application.[22] Their emphasis on incremental legal advances accentuated historical development as continuity instead of change.

In contrast, the emergence of a static Constitution focused America's legal minds on a specific historical document from a discrete period. Its canonization, a process that began almost immediately after ratification and accelerated in subsequent decades, exalted the founding era to rival the importance of the biblical past, which initiated a unique historical conversation.[23] The canonization process directed adherents to look to the set period of revolution and ratification for political and legal direction. The increasing focus on this period promised to raise far-reaching questions about how events, people, and documents from that eighteenth-century past spoke to the needs of the nineteenth-century present. Addressing such questions carried unique potential to historicize the founding era and instill a sense of historical distance from that relatively recent and erstwhile familiar period.

Americans imbued both biblical and founding pasts with special relevance and even tied them together; in the American imagination, the era of

---

[22] Kunal M. Parker, *Common Law, History, and Democracy in America, 1790–1900: Legal Thought before Modernism* (New York, 2011), 117–218; Stuart Streichler, *Justice Curtis in the Civil War Era: At the Crossroads of American Constitutionalism* (Charlottesville, VA, 2005), 18–22.

[23] See Jonathan Gienapp, *The Second Creation: Fixing the American Constitution in the Founding Era* (Cambridge, MA, 2018). See also David Ray Papke, *Heretics in the Temple: Americans Who Reject the Nation's Legal Faith* (New York, 1998), 1–23.

revolution and ratification was understood as the culmination of an Old Testament drama and the starting point of a new Christian nation. These pasts became even further linked in the biblical and constitutional debates over slavery, both of which partook of and contributed to the move toward contextual interpretation.

The distinct natures of the biblical and founding pasts and the differences in time between them and the present meant that unique points of emphasis would indicate historical distance. The revolutionary era was a blip in time compared to the vast chronological expanse of the biblical past, and the decades dividing the nineteenth-century present from the late eighteenth-century founding were insignificant compared to the centuries separating that present from the ancient pasts. And while the canonization, sacralization, and historicization of the Bible took place over the course of centuries, a series of forces compressed this process into a matter of decades for the Constitution.

Even still, a number of forces mitigated some of these differences. The dominant Protestant hermeneutic, which stemmed from a determination to lay aside traditions and glean Christian meanings from the biblical text itself, conflated thousands of years of biblical history and ignored the nearly two millennia that divided the present from the biblical past. Many Christians read the Bible as if the nineteenth century had immediately followed the first. The focus on the text itself meant that when scholars began to illuminate biblical eras with historical research, they revealed historical distance more through a realization of distinct biblical contexts than through a realization of historical change. Such research also drew attention to the intervening centuries separating past from present, but a sense of distance emerged less through a recognition of all that had occurred since primitive Christian times and more through a realization of the historical particularities of biblical pasts.

In the case of the founding era, Americans' growing sense of distance from the past depended on their recognition of historical change as much as their awareness of historical particularities. Regardless of how much they knew about the context of the revolutionary era, American commentators readily voiced conflicting opinions about developments since that era. To contemporary readers, seeing both the spread of antislavery sentiment and the rise of the Slave Power indicated ambivalence about historical development. America's interpreters continued to believe that the present and the past were related, but rather than viewing them as somehow concurrent, they began to see the present as the product of a series of complex historical processes.

Prior generations had sensed history's uncertain direction, even as they also adopted understandings that allayed that sensibility. The Protestant narrative of decline and renewal that found receptive soil in colonial times and continued to bear fruit in later periods contributed to a realization of "supersessive change."[24] And the republican tradition that inspired the revolutionaries was shot through with the expectation of historical vicissitude.[25] But citizens of the new nation merged the providential and cyclical aspects of these narratives and believed that the nation – as the New Rome or the New Israel – was largely exempt from the political and religious decline of other republics. This checked understandings of the founding era as discrete and historical change from that period as unpredictable, or contingent.[26]

These beliefs persisted as the founding era took shape as a favored past. To antebellum Americans, the period seemed more present than past, which worked against its historicization. History, for many, was ancient and foreign, not modern and American. The new nation's historians introduced some distance by draping the Revolutionary War era in classical terms and lamenting the loss of classical virtue since that time, but those efforts brought the classical past forward as much as it pushed the founding era backward.[27] Furthermore, those celebrating change as the fruits of the founders' labors soon overwhelmed those lamenting corruption, which blunted a sense of contingent development, or an awareness that unpredictable change characterized history's course. And yet, relatively little time had passed since the founding era, and knowledge about that period was accessible and widespread. Consequently, in a period of historicization, the specters of historical difference and change hung over conversations about the era.

In this intellectual environment, even interpretive efforts to dismiss historical context and change as irrelevant raised questions about the Constitution's relationship to temporal evolution and reified the reality of those historical forces. When some readers denied the interpretive relevance of slavery in the founding era, they unintentionally highlighted – rather than dismissed – the prominent presence of slavery in that period.

---

[24] Anthony Kemp, *The Estrangement of the Past: A Study in the Origins of Modern Historical Consciousness* (New York, 1991), vi.
[25] J. G. A. Pocock, *The Machiavellian Moment: Florentine Political Thought and the Atlantic Republican Tradition* (Princeton, 1975).
[26] Eran Shalev, *Rome Reborn on Western Shores: Historical Imagination and the Creation of the American Republic* (Charlottesville, VA, 2009), 73–113.
[27] Ibid., 188–215.

When other readers rejected burgeoning antislavery sentiment as interpretively inconsequential, they inadvertently drew attention to this change in sentiment over time. Whether they were using historical distance or rejecting its importance, readers spoke of its presence. All of this began to suggest to readers that an unbridgeable temporal gap separated the present and the founding past.

The potential for historical distance to become widely recognized due to Americans' fixation on periods of religious and political founding remained suppressed until the mid-nineteenth century, when events pushed slavery to the political forefront. In seeking to resolve the growing crisis, Americans turned to their enduring favored pasts and their timeless sacred texts. As before, interpreters usually undertook this process for the purpose of uncovering permanent political, religious, and legal truths, but at this time, their efforts carried unprecedented potential to reveal the transient nature of biblical and founding pasts. In other words, attempts to use historical research to assert the timelessness of biblical teachings and constitutional imperatives on the issue of slavery inadvertently laid bare the immediate contexts of biblical passages and constitutional clauses and drew attention to the historical changes separating ancient and American pasts from modern times. This interpretive development, above all others, cultivated a sense of historical distance.

The deepening of historical awareness fueled new conversations about the place of the Bible and the Constitution in Americans' present. As some began to view the biblical and revolutionary pasts as distinct and distant periods of historical time, more than a few also reinterpreted these texts as malleable in relation to new historical contexts. The Civil War, along with scholars' assumption that antebellum Americans failed to reason historically, obscured these developments.[28] This study removes that occlusion by showing how slavery led American biblical and constitutional interpreters to sense that historical distances divided them from even their most favored pasts. This study also adds a crucial component to our understanding of the rise of a modern American historical awareness, showing that even the idea of thinking historically has a history.

Slavery and Sacred Texts revises conventional thinking about significant segments of nineteenth-century American intellectual life. Historians have yet to account for the range and depth of antebellum historical thought, in part because they have not examined its relationship to the debate over

---

[28] On this long-standing assumption, see Cheng, *Plain and Noble Garb*, 1–12.

southern slavery. The peculiar institution was singular in spurring and giving shape to an awareness of temporal dislocation, which became a central component of modern historical consciousness in America.

To be sure, other developments contributed to this intellectual transformation. The transition toward a modern historical awareness in the United States coincided with intellectual shifts in the Western world, including the emergence of an understanding of time as progressive and linear, a realization of the chronological depth of the earth's history, and the development of more mechanistic and materialistic approaches to the natural world.[29] Republicanism, common law, and political economy also played their own roles in teaching Americans about the uncertainties of time's movement. These and other far-reaching developments fueled the spread of historical consciousness in the United States.

Although some of these changes challenged traditional religious beliefs, religion contributed to the transatlantic deepening of historical awareness. A number of recent studies have disputed the assumption that modern modes of thought developed along purely secular lines by explaining the ways in which religious debates and religious sources contributed to the emergence of modern thought.[30] Some of this work shows how discussions over biblical interpretation, in particular, became enmeshed in historical writing and thought. In this vein, Thomas A. Howard argues that W. M. L. de Wette's historical-critical approach to the scriptures informed the development of German historicism through the scholarship of historian Jacob Burckhardt. This demonstrates that European Protestantism contributed to the rise of secular historical thinking.[31] In line with this work, I seek to uncover the theological roots of American historical awareness in showing how biblical interpretation, including

---

[29] See Martin J. S. Rudwick, *Bursting the Limits of Time: The Reconstruction of Geohistory in the Age of Revolution* (Chicago, 2005); and Martin J. S. Rudwick, *Worlds Before Adam: The Reconstruction of Geohistory in the Age of Reform* (Chicago, 2008).

[30] See, for example, J. G. A. Pocock, *Barbarism and Religion* (Cambridge, UK, 1999–2015); Eric Nelson, *The Hebrew Republic: Jewish Sources and the Transformation of European Political Thought* (Cambridge, MA, 2010); and Brad S. Gregory, *The Unintended Reformation: How a Religious Revolution Secularized Society* (Cambridge, MA, 2012).

[31] Thomas A. Howard, *Religion and the Rise of Historicism: W. M. L. de Wette, Jacob Burckhardt, and the Theological Origins of Nineteenth-Century Historical Consciousness* (New York, 2000). Frederick C. Beiser makes a similar argument in tracking the influence of Johann Salomo Semler's and Johann David Michaelis's biblical criticism on Johann Gottfried Herder's historicism. See Frederick C. Beiser, *The German Historicist Tradition* (New York, 2011), 98–167.

selective engagement with German biblical criticism, contributed to the shape of American historical consciousness.

Most scholars writing on American historical awareness, in particular, assert or assume that developments unique to the new republic, including the nature of American religiosity, hindered and delayed the emergence of modern historical consciousness.[32] Much of this scholarship has focused on the perceived shallowness of antebellum historical writing. Eileen Cheng has revised this view by highlighting the rich methodological debates among America's historical writers.[33] This book also challenges the traditional narrative, but it does so by turning that narrative's central assumption on its head: far from uniformly blunting historical thinking, American particularities deepened American historical consciousness in a number of important ways.

Antebellum debates about the Bible and the Constitution had unique power to both limit and drive historical awareness, and these interpretive debates often revolved around slavery. In this book, writings about the Bible and the Constitution provide the measure of historical consciousness, and debates over slavery serve as the lens through which to take that measurement. Scholars have correctly identified the distinctive religious, legal, and political peculiarities of the new nation: a biblically saturated culture, the reliance on a written Constitution, and a growing crisis over slavery. But rather than uniformly hinder American historical consciousness, as much of the existing literature on the topic either asserts or suggests, those peculiarities actually spurred that consciousness by encouraging a growing sense of historical distance. In short, I argue that the distinct religious and legal nature of American society created the conditions for the nation's profound confrontation with history – and that the slavery crisis ignited that historical conflict.

While the transition to modern historical awareness in the United States both converged and diverged from broader changes, and though it was in many ways symptomatic of the Western world's awakening to history, the precise nature of the transition was distinctly American. Historical awareness can result from intellectual awakenings, radical upheaval and revolution, and organic developments. In Europe, the spread of historical awareness came through enlightenments and

---

[32] See, for example, Dorothy Ross, "Historical Consciousness in Nineteenth-Century America," *American Historical Review* 89 (October 1984): 909–28; and Winterer, *The Culture of Classicism*, 91–2.

[33] See Cheng, *Plain and Noble Garb*.

romanticism, the French Revolution, and the Napoleonic Wars.[34] This relates to what Reinhart Koselleck describes as the "temporalization (*Verzeitlichung*) of history" – whereby individuals exhibited a sense of temporal difference – the culmination of which he locates in the nineteenth century.[35] These developments helped create the conditions for the spread of historical awareness in the antebellum United States. However, in that setting, biblical and constitutional debates over slavery were most responsible for signaling historical difference and change and spreading a sense of historical distance. The slavery debates internally drove this development.[36]

This book is not a study of the Bible and the Constitution, or even of slavery, per se, but rather an examination of the role interpretive debates over slavery played in historicizing America's sacred religious and legal texts and their venerated pasts. This is also not an examination of the full scope of antebellum historical consciousness or of the rise of modern American historical thought. Instead, it narrates how these interpretive religious and legal debates gave rise to a sense of historical distance, which became a crucial aspect of American historical consciousness.

Some historians have examined the religious aspects of this development. James Turner has shown that in the eighteenth and nineteenth centuries, American Christians unintentionally made unbelief viable by adopting the secular standards of their opponents.[37] Similarly, Michael Lee has demonstrated that during the same period theological conservatives used the methods of the Bible's critics and in doing so unwittingly prepared the way for the late nineteenth-century challenge to traditional

---

[34] See Hayden White, "Romanticism, Historicism, and Realism: Toward a Period Concept for Early Nineteenth-Century Intellectual History," in *The Uses of History: Essays in Intellectual and Social History*, ed. William John Bosenbrook and Hayden White (Detroit, 1968), 45–58; Georg G. Iggers, *The German Conception of History: The National Tradition of Historical Thought from Herder to the Present* (Middletown, CT, 1968), 3–89; Peter Hanns Reill, "Science and the Construction of the Cultural Sciences in Late Enlightenment Germany: The Case of Wilhelm von Humboldt," *History and Theory* 33 (1994): 345–66; Jonathan Knudsen, "The Historicist Enlightenment," in *What's Left of Enlightenment? A Postmodern Question*, ed. Keith Michael Baker and Peter Hanns Reill (Stanford, 2001), 39–49; and Peter Fritzsche, *Stranded in the Present: Modern Time and the Melancholy of History* (Cambridge, MA, 2004).

[35] Reinhart Koselleck, *Futures Past: On the Semantics of Historical Time*, trans. Keith Tribe (New York, 2004), 11.

[36] In examining slavery as an intellectual problem and a force for intellectual change, this book takes its cue from the work of David Brion Davis.

[37] James Turner, *Without God, Without Creed: The Origins of Unbelief in America* (Baltimore, 1985).

views of scripture.³⁸ A few historians have examined how the slavery debate impinged on this development. Eran Shalev points out that the biblical argument over slavery revealed deep cultural divides between ancient Israel and modern America, while Molly Oshatz contends that antislavery Protestants developed the idea that God gradually revealed slavery's sin in relation to varied contexts of human experience.³⁹ In different ways, each of these studies provides a useful corrective to the caricature of shallow antebellum historical awareness.

While this scholarship tracks developments that threatened to undermine the Bible as a sacred text, the scholars explain that the threat did not fully materialize until the Civil War or the decades after. To be sure, some radical voices in antebellum America rejected the Bible, but their Christian counterparts drowned them out with valiant defenses that insisted on the relevance of the biblical texts.⁴⁰ Such efforts made the Bible even more sacred, but, as noted earlier, that effort – which drew the biblical past into the present – created the potential for an even greater sense of dislocation when research exposed historical differences between the favored past and the present. Increased sacralization deepened the potential for historicization.

This book builds on the abovementioned works by showing that the antebellum era saw the emergence of approaches that had the potential to expose the Bible's archaism. I demonstrate that both heterodox and orthodox thinkers adopted the historical lessons of European biblical criticism – especially the emphasis on the ways in which contexts and circumstances shaped biblical language – and I also track how they contributed to the process of making sacred texts historical. Their biblical debates over slavery, in particular, began to historicize the Bible as a whole, which troubled Americans' New and Old Testament uses and associations. While showing that the Bible maintained a sacred status throughout the antebellum era, I argue that these debates contributed to a growing perception that an unbridgeable gap separated the present from ancient pasts, including not just Old Testament eras but also primitive Christian times.

---

³⁸ Michael J. Lee, *The Erosion of Biblical Certainty: Battles over Authority and Interpretation in America* (New York, 2013).

³⁹ Eran Shalev, *American Zion: The Old Testament as a Political Text from the Revolution to the Civil War* (New Haven, 2013); Molly Oshatz, *Slavery and Sin: The Fight against Slavery and the Rise of Liberal Protestantism* (New York, 2012).

⁴⁰ See Christopher Grasso, *Skepticism and American Faith: From the Revolution to the Civil War* (New York, 2018).

This book's most innovative move is to show how the interpretive shift in biblical debates over slavery corresponded to a similar shift in constitutional debates over slavery. Placing these interpretive debates in direct proximity highlights American interpreters' growing awareness of historical distance from their favored pasts. These biblical and constitutional debates had some clear overlap both in terms of the individuals who participated in them and in the methodologies those individuals used. However, in this narrative I am deliberately creating an even closer relationship between these debates, thus creating a kind of artificial relationship grounded in historic reality. In other words, I did not simply happen upon this relationship; instead I observed, analyzed, and underscored from afar the powerful rhetorical links between antebellum biblical and constitutional interpretation. I am not suggesting that the biblical debates led to the constitutional debates, but rather that the historical nature of the biblical discussions set the stage for a similar constitutional drama. As I track this development, I illuminate the theological origins of the constitutional crisis that was also a historical crisis.

This approach sheds new light on the role of history in antebellum legal thought. With some exceptions, studies on law and history in nineteenth-century America focus on the later decades, reifying the assumption that historical thought remained underdeveloped in prior eras.[41] In recent studies, both Jonathan Gienapp and Simon J. Gilhooley complicate this view by tracing the contingent process by which the Constitution became an archival text. In analyzing late eighteenth-century developments, Gienapp shows that the Constitution was not born a legal creed. At the framing, constitutional architect James Madison and his colleagues thought of the nation's new constitution less as a complete legal text and more as an imperfect system of government, subject to refinement. Gienapp contends that early congressional debates created the idea that the document was fixed in time and in need of historical excavation. In the process, politicians, including Madison, reimagined the Constitution as a static and sacred text. Early on, then, the idea of the Constitution as historical contributed to its sacredness.

As the Constitution became even more sacred in succeeding decades, the idea of the text as historical began to threaten that sacredness.

---

[41] See, for example, Johnathan O'Neill, *Originalism in American Law and Politics: A Constitutional History* (Baltimore, 2005); and David M. Rabban, *Law's History: American Legal Thought and the Transatlantic Turn to History* (New York, 2013). For an exception, see Parker, *Legal Thought before Modernism*.

Gilhooley demonstrates that during the 1830s, participants in the slavery debates began making extratextual appeals to the spirit of the founding era, a gradual and contingent development that cemented the view of the Constitution as a historical artifact.[42] I track a similar development in showing that the historical nature of the constitutional conversation reached a new level once the founding generation began to pass away and new generations could not remember ratification. The passing of the founders spurred a growing emphasis on the importance of their words, especially those found in Madison's papers. During the 1840s and 1850s, as politicians increasingly looked to the Constitution to solve the nation's problems, the crisis over slavery enhanced the idea that interpreters must use founding-era sources to understand the framers' intentions and to interpret the Constitution accordingly. In turn, historical debates over the Constitution became more politically and historically determinative than ever before. Even biblical scholars such as Moses Stuart conceded and even insisted that constitutional interpretation mattered most.

This had important implications for historical consciousness. The political and public nature of the resulting debate opened the door for a growing number of Americans to recognize historical difference and observe historical distance. When Taney insisted on a thoroughly historical decision in *Dred Scott*, a number of commentators felt confident in meeting him on those grounds. Americans felt more comfortable voicing opinions on questions of constitutional interpretation than on those of biblical interpretation, particularly in light of the growing emphasis on historical readings of the Constitution. As one observer wrote, the *Dred Scott* decision "does not rest so much upon any interpretation of the law as it does upon a construction of the facts of history."[43] As the slavery debate reached its tipping point, the archival nature of the document, and the excavation required to understand it, began to create a sense of historical distance. In other words, what made the Constitution sacred in the first decades of its existence started to desacralize it as time wore on. This opened it up to new readings, including ones such as Lincoln's, which took historical distance into account.

These readings focused on what I term *original expectations*. Constitutional theorist Jack Balkin has used these words to describe an

---

[42] Simon J. Gilhooley, *The Antebellum Origins of the Modern Constitution: Slavery and the Spirit of the American Founding* (New York, 2020).
[43] "History, as Expounded by the Supreme Court," *Putnam's Monthly Magazine of American Literature, Science, and Art* 9 (May 1857): 541.

originalism that restricts meaning to the framers' era-specific intentions. Against this limiting originalism, he articulates a living originalism in relation to the flexible governmental framework and general principles he finds in the text.[44] In the twenty-first century, when language is understood as fluid and intent as rigid, Balkin's application of the term *original expectations* to era-specific intentions serves to highlight the adaptability of his textual originalism.

But this formulation does not fit the antebellum era, when readers often appealed to the text, along with original intent and understanding, to delimit meaning. To be clear, some did cite the framers' anticipation of new conditions as a reason to set aside change and insist on traditional readings, and in such cases the appeal to original expectations functioned like an appeal to era-specific intentions. However, as I demonstrate, some antislavery readers appealed to the Constitution's general principles and the framers' expectation of eventual abolition to advance new readings. While positing that the framers had anticipated a new historical setting, these readers insisted on interpreting the text in light of the framers' expectation, even though and especially because that original expectation had not been realized. I use the term *original expectations* to describe this kind of appeal and show how such appeals encouraged interpreters to advance readings open to change. While much distinguished these innovative antislavery readings from the living originalisms that emerged later, I suggest that they set in motion the very developments that made Balkin's reading possible.

While providing a new perspective on the evolution of historical awareness in America, examining antebellum religious and legal interpretation in tandem also sheds light on core concerns in American intellectual and cultural life. These interpretive practices constitute the foundations on which the American traditions of progressivism and conservatism have taken shape. Both projects were preoccupied with uncovering the "original meanings" of sacred texts from hallowed historical eras. Jaroslav Pelikan, who has explored this relationship in general terms, notes that "both the New Testament and the Constitution are set within historical periods that are endowed with a special aura by their traditions and that carry a unique authority for their communities."[45] Tracing a clear interpretive overlap in antebellum biblical and constitutional

---

[44] See Jack M. Balkin, "Abortion and Original Meaning," *Constitutional Commentary* 24 (2007): 291–352; and Jack M. Balkin, *Living Originalism* (Cambridge, MA, 2014).
[45] Jaroslav Pelikan, *Interpreting the Bible and the Constitution* (New Haven, 2004), 85.

readings grounds this discussion. By analyzing these interpretive traditions together, I demonstrate just how pervasive an emphasis on recovering "original meanings" through historical interpretation had become in antebellum America.

This examination of biblical and constitutional debates over slavery outlines the rise and development of historical awareness in antebellum America and gives shape and specificity to an often broad and loose notion of historical consciousness. It shows that some Americans' historical thinking took the form of an awareness of qualitative historical distances from revolutionary and biblical pasts; it also indicates that interpretive debates over slavery played a central role in this complicated but clear intellectual process. In this book, I explain how these debates revealed historical distance from favored pasts, and thus I offer a narrative that corrects longstanding assumptions about the shallowness of antebellum historical awareness. In doing so, this book invites readers to consider the deep roots of their own historical reasoning.

As I illuminate the previously unexamined relationship between antebellum religious and legal interpretation, I attend to both familiar and obscure thinkers. I reorient the discussion away from the writings of self-conscious historians and toward the biblical and constitutional commentaries of ministers, theologians, lawyers, reformers, judges, and politicians. Transcendentalist Theodore Parker, a key figure in both the biblical and constitutional debates over slavery, serves as a kind of narrative hinge. Other central characters include biblical scholars Andrews Norton, Moses Stuart, and Charles Hodge; abolitionists William Lloyd Garrison, Lysander Spooner, and Frederick Douglass; Justices Roger B. Taney and Benjamin R. Curtis; and politician Abraham Lincoln.

While I devote many pages to their writings and speeches, I also show that the historical nature of their interpretive debates drew responses from non-specialists and those at the margins of American public life, who articulated popular biblical readings and popular constitutionalisms.[46] Taney's deciding opinion in *Dred Scott*, in particular, gave rise to historical counternarratives from a range of individuals, including African American intellectuals such as William C. Nell. Even Americans who

---

[46] While Michael Conlin depicts popular constitutionalism as a static phenomenon in the antebellum era, I aim to show that popular constitutionalism developed in relationship to the debates over slavery and to interpreters' emerging insistence on historical readings. Michael F. Conlin, *The Constitutional Origins of the American Civil War* (New York, 2019).

were unaware of these debates were nonetheless deeply invested in sacred texts and slavery; these discussions had far-reaching implications. The focus on the writings and interpretive debates of the aforementioned thinkers, and the political contexts from within which they wrote and spoke, offers an alternative means of gauging antebellum historical thought.[47]

Because these sources do not generally contain explicit expressions of historical awareness, I read them in search of their multivocalities, their unwritten assumptions, and their complex relationships to various contexts, especially other texts. Taking a methodological cue from Dominick LaCapra, I examine the intersections among these thinkers and their texts, and between them and their antebellum and transatlantic contexts.[48] Within each text I locate the presence of approaches, narratives, and ideas that indicate historical distance. Although an abstract concept like historical consciousness can be difficult to measure, a careful reading of biblical and constitutional interpretation reveals much about the development of antebellum Americans' historical understandings.

Participants in the biblical and constitutional debates over slavery did not create American historical consciousness but rather contributed to its shape in relationship to broader cultural forces that constrained and stimulated their historical understandings. These participants worked within an intellectual environment where a series of factors, both transatlantic and national, combined to constrict historical thought but also allow for the kinds of historical reasoning that introduced a sense of distance from biblical and American pasts.

Far from being total and complete, the spread of historical awareness in antebellum America was piecemeal and uneven. Most Americans retained some traditional historical views, linking vast periods of time with grand narratives – such as providentialist millennialism or Whiggish progressive liberalism. Both of these schemes contained a sacralized epoch and a sacred text: the biblical era and the Bible, and the

---

[47] For other studies that examine a range of sources in measuring antebellum historical consciousness, see George H. Callcott, *History in the United States, 1800–1860: Its Practice and Purpose* (Baltimore, 1970); Thomas M. Allen, *A Republic in Time: Temporality and Social Imagination in Nineteenth-Century America* (Chapel Hill, 2008); Lloyd Pratt, *Archives of American Time: Literature and Modernity in the Nineteenth Century* (Philadelphia, 2010); and Shalev, *Rome Reborn* and *American Zion*.

[48] Dominick LaCapra, "Rethinking Intellectual History and Reading Texts," *History and Theory* 19 (October 1980): 245–76.

revolutionary era and the Constitution. As Americans continued to receive their sacred texts as timeless, this perspective contributed to an intellectual atmosphere in which periods of time did not seem significantly different; a nineteenth-century American might consider Moses or Madison as contemporaries, each uttering truths that were as valid and clear in 1857 as they had been in 1500 BC or 1787. Such assumptions partook of the long-standing "myth of the eternal return."[49] The Puritans believed their generation may have broken an ancient covenant or fallen from a primordial Eden, but they also believed obedience to timeless laws could immediately turn back the clock of declension. In their eyes, Puritan New England lay closer to the ancient truth than did medieval Rome.[50] Even American revolutionaries, who hoped to restore the glories of classical Rome, or to recreate the nonfeudal Saxon period, seemed set on measuring their progress in terms of the past.[51] Such historical approaches understood past and present times as fluid and interchangeable eras of temporal conflation rather than impenetrable and discrete epochs of temporal distinction. These sorts of ahistorical understandings persisted throughout the antebellum era.

However, the durability of such views did not preclude the emergence of new historical understandings. Slavery, above all else, led Americans to rethink their relationship to favored pasts and to reinterpret sacred texts. Even conservative and moderate readers – who set aside historical distance to assert the applicability of Jesus's or Madison's words – inadvertently drew attention to the vast differences dividing biblical and revolutionary pasts from the present. The need to account for a sense of historical distance inspired interpretive innovations. When it proved exegetically impossible for abolitionists to deny that Jesus tolerated slavery in primitive Palestine, or that Madison sanctioned it in the nascent United States, they faced two choices: reject the Bible and the Constitution as worn out and obsolete (and some did just that) or insist that they were written in fundamentally different historical circumstances and that one must be hermeneutically attuned to that fact (more did this). Regardless of how readers used historical distance, their readings drew attention to its

---

[49] Mircea Eliade, *The Myth of the Eternal Return: Or, Cosmos and History* (New York, 1954).
[50] Theodore Dwight Bozeman, *To Live Ancient Lives: The Primitivist Dimension in Puritanism* (Chapel Hill, 1988).
[51] Trevor Colbourn, *The Lamp of Experience: Whig History and the Intellectual Origins of the American Revolution* (Chapel Hill, 1965).

presence. In addressing slavery, America's interpreters became aware of such distance to a degree unmatched by their predecessors.

This book offers a chronological account of these developments. Because the thinkers studied herein only conveyed historical awareness indirectly through their interpretive debates, I have not grouped them in the narrative based on the rigor of their historical investigations or the depth of their historical consciousness. Instead, I have measured their historical awareness in relation to their interpretive contestations over time. Grouping thinkers according to the sophistication of their contextual readings, the depth of their historical consciousness, and the degree to which they used historical distance in interpretation would have resulted in a neater narrative, but detailing important ideational distinctions between and among thinkers allows me to give readers a feel for their intellectual discussions and debates. The debates, in a sense, are just as much characters in this narrative as are the historical actors. This organizational choice, which demands some patience from the reader, also reveals the central argument of the book: that immediate contexts in antebellum America – and the interpretive debates over southern slavery in particular – created a sense of historical distance.

In the first six decades of the nineteenth century, America's biblical and constitutional interpreters waged their hermeneutical battles on historical grounds. The turn to historical explication in biblical interpretation began in earnest during the first few decades of the nineteenth century, when the lessons of German biblical criticism infiltrated influential segments of America's religious society. Biblical scholars across the antebellum religious spectrum, from orthodox Charles Hodge's Calvinism to heterodox Theodore Parker's Transcendentalism, began to insist that a proper reading of the Bible rested on a clear recognition of historical differences. This development, which challenged conventional readings that ignored historical specificity and flattened out time, sparked debate about the pertinence of biblical texts and the permanence of their teachings. The historicizing process began with the Old Testament, but during the 1830s the resurfacing slavery issue increased the urgency to explore biblical pasts for answers, an endeavor that began to unmistakably expose the archaism of even the New Testament past. To be sure, some still posited the relevance of the Bible as a whole, and others rescued a Testament, a text, or a teaching, but they did so in the face of historical distance. In this setting, some proved willing to let the old canon drift into the past.

These relatively isolated biblical discussions had far-reaching implications. Although somewhat recondite, they readied participants for the more public constitutional debates that followed. In fact, a number of the individuals who participated in the shift toward historical readings of the Bible, including Parker, contributed to a similar move in constitutional interpretation. The growing slavery crisis, which raised the stakes in both biblical and constitutional interpretation, brought these distinct traditions together in a process that placed an unprecedented amount of pressure on both texts.

During the 1830s, the antislavery agitation of Garrison and others stirred the ghosts of the founding era and set in motion the period's historicization. The passing of the framers also spurred this development, as it cultivated great interest in founding-era sources; the framers' bodily absence induced anxious attempts to restore their written presence. After James Madison died in 1836, a range of observers discussed the need to rescue the framers' writings and to understand their original intent. This sentiment inspired the publication of the *Papers of James Madison* (1840), which most interpreters came to value as paramount. In the 1840s and 1850s, the slavery debates reached a fever pitch and directed those on all sides of the issue to confront the historical grounds of debate and craft historical readings of the founding legal text. Even when antislavery constitutionalists like William Goodell and Lysander Spooner rejected the emphasis on contextual interpretation, their accounts highlighted slavery's presence at the founding and traced the anachronistic rise of the Slave Power since that period – they deemed the spread of slavery and the rise of the Slave Power as aberrant. Those who hoped to reclaim historical personalities and recover static original meanings inevitably dug up unexpected historical facts. These facts revealed historical difference and distance.

When the Fugitive Slave Law of 1850 and the Kansas-Nebraska Act of 1854 nationalized the slavery issue, the pressure on constitutional interpreters increased and the past to which they looked became further historicized. Readers ranging from radical abolitionists to prominent politicians strove to recover and use the framers' intent. As American political culture expanded, the issue of slavery was constitutionalized; commentators came to believe the national crisis would be resolved through a proper reading of the Constitution. This development peaked in *Dred Scott*, when politicians looked to the Supreme Court to adjudicate the matter. Taney's historical reading marked the culmination of decades of interpretive emphasis on context. Although he ignored historical facts and set aside historical distance, his interpretation again highlighted that much had changed since the founding era. His decision was meant to settle the crisis, but instead it sparked further debate as Americans welcomed the chance to challenge Taney on historical grounds. Instead of resurrecting the past, his reading had conjured historical hauntings. He had hoped to embody shadowy spirits, but he had set them loose instead. Both obscure and prominent critics countered with historical narratives of their own, which further spotlighted the historical particularities of the founding era. Some continued to uphold the Constitution as an enduring national covenant or read it in light of the egalitarian promises of the Declaration of Independence, while others joined Garrison's call to dismiss it as outdated.

Still others developed readings that acknowledged and used historical distance. The ghosts of the founding era prompted them to consider new readings based in original expectations. This approach had roots in both biblical and constitutional interpretation. Since the 1830s, moderate antislavery interpreters had formulated sophisticated readings meant to recover timeless antislavery truths from transient proslavery contexts. Biblical scholars like William Channing and Francis Wayland contended that Christ and his apostles had inculcated principles meant to abolish slavery with time. In the 1840s, antislavery constitutionalists similarly contended that the framers had crafted their creation with the expectation that change would eventually remove the national blight of chattel slavery. This reading soon found powerful proponents in Frederick Douglass, Theodore Parker, and Abraham Lincoln, who aligned the founding-era anticipation of abolition with contemporary antislavery sentiment and contrasted those expectations with the rise of the Slave Power. The idea that historical figures had knowingly articulated universal promises that they themselves could not realize but that future generations would fulfill encouraged an emphasis on historical difference from and change since the biblical and revolutionary pasts. Furthermore, in tracing both moral progress in the form of rising antislavery sentiment and moral decline in the form of proslavery politics, Douglass, Parker, and Lincoln displayed ambivalence about history's direction. In the decades before the Civil War, interpretive debates over slavery spread not only a sense of historical distance but also a sense of historical contingency. These debates forced new confrontations with history, and the resulting historical awareness became a powerful interpretive guide in new historical settings.

In antebellum biblical and constitutional debates over slavery, some readers minimized and others maximized the interpretive importance of historical distance and change, but in either case their readings brought new attention to those realities. This process of historicizing America's sacred texts and favored pasts – historical documents and eras with seemingly timeless appeal – contributed to a growing sense that nothing existed outside of time and that everything bore the marks of temporal vicissitude.

In essence, the crisis over slavery in America became a crisis of historicity. This book narrates how that crisis came about and how readers of sacred texts responded to that crisis. While the deepening awareness of historical distance led some to repudiate the Bible and the Constitution as products of foreign pasts, it also inspired innovative approaches wherein interpreters read these documents as flexible guides to the present and future. This development would allow Lincoln to assert that the proper circumstances had emerged in which he was duty-bound to fulfill the antislavery promises of the founders. Thus, the antebellum confrontation with history complicated but did not discourage the use of the past; instead, it compelled many Americans to adopt new approaches to favored pasts and sacred texts.

I

"Recourse Must Be Had to the History of Those Times"

Two deaths gave life to American biblical criticism: the demise of former Massachusetts congressman Samuel Dexter in 1810 led to the execution of his will, which directed his testators to give $5,000 to Harvard "for promoting biblical criticism."[1] A year later, Dexter's trustees elected Unitarian minister Joseph Stevens Buckminster as Harvard's inaugural Dexter Lecturer, an appointment dedicated to biblical criticism.[2] The young Buckminster died of epilepsy before he could deliver his first lecture. His death, however, propelled the spread of biblical criticism in ways that his lectureship might not have. After Buckminster's passing, America's biblical scholars journeyed to Boston for the public sale of his library, which included works of biblical scholarship known for "their rarity in our country."[3] The sale placed these works into the hands of those who became America's foremost advocates of biblical criticism. Unitarians, such as William Ellery Channing and Edward Everett, attended the event, but so did Congregationalists, including Jeremiah Evarts and Moses Stuart. Stuart outbid his friend Everett for Johann Gottfried Eichhorn's five-volume introduction to the Old Testament, *Einleitung ins Alte Testament* (1780–83), an important text by a leading scholar in biblical criticism. This event indicated that orthodoxy's defenders would join advocates of liberal religion on the historical grounds

---

[1] "Biographical Notice of the Late Hon. Samuel Dexter," *The Monthly Anthology, and Boston Review* 9 (July 1810): 7.
[2] "Intelligence," *General Repository and Review* 1 (January 1812): 205.
[3] "Sale of the Library of the Late Rev. Mr. Buckminster," *General Repository and Review* 2 (October 1812): 392–94, quotation on 392.

prepared by biblical criticism and challenge them on questions of canon and doctrine on those grounds.[4]

Important doctrinal and canonical differences separated antebellum Unitarians, Congregationalists, and Presbyterians, and the biblical scholars among them promoted unique modes of historical explication. The liberal Unitarians accepted as canonical the New Testament texts that they believed could be authenticated through internal and external evidence and illuminated with interbiblical and extrabiblical knowledge. Unitarians denied plenary inspiration and emphasized the historical situatedness of authors, texts, and audiences to better understand the scriptures and to guard against ahistorical applications. This approach allowed for distinct approaches among Unitarians. While Buckminster upheld the chosen canon as uniquely accurate historical texts, Andrews Norton received the canon as occasionally flawed historical texts, in part because of the writers' accommodations and inability to fully transcend the characteristic ideas and notions of their times. The orthodox Congregationalists and Presbyterians affirmed, with some exceptions, the traditional canon and often appealed to internal and external evidences to assert its unity, historicity, and accuracy. They emphasized the historical situatedness of authors to better comprehend the Bible's universal meaning. While rejecting the idea that Jesus and the Gospel writers had accommodated to their audience, figures such as Moses Stuart and the Presbyterian Charles Hodge believed that God had accommodated to human language. Stuart privileged interbiblical knowledge over extrabiblical knowledge, and both he and Hodge approached biblical criticism with deep suspicion, but both accepted historical insight from extrabiblical sources.

In short, thinkers across the antebellum religious spectrum, from Hodge's orthodox Calvinism to Norton's liberal Unitarianism, accepted history as the favored battleground for rhetorical conflicts about the canon and religious truth. While most American Protestants remained oblivious to this development, biblical criticism led these and other prominent religious thinkers to defend their canonical choices with historical arguments, base their hermeneutics in historical analysis, and center their epistemologies in historical knowledge. Even those who rejected aspects

---

[4] For more information on the auction, see Jerry Brown, *The Rise of Biblical Criticism in America, 1800–1870: The New England Scholars* (Middletown, CT, 1969), 27–29; see also E. Brooks Holifield, *Theology in America: Christian Thought from the Age of the Puritans to the Civil War* (New Haven, 2003), 191.

of historical interpretation recognized the need to address these kinds of readings. Whether in using historical readings or in dismissing them as dangerous or problematic, biblical interpreters' efforts highlighted crucial contextual differences between their world and the biblical world they looked to for guidance. Unlike most of their hermeneutical predecessors, many nineteenth-century American interpreters came to realize that the Bible's authors did not always write "for the instruction of all succeeding time."[5] To be sure, a priori assumptions about the word of God shielded readers from biblical criticism's threat of textual and moral relativism; most readers continued to rely on the Bible's perceived atemporal truths despite the attention to its time-bound features. But the process of using the historical tools of biblical criticism began to show that a sacred text from a favored past was also a set of historical documents from an ancient era. In short, the stress on historical difference in biblical interpretation carried with it the threat of raising questions about the Bible's relevance.

In this chapter, I demonstrate that a broad range of antebellum religious thinkers used the historical tools of biblical criticism, and in doing so I argue that such efforts signaled a growing awareness of historical distance from biblical times. The history of biblical criticism in America, when explored in terms of its contribution to contextual interpretation, suggests that European biblical scholarship had a greater influence in antebellum America than previously thought. While casting aspersions on European thinkers, including English deists and German liberals, American biblical scholars also incorporated a number of European hermeneutical lessons, especially in the use of historical reasoning to determine the authenticity and meaning of biblical passages. The next two chapters show that historical explication became standard among a wide variety of religious thinkers; thus, these chapters challenge our perception of both orthodox and liberal thinkers, who used contextual interpretation to cultivate faith in atemporal truths.

This chapter details a variety of interpretive approaches used by a range of readers from different religious denominations. Discussing these approaches in close proximity can create confusion, but such discussions provide the reader a window into actual historical conversations. This narrative decision also allows me to highlight the biblical readers' distinctive interpretive approaches as well as their shared emphasis on historical explication. The Unitarians, Congregationalists, and Presbyterians

---

[5] Joseph S. Buckminster, "Philemon," in *Sermons by the late Rev. Joseph S. Buckminster*, 2nd ed. (Boston, 1815), 84.

discussed herein differed on crucial canonical and theological issues and varied in their level of engagement with European biblical criticism, but each of them incorporated aspects of biblical criticism's emphasis on contextual interpretation. In tracing this emphasis, this chapter prepares the way for the examination of a series of interpretive battles over the issue of slavery. While it took a civil war to resolve a question that theologians could not – whether American slavery was indeed anachronistic – these prewar rhetorical engagements along religious lines nourished an emerging historical consciousness while also creating the conditions for a constitutional debate with similar implications.

HISTORICAL KNOWLEDGE IN SEVENTEENTH- AND EIGHTEENTH-CENTURY HERMENEUTICS

The rise of biblical criticism in early nineteenth-century America followed developments in European biblical interpretation. Christianity had originated as a faith grounded in historical texts and figures, but the shakiness of those foundations began to appear only in relation to seventeenth- and eighteenth-century epistemological and methodological transformations that privileged historical explanations of the Bible. The Reformation's major thinkers, including Martin Luther and John Calvin, had believed that the Bible's content corresponded to actual historical realities and that substantive religious truths bound its two testaments together. In both literal and figurative interpretations, readers assumed that the words of the Bible reflected historical truths. Those readers received it as the sole source of divine revelation and trusted it as an authentic, accurate, and inclusive historical account of God's dealings with humankind.[6]

In the seventeenth century, a few thinkers began to challenge some of these underlying suppositions. This development corresponded with the rise of the term *hermeneutics* – the methodology of interpreting texts – which was quickly applied to the project of biblical interpretation. Practitioners of biblical hermeneutics included English philosopher Thomas Hobbes. In *Leviathan* (1651), Hobbes denied the Mosaic authorship of the Pentateuch and distinguished between the original writings of the apostles and the books that made up the New Testament. Furthermore, Hobbes supplanted the laws of God with the laws of nature.

---

[6] See Hans W. Frei, *The Eclipse of Biblical Narrative: A Study in Eighteenth and Nineteenth Century Hermeneutics* (New Haven, 1974), 18–37.

He still accepted the biblical texts as accurate historical accounts, based on the determinative word of the civil sovereign, but his reading demonstrated how using historical analysis to scrutinize the Bible could undermine traditional tenets.[7]

Dutch philosopher Baruch Spinoza went even further. In his *Theological-Political Treatise* (1670), he also rejected the Mosaic authorship of the Pentateuch. Spinoza dismissed affinities between Israelite wars and Dutch struggles for independence, just as Hobbes had disassociated Israel's theocratic government from both Puritan and Catholic rule in England. Rather than assume that past prophets spoke to people in all ages – an assumption that produced anachronistic readings – Spinoza contended that biblical texts must be understood in relation to the historically conditioned intentions of their authors. In contrast to Hobbes, who placed the power of interpretation in the civil sovereign, Spinoza aimed to wrest authority from public purveyors of biblical understanding and exalt individual readers as interpreters. He did not mean to suggest that the Bible contained no truth or that all truth was relative; instead, he suggested that all truth, including biblical teachings, should be subjected to reason. Spinoza allowed that historical and religious truth might align but did not believe religious meaning depended on the historicity of biblical texts.[8]

Oblivious to these isolated discussions, most biblical readers assumed that the Bible faithfully recounted historical occurrences, conveyed a cumulative story, and embraced all of human existence. But thinkers continued to challenge these views. In the late seventeenth century, English philosopher John Locke incorporated narrow biblical narratives into an expansive human story rather than cramming world history into a presumably all-encompassing Bible. In the next century, deism, empiricism, and historical criticism posed new challenges to traditional readings. Deist Anthony Collins dismissed typological interpretations of the Old Testament as meaningless and literal readings as false. In response, inheritors of the figurative approach used providentialist readings to establish a bridge of religious meaning across the chasms of historical difference that divided the Old and New Testaments. Meanwhile, successors to the literalist approach strove to capture the original sense of

---

[7] Paul D. Cooke, *Hobbes and Christianity: Reassessing the Bible in Leviathan* (Lanham, MD, 1996), esp. chaps. 6–7.

[8] Samuel J. Preus, *Spinoza and the Irrelevance of Biblical Authority* (New York, 2001). See also Frei, *Eclipse of Biblical Narrative*, 42–46.

scriptural passages and to determine their relationship to historical facts. Increasingly, hermeneutics revolved around the relationship between religious meaning and historical referent. While conservative interpreters read biblical narratives as factual sources of revealed truth, their liberal counterparts read them as dubious accounts of questionable inspiration. In either case, efforts to discern religious meaning became a question of understanding historical contexts. In short, historical reasoning began to control biblical interpretation.[9]

Historians often assume colonial America was isolated from the more dangerous undercurrents of these developments, but recent scholarship shows that Calvinist preacher and theologian Jonathan Edwards was drawn into those undercurrents.[10] In contrast to deists and Quakers, who derived religious knowledge from a priori understandings, he looked to scripture for religious instruction. Drawing on Locke's sensationalism, Edwards posited a kind of *divine* intuition, which he believed the Bible cultivated. And yet, deist critiques of an epistemology based in revelation led him to conclude, as Robert Brown notes, that "historical religious knowledge was the only source of *human* ideas about religion."[11] Aligning religious understanding with historical knowledge made it paramount for Edwards to defend the Bible and the Christian religion on historical grounds.

Writing in a notebook in the mid-1750s, Edwards upheld Hebrew scripture with historical arguments. Like earlier interpreters, he accepted the Bible's authenticity simply because it presented itself as historical. For example, because "some of the STATUTES of the Law [of Moses] are delivered in the FORM OF HISTORY," Edwards read those statutes as accurate accounts of past events. But Edwards also used profane knowledge to confirm the truth of the Bible.[12] He cited the history of pagan religions, for instance, to verify the accuracy of the Pentateuch and to favorably compare its contents. This kind of historical apologetic shows up throughout Edwards's "Notes on Scripture" and his early

---

[9] See Frei, *Eclipse of Biblical Narrative*, 66–104; see also Lee, *Erosion of Biblical Certainty*, 11–24.
[10] Michael Lee has shown that Cotton Mather also selectively appropriated new interpretive methods. Lee, *Erosion of Biblical Certainty*, 26–51.
[11] Robert E. Brown, *Jonathan Edwards and the Bible* (Bloomington, IN, 2002), 27–87, quotation on 55 (emphasis mine).
[12] Jonathan Edwards, "Defense of the Pentateuch as a Work of Moses," in *Works of Jonathan Edwards Online, Volume 28, Minor Controversial Writings* (Jonathan Edwards Center at Yale University, 2008).

"Miscellanies." The latter, for example, includes the entry "History of the Old Testament from Moses' time confirmed from heathen traditions and records."[13] His catalogue of books, which references both ancient and contemporary historical sources, also shows Edwards's commitment to historical reasoning.[14] Although he remained apologetic in his reasoning and still prioritized divine intuition, he waged much of his biblical defense on the historical grounds that had been prepared by figures such as Hobbes, Spinoza, and Locke.[15] Indeed, precisely because Edwards believed the Bible to be the primary repository of divine revelation and the gauge of religious truth, sometimes he seemed to value historical reasoning even more than the Bible's critics.

In his "Work of Redemption," a collection of sermons he first delivered to his Northampton congregation in 1739 and then revised during the remainder of his life, Edwards contended that the historical nature of the Bible confirmed its revelatory status. In his sermons, he focused on Christ's salvific providences in the form of revivals. Rejecting the enlightenment-inspired mechanical philosophy of time and its anthropocentric view of progress toward a millennium, Edwards argued that God maintained sovereign control over historical development through continual redemptive workings. He believed that divinely directed revivals effected change toward a Christian culmination. This holistic historical view influenced Edwards's reading of the Bible.[16]

Even though he used extrabiblical sources and acknowledged human experience outside of the Bible, Edwards maintained that all human existence, past and present, fit within the biblical framework. Thus, he held that "the Bible is the most comprehensive book in the world."[17] In his first sermon, he noted that the work of redemption "'tis all but one work, one design. The various dispensations and works that belong to it are but the several parts of one scheme."[18] In his tenth sermon, Edwards again

---

[13] Jonathan Edwards, *Works of Jonathan Edwards, Volume 20, The "Miscellanies," 833–1152*, ed. Amy Plantinga Pauw (New Haven, CT, 2002), 351–53.
[14] Jonathan Edwards, *Works of Jonathan Edwards, Volume 26, Catalogues of Books*, ed. Peter J. Thuesen (New Haven, CT, 2008).
[15] See Brown, *Edwards and the Bible*, 88–163; see also Lee, *Erosion of Biblical Certainty*, 71–85.
[16] Avihu Zakai, *Jonathan Edwards's Philosophy of History: The Reenchantment of the World in the Age of Enlightenment* (Princeton, NJ, 2003). On "Work of Redemption," see also Brown, *Edwards and the Bible*, 164–96.
[17] Jonathan Edwards, *Works of Jonathan Edwards, vol. 9, A History of the Work of Redemption*, ed. John F. Wilson (New Haven, 1989), 291.
[18] Ibid., 9:118.

explained that the Bible contained "an account of how the Work of Redemption is carried on from the beginning to the end." Aware that new historical information attested to extrabiblical peoples and settings, he admitted that "the Scripture don't contain a proper history of the whole," but taught that "there is contained the whole chain of great events by which this affair has been carried on from the foundation soon after the fall of man to the finishing of it at the end of the world."[19] In cases where the Bible did not offer a "proper history" of its own subjects, Edwards believed God "took care that there should be authentic and full accounts ... preserved in profane history," which, he argued, "wonderfully agree with the many prophecies that we have in Scripture of these times."[20]

While using extrabiblical historical sources to confirm the Bible's factuality, Edwards felt a need to account for its historical nature and distinguish it from other historical sources. He set out to do this in his thirteenth sermon. In response to readings that placed the biblical texts alongside other histories and thus threatened to desacralize them, Edwards posited that "though they are histories, yet they are no less full of divine instruction ... than other parts of the holy Scriptures that are not historical. To object against a book's being divine merely because it is historical is a silly objection."[21] Indeed, Edwards continued, the notion was "so far from being a weighty objection against the historical parts of Scripture being the word of God that 'tis a strong argument" in its favor. If reason led "all civilized nations to keep records," he wondered, "how much more may we expect that God gives the world a record of the dispensations of his divine government."[22] Edwards insisted that revelatory eras deserved historical accounts. And these accounts offered unique insight into the ancient past: "the times of the history of the Old Testament are times that no other history reaches up to."[23] While observing that the Bible provided historical depth, Edwards believed that its unmatched narration "of the grand scheme of divine providence" was what distinguished it and ensured its continued relevance.[24]

The lens of redemptive workings provided Edwards with an answer to the problem of distance that historical research had begun to expose. "Some," he bemoaned, "are ready to look on the Old Testament as being, as it were, out of date and as if we in these days of the gospel had but little to do with it." While some Christians perceived an insurmountable

---

[19] Ibid., 9:242.   [20] Ibid., 9:243.   [21] Ibid., 9:284.   [22] Ibid., 9:285.
[23] Ibid., 9:285–86.   [24] Ibid., 9:284.

distance between modern Americans and ancient Hebrews, Edwards insisted that "both Old Testament and New, is filled up with gospel, only with this difference, that the Old Testament contains the gospel under a veil."[25] This typological reading protected the relevance of the Hebrew scriptures. While acknowledging extrabiblical sources and using them to confirm the authenticity of biblical texts, Edwards incorporated both the Bible and extrabiblical sources into God's all-encompassing work of redemption. This approach ensured the present era's hold on the biblical past. In the short term, this reading guarded against the threat of historical distance as an interpretive problem. However, by meeting his opponents on historical grounds, Edwards helped set the stage for new developments in historical readings of the Bible. Within a few generations, some American exegetes began to argue that the Bible's divinity rested on its historicity and insisted that a proper interpretation required contextual readings. This placed the sacred biblical texts in a precarious position, threatening to further expose the archaism behind the veil.

Much of this development depended on advances in European biblical scholarship. As deism directed America's preeminent theologian to prize historical knowledge, so it also contributed to the rise of biblical criticism as an autonomous academic discipline. In the 1770s, German enlightenment scholar Gotthold Ephraim Lessing published portions of a work in which deist Hermann Samuel Reimarus denied the historical accuracy of the New Testament texts and dismissed Jesus's miracles. In response, Johann Salomo Semler, a professor of theology at the University of Halle, defended the miracles' factuality by appealing to historical context. One of Semler's students, Johann David Michaelis, who became a professor of history at the University of Göttingen, embraced the historical approach to the Bible, as did his student Johann Gottfried Eichhorn. Halle and Göttingen provided nourishing institutional seedbeds in which German biblical criticism flourished. In their historical introductions to the New and Old Testaments, Michaelis and Eichhorn provided the first thorough treatments of the anticipatory questions that had been raised by Spinoza, Hobbes, and Locke.

Acknowledging the historical nature of the Bible's content, these German critics used philological and historical tools to ascertain the origin, context, and factual veracity of biblical narratives. Rather than draw a straight line from historical content to religious meaning, as had their predecessors, they sought to recover historical conditions to

[25] Ibid., 9:290.

determine the enduring religious value of biblical passages. In their view, religious meaning was distinguishable from historical facts and could not be wholly explained through reference to historical contexts, but facts provided a basis for belief, and context acted as a gauge of truth. In championing contextual interpretation of biblical and also classical texts, these moderate German scholars demonstrated awareness of historical distance from ancients such as Plato, Homer, and Moses.[26] Johann Gottfried Herder, in particular, assumed historical distance in viewing each era, including the biblical pasts, as unique. He argued that because each past period and people had distinct value, historians must approach them sympathetically.[27] Such attention to historical distinctions raised questions about the canon's unitary meaning. Even before Lessing published Reimarus's work, Semler had divided up biblical books based on what contextual investigation indicated about their religious value. Unlike Edwards, Semler did not think each biblical text preached of Christ. These varied uses of historical reasoning opened the door to Johann Philipp Gabler's biblical theology. Gabler contended that religious meaning depended on textual referents in the form of facts authenticated through historical research.[28] In these ways, German biblical critics made contextual reading central to the project of biblical interpretation.

Within a few decades, these developments began to shape American biblical scholarship, which had already begun leaning toward an emphasis on historical reasoning. In general, American biblical scholars were less critical than their German counterparts, but the Americans became even more invested in the historical nature of biblical texts during this period. Scottish realism encouraged that investment. In revising Locke's sensationalist epistemology to combat David Hume's skepticism, Glasgow native Thomas Reid asserted that ordinary human experience laid bare the universal presence of internal first principles. According to Reid, these principles revealed the self and attested to the reality of objects perceived via the senses. American proponents of evidential Christianity used this bolstered sensationalism, along with the empiricism of Francis Bacon, to marshal internal and external evidences in defense of the reasonableness of the Bible. This provided them with a viable response to radical deists such as Thomas Paine, who battered the Bible as irrational. Orthodox

---

[26] Michael C. Carhart, *The Science of Culture in Enlightenment Germany* (Cambridge, MA, 2007).
[27] Beiser, *The German Historicist Tradition*, 110–20.
[28] See Frei, *Eclipse of Biblical Narrative*, 60–65, 105–64.

belief guarded most of America's biblical scholars from the undermining potential of biblical criticism, but as with Edwards before them, their strenuous efforts to evidence the truth of Christianity drew together historicity and religious meaning. Historical reasoning became a principal concern for American exegetes, which created the conditions for the qualified introduction of biblical criticism in antebellum America.[29] Thus began the exegetical march toward reading the Bible as a historical text and the resulting sense of historical distance, two developments that challenged assumptions of easy transference between biblical past and American present.

JOSEPH S. BUCKMINSTER'S "HISTORICAL EXPLICATION"

The same sources that shaped biblical criticism in Europe informed its institutional arrival in America. Convinced that "deistical publications" obscured Christian truths, Samuel Dexter set aside $5,000 in his will for Harvard to promote "that most useful branch of learning, the critical knowledge of the holy scriptures."[30] He directed the testators to acquire scholarly works, purchase and support the production of new translations, and fund learned lectures "for the purposes of *critically* explaining either the *history*, *doctrines*, or *precepts*, of the gospel." History figured prominently in Dexter's plans, as in his emphasis on the "usefulness of explaining idioms, phrases, and figures of speech, which abound in the scriptures; and the usages and customs therein referred to; and of clearing up the difficulties in sacred chronology and geography."[31] Dexter understood that biblical criticism was often a historical endeavor.

In 1811, the year after his death, Dexter's trustees elected Joseph Buckminster as Harvard's Dexter Lecturer of Biblical Criticism, the first American academic appointment of its kind.[32] When notified of his election, the New Hampshire native wrote to Harvard President John Thornton Kirkland of the "unexpected appointment." The young Unitarian minister expressed his conviction that perhaps the lectureship

---

[29] See Holifield, *Theology in America*, 174–95.
[30] "Intelligence," *General Repository and Review* 1 (January 1812): 204, 205. The *Repository*'s Unitarian editors introduced readers to biblical criticism, providing them with an English translation of Eichhorn's biography of Semler, discussions about critical editions of the Bible, and reviews of histories and geographies of the New Testament.
[31] Ibid., 205, emphasis in original.
[32] Ibid., 208–9. For more on Buckminster's role in propagating biblical criticism in America, see Brown, *Rise of Biblical Criticism*, 10–26.

should be "entrusted to some one whose age and acknowledged merits in theology will gain for them more consideration than will probably be secured by the present appointment." If the trustees were set on Buckminster, however, he stood ready "to execute as well as the time allows and my own health will permit."[33] Neither time nor his health complied. In 1812, before beginning his lectureship, the promising twenty-eight-year-old died of epilepsy. Nonetheless, Buckminster had already contributed to the development of American biblical scholarship. As minister of the prominent Brattle Street Church and as Boston's foremost orator, he had displayed a respectable grasp of German biblical criticism and put it to use. While he upheld the Bible as the final authority on religious truth, Buckminster called upon historical insight to explain its teachings.

Buckminster developed an interest in both history and biblical scholarship at an early age. He learned Greek and Latin as a child and graduated at the age of sixteen from Harvard with both a bachelor's and master's degree. As a student, he wrote an essay entitled "Biblical Criticism." It contained passages copied from Herodotus and Thucydides, extracts from evidentialist Samuel Clarke's writings on Homer, and notes on Hebrew grammars. While the essay reflected the period's overlapping interest in classical works and the Bible, it contained little of what Buckminster learned in subsequent years from German scholars.[34]

In a more illuminating essay titled "Study of History," Buckminster demonstrated a youthful fascination with the utility of the past. Allowing that metaphysics offered delight, and that poetry and oratory provided ornamentation, he proposed that "to History alone can we resort in circumstances the most intricate and situations the most hazardous. Here is collected in one vein the universal experience of human nature." Buckminster's idea of history as a guide to human endeavor echoed the axiom, famously expressed by Lord Bolingbroke and repeated throughout the eighteenth and nineteenth centuries, that "history is philosophy teaching by examples."[35] History gifted the present the collective wisdom of generations past. According to Buckminster, the universality of human nature ensured history's continued usefulness: "the utility of the study of

---

[33] Joseph S. Buckminster to John Thornton Kirkland, n.d., Joseph Stevens Buckminster Papers, Boston Athenæum (hereafter BA).
[34] Joseph S. Buckminster, "Biblical Criticism," Joseph Stevens Buckminster Papers, BA.
[35] Bolingbroke attributed the idea to the Greek historian Dionysius of Halicarnassus. See Henry St. John, Viscount Bolingbroke, *Letters on the Study and Use of History* (London, 1752), 1:15.

history results from the truth of this principle, viz. that human nature remains throughout all ages essentially unaltered." While acknowledging that "precisely the same circumstances can never twice occur, and consequently precisely the same line of conduct can never be wisely attempted," he believed that "where a strong analogy or resemblance can be traced we are justified in similar conduct of sentiment." While exhibiting a traditional belief in human nature as static, this short student essay also displayed a more modern awareness of distinct historical contexts. The recognition of particular circumstances in a search for universal truths became a central component in Buckminster's approach to biblical texts.[36]

In 1806, two years after Buckminster became minister of the Brattle Street Church, he made a trip to Europe, as Harvard graduates often did, and amassed a huge library of biblical studies. An 1810 letter from Buckminster to Herbert Marsh, an English bishop who had studied with Michaelis and had translated his mentor's introduction to the New Testament, shows that Buckminster obtained works such as the manual edition of Johann Jakob Griesbach's two-volume study of the New Testament, *Novum Testamentum Græce* (1774–75).[37] In 1809, Buckminster published the first American edition of Griesbach's study.[38] Buckminster's sermons suggest that he not only bought and published such works but also read and used them in preaching to his Boston congregants, who heard him articulate a historical approach to the Bible.[39]

A passage from a set of Buckminster's undated sermon notes "On Studying the N.T. as a historical record" encapsulates his approach to the Bible as a historical text. Buckminster wrote,

To many xtns [Christians] it appears superfluous and vain to insist so much as we do on the study of the books of the N.T. as historical records. We do this however not only because the importance of the facts there recorded justifies and demands the closest attention, but because this is the only method by wih [which] we can arrive at the understanding of the primitive simplicity of xtnity [Christianity], and correct there mistakes into wih [which] we are continually led by the sound of words and phrases taken out of their connexion, and by the misapplication of

---

[36] Joseph S. Buckminster, "Study of History," Joseph Stevens Buckminster Papers, BA.
[37] Joseph S. Buckminster to Herbert Marsh, May 13, 1810, Joseph Stevens Buckminster Papers, BA.
[38] See Lee, *Erosion of Biblical Certainty*, 130–36.
[39] On the European influences of Buckminster's emphasis on contextual readings, see Lee, *Erosion of Biblical Certainty*, 144–53.

phrases appropriate to certain times and circumstances to the all ages, and all the world.

Understanding the historical nature of biblical texts and the contextual nature of biblical language, Buckminster aimed to avoid anachronistic readings and applications as he strove to recover religious truth. He exhibited a historicist confidence that once the interpreter recognized historical distance, he could use research to overcome that distance for himself and his contemporaries. In writing that "it is only so far as his hearers take an interest in the same inquiries and are furnished with similar information that his discourses can be truly profitable," Buckminster hoped his congregants would join him in recognizing the importance of a historical exegesis of the New Testament. Because he believed "the circumstances of the first chhs [churches] of xt [Christ], to wih [which] Pauls epistles are directed, make a very interesting and profitable subject," Buckminster made those circumstances the focus of his historical explication.[40]

Buckminster's mode of historical explication assumed the canon's authenticity. He followed Michaelis in drawing distinctions between the two testaments, and he received the Gospels as canonical based on apostolic authorship, which he believed was confirmed by internal consistency and external evidences such as miracles and fulfilled prophecies. For Buckminster, intertextual analysis ensured historical accuracy, and extratextual historical evidence confirmed, but could not unsettle, the canon. Using textual evidence alone to authenticate the canon limited the extent to which extrabiblical evidence could shape Buckminster's views. Even still, he advanced a contextual approach that drew attention to the historical differences among biblical pasts and, especially, between those pasts and his American present.

In a sermon on Philemon, probably delivered sometime between February 1809 and August 1810, Buckminster described biblical exegesis as a historical endeavor. He used the Gospels to authenticate other New Testament texts, and Paul's epistle to Philemon passed the test. After a quick verse-by-verse analysis of the text, wherein Paul returns Onesimus, a slave, to his master, Buckminster proposed that "an historical explication of the writings of the New Testament" provided "the most interesting and satisfactory mode of studying them."[41] What did

---

[40] Joseph S. Buckminster, "On Studying the N.T. as a historical record," Joseph Stevens Buckminster Papers, BA.

[41] Buckminster, "Philemon," 78–92, quotation on 83.

"historical explication" signify? He explained: "instead of looking into every text, separated from its context, to find something which may bear upon a favourite system, we should be content to understand the apostles, as they meant to be understood by those to whom they wrote." Challenging conventional understandings, Buckminster insisted that the apostles "were not, on every occasion, delivering a system of dogmas for the instruction of all succeeding time."[42] This approach paralleled the arguments of figures such as Herder. To avoid the pitfalls of conventional readings, which often ignored historical differences and collapsed historical distance, Buckminster stressed the need for contextual interpretation; he insisted that historical context rather than present concerns should direct analysis. This attention to temporal disjuncture marked a departure from readings that assumed the timelessness of biblical words.

In emphasizing context, Buckminster suggested that readers focus on the intentions of historical authors and the reception of historical audiences. A similar emphasis on original intent and meaning also developed in legal interpretation, where constitutional interpreters began to stress the need to understand Madison's founding-era context. Focused on Paul's context, Buckminster wrote that the ancient apostle "consulted the circumstances of his correspondents, reasoned with them sometimes on their own assumptions, and sometimes upon prevailing hypotheses, now according to their peculiar habits of interpretation, and then upon suppositions and accommodations of his own."[43] Buckminster hoped his audience would adopt the view that Paul inhabited a different world. Acting as a guide in a foreign country, Buckminster used works such as Michaelis's studies on the New Testament to help orient readers during their sojourn. Buckminster's emphasis on context as determinative, and his efforts to illuminate that context, indicated that the New Testament past was distinct and unfamiliar.

This approach raised a difficult question: if the Bible's writings were subject to the same constraints as other texts, how could one be sure it taught eternal truths? Buckminster rejected the popular notion of plenary inspiration: he believed apostolic writings constituted the word of God but that God did not inspire his authors in every particular. Still, Buckminster held that God "would not suffer them, in writing on any occasion in which his revelation was even remotely concerned, to give a false or mistaken statement of his truth."[44] While at pains to ground the texts in local circumstances, he assured his congregants that an eternal

[42] Ibid., 83–84.   [43] Ibid., 84.   [44] Ibid., 85.

God guarded his temporal servants from error. Like Edwards's appraisal of the Old Testament, Buckminster believed the apostles' writings held unique historical value. They throw "light upon the early history of the gospel," he proposed, and assist "us in judging of the probability of the principle facts mentioned ... in one word, they are documents which awaken an interest in, and add confirmation to the wonderful history of Jesus and his apostles."[45]

While using the apostolic epistles to confirm the message of the Gospels, Buckminster continued to caution against assuming affinities between past and present. He acknowledged that Christians would like to know "what the apostles thought upon some subjects of modern speculation," but he cautioned that "it is likely that few [of those modern subjects], perhaps none of them, ever once entered their minds." In focusing on differences in thought, Buckminster noted that the apostles' writings must be read as historically situated records, written "in a popular style, influenced ... by the prevailing notions of their own age and nation; a style by no means nicely accommodated to the metaphysics of our times."[46] Buckminster told his congregants that in most instances, ideas specific to the apostles' own distinct era – one distant from the present age – shaped their teachings.

Buckminster's historical explication alternated between emphasizing context and authenticating text. Turning his attention to the content of Paul's letter, he demonstrated how comparing New Testament texts could confirm their histories and religious truths. He asked his audience to imagine the following: the executor of Philemon's estate reads the book of Acts, peruses Paul's letter to Philemon, and listens to a public narration of his correspondence to the Colossians. Such experiences, Buckminster suggested, would verify the "history of the apostle."[47] Buckminster contended that intertextual analysis authenticated New Testament texts.

In a move reminiscent of Edwards, Buckminster also appealed to a contemporaneous nonbiblical text to elevate Christianity above other belief systems and to confirm the plausibility of Paul's decision to return the slave Onesimus to his master, Philemon. Noting that the Roman author Pliny the Elder "lived in the same age with the apostle," Buckminster cited an extant letter that Pliny had "addressed to one of his friends, upon an occasion precisely similar to this of Paul,

[45] Ibid., 86.   [46] Ibid.   [47] Ibid., 88.

interceding for the pardon of a runaway slave."⁴⁸ According to Buckminster, the affinities between the sources corroborated Paul's account. In comparing the accounts, Buckminster noted that Pliny's epistle, though written by a man of literary learning, "is altogether inferiour."⁴⁹ Buckminster used remainders of the classical past to attest to both the factuality and the superiority of the New Testament past. Given the text's historical accuracy and superior literary value, the author's magnanimity, and Christianity's greatness, he wondered "what ideas would the reader of this letter [to Philemon] form of the nature and spirit of christianity?"⁵⁰

Christian universalism was among the religious truths that Buckminster extracted from Paul's letter. Here the reader "would learn, that the soul, even of a fugitive slave, is not unworthy of being rescued from the tyranny and misery of sin; that the gift of eternal life … is no less important to Onesimus, than to his master." But freedom from sin did not signify freedom from slavery. "In remarkable coincidence with the doctrine of the apostle in other epistles," the reader "would find, that Christianity made no alterations in the civil or political relations of the converts."⁵¹ Buckminster had highlighted congruencies among apostolic texts to authenticate Paul's letter, marshaled extrabiblical historical evidence to confirm its history, and then made Paul speak for "all succeeding time" on slavery and *fugitive slaves* – a contemporary term applied to an ancient figure.⁵²

Buckminster's contextual interpretation of Philemon itself demands further contextualization. Providing a historical explication of a text in which Paul returns Onesimus, a slave, to Philemon was not an arbitrary choice. In 1808, a year or two before Buckminster's speech, Congress used section 9 of article 1 of the Constitution to pass an act prohibiting the importation of slaves. Illegalizing the transatlantic slave trade made southern slaveholders more dependent on the domestic slave trade and more reliant on the enforcement of the Fugitive Slave Act of 1793, which had bolstered the Constitution's fugitive slave clause. In this context, Buckminster wrote of Paul's return of Onesimus to Philemon: "how unlike the customs and the spirit of modern society!"⁵³ His reading, which paralleled a conventional constitutional reading urging the

---

⁴⁸ Ibid., 89, 89–90. For similar uses of nonbiblical sources see, for example, Joseph S. Buckminster, "The Fitness of the Time of the Introduction of the Gospel," in *Sermons by the late Rev. Joseph S. Buckminster*, 3–4.
⁴⁹ Buckminster, "Philemon," 90.   ⁵⁰ Ibid., 91.   ⁵¹ Ibid.   ⁵² Ibid., 91–92.
⁵³ Ibid., 92.

maintenance of the status quo, condemned those antislavery contemporaries who failed to collapse historical distance and live as Paul had.

Buckminster believed that certain human relations – including that between enslaver and enslaved – remained constant despite profound changes in thought, language, and custom. His reading of Philemon would echo loud and clear in subsequent decades, culminating in defenses of the Fugitive Slave Law (1850), and finding a legal corollary in constitutional readings that also acknowledged and then set aside historical change. Nineteenth-century concerns constrained biblical readers' views of Christian freedom – as they would later inhibit constitutional readers' ideas of American freedom – and encouraged individuals in both groups to ignore historical distance in the application of original proslavery biblical and legal truths.

Buckminster's biblical criticism was synonymous with his historical explication, which he used to uncover universal truths. He began with the acknowledgment that New Testament Christianity "is conveyed to us in the historical form" and built from an assumption of the biblical texts' historicity.[54] Arguing for the need to understand the historical situation in which these texts were produced, Buckminster proceeded to extract timeless religious truths from transient temporal facts. His emphasis on the need to recognize the historical situatedness of an apostolic author, his text, and his audience and the historical distance between said author, his text, and the present yielded to the idea that on crucial issues, such as the relationship between enslaver and enslaved, the canon transcended time. In this way, Buckminster conceived of historical understanding and religious truth as allies.

However, in making religious truth epistemologically dependent on "an historical explication," Buckminster's reading had the potential of arming historical understanding against religious truth. What happened, for example, when historical insight undermined the authenticity of a biblical text or the permanence of its teachings? Buckminster believed attention to historical differences would yield more accurate readings and make it easier to understand and apply universal truths, but his contextual emphasis laid bare the temporal nature of biblical eras and drew attention to distance from those favored pasts. The realization of historical distance could complicate assertions of the Bible's relevance.

---

[54] Joseph S. Buckminster, "Acts 10:34–35, February 1812," Joseph Stevens Buckminster Papers, BA.

At this point, biblical interpreters such as Buckminster seemed unaware of the interpretive challenges their attention to historical differences might pose. And indeed, as an alternative to a firmly entrenched ahistorical approach to scripture, Buckminster's historical explication stood little chance of spreading awareness of historical distance in ways that might challenge the Bible's moral authority. Buckminster worried about winning over audiences who were skeptical of his approach rather than warning them about the skepticism that might follow historical exegesis. And yet, his version of historical explication marked the beginning of a broad development toward reading the Bible in ways that drew attention to the temporal and transient nature of the sacred text's content. Such historical readings opened the door for later interpreters to use a newfound sense of historical distance to question the modern relevance of ancient scriptures.

Over the next few decades slavery maintained and then increased its hold on the national consciousness, fueling efforts to provide historical readings of the Bible and thus increasing the potential for readers to recognize the problem distance posed to their interpretations. Using historical facts to confirm religious truths made the interpretive challenge of temporal distance difficult to ignore. Before that challenge was drawn out into the open, however, an array of biblical scholars began to adopt and promote the same kind of historical explication that Buckminster had advanced.

RELIGIOUS LIBERALS IN THE BATTLE FOR THE ELEVATED GROUNDS OF HISTORY

The influence of Buckminster, America's foremost proponent of biblical criticism in the first decade of the nineteenth century, remained mostly limited to his Brattle Street congregation. His appointment as Dexter Lecturer promised to spread his principles to a more engaged audience. Death robbed him of the opportunity, but it also gave life to biblical criticism in the United States. The public sale of his library brought together some of America's most prominent and promising biblical scholars, and when they parted ways, they left with works of European biblical criticism. While they approached biblical criticism in distinct modes and used new insights to different ends, most of them began to privilege a form of what Buckminster had called "an historical explication" of scripture.

Although Unitarianism was a newer feature of the American religious landscape, and while Unitarians were relatively few in numbers, they figured most prominently in promoting historical explication in the antebellum era. American Unitarianism had emerged gradually from the divide that had developed between conservative and liberal congregationalist churches in New England. In the eighteenth century, liberal ministers such as Jonathan Mayhew had valued reason over enthusiasm and had called into question the creedal belief in the Trinity. Despite Jedidiah Morse's later claims, American Unitarians did not adopt the views of English Unitarians such as Joseph Priestley, who relegated Jesus to the status of a human teacher. However, they did set aside a belief in God's meddling providence in favor of an emphasis on his paternal benevolence and replaced the idea of original sin with human virtue. They also insisted that a reasonable reading of the New Testament would highlight these truths.

The Unitarian emphasis on reason usually carried with it an attention to context, as demonstrated in the sermons of figures such as Buckminster and Samuel Cary. In January 1809, Cary became the pastor of King's Chapel in Boston. A few years earlier, he had served as the assistant minister at King's Chapel, a position Buckminster had turned down. In July 1809, Cary was present with Buckminster at the founding of the Massachusetts Bible Society (MBS). Cary and Buckminster had similar associations and advocated the same brand of biblical criticism.

In an 1814 sermon given first at King's Chapel and then at the Brattle Street Church, Cary promoted historical explication. Accepting the Bible as "an authentick record of what God has revealed to mankind," he outlined the historical nature of the biblical record.[55] He attributed scriptural ignorance to the idea that "most christians are but imperfectly acquainted with the facts ... which have been brought to light by the researches of biblical criticism."[56] According to Cary, in order to understand "the works of men who lived at a very remote period, and who wrote with particular objects in view, and are known to have accommodated themselves to the circumstances of their own time; it is manifestly necessary, that we should know something of the state of the world at that period."[57] In this era, biblical scholars frequently used the term *accommodate* to describe how God or biblical speakers and writers used the language and ideas of their own times to be understood by their contemporary audiences. With this in mind, Cary emphasized that readers

---

[55] Samuel Cary, *Ignorance of the True Meaning of the Scriptures, and the Causes of It* (Boston, 1814), 5.
[56] Ibid., 14–15. [57] Ibid., 15.

must recognize the "particular" nature of the Bible's contents, which, he explained, often "can have no reference whatever to any circumstances now existing in christian societies." As with Buckminster, Cary insisted on the need to separate "the mere local precepts from those which are of universal and perpetual obligation."[58] This practice of dividing the particular from the universal promised to bring religious truths to the fore, but in the process it also began to draw new attention to just how different the biblical pasts were from the present.

Like Buckminster, Cary died young. He passed away in 1815 at the age of twenty-nine, leaving the work of promoting biblical criticism to other Unitarians, including William Ellery Channing, who had been the pastor at Boston's Federal Street Church since 1803. Channing was another Harvard graduate who attended MBS meetings, and he succeeded Buckminster as Dexter Lecturer from 1812 to 1813. Channing's most successful efforts to publicize the Unitarian approach to scripture came not during his time as Dexter Lecturer in Cambridge but instead through a sermon he gave at the ordination of fellow Harvard alumnus Jared Sparks in Baltimore. On that occasion in 1819, the thirty-nine-year-old Unitarian luminary prioritized apostolic texts and upheld the reasonable use of historical knowledge as indispensable in interpretation.

Channing asserted that because God conformed to human language, "every word and every sentence must be modified and explained according to the subject ... the purposes, feelings, circumstances and principles of the writer, and ... the genius and idioms of the language which he uses."[59] Not even the Holy Spirit, he explained, suspended "the peculiarities of their minds."[60] One hears Buckminster and Cary in Channing's caution that "the different portions of this book ... refer perpetually to the times when they were written, to states of society, to modes of thinking, to controversies in the church, to feelings and usages which have passed away, and without the knowledge of which we are constantly in danger of extending to all times, and places, what was of temporary and local application."[61] Like the first Dexter Lecturer, Channing encouraged readers to avoid anachronistic applications and insisted that they must recover and use the historical context in which the apostles operated to

---

[58] Ibid., 16.
[59] William Ellery Channing, *A Sermon Delivered at the Ordination of the Rev. Jared Sparks* (Boston, 1819), 5. On Channing's role in propagating biblical criticism in America, see Brown, *Rise of Biblical Criticism*, 28–29, 60–74.
[60] Channing, *Sermon*, 7. [61] Ibid.

successfully separate general timeless truths from particular temporal facts. That insistence indicated historical difference.

As explained later, Channing's emphasis on context and his insistence on historical difference would allow him to posit that the apostles had taken expedient measures in addressing slavery's evil: rather than damn the institution outright, he would argue, the apostles had sowed abolitionist principles. Believing in the progress of those principles also led Channing to insist that the Constitution must be brought into accord with the antislavery spirit of the times. In both interpretive instances, Channing's readings implied that historical distance required the interpretive use of historical knowledge and reason.

But historical distance became an interpretive problem before it became an interpretive force, and both developments followed from biblical debates. In 1813, Andrews Norton, another Harvard graduate, replaced Channing as Dexter Lecturer. About six years later, around the same time as Channing's sermon, the Dexter Lectureship became the Dexter Professorship of Sacred Literature, and Norton filled the position. His appointment ensured the continuing spread of a historical approach to the Bible, as well as the deepening of religious divides. Whereas Channing had healthy exchanges with conservatives such as Moses Stuart and radicals such as Theodore Parker, the contentious Norton often engaged in more heated debates with his Christian contemporaries. In working to position Unitarianism against Calvinism on the right and Transcendentalism on the left, Norton went further than most American interpreters in advocating for a historicist approach to the scriptures.

Norton began by upholding what he described as the liberal approach to scripture over and against his understanding of the orthodox approach. In 1812, he opened the *General Repository* with an attack on orthodox interpreters, who, he argued, "pay but little regard to the circumstances in which [the author] wrote, or to those of the persons, whom he addressed."[62] In contrast, Norton posited, liberals rightly attend "to all these circumstances."[63] Like Buckminster before him, Norton insisted that interpreters must consider the circumstances of the ancient authors and their ancient audiences. As a Unitarian, he

---

[62] Andrews Norton, "A Defence of Liberal Christianity," *General Repository and Review* 1 (January 1812): 2. On Norton's role in propagating biblical criticism in America, see Brown, *Rise of Biblical Criticism*, 29–35, 69–93; see also Lee, *Erosion of Biblical Certainty*, 153–72.

[63] Norton, "Defence of Liberal Christianity," 3.

believed the New Testament to be the source of Christian truth and stressed the importance of historical explication in attempts to grasp the meaning of its texts.

While Norton articulated the liberal approach to scripture in relationship to more orthodox American interpreters, his emphasis on contextual readings developed in relationship to a foreign foe: the German critics. Norton's journal shows that in early 1818, perhaps in anticipation of his new appointment, he began reading and taking notes on works by Eichhorn and other German scholars. The depth of German criticism threatened Norton's beliefs and those of his American contemporaries. Rather than use contextual reasoning to better understand the religious truths of the Bible, German critics often applied such reasoning to explain and dismiss biblical texts as factually inaccurate products of their time. In light of this threat, Norton told a young George Bancroft that "there is nothing more abhorrent to our natures than German sentiment."[64] Bancroft had recently graduated from Harvard and was pursuing his doctorate under the tutelage of German scholars at Göttingen. Bancroft and a number of other Harvard graduates attended German universities with plans to begin a career in the ministry, but upon their return, they opted for other occupations, in part because of the cracks German biblical criticism had exposed in their Christian foundations. Norton had sensed the danger the Germans posed and warned Bancroft. Now Norton also began preparing a robust response.

Even as Norton started to formulate an answer to the threat of biblical criticism, he embraced much of its emphasis on historical reasoning and turned it to his own purposes. Late in 1818, he "commenced a work on the genuineness of the Gospels."[65] The next May, he notified Bancroft of Channing's recent sermon and explained that he, Norton, had been elected "Professor of biblical literature."[66] In subsequent letters, Norton sought clarification on the state of biblical scholarship in Germany and asked Bancroft to send German-authored works. In his journal, Norton continued to take notes on such works and tested his own arguments. This marked the beginning of an effort that culminated in his three-volume

---

[64] Andrews Norton to George Bancroft, December 29, 1820, Andrews Norton Papers, MS Am 1089, Houghton.
[65] Andrews Norton, Journal, December 31, 1818, Andrews Norton Papers, MS Am 1089, Houghton.
[66] Andrews Norton to George Bancroft, May 24, 1819, Andrews Norton Papers, MS Am 1089, Houghton.

Evidences of the Genuineness of the Gospels (1837–44).[67] In this mature work, Norton would marshal historical evidence to defend the Gospels as authentic.

In the earliest stages of this project, Norton focused less on answering the critics and more on convincing students of the correctness of the historical approach. If America's rising biblical scholars were going to beat the skeptics, they first had to learn how to play the game. Norton thus spent much of his time and energy emphasizing the importance of attending to circumstance and context in interpretation.

In this effort, Norton, like Buckminster, did not lose sight of the faith-affirming purpose of scriptural interpretation. He privileged historical understanding to highlight transcendent truth. In his "Materials for Lectures on Biblical Criticism," Norton even suggested that Jesus sometimes articulated ideas meant to be understood not "by his hearers at the time, but only afterward."[68] This indicated that Jesus, unlike his audience, sometimes transcended the limits of his immediate context and spoke across the centuries. The idea that some historical actors addressed future audiences bore some semblance to the antislavery biblical and constitutional readings later advanced by Channing and others, who argued that the Christian founders and the founding fathers had planted the seeds of abolition for their Christian and American descendants to cultivate. Before that development, Norton used the idea to signal the transcendence of Christ's message.

While Norton allowed that Christ sometimes taught in anticipation, he seemed intent on making sure his students understood the ways in which context constrained the teachings contained in the Bible. Citing various scriptures, he aimed to demonstrate that biblical teachings are best "explained by a consideration of circumstances."[69] Norton fleshed out these ideas in his lecture notes, in which he held that "the fundamental principles of religion and virtue are always the same" even as he affirmed that "the particular rules derived from these vary with the varying circumstances of men." He outlined three kinds of information needed to understand scripture, including "a knowledge of the circumstances under which the discourses of our Saviour were delivered, and the writings of

---

[67] Andrews Norton to George Bancroft, April 29, 1820, Andrews Norton Papers, MS Am 1089, Houghton.

[68] Andrews Norton, "Materials for Lectures on Biblical Criticism," Notebooks of Andrews Norton, Andrews Norton Papers, MS Am 1089, Houghton.

[69] Ibid.

the evangelists and apostles [were] composed," an understanding of the biblical writers' style, and a knowledge of the meanings behind their words and phrases. Norton indicated that all of this interpretive information had to be obtained through historical reasoning.[70]

In Norton's view, the particular revealed the eternal, which readers might miss if they assumed the Bible's relevance. He thus taught his students to read New Testament writings in relation to their authors' circumstances, explaining that "we must know the situation and character of those to whom any particular rules are addressed, before we can judge ... of the extensiveness of their application to others." Norton warned, "We shall interpret all these [scriptures] very erroneously if we neglect their original application, and suppose them to have a direct relation to ourselves." He wanted his students to understand that failing to take note of controversies "which have become long since wholly obsolete" and supposing that the apostles wrote "with the express design of affording instruction to all Christians in all ages" obscured original and universal truths. So, again and again Norton emphasized that readers "must be careful to understand" a text's "words in their original sense, and not that which they have acquired in modern times."[71] In most cases, he explained to his pupils, Christ and his apostles addressed the specific needs and problems of specific audiences. Norton's students learned to assume historical difference in and distance from the New Testament past.

Student notes on Norton's lectures confirm his insistence that readers use historical reasoning and indicate that he taught this approach as the corrective to enduring traditional readings. Alexander Young attended Harvard Divinity School from 1821 to 1824 and took Norton's course on biblical criticism. His notes are replete with references to the need for interpreters to take into account "particular" and "peculiar circumstances" and to avoid substituting "the modern for the original" meanings. Young recorded that "the fathers did not attend to these things ... they were inattentive to the peculiarities of the style of the N.T." While referencing prior generations, Norton's incessant instruction that "external circumstances ... should qualify the meaning" of scripture suggests that he also had in mind his contemporaries, including some of his students, who – like their fathers – imagined "a general and permanent state of things" and assumed that each passage was "intended for all men"

---

[70] Norton, Lecture 5, Notebooks of Andrews Norton, Andrews Norton Papers, MS Am 1089, Houghton.
[71] Ibid.

and "miraculously inspired for the use of all future ages."⁷² In Norton's lectures, students such as Alexander Young, Jared Sparks, John G. Palfrey, and Samuel J. May learned to resist the universal application of particular teachings and instead assume historical distance from the biblical past.

Norton's adoption of historical reasoning at Harvard preceded a similar development among other biblical scholars at other universities. Such reasoning also became bound up with debates about the relationship between biblical and American slaveries. Furthermore, the emphasis on original meanings later emerged as a central component in the constitutional debate over the peculiar institution, in which figures such as Palfrey and May were very involved. In the meantime, the stress that figures such as Norton placed on "temporary and transient circumstances" and "particular incidents and situations" suggested that historical differences set off biblical pasts from the present.⁷³

In proposing that "the whole preaching of our Saviour and his apostles must have been accommodated to the understandings, to the character, and to the situation of those whom they addressed," Norton was entering a popular interpretive debate. While some damned the German-born "theory of accommodation," which insisted that Jesus and the Gospel writers had accommodated to their audience, a growing group of American scholars accepted and advanced aspects of that same theory. Norton suggested that "we have ... no reason to believe that the minds of the apostles themselves were unaffected by the intellectual character and prevailing opinions of the age."⁷⁴ As an example, Young heard Norton teach that "the apostles held the common opinions of demoniacal possessions."⁷⁵ Norton spent more time teaching that the apostles must have "conformed themselves as far as possible to the apprehension of their disciples." He emphasized that the "great truths of our religion ... are of permanent and universal interest" but maintained that "the manner of their exhibition was conformed to temporary and local circumstances." The sacred writers, he repeated, "had in mind no readers but their contemporaries" and anticipated "none of those difficulties which would occur to other men than those in their own age." Like Herder, Norton believed that the interpreter must "forget our modern doctrines, and prejudices, and associations. He must make himself familiar and

---

⁷² Alexander Young, Notes on Professor Andrews Norton's Lectures, Andrews Norton Papers, MS Am 1089, Houghton.
⁷³ Norton, Lecture 5.   ⁷⁴ Ibid.
⁷⁵ Young, Notes on Professor Andrews Norton's Lectures.

contemporary with" historical actors.⁷⁶ Norton exposed the foreign nature of the biblical characters' past and then posited that historical research allowed the scholar to inhabit the biblical characters' mental world.

Norton's approach contained a historicist sensibility. In highlighting the historical situatedness of New Testament authors and audiences, he placed distance between Christian Americans and New Testament Christians. Then, once he had severed the assumed connection with biblical times, he suggested that the modern reader could build a bridge to the ancient past. The shift from assuming a fluid relationship with a familiar biblical past to the belief that one could construct a link to an ancient historical era indicated a profound transformation in historical awareness. The assumption of historical distance and the belief that one can shed modern sensibilities and use historical knowledge to bridge that distance is a central assumption of modern historical research. Even more than Buckminster, Norton expressed the optimism of the historicist position.

Norton did not appear worried that historical distance might pose an interpretive problem. Indeed, in a period when many still viewed the favored biblical past as familiar, he focused on its foreignness, spending most of his time lecturing on the particular nature of the Bible's content. He believed that the Bible's "meaning appears more distinctly" through his approach, ultimately giving readers "more reason to admire the simplicity, the purity, and the sublimity of it's [sic] moral precepts and it's [sic] religious doctrines." Norton maintained that rigorous historical research revealed simple eternal truths, but his emphasis on the historical nature of biblical pasts had the potential to complicate efforts to recover such truths. In other words, Norton's repeated stress on the distance from biblical periods threatened to undermine his familiarizing project.

When Norton did worry about historical research, his worries centered on arguments that might challenge the authenticity of the Gospels rather than ideas that might call into question the relevance of their teachings. He answered those worries with historical arguments, contending that the historical peculiarities of New Testament texts reinforced their genuineness; their archaic components, he asserted, signaled their historicity. Norton knew that many of his contemporaries still assumed that the canon had been written for "Christians in all ages and countries; and ... should contain little or nothing of a merely local or temporary

---

⁷⁶ Norton, Lecture 5.

nature," but he explained that if a presumed historical text lacked historical peculiarities, it would raise questions about its authenticity. So God, in his providence, allowed the sacred writer to have "nothing in view, but to be understood by the person or persons whom he is addressing." Norton observed that historical distinctions authenticated other ancient texts as well, such as Cicero's letters, and, like Buckminster, Norton compared biblical and classical texts to authenticate New Testament writings. Norton seemed unaware that this comparative approach could demote the Bible, making it one of a number of historical texts. More significantly, he did not see how his appeal to the canon's historical peculiarities could call into question the relevance of its teachings. When the issue of slavery imbued the biblical debate with new relevance, some figures, including Theodore Parker, would use historical distance to dismiss the Bible as outdated.[77] In the meantime, liberal and conservative biblical scholars competed on the new grounds of historical reasoning.

RELIGIOUS CONSERVATIVES IN THE BATTLE FOR THE ELEVATED GROUNDS OF HISTORY

In the period after Norton's appointment, religious liberals and conservatives remained focused on issues of canon and interpretation. Although the raging Missouri Crisis gave new life to political conversations about slavery, the biblical debate over slavery remained subdued. Channing's 1819 ordination sermon fueled interpretive debates between Harvard's Unitarians and their religious competitors at Andover Theological Seminary, which a group of orthodox Congregationalists, including Jedidiah Morse, had founded in 1807. The founding of this new seminary came as a partial response to Harvard's appointment of the liberal Henry Ware as Hollis Chair of Divinity two years earlier. To further stem the Unitarian tide, those at Andover promptly appointed New Haven pastor Moses Stuart – a Yale graduate who would quickly become the nation's most competent Hebrew and Greek grammarian – as Professor of Sacred Literature.

While Stuart's brand of biblical criticism focused on its more benign principles, he too began to emphasize the need to attend to context. As with the Unitarians, his qualified embrace of historical reasoning occurred in connection to an engagement with German scholarship and through dialogue with his religious opponents. In his published response to

[77] Ibid.

Channing's 1819 sermon, Stuart demonstrated a keen awareness of German scholarship, an interest in which had led him to learn German. Andover's studied appointee did not shy away from the doctrinal differences and canonical distinctions he perceived among his contemporaries; he worried that Channing too easily dispatched the Old Testament, which Stuart believed the Gospels authenticated. Even still, Stuart prized parts of the Unitarian's rules of interpretation; "with all [his] heart" he embraced the directive to interpret biblical passages according to the authors' specific subjects, motivations, and "special circumstances."[78] For example, Stuart noted that he interpreted John "just as I do any other author, ancient or modern, by the general rules of interpretation modified by the special circumstances and dialect in which he wrote."[79] In short, Stuart agreed with the Unitarians that interpreters should read the Bible as a historical text and that its words needed to be understood in "relation to the context."[80]

Stuart maintained that a close grammatical analysis mattered most; this view drew criticism from some quarters. Distinguishing general interpretive rules from the use of extrabiblical knowledge, he wrote that "whatever aid I may get from other sources ... must be that which is superadded to the explanation that these rules will afford."[81] The move to privilege an examination of the Bible's words over the use of extrabiblical sources found a close parallel in constitutional interpretation. Some later antislavery writers valued a strict reading of the Constitution's words over the use of extraconstitutional sources. The new stress on contextual readings in biblical interpretation made Stuart's distinction subject to critique; Norton believed that Stuart ignored historical circumstances in emphasizing a grammatical interpretation.

In printed responses to Stuart, Norton criticized what he understood as the orthodox inattention to context. Airing ideas he had scribbled in journals and presented in lectures, Norton promoted a liberal attention to historical circumstance. He argued that an interpreter must account for "the general state of things in which [the writer] lived, the particular local and temporary circumstances present to his mind while writing, [and]

---

[78] Moses Stuart, *Letters to the Rev. Wm. E. Channing, Containing Remarks on His Sermon Recently Preached and Published at Baltimore* (Andover, 1819), 23. On Stuart's engagement with biblical criticism, see John H. Giltner, *Moses Stuart: The Father of Biblical Science in America* (Atlanta, 1988); and Brown, *Rise of Biblical Criticism*, 43–59, 64–73, 94–110.

[79] Stuart, *Letters to the Rev.*, 143.   [80] Ibid., 50.   [81] Ibid.

the character and conditions of those for whom he wrote."[82] Implying that biblical pasts were unfamiliar places, Norton seemed to value learning unique cultural languages more than he valued learning Greek in the effort to understand biblical passages. In a note, he drew attention to Stuart's use of certain German scholars whom Norton found "defective" in their failure to address historical circumstances. "*It is necessary,*" he emphasized, "*to have just notions of the intellectual and moral character of our Saviour and his apostles, and of the circumstances under which they spoke or wrote.*"[83] In deriding Stuart for his apparent neglect of context, Norton failed to notice that Stuart and the German critics he had referenced also stressed the historical situatedness of biblical texts.

Norton's critique belied the similarities between the Unitarian modes of interpretation he cherished and the German modes of interpretation he considered dangerous. Indeed, his awareness of the similarities might have directed his effort to disassociate them; Norton's contempt for all things German might be attributable to an intellectual "narcissism of small differences." Sigmund Freud posited that "it is precisely the little dissimilarities in persons who are otherwise alike that arouse feelings of strangeness and enmity between them."[84] This might explain Norton's effort to contest the claim that Channing was traveling down a heretical path staked out by figures such as Semler, Eichhorn, and Wilhelm Martin Leberecht de Wette. It also might account for the rhetorical darts Norton later directed at Theodore Parker, whose German-inspired religious beliefs seemed to confirm everything that conservatives feared liberal religion would lead to and everything Norton assured them it would not. Regardless of the reasons, Norton distrusted German scholars. He failed to acknowledge that he was indebted to them for his approach and proceeded to fault them, as well as Stuart, for neglecting context in emphasizing grammar. But as Norton well knew, grammatical issues were bound up with historical questions.

While privileging a grammatical approach, Stuart protected himself against critiques of inattention to context. In the third edition of his response to Channing, he added a few sentences that further exhibited his appreciation for historical knowledge. In place of his statement about

---

[82] Andrews Norton, *A Statement of Reasons for Not Believing the Doctrines of the Trinitarians Respecting the Nature of God and the Person of Christ* (Boston, 1819), 42. Norton first responded to Stuart in two articles published in the *Christian Disciple*. He published an expanded edition of *Statement of Reasons* in 1833.

[83] Norton, *Statement of Reasons*, 43, emphasis in original.

[84] Sigmund Freud, *Sexuality and the Psychology of Love* (New York, 1997), 66.

"aid ... from other sources," he wrote, "I may obtain aid from many sources, to throw light upon the meaning of words and sentences. From a knowledge of the geography of any country ... as well as of the manner, customs, laws, history, &c. of its inhabitants, I may obtain assistance to explain its language, and must obtain it, if I mean to make out a satisfactory interpretation." Stuart signaled his belief that a correct interpretation required the use of available historical knowledge. "But," he interjected, "I can never dispense with the laws of grammatical analysis."[85]

Stuart granted primacy to grammatical rules in part because he felt confident in uniformly applying them independent of extrabiblical findings, which were relatively scarce and often unverifiable. "Admitting these rules to be the best and surest guide to the meaning of language," Stuart wrote, "we cannot supersede them, by *supposing*, or *conjecturing* peculiarities in a writer. It is only when these peculiarities are proved, or, at least, rendered probable, that they can be admitted to influence our interpretation."[86] Even as interpreters began to stress contextual readings, some of them pointed out the difficulties involved in recreating contexts. This was also true in the development of historicism in historical writing; even Herder was skeptical about historians being able to achieve historical understanding.[87] Stuart's caution matched that of some other biblical scholars, including Parker. This caution also foreshadowed later constitutional debates in which some antislavery interpreters highlighted the conjectural nature of historical research to cast doubt on proslavery contextual readings, including the one Stuart himself provided amid the uproar over the Fugitive Slave Law. But Stuart's 1850 reading was not a stark departure from his earlier statements on interpretation. As the period's preeminent popularizer of the grammatical–historical method, Stuart did not privilege ahistorical grammatical rules over historical explication. Instead, he was prizing a demonstrable interbiblical and language-based historical explication over a dubious extrabiblical one.

Stuart articulated his approach against a presentism he had observed in his contemporaries. He associated this presentism with the theory of accommodation advanced by Semler, who had proposed that Jesus and the Gospel writers had accommodated their teachings to the ignorance of the Jews. Stuart held that critics such as Semler, Eichhorn, and Ferdinand

---

[85] Moses Stuart, *Letters to the Rev. Wm. E. Channing, Containing Remarks on His Sermon Recently Preached and Published at Baltimore*, 3rd ed. (Andover, 1819), 57.

[86] Ibid., emphasis in original.   [87] Beiser, *German Historicist Tradition*, 116–18.

Bauer relied on this approach to explain away the Genesis account of the Creation and the Fall as poetical, to naturalize the Gospel's miracles, and to dismiss doctrines that failed to align with their own philosophical and theological positions. But, as far as Stuart could tell, "*accommodation* ... itself [had been] *accommodated*" and was being put to new uses.[88] Now, rather than assigning distasteful teachings and supposed miracles to Jewish ignorance, some critics explained them according to "the idiom and ignorance of antiquity in general, and ... of the sacred writers themselves."[89] Norton himself had accepted this view in part; he taught that, in some cases, historical circumstances influenced the apostles' teachings. According to this idea, New Testament audiences *and* authors held outdated beliefs. Parker later made similar claims about both New Testament and founding-era audiences and authors. This reading depicted entire historical periods, rather than portions of them, as bound up in time. The temporal threatened to engulf the eternal.

Stuart observed and dismissed this deep historicist threat. He believed that if one accepted the theory of accommodation, then one had to be willing to grant its application to both audiences and authors as the more sound historical approach. But he rejected the theory, finding it more telling of modern views than ancient beliefs. Studying the Germans left him even more convinced "that we need nothing more than the simple rules of exegesis, and a candid, believing heart, to see in the Scriptures ... all the substantial and important doctrines, which have commonly been denominated *orthodox*."[90] While admitting he could no longer "rely for the proof of doctrines on some texts which I once thought contained such proof," Stuart still believed that "the real truth and importance of evangelical doctrines ... are greatly strengthened" by the grammatical–historical method.[91] Like Edwards, his denominational and theological forebear, Stuart held that history sanctioned the Christian canon. Returning the critique of presentism, he charged Channing with using the principle of accommodation to twist ancient and authoritative writings in support of newly propounded ideas. The Unitarians, Stuart held, neglected the Germans' redeeming interpretive methods while embracing their damning liberal sentiments. Such efforts threatened to banish the sacred canon to a dark past.

While departing with Channing in the application of scripture, Stuart shared the Unitarian's focus on historical explication. He maintained that

---

[88] Stuart, *Letters to the Rev.*, 155, emphasis in original.   [89] Ibid., 151–52.
[90] Ibid., 158, emphasis in original.   [91] Ibid., 159.

"we are agreed as to *principles* of interpretation, in most things that are of importance."[92] In Stuart's lectures, he insisted that history "must come in to the aid of the grammatical principle." His instruction at Andover stressed the presence of historical distance. Like Norton, he urged ascription "to every sacred writer, views on such subjects consonant with his character and his age – and to reject the monstrous exegesis which explains him as though he spoke but yesterday and with all our feelings and prejudices."[93] Stuart's attention to grammar and language corresponded to his interest in promoting historical consciousness. In this period, the effort to learn languages such as Greek opened up ancient worlds.[94]

To be sure, Stuart articulated a qualified historicism, but it nonetheless contributed to a rising sense of historical distance. His orthodoxy informed his belief in the Bible's primacy and unity, his defense of plenary inspiration, and his move to assign accommodation to God rather than his scribes. Stuart indicated that "on all subjects, *not pertaining directly to the development of moral or religious truth*, you find in the sacred writers, the common views of their age & time." On certain issues, he set aside his own instruction to not assume nineteenth-century relevance and wrote of Paul "as though he lived at the present day."[95] As noted earlier, Stuart later echoed Buckminster's reading of Philemon to criticize those opposed to the Fugitive Slave Law. In upholding historical explication as the premier exegetical mode while also insisting on static meanings of certain biblical passages, Stuart and his liberal counterparts inadvertently backed into an awareness of historical distance from biblical times. In turn, that distance became difficult to ignore in their applicative efforts; their general emphasis on historical readings undercut their insistence on the enduring significance of specific passages. This armed more radical readers, including abolitionists who were willing to question the contemporary value of an ancient text.

Other conservative religionists also valued historical explication. Stuart's engagement with German scholarship did draw suspicion from colleagues, many of whom preferred to read the Bible without engaging German heresies, but Stuart was not the only Congregationalist who read the scholarship coming out of Europe. Yale graduate Jeremiah Evarts was

---

[92] Stuart, *Letters to the Rev.*, 3rd ed., 56, emphasis in original.
[93] Moses Stuart, Lecture 6, Lectures on Hermeneutics, Moses Stuart Papers, Franklin Trask Library, Andover Newton Theological School.
[94] See Winterer, *The Culture of Classicism*, 77–98. [95] Stuart, Lecture 6.

present at the landmark auction of Buckminster's library, where Evarts purchased works on the New Testament by Göttingen scholar Johann Friedrich Schleusner and Semler disciple Johann Jakob Griesbach. While suspicious of biblical criticism, figures such as Evarts valued the use of historical information to understand the Bible.[96]

As editor of the *Panoplist*, a religious monthly magazine created to challenge Unitarian influence, Evarts acknowledged the need to use historical research in reading the Bible. While he gave little space to biblical criticism except to counter its unsettling historicization of the canon's creation and transmission, in 1811 – the same year that Buckminster became Dexter Lecturer – the *Panoplist* diverted attention from its evangelical emphasis to praise Englishman Thomas Scott's *Commentary on the Whole Bible*.[97] "Scott's Family Bible," introduced to the American market in 1804, anticipated a bourgeoning book trade of new Bible translations; Bibles buttressed with commentaries, introductions, illustrations, and maps; and geographical studies such as William Thomson's *The Land and the Book* (1858). The deepening of historical awareness in this period depended on the publication and dissemination of historical knowledge about America's sacred texts. While intended to expand the Bible's reach and appeal, these works also contributed to its historicization. As historian Paul Gutjahr puts it, "While many still believed it to be 'the book of books,' it was equally true that the Bible was increasingly a book among books."[98]

Orthodox figures such as Evarts and the *Panoplist*'s publisher, Jedidiah Morse, upheld the Bible as "the standard, and only standard, of truth," but they recognized "that the Bible abounds with allusions to manners, customs and facts," the explication of which requires "knowledge, drawn from other sources, of the general history of the ages and countries in which the Scriptures were written."[99] Morse, who was a major figure in the divide between religious conservatives and liberals in New England,

---

[96] For an example of the *Panoplist*'s response to biblical criticism, see "On the Canon of Scripture," *Panoplist* 2 (May 1810): 559–60.

[97] See Lee, *Erosion of Biblical Certainty*, 132–36. As Lee demonstrates, antebellum biblical scholars sometimes attended to the Bible's textual history, but I am more interested in their emphasis on contextual explication.

[98] Paul C. Gutjahr, *An American Bible: A History of the Good Book in the United States, 1777–1880* (Stanford, 1999), 2. On "The Threat and the Promise of History" in the early republic's canonical debates, see David F. Holland, *Sacred Borders: Continuing Revelation and Canonical Restraint in Early America* (New York, 2011), 104–14.

[99] "Reviews," *Panoplist, and Missionary Magazine* 4 (September 1811): 161–69, quotations on 162 and 163.

agreed with the Unitarians on at least one point: the peculiarities of biblical pasts necessitated the use of historical guides. While America's biblical interpreters varied in their responses to biblical criticism, their exposure to it and debates about it demanded that they attend to and account for the particularities of the biblical past.

Even Orthodox Calvinists contributed to the growing emphasis on contextual interpretation. Charles Hodge, described as "the Pope of Presbyterianism" by his biographer, was more leery of biblical criticism than either the Unitarians or the Congregationalists.[100] He was among the first cadre of students to attend Princeton Theological Seminary when it opened in 1812. At the seminary, which was more conservative than the Congregationalist institution of Andover, Hodge learned biblical languages and came to appreciate the importance of historical readings. In 1820, before he began teaching at his alma mater, he traveled to New England, where he visited with Stuart. Stuart encouraged his Presbyterian counterpart to learn German to combat the Unitarians. Hodge obliged and, the next year, formed a society for the improvement of biblical literature. As president, he presented and published the society's first dissertation. In addressing the interpretation of biblical texts, Hodge stressed the need to understand "the character and history of the several sacred writers, with the state of opinion in the age in which they lived.... [And] the manners and customs, laws, character, and circumstances of the persons to whom the sacred writings were addressed."[101] Not unlike Norton and Stuart, Hodge instructed his audience to attend to the sacred authors' "peculiar circumstances," explaining that they addressed audiences "whose situation, habits, laws &c. were so different from our own."[102] While urging caution in reading German works, some of which approached the Bible as a purely human production, Hodge nonetheless accepted their interpretive emphasis on context as crucial.

In an effort to both counter writings coming out of Cambridge and "excite a spirit for Biblical Studies," Hodge formed the *Biblical Repertory* in 1825 and edited it for nearly five decades. He envisioned the quarterly "as a substitute, for the possession or perusal of works, which ... it may

---

[100] Paul C. Gutjahr, *Charles Hodge: Guardian of American Orthodoxy* (New York, 2011), 3.
[101] Charles Hodge, *A Dissertation, on the Importance of Biblical Literature* (Trenton, 1822), 25–26.
[102] Ibid., 32–33.

neither be easy nor desirable to put into general circulation."[103] While Unitarians engaged the broad spectrum of new biblical scholarship issuing from Germany, more conservative figures, such as Hodge, thought it best to selectively disseminate "interesting articles on the manners, customs, institutions, and literature of the East – on various points in Biblical Antiquities – and on the Literary History of the Sacred Volume."[104] Hodge hoped to extract faith-affirming content and distill it for his readers. He aimed to use biblical criticism's harmless principles to counter its lethal lessons. While engaging biblical scholarship in this conservative way, Hodge maintained the essential neutrality of critical study and, like his religious counterparts, valued the use of historical knowledge in interpretation.

The articles published in the *Biblical Repertory* demonstrated Hodge's commitment to using historical information. The opening issue included partial translations of German philologist Christian Daniel Beck's work on the New Testament, *Monogrammata Hermenuetices Novi Testamenti* (1803), and German theologian Charles Christian Tittmann's commentary on the Gospel of John, *Meletemata Sacra* (1816). Both of these works grounded biblical exposition in historical explication. Hodge wrote that the Beck selection gave "an account of the character, age, origin, and history of each particular book."[105] Beck himself informed readers that "those passages which are inconsistent with the Christian religion or history ... are to be regarded as spurious" and the content and style of the texts are to be judged "according to the opinions and manner of writing prevalent in the times of the sacred penmen."[106] Because "much belongs to the means of determining the *historical sense*," he encouraged the acquisition of "the knowledge of history and antiquities of the Jews, Greeks, and Romans, especially of the age in which the Sacred Writers lived."[107] All of these insights illuminated the language and teachings of the New Testament authors, who, Beck explained, accommodated themselves "in some measure, to the character of their readers."[108] Although he did not advocate the radical theory of accommodation – which posited

---

[103] Charles Hodge, "Proposals for the Periodical Publication of a Collection of Dissertations, Principally in Biblical Literature," *Biblical Repertory: A Collection of Tracts in Biblical Literature* 1, no. 1 (1825): 1.
[104] Ibid., 1–2.
[105] Charles Hodge, "Introduction," *Biblical Repertory* 1, no. 1 (1825): vi.
[106] Christian Daniel Beck, "Outlines of Hermeneutics," *Biblical Repertory* 1, no. 1 (1825): 53, 54.
[107] Ibid., 77, 99, emphasis in original.   [108] Ibid., 19.

that notions prevalent during the time of the apostles had shaped the apostles' understanding of gospel truth – Beck proposed that of necessity the "Sacred Writers" had to conform to the views of their historically situated audiences.

In the second selection, Tittmann sought to dismantle the theory of accommodation that aimed to discover "not what [the New Testament authors] taught, but what the measure of light then in the world, and their own talents, enabled them to teach."[109] Similar to Stuart, Tittmann upheld the grammatical mode of interpretation as the best and recognized that it "is for the most part Historical." He explained that the interpreter must attend to the *usus loquendi*, or the customary manner of speaking, which revealed "the import of every expression, at every different period ... with each particular author and nation ... all which are historical facts, which history only can teach us."[110] Tittmann asserted that in deciphering both doctrinal and historical passages, "recourse must be had to the history of those times ... and in this way, and in no other, can the true meaning of the passages be evinced." Like Stuart, he renounced the purely "historical mode of interpretation" as presentist but granted "that the Sacred Writers ... so accommodated themselves to the genius of their age, as to use a style and language which they would not have used, had they written for different people, and at another time."[111] Allowing accommodation in form rather than content, Tittmann directed the interpreter to "discover in what instances Sacred Writers have accommodated themselves to the genius of their age."[112] Hodge's Beck and Tittmann selections indicated that regardless of just how the New Testament authors had accommodated, they lived in a different world. And the historical comprehension of that world was a prerequisite to understanding their words.

In the years after publishing the first issue of the *Biblical Repertory*, Hodge remained abreast of scholarship – he even traveled to Europe to study at Halle – and continued to answer the threat of biblical criticism by making apologetic use of scholarship. In works such as his *Commentary on the Epistle to the Romans* (1835), for example, Hodge drew heavily on historical sources to back his reading of that text.[113]

---

[109] Charles C. Tittmann, "C. CHS. Tittmann, on Historical Interpretation," *Biblical Repertory* 1, no. 1 (1825): 136–37.
[110] Ibid., 130.   [111] Ibid., 131.   [112] Ibid., 132, 133.
[113] Charles Hodge, *A Commentary on the Epistle to the Romans* (Philadelphia, 1835). See also Gutjahr, *Charles Hodge*, 143–45.

Hodge's clearest articulation of historical explication came much later in his magnum opus, *Systematic Theology* (1871–73), in which he echoed the translations that he had included in the first issue of the *Biblical Repertory* decades earlier. As a believer in plenary inspiration, Hodge continued to reject the idea that the cultures of the sacred writers had shaped the content of their writing and that the role of the interpreter was to use reason to "separate the wheat from the chaff."[114] Hodge nonetheless valued historical context even as he condemned the move to confine the Bible's meaning to that context. While affirming that the words of the Bible reflected God's mind, Hodge insisted that God did not suspend the sacred writers' "self-consciousness" and that they "impressed their peculiarities on their several productions" and used their own "language and modes of expression."[115] In short, he granted that the "words are to be understood in their historical sense.... We must not interpret the word or the fact," he explained, "according to our theories of the relation of God to the world, but according to the usage of antiquity."[116] Hodge repeated this point at various places in the text, where he indicated that the first and "fundamental principle of interpretation of all writings, sacred or profane, is that words are to be understood in their historical sense; that is in the sense in which it can be historically proved that they were used by their authors and intended to be understood by those to whom they were addressed." Hodge's historical approach stressed the importance of original audiences. "We are bound," he wrote, "to take [the sacred writings] in the sense in which those to whom they were originally addressed must inevitably have taken them."[117] Like Stuart, Hodge believed proper interpretation demanded that readers recognize the ways in which God, as the final author of sacred scripture, had accommodated to the language of the sacred writers and their audiences.

Hodge, a Presbyterian, displayed much of the same historical awareness that Unitarians and Congregationalists exhibited, while similarly ignoring historical distance when it came to core truths. He often echoed Tittmann's criticism of the idea that scriptural truth "is not to be considered as pertaining to all Christians, and that the doctrines thus revealed are by no means common, and necessary to every age, in such a manner as to be a perpetual rule of faith and practice."[118] And, with Tittmann, Hodge insisted that religious truth "is equally applicable to all men, in

---

[114] Charles Hodge, *Systematic Theology*, 3 vols. (New York, 1871–1873), 1:40.
[115] Ibid., 1:157.   [116] Ibid., 1:158.   [117] Ibid., 1:376, 377. See also 1:187.
[118] Tittmann, "C. CHS. Tittmann, on Historical Interpretation," 131.

every age."[119] While fully acknowledging the differences between biblical pasts and American present in terms of language and modes of thought, these conservative interpreters strongly objected to the idea that the Bible could simply be set aside as a human creation of ancient pasts. In the short term, they were largely successful in warding off the complete historicization of the Bible. However, their attention to historical differences began to reveal historical distance as an interpretive problem. Efforts to ignore the distance in application highlighted its presence. The consistent emphasis on context, circumstance, and accommodation contributed to a new understanding that the sacred religious text to which Christians looked had been produced in a very different time and among a very different people.

In the antebellum United States, a range of liberal and conservative biblical scholars recognized the need for a historical exegesis. While these thinkers varied in how to best explain and apply scripture – and though many of their coreligionists were unaware of their engagement with biblical criticism – it is important to emphasize that each of them accepted history as the grounds of debate. Jonathan Edwards's affirmative answer to the question of whether the Bible could be historical and divine had been replaced by the assumption that its divinity rested on its historicity. More than ever, America's pious biblical scholars valued the canon as historical texts in need of historical illumination.

While their qualified engagement with biblical criticism cultivated an understanding of interpretation as a historical endeavor, their unprecedented focus on the historical nature of the biblical texts drew new attention to the distance separating their ancient setting from their modern audience. As David F. Holland notes, "both sides committed themselves to careful examinations of the Bible's history – and in the course of their conflict, they drove the historical distance of the ancient scriptures deeper into the center of Americans' religious thought."[120] Questions about eternal truths inspired greater interest in the historical facts that had become the foundation for knowledge about those truths, and the recognition of historical distance that resulted reinforced the value of and desire for historical knowledge. Even when interpreters believed their efforts could overcome the distance their readings revealed, their historical search for universal truths exposed the vastness of the Bible's transient past.

[119] Ibid., 132.   [120] Holland, *Sacred Borders*, 105.

Biblical scholars were most responsible for cultivating a perception of historical distance, but this perception also grew among Americans with little or no direct exposure to biblical criticism. Early followers of Joseph Smith, for example, highlighted the distance between biblical pasts and American present to prioritize new scripture and new revelation. As Reverend Benton Pixley observed in an 1832 letter to the *Christian Watchman*, Sidney Rigdon, a prominent Mormon preacher, proclaimed that "the Epistles are not and were not given for our instruction, but for the instruction of a people of another age and country, far removed from ours, of different habits and manners ... and that it is altogether inconsistent for us to take the Epistles written for that people at that age of the world, as containing suitable instruction for this people at this age of the world."[121] The correspondent quoted Rigdon without comment – the absurdity of the belief did not need to be explained. And yet, while some scoffed at the idea that biblical texts were no longer relevant and that new times called for new revelations, a range of biblical scholars had begun to read the Bible in ways that pushed biblical times further into the past. In succeeding decades, as the slavery debates brought increased attention to the meaning of biblical passages, historical readings were drawn out into the open, which increased the potential for Americans to sense historical distance from the biblical pasts.

The growing perception of distance encouraged some biblical interpreters to do just what Hodge forbade: "separate the wheat from the chaff." In other words, some interpreters used the lessons learned through biblical criticism to reject the historicity of certain biblical texts and, in the case of the more liberal minded, to dismiss certain teachings as antiquated. This process of separating out specific biblical books and principles expanded the sphere of the temporal and shrunk the sphere of the timeless.

The subsequent biblical debates over slavery further encouraged interpreters to make canonical distinctions and to differentiate transient from permanent teachings. A similar development soon emerged in constitutional debates over slavery, when some appealed to the Declaration of Independence rather than the Constitution or aimed to extract permanent truths from transient legal precepts. In both debates, those involved aimed to rescue and apply universal ideas. In the biblical discussion, even attempts to challenge certain texts and teachings most often prefaced

---

[121] B. Pixley, "Intelligence Respecting Mormonites," *Christian Watchman* (November 9, 1832): 177.

a more urgent effort to establish a canon and present its timeless truths. History was more often used to reveal rather than question a text's meaning. Once the Unitarian, Congregationalist, and Presbyterian expositors had established their versions of the canon, historical knowledge assisted them in recovering God's eternal verities. Even those who believed that most of the Bible's content described a now-irrelevant past also asserted that the canon's universal truths were just as applicable in the present. Rational supernaturalism was, in many ways, historical supernaturalism. The temporal revealed the eternal. But, as Transcendentalist Theodore Parker soon made clear, the transient could also undermine the textual source of the permanent.

2

"The Ground Will Shake"

In a February 1839 letter addressed to his mentor and fellow Transcendentalist Convers Francis, Theodore Parker freely expressed his view that the Bible was a historical text. "Let any sober man read *de Wette's* Biblical Dogmatics," he wrote to his friend, "and he will be astonished to see how many doctrines are taught in the Bible which enlightened men cannot believe. I must think that by and by, centuries hence, the O.T. will be dropped out from the church, then the N.T. will follow, or only be used as we now use other helps. I cant [sic] but wish with you, that Jesus had written his own books, but even then, they must have contained some things local and temporary." According to Parker, the passage of time and the progress of religious sentiment made sacred historical texts obsolete, and not even Jesus could have ensured their timelessness. In an attempt to articulate the difference between his own Transcendentalist beliefs and those of traditionalists, Parker wrote that "the orthodox place the Bible above the Soul. We the Soul above the Bible." He believed that the soul, unlike the Bible with its myriad mediations, enjoyed a direct connection with the divine. Thus, he answered the questions of whether "'the canon was closed'" and "revelation is at an end" with a resounding no.[1] While biblical criticism dictated that America's biblical scholars rest their arguments on historical grounds, biblical criticism also directed one of the nation's most heterodox thinkers to abandon those transient grounds in favor of what he understood to be a transcendent moral sphere.

---

[1] Theodore Parker to Convers Francis, February 9, 1839, Theodore Parker Papers, Massachusetts Historical Society (hereafter MHS).

Parker used historical knowledge to replace transitory biblical texts and figures with a divine intuitive sense as the source of unchanging religious truth. Theological understandings shaped Parker's historical sensibilities and those of his contemporaries. However, he held an abstract and minimalist belief – "no master but God, no creed but Truth, no service but Love" – and thus distinguished between permanent truths and mutable doctrines, ceremonies, structures, and texts.[2] While Charles Hodge, Moses Stuart, and Andrews Norton sought to avoid or mitigate the undermining potential of historical criticism, Parker's minimalist belief allowed him to sidestep the conflict. Sure of his direct connection with a timeless God, Parker confidently used historical arguments to unchain eternal truths from temporal facts. Once America's leading biblical scholars placed the Bible on a presumably firm historical footing, Parker revealed the footing's cracks and its susceptibility to wear and tear. His approach demonstrated that historical evidence could not only authenticate a sacred text but also falsify the text and render it banal. Rather than rest his faith on those unstable grounds, Parker centered his belief in an atemporal religious sense. Thus, when historical evidence indicated that a text sat on a faulty historical foundation, he painlessly dispatched it as inauthentic. And when historical distance demonstrated the temporariness of an authentic text's teachings, he summarily rendered them outdated. Rather than set aside historical differences in the application of sacred texts as orthodox and liberal religionists did, Parker used that distance to disregard teachings that conflicted with his conscience. He believed that portions of the Bible remained useful as the historical expression of true religion and often used these passages to demonstrate the universality of an innate religious sense, but his beliefs freed him from allegiance to static meanings.

The debates over slavery, in which Parker became embroiled during the 1840s and 1850s, cemented his approach to biblical texts as useful but ultimately dispensable. He could accept a contextual reading of Paul's epistle to Philemon, which affirmed that Paul had directed a slave to return to his master, as historically accurate. And he could then reject that outdated original meaning in favor of a universal one that he believed had emerged through both the development of religion and the progress of freedom. While Parker's religious opponents used historical stasis, grounded in a founding religious text, to combat change, he used historical change, informed by an illuminated conscience, to combat stasis. In the process, both sides of the

---

[2] Theodore Parker, *A Discourse of Matters Pertaining to Religion* (Boston, 1842), 377.

debate brought new attention to historical distance. One did so inadvertently in an attempt to set distance aside in application, and the other did so explicitly by using it to dismiss the sacred texts, and their teachings, as antiquated. Perceiving temporal distance made it easier for Parker to privilege what he identified as present imperatives over past teachings. This approach, which Parker later extended to the recent founding era and the Constitution, became most clear in his contention that whatever the position of the prophets and apostles or the founders and framers, the present age, as an age of freedom, demanded slavery's abolition. Historicity, it turned out, was a double-edged sword; it could be used to authenticate a sacred text or dispatch that text as archaic. In this Transcendentalist's hand, one edge of the sword seemed sharper than the other.

As with other antebellum biblical scholars, Parker's search for religious truth drew attention to historical distance. Like those other scholars, he sought the eternal, though he found it in a different source. Norton, Stuart, and Hodge asserted the transcendence of their canon and the timelessness of certain biblical truths: they argued that these truths trumped historical change. Parker, on the other hand, asserted the transcendence of conscience and the timelessness of intuited truths: he argued that these truths trumped the historical canon. Both Parker and his opponents used historical insights to reveal the eternal, but as those insights began to expose permanent truths as transient facts, they threatened to reveal the unsettled nature of the Bible's historical foundations. To an extent, even Parker's position was suspect. When contextual exegesis indicated the local and transient nature of sacred biblical teachings, it suggested the potential transiency of all truth. Even if Parker's temporally transcendent position protected his truths from historicization for a time, the ongoing conversations about truth and history contributed to the idea that all truth is historically constructed and temporally limited, a concept that gained ground in the late nineteenth century. Distinct paths led to the same destination; regardless of where these thinkers located the source of religious truth, their biblical approaches contributed to new kinds of historical thinking. In the short term, their contextual interpretations drew attention to the historical differences and distances separating peculiar biblical pasts from the nineteenth-century American present, while also creating the intellectual conditions for a similar process that spread an awareness of historical dislocation from the founding era.

Many scholars have stressed the ahistorical aspects of Transcendental belief and emphasized the ways in which Transcendentalism outgrew its Unitarian roots. In doing so, however, they have too often neglected to note how historical arguments freed heterodox thinkers such as Parker and Ralph Waldo Emerson in their attempts to build atemporal worlds. As I traced in the first chapter of this book, historical argumentation became standard among thinkers across the antebellum religious spectrum. Most biblical scholars, especially Unitarians, used it to ground universal truths in a biblical past, but these Transcendentalists employed historical explication to unmoor such truths from that historical setting. While others aimed to recover eternal verities with the help of temporal facts, Parker and Emerson strove to separate timeless truths from transient biblical pasts. The growing perception of historical distance assisted them in that effort.

Transcendentalism's break with old and new branches of New England orthodoxy was not a wholesale renunciation of the past and its lessons but rather a deep historical critique of the ancient book and world on which Trinitarians and Unitarians grounded their beliefs. While the level of the Transcendentalists' critique was unique, it followed a long tradition of rejecting the authority of more recent historical eras for that of a purer past. During the Reformation, Protestants found change and corruption where Catholics posited continuity. Luther cast aside that claim of constancy and replaced it with a call to read the Bible and recover the teachings of the primitive church. This sensibility crossed the Atlantic with the Puritans, who in turn found corruption in Protestant England and reclaimed the early Christian past. Later American restorationist movements, such as the Disciples of Christ and the Latter-day Saints, repeated this narrative of corruption and renewal, repudiating the elongated immediate past and seeking union, or at least correspondence, with a distant biblical one.[3] The Latter-day Saint case, in particular, highlights the contrapuntal American fascination with both the old and the new, both restoration and innovation. A similar but distinct attitude emerged among Transcendentalists. While the Latter-day Saints aimed to reclaim the primitive Christian and even the ancient Old Testament past, Transcendentalists preferred, as Emerson put it, an "original relation to the universe."[4]

---

[3] See C. Leonard Allen and Richard T. Hughes, *Discovering Our Roots: The Ancestry of Churches of Christ* (Abilene, TX, 1988), 94–97; and Samuel Brown, "Mormonism as Restoration," in *Mormonism: A Historical Encyclopedia*, ed. W. Paul Reeve and Ardis E. Parshall (Santa Barbara, 2010), 365–71. See also Jordan T. Watkins, "Early Mormonism and the Re-Enchantment of Antebellum Historical Thought," *Journal of Mormon History* 38 (Summer 2012): 195–201.

[4] Ralph Waldo Emerson, *Nature*, in *The Collected Works of Ralph Waldo Emerson*, ed. Robert E. Spiller, et al., 10 vols. (Cambridge, MA, 1971–2013), 1:7 (hereafter cited as *CWRWE*). On these developments, see Kemp, *Estrangement of the Past*.

The Transcendentalists sought a past that extended backward but their search for timeless truths also extended upward beyond temporality in ways that devalued the favored biblical era's claims on the present. Although their approach to the divine partook of a long tradition of restoration and renewal, their emphasis on the present moment broke from that tradition. They were not claiming contemporaneity with a pure past or golden age but rather positing that the present – the eternal now – was pregnant with promise.[5] To be sure, they did not dismiss as fiction what their intellectual predecessors had upheld as fact; Emerson and Parker maintained that the Gospels and their Jesus rested on a foundation of some historical truth.[6] Historicity, however, signified temporal limitation and revealed historical distance. Once America's Christian theologians linked religious truth and authority to a historical text, it was left to thinkers such as Emerson and Parker to point out the insecurity of that connection and to center truth in a more intimate and innate source. As these thinkers drew attention to the shiftiness of historical evidence, the limitations of time, and the remoteness of the past, they exposed the transience of the historical grounds on which Americans based their faith.

THE PARTICULAR AND THE UNIVERSAL IN EMERSON'S VESTRY LECTURES

Transcendentalists engaged German biblical criticism with a vigor unmatched by any other collection of individuals in antebellum America. Emerson's and Parker's writings on the topic highlight their varying approaches to biblical scholarship and demonstrate distinct implications for a growing awareness of historical distance. Their interest in biblical criticism's historical critique emerged within a faithful tradition, as seen in their early uses of biblical scholarship, but the potential for dissension was present from the start. Emerson's brother William – along with fellow Bay Staters George Ticknor, George Bancroft, and Edward Everett – encountered Johann Eichhorn's biblical criticism firsthand as a student at Göttingen, a hub of biblical scholarship in the heart of Germany. Although Eichhorn advocated a constructive approach to biblical criticism, many of his American students perceived that his

---

[5] See James R. Guthrie, *Above Time: Emerson's and Thoreau's Temporal Revolutions* (Columbia, MO, 2001).
[6] See Elisabeth Hurth, *Between Faith and Unbelief: American Transcendentalists and the Challenge of Atheism* (Leiden, NL, 2007), 31–76.

criticism might undermine a faith grounded in historical fact. Shaken by that potential, they passed up careers in the ministry and pursued occupations as literature professors, orators, statesman, and historical writers. Ralph Waldo Emerson's own engagement with biblical criticism seems to have led him to give up the ministry as well, but not before a short stint as a pastor in Boston's Second Church from 1829 to 1832.

Emerson had already received a profound education in grief. Just weeks before his eighth birthday, his father, a Unitarian minister, died. Emerson's mother, Ruth, raised him with the help of his aunt, Mary Moody Emerson. At fourteen, he attended Harvard College, and after his brother William left for Göttingen he entered Harvard Divinity School. Waldo did not graduate but was licensed to preach in 1826. In January 1829, he accepted an appointment as junior pastor of the Second Church. Among the sermons he gave there include the Vestry Lectures, a series of nine discourses on the Bible delivered to his congregation's youth in the spring of 1831, just one month after Ellen Tucker, his wife of only a year and a half, died of tuberculosis. Perhaps the lectures acted as a distraction for the grieving Emerson. He presented the first sermon on March 8, one week after the dedication of the Second Church Vestry, and he gave the last sermon two months later on May 3. In the lectures, only six of which are extant, Emerson discussed the authors of the first three Gospels (Matthew, Mark, and Luke), outlined the transmission of their accounts, and analyzed the early chapters of Matthew. In these sermons, Emerson made apologetic use of works by scholars such as Johann Michaelis and his students, including Eichhorn and Herbert Marsh, but he also used the historical lessons of their works – including an interpretive focus on ancient contexts – to emphasize the inestimable value of individual conscience. While experiencing the deep despair accompanied by his wife's death, Emerson ardently sought an unmediated connection with the divine.[7]

Emerson attended to both the historical nature of the Gospels and the history of their transmission, which had the potential to instill a sense of temporal dislocation. In his first lecture, he noted that "St. Mark wrote for the immediate use of the Romans."[8] Like his Unitarian counterparts,

---

[7] On Emerson's studies and the immediate background to these lectures, see Robert D. Richardson Jr., *Emerson: The Mind on Fire* (Berkeley, 1995), 63–113.

[8] Ralph Waldo Emerson, "Emerson's Six Vestry Lectures of 1831," in *Transcendental Epilogue: Primary Materials for Research in Emerson, Thoreau, Literary New England, the Influence of German Theology, and Higher Biblical Criticism*, ed. Kenneth Walter Cameron (Hartford, CT, 1965–82), 2:722.

Emerson believed that the biblical authors had created their sacred accounts for historically situated audiences. Turning to the transmission of the biblical texts in his third lecture, he traced a neat line from the creation of the King James Bible backward through the efforts of William Tyndale and Myles Coverdale to Saint Jerome and early church fathers, including Origen and Irenaeus. Emerson supposed that "an unbroken chain of evidence" connected "the books from which we now draw our rule of faith and duty with the books first written by the four apostles 1800 years ago." Scholarship focusing on the Bible's transmission soon problematized such streamlined accounts, calling the canon's integrity into question. At this stage, though, the idea of Catholic corruption posed a greater threat than that of textual transmission. Emerson asserted that Providence had protected Christianity's sacred texts, which "outlasted the barbarous institutions of the middle ages – and have now come down safe ... across the vast tract of so many ages of war and ignorance."[9] Emerson reasoned that God had guarded the texts from temporal corrosion. The Christian insistence on the canon's enduring integrity proliferated alongside widespread Christian assertions of its teachings' continued relevance. In both cases, however, the historical nature of these two arguments brought new attention to historical differences and distance. Even Emerson's discussion of early church fathers highlighted temporal distinction. He mentioned, for example, that Irenaeus wrote "very much in the mystical style of the age."[10] This attention to textual transmission and ancient contexts indicated temporal distance from the Bible and its peoples and cultures.

Antebellum biblical scholars paid more attention to the contexts of the biblical writers than to the transmission of their texts. In a nation where Christians focused on the words of the Bible, scholarship centered on its meaning rather than the lives of its texts, which had more potential to reveal historical distance. In other words, the emphasis on the historical peculiarities of biblical pasts accounted more for biblical scholars' growing perception of historical distance than did a narration of developments since biblical times. In later constitutional debates, narrations of change spread a sense of distance from the founding era as much as contextual readings of the nation's supreme legal text. In part, this was a question of proximity. Although the Constitution – a much smaller and more recent text than the Bible – did not have a similar tradition of transmission, the political need to establish ties to the recent founding era alerted

---

[9] Ibid., 2:727.   [10] Ibid., 2:726.

commentators to perceived changes since that time, the narration of which proved an easier task. In the biblical debates that preceded and overlapped with the constitutional discussions, participants spent their time emphasizing the interpretive importance of ancient contexts.

In Emerson's vestries, attention to historical differences and changes went hand in hand. In his fourth lecture, he outlined various theories to explain the similarities between the synoptic Gospels, citing arguments that the authors had the various texts in their possession or drew from a common written source. He preferred the alternative explanation provided by Johann Karl Ludwig Gieseler, another Göttingen scholar, who drew attention to, in Emerson's words, a crucial "difference of circumstance" in his explanation that "*oral instruction* was the great mode of communication in that age." This approach, Emerson believed, showed that some biblical criticism "has served to confirm rather than shake the faith of inquirers."[11] He noted that the prominence of an oral tradition accounted for the similarities and differences between the accounts. As with many of his contemporaries, the early Emerson believed that historical readings authenticated the Bible.

In his fifth lecture, Emerson retained his apologetic tone to address the background of Matthew's Gospel. While noting "usages so peculiar" to the Jews, he argued that Jewish laws "presuppose the truth of the history and [are] connected too with historical actions and confirmed by [the] concurrent history of other nations."[12] Emerson's use of extrabiblical historical knowledge paralleled the earlier uses of Joseph Buckminster and Jonathan Edwards. In his eighth lecture, Emerson referred to the historical writings of Josephus and noted that ancient accounts of the Holy Land compared well with those of modern travelers, which attested to the veracity of Mathew's record. Like his predecessors, Emerson used historical research to preserve the canon's authenticity, but that effort drew attention to the different circumstances and historical peculiarities of biblical pasts.

Much like other American scholars, Emerson aimed to discern permanent truth in the biblical record, but he believed that the central truth he sought existed independent of the Bible. His Transcendentalist leanings, as much as his inherited Unitarian faith, informed his search. In his discussion of the first few chapters of Matthew, Emerson posited that "the human mind is the same when it opens itself to the light in Judea or in Greece [or in] Rome or in America."[13] The belief in a universal religious

---

[11] Ibid., 2:729, emphasis in original.   [12] Ibid., 2:730.   [13] Ibid., 2:731.

sentiment fast became a central pillar of Transcendentalism and soon supported the idea that though historical and uniquely useful, even the New Testament and its Christ were unessential to individual salvation. This sentiment signaled a significant break from Unitarian teachings. At this stage, Emerson's interest in a universal truth – present in but independent of the Bible – informed his attention to the New Testament's temporal features.

As was common, Emerson accounted for historical differences by appealing to accommodation. He explained that although Jesus taught universal truth, he had "adopted [the Jews'] language to impart a new and a sounder sense," and thus, interpreters should guard against strict literal readings and recognize that such accommodations had introduced mistaken beliefs into the text.[14] As an example, Emerson cited Matthew 4:24, which references demonic possession. Anticipating discussions surrounding the miracles controversy that broke apart American Unitarianism, he attributed this idea to views prevalent in biblical times. "It is maintained," Emerson wrote, "that this was a popular superstition of the Jews ... and that Jesus accommodated his words to the usual modes of speech." Emerson noted that "the apostles and evangelists" also used "these expressions which in their time were in common use." Like William Ellery Channing and Andrews Norton, Emerson found accommodation in both language and meaning. This prepared him to view the Unitarian investment in biblical miracles, which historical evidence might disprove at any time, as misplaced.[15]

In an addendum to Emerson's lectures, he identified the permanent truths he valued most, a move that laid bare the transience of all else. In referencing the love at the heart of Christ's beatitudes, he wrote that "it is this sense that fits the Gospel to all countries and times." Emerson contrasted this universal love to the limitations of "the Jewish code," which he described as "a local code fit for that particular region." He contended that, "With the law of *love* at the bottom, [the Sermon on the Mount] is as good at Rome as [at] Jerusalem – at Boston as at either. It is for all places where the human heart beats.... It is for the soul. If this whole system of worlds ... should pass away it would still be eternally true that purity and love and wisdom would be heaven ... as it was nineteen centuries ago to the little company of poor Jewish peasants whom Jesus Christ addressed."[16] By reducing the permanent component of the Bible to one

---

[14] Ibid.   [15] Ibid., 2:735.   [16] Ibid., 2:738, emphasis in original.

basic element of Christian love – and in essence severing the dependent link between religious truths and the Bible itself – Transcendentalists such as Emerson and Parker advanced minimalist positions that designated most of the Bible's content as transient. This preceded a similar development in relation to the founding era, when abolitionists appealed to the Declaration of Independence's universal egalitarian ideas – eternal verities rescued from a sea of temporalities. In robbing the Gospels and Christ, and later the Constitution and its framers, of their exceptional historical roles, this position cultivated greater cognizance of temporal distance from favored pasts.

Emerson's attention to the transience of biblical teachings carried over to his view of religious rituals. By the early 1830s, he had read a number of works that undermined the Christian story of Adam's fall and Christ's sacrifice. He also had engaged Quaker descriptions of the Last Supper as a one-time event. At the close of Emerson's brief ministerial career, the question of Communion stood in for the larger question of Christian faith. Binding religious belief to certain narratives, figures, texts, and practices had become cumbersome for one who desired an immediate relation with the divine. In the summer of 1832, Emerson requested that his church allow him to do away with Communion. That June, his church denied his request. Months later, Emerson delivered a final sermon and resigned as pastor at the Second Church.[17]

Emerson's sermon on the Lord's Supper drew even more attention to the transient nature of the Christian past than his vestries. His survey of commentary on the topic led him to conclude "that Jesus did not intend to establish an institution for perpetual observance."[18] His recent studies of the Gospels supported this idea. In his discussion of a passage in Luke, Emerson allowed that Jesus may have wanted his disciples to use the ritual to remember him, but could not accept that "he looked beyond the living generation."[19] Reading the passage in the context of the Jewish Passover and comparing it to the washing of feet, Emerson concluded that the Lord's Supper was "local ... and does not concern us."[20] Emerson reasoned that context confined the Lord's Supper to the New Testament

---

[17] See Richardson, *Emerson*, 118–27.
[18] Ralph Waldo Emerson, "Sermon CLXII," *in The Complete Sermons of Ralph Waldo Emerson*, ed. Albert J. von Frank and Wesley T. Mott, 4 vols. (Columbia, MO, 1989–92), 4:186.
[19] Ibid., 4:187. See Luke 22:19.   [20] Emerson, "Sermon CLXII," 4:189.

past. Such reasoning had a parallel in discussions about the South's peculiar institution. Some commentators allowed that slavery suited crude Old Testament times but began to insist that it had no place in an enlightened nineteenth century.

Sounding like Buckminster, Norton, and Stuart on certain biblical teachings, Emerson rejected the notion that Jesus had intended to "fasten [Communion] upon men in all times." Paul believed it to be a perpetual institution, Emerson admitted, but that "does not settle the question for us."[21] This line of reasoning led to Emerson's most determinative objection to the Lord's Supper. While this means of remembrance might be "suitable to the people and the modes of thought in the East," he stated, it "is foreign and unsuited to affect us." Symbolic practices, he argued, did not move Westerners. Emerson believed that both temporal and spatial difference robbed Communion of its relevance, and it was for these reasons "alone" that he rejected "the ordinance."[22] In a final objection, he severed the "spirit of Christianity" from its "forms," arguing that "its institutions should be as flexible as the wants of men."[23] The idea of flexible forms later arose in political debates over slavery during the 1850s, when Emerson criticized an inflexible approach to the Constitution. In 1832, his historical reading of the Bible led him to characterize the Lord's Supper as a local practice and his appeal to distance allowed him to declare it outdated and irrelevant.

Emerson preached on a number of occasions during the next eight years, but with his 1832 resignation from Second Church, he left behind much of his interest in biblical scholarship. Like a number of Harvard graduates, including his brother William, Ralph Waldo Emerson began to pursue a career outside the ministry. His philosophical stance in the late 1830s and early 1840s assumed temporal dislocation from biblical pasts, but he was no longer interested in debating the meaning of the Bible's passages. Biblical scholarship had served its purpose for this Transcendentalist: it had laid bare the idea that he could best discern truth with his own conscience.[24] Emerson turned to other pursuits, including literature and oratory, but his early contextual readings and use of distance to dismiss certain biblical practices anticipated the arguments of another Transcendentalist, Theodore Parker.

---

[21] Ibid., 4:191.   [22] Ibid., 4:192.   [23] Ibid., 4:192, 4:193.
[24] See Philip F. Gura, *American Transcendentalism: A History* (New York, 2007), 43–44.

THEODORE PARKER AND THE TRANSIENCE OF THE TESTAMENTS

While Emerson chose to leave the ministry and set aside serious attention to biblical interpretation, Theodore Parker determined to preserve a place at the pulpit, and he retained a keen interest in biblical studies. As a Transcendentalist committed to biblical interpretation, Parker's sense and use of distance from biblical pasts was especially pronounced. His engagement with biblical criticism ultimately informed his use of historical distance to reject proslavery biblical teachings. A similar approach later emerged in his constitutional readings. While historical distance became an interpretive problem for some, it became an interpretive solution for others, including Parker.

Similar to Emerson, Parker's early writings on biblical topics show that his rather orthodox understanding of scripture gave way to a more critical approach. Within the period of a decade, he moved far beyond the Unitarians' liberal exegetical positions. One way to trace this development is through Parker's engagement with the biblical criticism of two German scholars: Wilhelm Martin Leberecht de Wette and David Friedrich Strauss. De Wette identified historical problems with Old Testament texts while also cultivating belief in an innate religious sense, and Strauss leveled historical critiques at the Gospels. Parker held some reservations about the most troubling aspects of German scholarship, including Strauss's approach to the Gospel accounts as myths, but his religious convictions allowed him to uniquely engage some of the era's most devastating biblical strictures without fear of losing his faith. In turn, Parker became less attached to the Bible and more willing to dismiss its texts and teachings as curiosities of the past.[25]

For a short period in the early 1830s, Parker read the Hebrew Bible as an accurate historical account of an ancient sacred past. In an 1832 text written for his students at the school he opened in Watertown, Massachusetts, he presented a straightforward reading of the Old Testament and an orthodox acceptance of its miracles. However, during Parker's time in Watertown, the Unitarian minister Convers Francis introduced him to some of the biblical scholarship of their coreligionists, including that of Norton and Channing, and soon Parker adopted a more critical approach to the Bible.[26]

---

[25] On Parker's prolonged engagement with biblical criticism, see Dean Grodzins, *American Heretic: Theodore Parker and Transcendentalism* (Chapel Hill, 2002).
[26] Grodzins, *American Heretic*, 31–34.

In March 1834, Parker closed his academy, and the next month he moved to Cambridge, where he began a more thorough engagement with biblical criticism. After completing a few semesters at the Divinity School, Parker began coediting Ezra Stiles Gannett's *Scriptural Interpreter*, which fed subscribers a steady diet of biblical criticism. This editorial work familiarized Parker with German thinkers. In contrast to his contemporaries, who often dismissed and condemned them as infidels and atheists, Parker believed that the Germans thinkers possessed native religious inclinations.[27]

Parker's 1836 "A Report on Germany Theology," which he read before the Philanthropic Society, shows his early appreciation for German thought. Parker narrated the history of German theology and biblical scholarship from Martin Luther up to the more recent writings of Hermann Reimarus, Johann Michaelis, Johann Semler, Immanuel Kant, Johann Herder, Johann Eichhorn, Johann Gottlieb Fichte, Friedrich Schleiermacher, Friedrich Wilhelm Joseph Schelling, Wilhelm Martin de Wette, and Ferdinand Bauer.[28] Parker dedicated most of his space to contemporary thinkers he described as *rationalists*, whom he divided between those who based religion in understanding and those who centered it in feeling.

This division represented two strands of the German Idealism that fired the imaginations of American Transcendentalists, who began to meet at the home of George Ripley in the very year that Parker delivered his report. German Idealism had emerged from Kant's response to Lockean sensationalism and empiricism. Positing a difference between the perception of a thing and the nature of the thing itself, Kant argued that knowledge depended on transcendental mental categories – space, time, and causality – which gave shape to information perceived via the senses. Kant's philosophy focused attention on the mind, which inspired some, such as Georg Hegel, to privilege reason, and others, such as Schleiermacher, to privilege feeling. Transcendentalists embraced the primacy that German Idealists granted the mind, even as they continued to value the Scottish philosophers' teaching that some knowledge could be obtained via intuition. Transcendentalists also looked to the English Romantic Samuel Taylor Coleridge, whose novel distinction between Understanding – by which humans obtained knowledge via

---

[27] On the fear of German thought, see Hurth, *Between Faith and Unbelief*.
[28] Theodore Parker, "A Report on German Theology Read Before the Philanthropic Society in Divinity College, Harvard University," in *Transcendental Epilogue*, 2:706–720.

the senses – and Reason – by which humans accessed knowledge beyond the senses – provided them a more robust basis for trusting their own minds. Inspired by these and other European-born philosophies that prized the mind's power to intuit truth (including divine truth), Transcendentalists criticized Unitarianism's blind love affair with rationalism. Against Norton's insistence on proving religious truth through external evidences, individuals such as Emerson and Parker upheld intuition or conscience – Coleridge's Reason – as providing unmediated access to moral and religious truth.

In his 1836 report, Parker implied that he shared greater affinity with those, such as de Wette, who based religion in feeling, though he also appreciated the scriptural hermeneutic of the Germans who emphasized understanding. After happily observing, "The fact that religion does originate in the feelings is one of the grandest discoveries of modern times," Parker referenced Ferdinand Bauer on the Old Testament and Heinrich Paulus on the New, explaining how both scholars accounted for biblical miracles by drawing attention to the age of the world in which the texts were written.[29] Parker agreed with this reading, noting that "what are miracles to one age are not so to another."[30] The mythical nature of biblical passages attested to the antiquity of the biblical texts, but it also highlighted the historical differences between the Testaments and the historical distances between biblical pasts and the present.[31]

Of all the German thinkers, the work of de Wette, in particular, gave shape to Parker's own views. While de Wette used a historical approach to interpret the Bible, the German thinker aimed to unhinge its religious significance from historical facts. Other scholars, such as Eichhorn and Bauer, had discarded unverifiable narratives regardless of their symbolic meaning in their efforts to find reliable historical information in the biblical record. In contrast, de Wette granted that biblical texts did not accurately depict past events but argued that they had captured moments of divine revelation. He read the Old Testament as religious poetry and viewed its reported miracles as mythic expressions of ancient Hebrew faith. He approached the New Testament similarly, preferring to measure the religious value of the ideas expressed therein according to an absolute religious ideal rather than in relation to historical events. Because he believed that the Gospels rested on a solid historical foundation, de Wette accepted Christ as the historical expression of the ideal. When Strauss published *Das Leben Jesu, kritisch bearbeitet* (*The Life of Jesus*,

---

[29] Ibid., 2:709.   [30] Ibid., 2:712.   [31] See Grodzins, *American Heretic*, 41–74.

Critically Examined) in 1835, de Wette granted that his compatriot had raised important questions about the historicity of the Gospels, but he believed that the scarcity of contemporary extrasynoptic and extrabiblical accounts arrested Strauss's critique. A lack of historical evidence, de Wette argued, undermined the mythological approach, and thus, he remained confident in Jesus's role as Christianity's founder. Once again, historical skepticism could undermine the work of the skeptic. Even still, because de Wette distinguished religious truth from historical fact, his religious position did not rest on the authenticity of biblical texts.[32]

Parker's engagement with de Wette encouraged him to separate the Old from the New Testament, as had Channing and Norton. A few months after leaving Cambridge, Parker initiated a seven-year project of translating an edition of de Wette's historical introduction to the Old Testament, *Lehrbuch der historisch-kritischen Einleitung in die kanonischen und apokryphischen Bücher des Alten Testaments* (Textbook of A Historical-Critical Introduction to the Canonical and Apocryphal Books of the Old Testament). Stuart had made the suggestion. In the spring and summer of 1837, Parker worked on his translation, married his fiancée, Lydia Dodge Cabot, and became minister at the Unitarian parish in West Roxbury. Francis preached the ordination sermon and Ripley welcomed Parker to the clerical fraternity. Even though he was ordained in a Unitarian church, Parker was embracing Transcendental ideas. During this time, he formulated a pair of sermons – delivered two years later – in which he outlined problems with the Old Testament. In the first sermon, he challenged the Testament's narration of the creation, its early depictions of God in physical form, and its moral contradictions, which anticipated his attention to ancient slavery. In the second sermon, Parker described the Bible itself as a contradiction. He believed that historical evidence required him to value the Greek over the Hebrew scriptures, but his emphasis on internal religion, which he located in the teachings and example of Jesus, directed that distinction. Parker had followed de Wette's move to center religion in feeling and measure truth according to the ideal, and in doing so Parker valued the New Testament over the Old. And soon, he began to wonder if the New Testament might be a collection of myths as well. Another German scholar, Strauss, whose critiques began to weigh on Parker's mind, would guide him down that path.[33]

---

[32] John W. Rogerson, *W.M.L. de Wette, Founder of Modern Biblical Criticism: An Intellectual Biography* (Sheffield, UK, 1992).

[33] See Grodzins, *American Heretic*, 150–65.

Parker first read Strauss's *The Life of Jesus* as he settled into pastoral life and began regularly attending meetings of the "Transcendentalist Club." Strauss's work posed a special threat to traditional Christian belief. Supernaturalists interpreted scripture literally and rationalists explained it naturally, but both believed in the historicity of the Gospels. In contrast, Strauss contended that these accounts had emerged through an unconscious myth-making process and thus reflected the beliefs of the times in which they were produced. This suggested that the Gospels revealed more about the mindsets of their writers than the actions and teachings of their subject. The question Strauss raised was not whether Christ had accommodated to the traditions and customs of the Jews but whether local beliefs and mentalities had led unwitting writers to mythologize a historical figure identified as Jesus. This kind of historicization laid bare the cultural differences separating modern and New Testament times and pushed the latter era deeper into the past. Strauss's views were the most unsettling iteration of the theory of accommodation to date. It undercut the historicity of the Gospels and threatened to leave scholars such as Norton, who had dug in his heels on historical grounds, sinking in quicksand.

The historicist component of Strauss's interpretation supported Parker's emerging view of the progress of religion. In January 1839 he asked Francis if he thought "the apostles understood Christianity as well as some in these times?"[34] In posing this question, which implied an affirmative answer, Parker went much further than liberal religionists such as Norton, who suggested that circumstances might have shaped some of the apostles' ideas. Parker aligned more with Emerson, who dismissed the apostles' views on matters such as Communion as irrelevant. The next month, Parker informed Francis that historical circumstances had also constrained Christ, resulting in erroneous teachings.[35] This approach supported Parker's move from a biblical dispensationalism to a more general belief in progress, which he nurtured throughout his life. With Emerson, Parker held that universal truth illuminated the souls of both past and present individuals and that the understanding of that truth became clearer over time in relation to more enlightened circumstances. Parker viewed the nineteenth century, in particular, as an era of progress and tied it to a rise in antislavery sentiment. In succeeding years, proslavery advancements introduced some ambivalence about historical

[34] Theodore Parker to Convers Francis, January 8, 1839, Theodore Parker Papers, MHS.
[35] Theodore Parker to Convers Francis, February 9, 1839, Theodore Parker Papers, MHS.

movement and gave Parker pause. However, he managed to retain his faith in progress by describing the Slave Power and its successes as aberrant and, in essence, anachronistic. This approach called attention to the circumstantial nature of religious understanding and highlighted historical distance from the favored biblical and, later, founding eras.

Parker valued much about Strauss's account, but he still raised objections to the German's views. By the time William Ware, editor of the *Christian Examiner*, asked him to critique Strauss's controversial publication, Parker was harboring doubts about New Testament miracles. In late March, he wrote Francis with a new question: "Is not Strauss right ... when he says the N.T. is a collection of myths?"[36] Francis answered in the affirmative, but added that all histories, including modern accounts, contained myths and reflected the beliefs of the times in which they were written.[37] Warned that Ware would not publish a controversial review, Parker repressed some of his private thoughts. Perhaps with Francis's letter in mind, he instead adopted an apologetic stance, labeling Strauss's publication a "conjectural history."[38] Like Stuart and de Wette, Parker referenced the conjectural nature of historical research to undermine the critic's work.

While leveling some criticisms, Parker did not hide the unsettling challenges the work presented to belief systems grounded in historical documents. In one of the era's clearest statements on how historical readings of sacred texts created a sense of historical distance, Parker wrote that "if a form of religion rest on written documents, sooner or later, there ensues a difference between the old documents and the modern discoveries and culture shown in works written to explain it."[39] This lucid statement about historical readings of biblical texts anticipated later developments in constitutional interpretation. Historical investigation of sacred texts drew attention to the dissonance between the American present and Americans' favored pasts. Of the distance from biblical pasts, in particular, Parker wrote that the critic may acknowledge the dissonance or "blind himself to this inconsistency, and seek merely to unfold the original meaning of the text."[40] In this striking statement, Parker implied that the interpreter should take distance into account

---

[36] Theodore Parker to Convers Francis, March 22, 1839, Theodore Parker Papers, MHS.
[37] Convers Francis to Theodore Parker, May 24, 1839, Theodore Parker Papers, MHS.
[38] Theodore Parker, review of *Das Leben Jesu, kritisch bearbeitet*, by David Friedrich Strauss, *Christian Examiner and General Review* 28 (July 1840): 273–316, quotation on 274.
[39] Ibid., 274.   [40] Ibid., 275.

when providing an interpretation. He later criticized proslavery readings for striving to uncover the Constitution's original meanings without accounting for developments since the founding era. In his review of Strauss's book, Parker articulated the sense of temporal dislocation that results from historical readings of sacred texts and encouraged attention to that historical distance in interpretation.

Parker's emphasis on temporal dissonance indicated an intellectual shift in viewing favored pasts as foreign instead of familiar, which complicated conventional readings of sacred texts even as it freed him to advance new readings of those texts. Parker's sense of distance did not include the idea, often attributed to postmodernism, that the past can only be approached in mediated ways. But as Francis's comments about the mediations of all historical accounts demonstrate, related ideas did begin to emerge in this period. However, like Buckminster and Norton, Parker worked under the historicist assumption that proper historical investigation would render objective understandings. This insistence on objective understandings transformed familiar pasts into foreign ones and raised questions about the staying power of sacred texts. While Parker's faith in an atemporal source of truth did allow him to set aside outdated documents, it also inspired him to read them in a new light. The ideas undergirding Parker's abovementioned statements about "old documents," some of the era's clearest on historical distance, surfaced again and again in his subsequent writings.

In turning to the content of Strauss's work, Parker summarized Strauss's mythical reading of the Gospel writers' accounts of the final three years of Jesus's life. Strauss regarded these accounts "as spurious productions of well-meaning men, who collected the traditions that were current."[41] This made the Gospels historical, not by evidencing their historical accuracy but by showing how they reflected the mentality of a specific time and place.

Strauss defined myths as unhistorical and fictive accounts, and he explained them by appealing to historical context. In his view, accounts were unhistorical if they countered the known laws of causality and contained circumstantial contradictions; they were fictive if they were poetical and agreed in substance "with the preconceived opinions of the community where [they] originate[d]."[42] Strauss applied this approach to Jesus's birth, public ministry, miracles, death, and resurrection. To explain Strauss's approach, Parker outlined Strauss's view of the

[41] Ibid., 281.   [42] Ibid., 283.

appearance of a "miraculous star," noting that, according to the German, "the whole story is mythical, and is derived from ideas and opinions commonly held at the time. The ancients believed a heavenly body sometimes appeared on great occasions."[43] An understanding of the ancient mythic mindset explained the miraculous. The same was true of possession: "It was a common opinion of the Jews, that certain diseases were caused by demons; Jesus himself seems to have shared this opinion."[44] In his letters to Francis, Parker had indicated that Jesus held the views of his contemporaries. The idea that biblical figures and writers held the opinions and beliefs of their era could authenticate teachings, as Bauer – and even Edwards – had shown with the Old Testament or as Norton had demonstrated with the New. As Parker noted, "Strauss thinks the controversial discourses of Jesus are genuine, because they correspond so closely to the spirit and tone of rabbinical explanations of Scripture, at that time."[45] But using the "spirit and tone" of past times to authenticate teachings put distance between those teachings and the present. In a way, Parker finished what Edwards had started, but instead of confirming the Bible's divinity, his use of historical evidence threatened to expose its temporality. Perhaps the Bible was authentic, but that also might mean it was irrelevant.

However, Parker did not render the entire Bible obsolete; he still found the permanent in the Gospels. He viewed the claim that the Gospels were inauthentic as more presupposition than proof, noting Strauss's reliance on internal evidence and his neglect of "the evidence of Christian, Heretical, and even Heathen Antiquity."[46] With de Wette, Parker believed Strauss had applied his mythical approach too liberally: "men do not make myths out of air, but out of historical materials." Adopting a middle path between mythical and supernaturalist approaches, Parker held that the New Testament "always rests on historical ground, though it is not common historical ground, nor is it so rigidly historical that no legendary or mythical elements have entered it."[47] He critiqued the effort to obtain "a complete, consistent, and thoroughly historical picture of the life of Christ" but argued that "if there was not an [sic] historical Christ to idealize, there could be no ideal Christ to seek in history."[48] Parker knew that historical interpretation had some limits but accepted it as the best approach. He was relieved to find that Strauss, in the third edition of the work, recognized the shortcomings of his own critique and left room

---

[43] Ibid., 287–88. [44] Ibid., 300. [45] Ibid., 297. [46] Ibid., 308. [47] Ibid., 309.
[48] Ibid., 310.

for a historical Jesus. While conceding that Strauss's text – "the production of the age" – had initiated an unprecedented crisis for Christian believers, Parker professed that it did not remove "the Redeemer's image" that "has been stamped ineffaceably on the hearts of men."[49] This affirmation did not signify a belief in the necessary authenticity of the Gospels but rather in the idea that essential Christianity had found historical expression in Jesus.[50]

Through his engagement with de Wette and Strauss, Parker came to the conclusion that some biblical texts stood on a firmer footing than others. He also followed de Wette in unhinging religious belief from biblical texts, which rested on grounds that new evidence might unsettle, and instead located the source of belief in an innate religious sense. This led Parker to appreciate the New Testament more than the Old. In the teachings of Christ, Parker discovered ideas that corresponded to the truths emanating from his own soul, and it was on this basis, and not on that of Christ's miracles, that he remained invested in the Gospels' historicity. In the years to come, that continued investment would only further indicate the distance from biblical pasts.

"I SEE NOT HOW A MIRACLE PROVES A DOCTRINE"

While Parker's review fit comfortably within the pages of the Unitarian *Examiner*'s July issue, he had grown uneasy with Unitarianism itself. Parker completed the review a few months prior, in early April – the same month in which Emerson delivered his final sermon. In a pseudonymous piece published late that month, Parker contributed to the growing division between Unitarians and Transcendentalists.

The division was the result of an earlier fracture in Unitarianism. In 1836 – the very year that Emerson published *Nature* – the acrimonious miracles controversy erupted. In November, Norton and his former student Ripley began a pamphlet war over the relationship between Christ's Gospel miracles and Christianity. In two separate reviews, Ripley had prized Schleiermacher's emphasis on intuition-based religious experience and praised James Martineau's move to sever the evidentialist tie between Jesus's miracles and his gospel message.[51] Norton damned Ripley's reasoning as heretical and forcefully asserted the necessity of a link between

---

[49] Ibid., 314, 316.   [50] See Grodzins, *American Heretic*, 129–90.
[51] [George Ripley], review of *Recollections of Schleiermacher*, by Friedrich Lücke, *Christian Examiner and General Review* 20 (March 1836): 1–46; and George Ripley, review of *The*

the reality of Christ's miracles and the truth of Christianity.[52] Within days of this exchange, Emerson's friend William Henry Furness published *Remarks on the Four Gospels*, in which he privileged "an internal moral evidence" over external evidence.[53] This added fuel to the debate. While Unitarians argued that Christian faith depended on the historicity and literality of the accounts describing Jesus's miracles, Unitarians-turned-Transcendentalists, who granted that such miracles might have happened, saw no such necessary relationship.[54]

Both Unitarians and Transcendentalists valued miracles but differed on what constituted a miracle, when miracles occurred, and how much authoritative weight miracles held. Unitarians prized Jesus's miracles as unique instances of the suspension of natural law and rejected all modern claims to miracles. This related to the broader belief among American Protestants that the Bible – and the New Testament, in particular – contained the special revelation of the gospel. In preserving the first Christian era as unique, Unitarians rejected their Congregationalist predecessors' understanding that the predecessors' era existed within a biblical framework and instead viewed their own period as one bereft of miracles. In contrast, Transcendentalists rejected the distinction between natural and revealed religion and between God's work in the biblical past and God's work in the present. Transcendentalists differed from each other in assessing the historicity and authority of Gospel miracles, but they joined together in rejecting these distinctions. In his publication, Furness recast divine miracles as natural, if little understood, and suggested that "the universe – all being – is miraculous."[55] Expanding the realm of the miraculous revalued all moments in time even as it diminished any single moment's power to claim special attention or enduring authority. What mattered most was that at any moment, an individual could experience the miraculous.

Rationale of Religious Enquiry, by James Martineau, *Christian Examiner and General Review* 21 (November 1836): 225–54.

[52] Andrews Norton, *Boston Daily Advertiser*, November 5, 1836. For Ripley's response, see *Boston Daily Advertiser*, November 9, 1836.

[53] "New American Publications," *Waldie's Select Circulating Library*, November 8, 1836, [4]; W[illiam] H[enry] Furness, *Remarks on the Four Gospels* (Philadelphia, 1836), 209.

[54] On the emergence of Transcendentalism in relationship to Unitarianism, see Holifield, *Theology in America*, 444–47; Dean Grodzins, "Unitarianism," in *The Oxford Handbook of Transcendentalism*, ed. Joel Myerson, Sandra Harbert Petrulionis, and Laura Dassow Walls (New York, 2010), 50–69; and Jordan T. Watkins, "Miracles, Transcendentalism and," in *Miracles: An Encyclopedia of People, Places, and Supernatural Events from Antiquity to the Present* (Santa Barbara, 2016), 398–99.

[55] Furness, *Remarks*, 146.

All of this had implications for interpreters' awareness of historical distance from biblical times. Unitarian reasoning implied a temporal divide between the favored New Testament past and the American present. Both the Unitarians' insistence on the uniqueness of this specific era and their efforts to understand it through the historical explication of biblical passages brought attention to temporal distance, which could undermine the idea that the New Testament had a special claim on Christian believers. Meanwhile, Transcendentalist reasoning implied that humans could access the divine in the nineteenth century just as well as in the first. On the surface, this position seems to reject the idea that a temporal divide separated present from New Testament past. However, the Transcendentalist focus on this specific concept – that souls in all eras have ready access to the divine – actually enhanced their sense of historical distance in allowing them to dismiss the many other biblical teachings and beliefs that did not transcend time. Prizing this one belief, in particular, and observing that progress in religious understanding brought it into the open gave adventurous Transcendentalists the ability to range far and wide in their historical investigations. It allowed them to look at the Gospel miracles as products of their age rather than the basis of Christian belief, which highlighted differences between the New Testament past and their own era.

In 1838, Emerson leveled a powerful blow in the battle over the relationship between Christ's miracles and Christian belief and threw his weight behind those who centered faith in an innate and internal religious sense. In his infamous address to Harvard Divinity School's graduating class, he taught that Jesus "saw with open eye the mystery of the soul" – that he saw a direct pathway from God, the divine fount of truth, to the individual. According to Emerson, Jesus "felt that man's life was a miracle." Emerson believed that verbal misuse had turned "Miracle" into an epistemological and theological "Monster."[56] The Galilean's salvific message rested not in supernatural occurrences or even in an atoning sacrifice but rather in the teaching that each human possessed divine attributes and a revelatory prerogative. Jesus's exceptional status depended on the fact that he was, as Emerson stated, "the only soul in history who has appreciated the worth of man."[57] Belief in Christianity, Emerson held, had mistakenly come to rest on whether or

---

[56] Ralph Waldo Emerson, "An Address Delivered Before the Senior Class in Divinity College," in CWRWE, 1:76–93, quotations on 81.
[57] Ibid., 1:82.

not Gospel miracles reflected ancient realities when it should rest on the indwelling presence of the divine in nature and, above all else, the "soul." Emerson appreciated "the Hebrew and Greek Scriptures" and their "immortal sentences," but not nearly as much as he cherished "that supreme Beauty, which ravished" ancient speakers and writers. He anticipated "the hour" when "those shining laws" would inspire a "new Teacher" to provide "new hope and new revelation."[58] In suggesting that this new revelation should align with both scientific and religious developments – with what both Understanding and Reason had uncovered – Emerson registered a belief in human progress that further diminished biblical authority. His address struck at the foundation of Unitarian, and even much of Christian, belief by exposing the shakiness of Christianity's supposedly firm foundations.

Christian commentators rushed to secure these foundations as righteous indignation rained down on Emerson from America's Christian watchtowers, from the Presbyterians at Princeton, to the Congregationalists at Yale, and to the Unitarians at Harvard. Norton, who had been in the audience as Emerson delivered his address, was at the forefront of those who spotlighted the rising specter of Transcendentalism. A year after Emerson's oration, "the Unitarian Pope" delivered an address of his own to the alumni of Harvard Divinity School. He aimed at the larger disease of which he believed Emerson was a symptom. Citing recent political and intellectual attacks on traditional institutions and modes of thought, Norton warned that a new form of infidelity, one that had been spawned in Germany, "has made its way among a very large portion of nominally Christian theologians."[59] Like Spinoza, Norton explained, these theologians used orthodox terms to mask heretical and even atheistic notions. What was at the heart of this infidelity? "It strikes directly at the root of faith in Christianity ... by denying the miracles attesting the divine mission of Christ."[60] In emphasizing the ultimate implications of that denial, Norton laid bare the historical roots of his faith: to "deny that a miracle is capable of proof," he stated, is "to deny the existence of God."[61] In Norton's theological calculus, miracles – as external evidences – proved God's reality, and Gospel miracles – as historical "facts" – proved Christianity's truth.[62]

---

[58] Ibid., 1:92.
[59] Andrews Norton, *A Discourse on the Latest Form of Infidelity* (Cambridge, MA, 1839), 9.
[60] Ibid., 11. [61] Ibid., 14–15. [62] Ibid., 18.

Even more than Edwards in the eighteenth century, Norton upheld historical evidence, understood through the use of reason, as the surest foundation of human knowledge about religious truth. He noted that some German scholars spoke of Gospel miracles as exaggerated natural events, or as "prodigies, adapted to rouse the attention of a rude people, like the Jews; but not required for the conviction of men of more enlightened minds."[63] He observed that others denied miracles outright. In response to such rampant disbelief, Norton argued that Christ's "whole history ... is miraculous." In his view, explaining away miracles was tantamount to throwing out the Gospels. Norton reasoned that "if the accounts of Christ's miracles are mere fictions," as some claimed, then no one can regard Christ himself "as an object of veneration, or ... consider his teachings ... as of any importance."[64] This was an all-or-nothing equation: either the miracles were factual occurrences and Christianity was true or they were fictitious and it was a farce. As Norton saw it, the Germans and their American followers "complain, that the solid earth is not solid enough for them to rest on. They have firm footing on the clouds."[65] Norton was not far off. Transcendentalists did deem historical grounds unstable and surely realized that their abstract footing was less susceptible to the unsettling potential of rigorous historical examination. Norton, though, contended that "there can be no intuition, no direct perception, of the truth of Christianity."[66] Intuition might not fall prey to historical criticism, but it provided no surer epistemology of truth. Indeed, to people like Norton, "conscience" seemed to lack any kind of foundation whatsoever.

In the appendix of the published address, Norton focused on the historical foundations of Christian faith. He pointed to de Wette and Schleiermacher as examples of theologians who placed faith in "a pious apprehension of things" rather than "a historical acquaintance with Christianity" and explained that Strauss went even further in arguing that the Gospels were "destitute of historical truth."[67] In Norton's mind, that conclusion demolished Christian faith.

Despite his heavy-handed critical approach, Norton was quite perceptive. These German thinkers, he explained, seemed to hold that "Christianity is no permanent thing, but must, with the advance of men, go on improving, and divesting itself more and more of its historical relations."[68] Proponents of this position had little to lose in the face of

---

[63] Ibid., 22. [64] Ibid., 23, 29. [65] Ibid., 30. [66] Ibid., 32. [67] Ibid., 41, 46.
[68] Ibid., 43.

historical distance, which actually supported their views. While Parker could agree with Norton that "true Christianity is always the same," Parker also held that the innate religious sense used to perceive atemporal Christian truths became less obstructed over time.[69]

Norton's observations about German and Transcendentalist belief in the progress of religion paralleled later developments in the debate over slavery. A sense of religious and moral progress proved influential for Parker and others who advanced a determinative antislavery reading. While granting that Christian apostles and American founders had sanctioned the practice of slavery, Parker and other antislavery writers stressed that historical contexts had blinded these historical figures to slavery's sin and that progress since their times had removed those blinders. In the debate over the Fugitive Slave Law, even Norton himself argued that the Constitution's fugitive slave clause had become obsolete.[70] Increasingly, contextual readings of both the Bible and the Constitution commingled with traditional narratives of progress from the biblical and revolutionary eras, all of which drew attention to and strength from perceived historical distance.

Norton's appeals to historical knowledge also anticipated the constitutional debate over slavery. In addressing objections to the idea that Christian faith rested on historical grounds, he asserted that "there is ... no other mode of establishing religious belief."[71] The airy epistemology of de Wette and his ilk was incomprehensible to the uninitiated, Norton scoffed, while historical knowledge, though ascertained by a "small portion" of learned men, could be distilled and enjoyed as "a common property and a common blessing."[72] This foreshadowed the response to *Dred Scott v. Sandford*, when a range of commentators called attention to the historical basis of Chief Justice Roger B. Taney's decision and asserted their right to provide alternative historical readings of the Constitution. Instead of relying on an elite group of scholars to learn about distant biblical pasts, however, they searched the recent American past unassisted and thus contributed to a developing culture of popular constitutionalism. The democratization of historical argumentation, through both scholarly presentation and popular participation, further highlighted the historical peculiarities of sacred texts.

Norton did not realize that in spreading the blessing of historical knowledge he was contributing to a growing awareness of the Bible's

[69] Ibid., 48.   [70] *Boston Daily Atlas*, November 26, 1850.   [71] Norton, *Discourse*, 53.
[72] Ibid., 55.

historical differences, which could be used to disprove and historicize the Gospels just as easily as they could be used to authenticate them. Unaware of that potential, he continued work on *The Evidences of the Genuineness of the Gospels* and subsequently published *Internal Evidences of the Genuineness of the Gospels* (1856). In this posthumous publication, Norton argued that the contradictions between the Gospels and the incompleteness of the accounts actually confirmed their authenticity, for such was the nature of historical accounts. This apologetic approach carried the dangerous potential to desacralize the Bible and place it alongside secular histories. Norton argued that the proofs authenticating the Gospels and their miracles "are of the same nature as the proofs on which we rely as to any other historical fact."[73] He then defended his faith with those proofs and, by doing so, drew attention to what he had worked so hard to remove, the obfuscating "distance of eighteen centuries."[74]

Norton's *Discourse* began a new volley of exchanges with Ripley and brought more combatants to the battle over the Bible's historicity.[75] Though critical of orthodox interpreters, Norton called on them to help combat the greater threat posed by Transcendentalism. The intensity of his contempt for this new movement was evident when he asked Hodge to reprint his coreligionists' biting critique of the movement, along with a portion of an article in which Hodge had strongly criticized Norton's reliance on miracles as the sole grounds of Christian belief.[76] Hodge accepted the invitation and suggested a few edits but then expressed his fear that Norton had taken the first steps down the Germans' heretical path by, at least in Hodge's mind, making "judgment of the genuineness of portions of Scripture to depend more on internal than external evidence."[77] The article on Transcendentalism exposed Emerson's affinities with the Germans and excoriated his exaggerated opinion of human

---

[73] Andrews Norton, *Internal Evidences of the Genuineness of the Gospels* (Boston, 1856), 142.
[74] Ibid., 237.
[75] For Ripley's responses, see George Ripley, *Letters on the Latest Form of Infidelity, Including a View of the Opinions of Spinoza, Schleiermacher, and De Wette* (Boston, 1840).
[76] [J. W. Alexander, Albert B. Dod, and Charles Hodge], *Transcendentalism of the Germans and of Cousin and Its Influence on Opinion in the Country* (Cambridge, MA, 1840). See also, "Review 3," *Biblical Repertory and Princeton Review* 9 (January 1839): 95–101.
[77] Charles Hodge to Andrews Norton, February 27 and March 12, 1840, Andrews Norton Papers, MS Am 1089, Houghton.

potential while Hodge's piece revealed the Hegelian nature of Emerson's philosophy and tied him to Strauss.[78]

When Norton used Hodge to combat Transcendentalism, Parker entered the fray, picking up where Emerson had left off. In April and May of 1840, Parker published a satirical announcement and a damning "Desultory Notice" of Norton's pamphlet, in which he dismissed Hodge for his reliance on Berlin biblical literalist E.W. Hengstenberg and chastised Hodge's coreligionists for their ignorance of German philosophy.[79] But it was in an essay published in late April of the same year, which Parker penned under the pseudonym of Levi Blodgett, that he struck at the heart of the debate.[80]

Parker attacked the idea that miracles formed the basis of Christian belief and attempted to establish the universal presence of an innate religious element, which, he contended, led to a belief in God. Rather than making historical evidence the basis of his faith, he used it to buttress his claims. In accounting for differences in past peoples' and prophets' use of the innate element – or what he referred to as the "higher faculties of the soul" – Parker emphasized the "progress and development of religion in man."[81] Parker posited that "as the tribe of race improves, the manifestations of religion become more perfect. The form changes to suit the culture of the age."[82] He believed that while religious truth remained constant, its expressions became clearer as religious forms developed in relationship to more enlightened circumstances. This emphasis on the progress of religion supported Parker's belief that some in the present understood Christian truth better than the primitive Christians. Similar to the enlightenment postulation of the progress of universal reason, this idea fostered an awareness of how historical differences and changes created distinct historical periods.[83]

Parker's belief in progress related to his sense that true religion adapted to new circumstances. He wrote that while some individuals who communicate with the divine "make religious epochs," they "are subject to

---

[78] See Gutjahr, *Charles Hodge*, 227–34. [79] See Grodzins, *American Heretic*, 190–99.

[80] Levi Blodgett [Theodore Parker], *The Previous Question between Mr. Andrews Norton and His Alumni Moved and Handled in a Letter to All Those Gentlemen* (1840), in *Transcendentalism: A Reader*, ed. Joel Myerson (New York, 2000), 260–80.

[81] Ibid., 266. [82] Ibid., 267.

[83] Some enlightenment-era thinkers understood historical development as cyclical, with alternative periods of rationality and irrationality. For example, some considered the classical era as a kind of golden age. See Dan Edelstein, *The Enlightenment: A Genealogy* (Chicago, 2010).

the various peculiarities of their nation, place and age." Because the peculiarities "perpetually change," he continued, "the old form of religion ... gradually becomes obsolete. A new teacher ... arises; starts from a higher stand and separating the peculiarities of the old form which adapted it to its age ... constructs a new form suitable to the altered condition of mankind."[84] These sentiments, which echoed statements Emerson had made in Cambridge in 1838, placed Parker at the far end of the spectrum of antebellum thinkers who accepted that the sacred writers had accommodated their messages to specific times and audiences. Stuart and Hodge granted God's accommodation to human language but continued to assert that the Bible remained the repository of divine revelation. Norton admitted that the apostles had accommodated to their audiences and even embraced some of their audiences' erroneous beliefs, but argued that the New Testament, and the Gospels in particular, formed the foundation of Christian faith. Parker agreed that the Bible contained religious truth, but only as circumstances allowed. True religion existed independent of time, but because it functioned in relation to the development of the soul, it also evolved in time. Parker held that truth itself accommodated. Although he and Emerson maintained the permanence of divine truth and of God as its originator, they placed religious development in human hands, which, to someone like Norton, was tantamount to the humanistic and atheistic positions spawned by Hegel, nurtured by Strauss, and perfected and unleashed by Ludwig Feuerbach.[85]

While Parker prized "true Christianity" as a historical instantiation of "the highest form of religion" and could conceive of "no more perfect moral and religious incarnation of God than Jesus of Nazareth," he would not designate Christianity "absolute religion" or label Christ "the ultimate incarnation of God."[86] Parker believed that "Jesus ... wrought miracles," but saw "not how a miracle proves a doctrine," which allowed him to sidestep "some historical difficulties in the way of establishing *all* the miracles which [Jesus] wrought."[87] These difficulties included contextual

---

[84] [Parker], *Previous Question*, 268, 269.
[85] See John Edward Toews, *Hegelianism: The Path toward Dialectical Humanism, 1805–1841* (New York, 1980). Elizabeth Hurth argues that "the tendencies toward atheism were inherent in Transcendentalist thought," but her careful attention to the distinctions between American Transcendentalists and individuals such as Strauss and Feuerbach complicates that argument. Hurth, *Between Faith and Unbelief*, 2. On the form of Transcendentalist religion and belief, see also David Faflik, *Transcendental Heresies: Harvard and the Modern American Practice of Unbelief* (Amherst, MA, 2020).
[86] [Parker], *Previous Question*, 271.   [87] Ibid., 274, 275, emphasis in original.

issues. Parker pointed to the "tendency to the marvellous ... among the Jews" and argued that the Evangelists' "inspiration did not free them from the notions of the age and nation."[88] In other words, the miracles of Jesus might be the product of a temporary mindset and thus could not serve as the foundation of faith.

Parker insisted that the issue was not whether Jesus had performed miracles but whether the truth of Christianity rested on the miracles he had presumably performed. His conviction that Christian truth flowed from an internal source did not necessarily imply a dismissal of Jesus's miracles as "fictions" of fabricated Gospel accounts. He assured his readers that he believed in "the *general* accuracy of [the Evangelists'] history of Christ."[89] But Parker would not place his faith in accuracies that research might later render inaccurate. So when scholars such as Norton, who accepted that historical circumstances shaped biblical content, failed to see that accounts of Christ's miracles might be productions of the age, Parker found them "at the mercy of scoffers, scholars and critics" who had dismantled the Old Testament miracles and discredited those of the New.[90] Signaling the instability of Norton's historical foundation, he wrote, "You make our religion depend entirely ... on strange events which happened ... two thousand years ago, of which we can never be certain."[91] In his review of Strauss's *The Life of Jesus* for the *Examiner*, Parker cited the limits of historical explication to neutralize the German critic, but in this pseudonymous publication he used the historical distance that historical explication had introduced to underscore the difficulties involved in upholding a faith based on facts. The Transcendentalist preferred a basis of faith that was less susceptible to deterioration and falsification.

Parker believed the endurance of the gospel message rested on its relationship to the universal religious sentiment, which had an atemporal standing. He stressed this conviction in a sermon entitled "The Relation of the Bible to the Soul." He first delivered this sermon in the summer of 1839 and then published it in two articles during the winter of 1840–41.[92] In the first article, Parker challenged the Bible's high status as "the Book of Books," arguing that it was "*not greater than Conscience and Reason.*"[93] The ancient biblical texts were not ancient enough, in

---

[88] Ibid., 276.   [89] Ibid., emphasis in original.   [90] Ibid., 277.   [91] Ibid., 278.
[92] See Grodzins, *American Heretic*, 180–200.
[93] Theodore Parker, "The Relation of the Bible to the Soul," *Western Messenger* 8 (December 1840): 337–40, quotations on 337 and 339, emphasis in original.

Parker's estimation. "Religion is older than the Bible," he posited, just as justice was older than legal tradition.[94] This was not a historical claim but an appeal to truths above time.

In making this appeal, Parker extended the comparison between religious and legal traditions. He explained that biblical passages, like legal codes, were "simply [the] historical form" of transcendent truths.[95] The legal parallel was potent in a nation preoccupied with law, especially at a time when Americans were vigorously debating slavery's constitutionality. Parker, who began to address slavery as a topic of reform during the 1840s, challenged the assumed tie between eternal juridical truths and sacred historical texts. He wrote, "men sometimes think the statutes of the land were providentially struck out, in some happy moment, which will never return – that if these should perish, so would Order and Justice decease from being."[96] This set the scene for Parker's later critique of the fixation on the favored founding era, which he believed the present far exceeded in terms of moral insight.

Drawing out the comparison between law and scripture, Parker wrote that men "say the same of the Bible, and assert that Morality and Religion would have been quite lost from the world, if the Bible had chanced to perish."[97] His absolute religion was ahistorical: "granting it were shewn ... that the facts related in the Gospels, were not facts, but fictions; that Jesus never rose from the dead; never died ... never wrought miracles, taught doctrines, or even lived – still Christianity would be as true, as lasting, as now it is, when environed by all these historical statements." Parker's formulation contradicted Norton's equation. His distinction between the truthfulness of the Gospels and the miracles recounted therein paralleled de Wette's distinction between historical facts and religious meaning. Parker's proposition, as with Emerson's salvo, shook the religious foundation of thinkers such as Norton, who rested their Gospel-centered faith on historical grounds. It undermined the exceptional status of the New Testament, of Christ's miracles, and even of Christ himself. Parker still valued the Bible, but he measured its teachings against "Reason and Conscience."[98] After all, he quipped in an allusion to Mark 2:27, "The Bible was made for man, not man for the Bible."[99]

Parker's modification of the passage in Mark foreshadowed a similar modification to the same passage by William I. Bowditch in the

---

[94] Ibid., 338.   [95] Ibid., 339.
[96] Ibid., 338. See Grodzins, *American Heretic*, 168–73, 333–40.
[97] Parker, "Relation of the Bible" (December 1840), 338.   [98] Ibid., 339.   [99] Ibid., 340.

constitutional debate. The modification came near the end of the 1840s and at the close of Bowditch's *Slavery and the Constitution*. Bowditch was a member of the Boston Vigilance Committee with Parker and helped house William and Ellen Craft, who had escaped from slavery. In his book, Bowditch voiced the higher-law position that "institutions were made for man, not man for them. Constitutions are the work of man, and man is to be reverenced before his works."[100] In both the biblical and the constitutional debate, the belief that conscience had clear access to divine truth made historical forms and figures secondary. This removed the need to see erstwhile favored pasts as familiar and pushed them further into the realm of the foreign.

In Parker's sermon, he continued his comparison between religion and law as he separated universal from temporal. He valued the Bible as Emerson had Christ: "It reveals the true idea of a *man*, the divine man.... It sets before him the noblest aim – 'Be perfect as God.'"[101] While extracting this teaching for continued use, Parker compared outdated Old Testament passages to "laws and political institutions," which "like old garments which were fine in their day ... are laid aside when their end is answered."[102] He agreed that Moses's laws were "wonderful for his age" but insisted that "it is only the true, the universal, the divine part of them, that ... still lives. All peculiar institutions of his system ... have long since fallen to decay." Parker's attention to context and his belief in a universal religious sentiment led him to dismiss much of Moses's teachings and to set aside appeals "to his old text-books."[103] Soon, Parker focused his contempt for the outdated on the South's peculiar institution. Once he conceived revelation as progressive rather than historical, he shined a spotlight on the discrepancies between ancient and modern views of servitude, as well as Americans' past and present attitudes toward slavery. These efforts highlighted historical distance, which, in turn, supported Parker's belief in progress and his call to abandon obsolete institutions.

Parker's emphasis on progress again directed him to question the relevance of the New Testament and its actors. "If the Old Testament ... has been superseded," he asked, "how do we know that the New Testament, the Gospel, nay, even Christianity itself, shall not

---

[100] William I. Bowditch, *Slavery and the Constitution* (Boston, 1849), 155.
[101] Theodore Parker, "The Relation of the Bible to the Soul," *Western Messenger* 9 (January 1841): 388–96, quotation on 388, emphasis in original.
[102] Ibid., 389.   [103] Ibid., 390.

one day be passed by and forgotten, having prepared the way for a more beautiful revelation of the divine image than Jesus himself?"[104] Parker was almost willing to leave behind the whole Christian past, in part because he believed that "there are men at this day who understand Christianity far better than it was understood by its teachers in the first ages of our era."[105] To Parker, progress made the original Christian truth clearer. He wrote that "the lights of old time, like lamps in the street, are passed by, diminished by the distance, and gradually lost sight of; while ... Christianity still shines with mild and tranquil light ... and is refined and elevated by the science and culture of successive ages." Distance rendered much of the past and its teachings obsolete, burnt up in "the furnace of time," even as progress made permanent Christian truth, "which knows nothing of time or space," more explicit.[106] Parker saw the passage of time as a sifter of truth.

Parker's reading not only indicated the presence of historical distance, it also made use of that distance. Mining out timeless gems drew attention to the time-bound mountain from which he had dug them. Parker believed that descriptions of the mountain and accounts of the return journey only served to highlight the true value of the rare gems. Increasingly, antebellum exegetes had to wrestle with the idea that substantial historical differences separated them from Old and New Testament eras. These individuals dealt with the emerging problem of perceived historical distance in different ways. Most of them dismissed it, but Parker turned it to his interpretive use.

While Parker attended to both sides of his interpretive equation, to both the transient and the permanent, he often focused on the former. He asserted that "the essence of Christianity can never change," even as he worked to show that "the form of Christianity will change, to suit the character and wants of different nations and ages."[107] He bemoaned, for example, his contemporaries' use of the writings ascribed to Moses to justify "war, capital punishment, [and] slavery." Parker retained a distinction between the Old and New Testaments in terms of religious value, but the limitations he found with ancient prophets also applied to the apostles: "Paul, and Peter, and James, and John, saw not all things; nor were they placed above the reach of passion, human weakness, the dreams of that age." Although sometimes prophetic, the biblical writers had existed in time and space and were subject to human weakness and temporal limitation. And yet, Parker noted, Christian ministers "will tell

[104] Ibid.   [105] Ibid., 391.   [106] Ibid., 392.   [107] Ibid., 393.

you the canon of revelation is closed – that you and I ... must be poor imitators of two or three men, who have incarnated in past ages, all of God's spirit."[108] Parker echoed Emerson's shocking statements at Harvard, in which the Sage of Concord had observed that "the divine nature is attributed to one or two persons, and denied to all the rest" and had lamented that "men have come to speak of the revelation as somewhat long ago given and done."[109] By encouraging his readers to use "the revelation made to others," Parker joined Emerson in directing the believer to "seek new ones in himself."[110] These Transcendentalists did not completely cast aside the past, but their awareness of the transient in and transience of the Bible supported their call for ongoing revelation.

During the late 1830s and early 1840s, Parker had detached his religious position from the historicity of the Bible. He had grown skeptical of Old Testament narratives and dismissed much of Hebrew scripture as the product of an outdated past with little present relevance. The miracles controversy allowed him to further articulate his position against that of Unitarians such as Norton, who asserted that Christian faith rested on the historicity of New Testament miracles. In contrast to this position, Parker posited that Christian truth existed independent of historical facts and flowed from an innate and ubiquitous religious sense that time had cultivated. He continued to distinguish between the Testaments only because he believed enough historical evidence existed to confirm that true religion found expression rather than embodiment in a person named Jesus. He was willing to suggest the transience of even that particular historical expression.

THE TRANSIENT JESUS AND THE PERMANENT CHRIST

Parker's sustained engagement with German literature and his ongoing effort to translate de Wette's *Introduction* shaped the themes in his sermons and writings from this time period, which served as the intellectual backdrop to his most important works on the relationship between history and Christianity: *A Discourse on the Transient and Permanent in Christianity* and *A Discourse of Matters Pertaining to Religion*.[111] The first resulted from a sermon Parker preached in May 1841 and the second from a series of lectures he delivered that fall. These writings, as much as

---

[108] Ibid., 394. [109] Emerson, "Address," 1:80, 84.
[110] Parker, "Relation of the Bible" (January 1841), 396.
[111] See Theodore Parker, "German Literature," *The Dial* 1 (January 1841): 315–39.

any other antebellum source, show a thinker whose exposure to biblical criticism created an acute sense of the transience of the Bible and its Christ.

In Parker's May 1841 sermon, which paid homage to Strauss's article "Über Vergängliches und Bleibendes im Christenthum" (On Transiency and Permanency in Christianity), Parker argued that historical expressions of permanent truths often obscured more than they revealed and thus held little purchase in the present.[112] He located the permanent in Christ's eternal words rather than in his temporal person. Distinguishing between divine religion (the permanent) and the religion of man (the transient), Parker explained that the latter "has never been [in] any two centuries, the same thing, except only in name."[113] This insistence on temporal distinctions, which exposed deep historical divides, gave shape to Parker's belief in progress. In contrast to Christian restorationists, he found efforts to reclaim religious forms futile: "neither God nor the world goes backward."[114] Insisting that true religion, like the law of nature, transcends temporality, he observed that the rites of religion, like the outward facts of nature, pass away.

Parker applied the same reasoning to Christian doctrines. "Nothing changes more from age to age than the doctrines... insisted on as essential to Christianity," he stated.[115] He used familiar examples – the authority of the Bible and of Christ – to make his point. Tracing the deep tradition of belief in the infallibility and unmatched authority of the Bible, he observed with some relief that "modern Criticism is fast breaking to pieces this idol which men have made out of the Scriptures." In showing that biblical authors "shared the darkness of their age," historical readings had begun to break Bible's spell.[116] Parker also outlined changing views of Christ to evidence the "transitoriness" of the belief that "Christianity rest[ed] on the personal authority of Jesus."[117] He conceded that Christianity "depends on [the New Testament] for the historical statements of its facts" but insisted that "we do not require infallible inspiration on the part of the writers, more than in the record of other historical facts." Parker was still convinced that the Gospels rested on historical grounds,

---

[112] See Grodzins, *American Heretic*, 242–43.
[113] Philip F. Gura, "Theodore Parker and the South Boston Ordination: The Textual Tangle of 'A Discourse on the Transient and Permanent in Christianity,'" *Studies in the American Renaissance* (1988): 164. Gura reconstructs the sermon text based on the appendix Parker included in the second edition of the pamphlet, in which he listed hundreds of changes he had made before sending the manuscript to the printer. Parker published the appendix to confront claims that he had altered the sermon's meaning.
[114] Ibid., 164.   [115] Ibid., 165.   [116] Ibid., 167.   [117] Ibid., 168.

"The Ground Will Shake" 103

but his faith was not built on them: "If it could be proved ... that the gospels were a sheer fabrication, that Jesus of Nazareth had never lived, still Christianity would stand firm." Christianity, he proposed, was "tried by the oracle God places in the heart" rather than the evidence offered by the critic.[118] Parker agreed with contemporary interpreters such as Stuart and Norton that the Bible should be read as a historical text but refused to base his belief on that text or the people and events it described. In a striking later addition to the sermon, he noted, "we live too late in the world to settle questions by texts."[119]

In reaction to critical reports, Parker issued a pamphlet edition in June.[120] In the pamphlet, Parker further argued that freedom from transitory doctrines allowed believers to approach the Bible and Christ as God intended them to. Discerning differences between the preached and pamphlet version of the sermon, his critics asserted that he had intentionally obscured the content. Parker insisted the changes were cosmetic.[121] In a second edition, published the next month, Parker included an appendix outlining all differences between the sermon as preached and published. If anything, Parker's ideas were clearer in the pamphlet editions. He agreed that when read with "Reason, Conscience, and Faith fully active," the Bible presented a "whole library of the deepest and most earnest thoughts and feelings, and piety and love, ever recorded."[122] When viewed in such light, Christ's words "solve the questions of this present age."[123] While rejecting the transient as outdated, Parker affirmed the relevance of the permanent. On this basis, he later argued that the spirit of Christianity condemned slavery. He pointed out cultural differences between past ages and his own but upheld as ahistorical the essential Christian truth that taught the "method of attaining oneness with God."[124] Part of attaining oneness with God depended on cultivating divinity within oneself.

Parker had added a couple of paragraphs to the pamphlet on Jesus as an exemplar of how to access the divine. His qualified view of the Christian founder had begun to emerge in relation to his emphasis on religious progress. About a year and a half earlier, in January 1840, after Parker

---

[118] Ibid., 169. [119] Ibid., 176n13.
[120] Theodore Parker, *A Discourse on the Transient and Permanent in Christianity* (Boston, 1841).
[121] See Gura, "Parker and the South Boston Ordination," 149–60.
[122] Theodore Parker, *A Discourse on the Transient and Permanent in Christianity*, 2nd ed. (Boston, 1841), 19–20. Parker did not make changes to the second edition of this pamphlet.
[123] Ibid., 21. [124] Ibid., 24.

had preached a new sermon on the universality of inspiration, the Unitarian minister Francis Parkman confronted him. "When you talk about future Christs," he complained, "I can't bear ye."[125] In July 1840, the *Dial* had published an expanded version of Parker's sermon, in which he praised Christ as possessing the "greatest measure of Inspiration" but again spoke of the potential of "future Christs."[126] A year later, when Parker published his *Discourse on the Transient and the Permanent*, he echoed Emerson, writing that in making Jesus "the Son of God in a peculiar and exclusive sense – much of the significance of his character is gone."[127] In both the preached and pamphlet version of this sermon, Parker explained that "there was nothing between [Jesus] and the Father of all.... He would have us do the same; worship with nothing between us and God."[128] Parker believed this teaching, which he located in the Bible, provided an enduring basis of faith, while other teachings crumbled beneath history's weight. He warned that "the ground will shake" under the feet of those focused on "the surfaces of things."[129] In the preached version of the sermon, Parker had noted that "the form Religion takes ... can never be the same in any two centuries."[130] He later added that "the *Christianity holy men feel in the heart* – the Christ that is born within us, is always the same thing to each soul that feels it."[131] The Christ born within existed independent of the Christ born in Bethlehem.

Parker continued to preach and write on the transient and the permanent despite mounting opposition. Convers Francis praised Parker's work as "a better defence of Christianity, than the many volumes on the 'Evidences,'" but the orthodox press damned Parker as a duplicitous deist, and most Unitarian ministers refused to share the pulpit with him.[132] He was shocked and hurt by this development. He had no intention of creating a firestorm. Parker resisted the urge to meet his critics head-on, but he did not retreat.[133] At the invitation of Boston Unitarians, he delivered a series of lectures in the fall of 1841, which he then published

---

[125] Theodore Parker, Journal, January 2, 1841, in *Life and Correspondence of Theodore Parker: Minister of the Twenty-Eighth Congregational Society, Boston*, ed. John Weiss, 2 vols. (New York, 1864), 1:142 (hereafter cited as *Life and Correspondence*). See Grodzins, *American Heretic*, 184.
[126] [Theodore] P[arker], "The Divine Presence in Nature and in the Soul," *The Dial* 1 (July 1840): 64, 65.
[127] Parker, *Discourse on the Transient*, 2d. ed., 21. [128] Ibid., 24. [129] Ibid., 27, 28.
[130] Gura, "Parker and the South Boston Ordination," 173.
[131] Parker, *Discourse on the Transient*, 2d. ed., 25, emphasis in original.
[132] Convers Francis to Theodore Parker, June 30, 1841, Theodore Parker Papers, MHS.
[133] See Grodzins, *American Heretic*, 242–65.

in his first book, *A Discourse of Matters Pertaining to Religion*, in May 1842.

The book, which closely followed the lectures, represented a kind of culmination of Parker's thoughts on the timebound and the timeless. In the preface, he proposed to recall "men from the transient shows of time to the permanent substance of Religion."[134] He revisited and expanded the familiar themes of the innate religious element and its relationship to God (inspiration), Jesus (Christianity), the Bible, and the church. At the outset, Parker announced the historical implications of his discussion, declaring that "our reverence for the Past, is just in proportion to our ignorance of it."[135] Historical ignorance, he believed, had led Christians to make idols out of a historical text and its central figure, obscuring their own direct connection to religious truth. Parker persisted in using history to confirm, rather than to ground, his beliefs.

Once again, Parker sought to establish the universal presence of the "religious element," and he did so by an appeal to "historical argument."[136] He referred to historical development, in particular, to explain differences in the presence of this element. In the winter of 1841–42, as Parker prepared to publish his sermons, his reading of French philosopher August Comte convinced him that human existence started in an uncivilized state and progressed to higher levels of being. This supported his ideas about the progress of religion. It also led him to associate golden age thinking with Old Testament mythmaking.[137] Such thinking, Parker lamented, shut communication with God between the two lids of the Bible. Again echoing the words Emerson had spoken at Harvard a few years earlier, he proposed that "now, as in the days of Adam, Moses, Jesus, he that is faithful to Reason, Conscience, and Religion, will, through them, receive inspiration."[138] Parker believed that although the Bible contained historical expressions of absolute religion, the Bible did not embody absolute truth. This kind of thinking allowed for and encouraged an openness to historical differences and distance.

Temporal distance introduced epistemological problems for those reliant on texts. Parker emphasized that it was more difficult to obtain "knowledge of the doctrine taught by any teacher of ancient times" than it was to learn truth via intuition.[139] In later constitutional debates, temporal proximity created different problems as antislavery interpreters,

---

[134] Parker, *Discourse of Matters*, iii.   [135] Ibid., 5.   [136] Ibid., 31.
[137] See Grodzins, *American Heretic*, 281–83.   [138] Parker, *Discourse of Matters*, 234.
[139] Ibid., 246.

including Parker, asserted the framers' lack of consensus on important questions. Investigating the framers' views, in turn, spread a sense of distance from the founding era. That distance required an awareness of the framers' constraining context.

Parker made this point about the biblical writers: "Their national, sectarian, personal prejudices must color their narrative."[140] Hence, there was a problem, he explained, with making the reality of Christ's miracles – a "purely historical question" based on "scanty" evidence – the basis of Christianity.[141] And the miracle problem implicated the miracle worker. If the Evangelists were to be trusted, Parker noted, Christ himself had held erroneous opinions. Parker agreed with Emerson that baptism and the Last Supper might "have been an accommodation," on the part of Christ, "to the wants of the times" but argued that Jesus was "mistaken ... in the doctrine of demons, in the celebrated prediction of his second coming and the end of the world."[142] As with the Old Testament and its prophets and the New Testament and its apostles, the Christ of the Gospels could not escape temporal limitations. But that fact left Parker unshaken. Again, he averred: "Let it be shewn ... that the Gospels are false, and Jesus mistaken, still Christianity is eternally true if it be the Absolute Religion."[143]

Parker still believed in the historical basis of the Gospels; in them he found the summation of Christianity: "Love to Man – Love to God."[144] This simple truth set Christianity apart as absolute religion and absolute morality. Parker rested his religion in universal principles rather than particular peoples and precepts, and he encouraged his contemporaries to "worship with no master but God, no creed but Truth, no service but Love."[145] To this, he added the universal privilege of inspiration, declaring that Jesus "never speaks of his connection with God as peculiar" but rather "represents himself as but the type of that relation which all good men sustain to God."[146] As Emerson listed Boston alongside Rome and Jerusalem, so Parker posited that "the light that shone at Nineveh, Egypt, Judea, Athens, Rome, shines no more from those points; it is everywhere."[147] Parker's religion was not restricted to a place, a past, a book, or a man. "The inward Christ, which alone abideth forever," he wrote, "has much to say which the

---

[140] Ibid., 248–49.   [141] Ibid., 271, 272.   [142] Ibid., 259, 265–66. See also pg. 290.
[143] Ibid., 280.   [144] Ibid., 253.   [145] Ibid., 377.   [146] Ibid., 255, 256.   [147] Ibid., 376.

Bible never told," or, as he later added, "much which the historical Jesus never knew."[148]

By the early 1840s, the intellectual framework was in place for Parker to critique what he viewed as his contemporaries' overreliance on the archaic teachings of sacred religious and legal texts from favored pasts. He clung to an idea of universal and unchanging religious truth as much as Channing, Norton, Stuart, Hodge, and other antebellum Christians, but he unbound that truth from historical facts, events, and figures. His willingness to travel down the paths of historical criticism paved by de Wette and Strauss informed his urgent rejection of the idea that the permanent relevance of religious truth rested in historical texts and actors.

America's biblical scholars existed on a spectrum, from those retaining faith in the Bible as a whole, such as Stuart and Hodge, to those trusting the New Testament or the Gospels alone, such as Channing and Norton, to those focused on the actions and teachings of Jesus himself. Each person on the spectrum granted that his chosen canon contained both time-bound teachings meant for a particular ancient audience *and* timeless teachings relevant to modern American audiences. Parker stood at the far end of this spectrum. He accepted a few specific messages gleaned from Christ's teachings as permanent religious truths and let all else drift away into the sea of the distant past. The crucial difference between Parker and his contemporaries was that he centered his faith in an atemporal sphere of conscience while his contemporaries rooted their faith in the historical grounds of a biblical past.

Despite important interpretive differences, each of the biblical scholars mentioned in this chapter contributed to a growing sense of distance from biblical pasts. Liberal and conservative scholars recognized the need to attend to historical context in discerning the meaning of scriptural passages. In doing so, they exposed the real temporal divide separating the pure primitive Christian era from the American present. Parker went even further than his contemporaries in how he used the distance his readings revealed. Rather than attempt to mute its presence in scriptural application, he used distance to measure the transient and the permanent according to conscience. In other words, while most biblical scholars approached distance as an interpretive problem, Parker saw it as a solution. Historical distance supported his insistence

---

[148] Parker, *Discourse of Matters*, 376; Theodore Parker, *A Discourse of Matters Pertaining to Religion*, 4th ed. (Boston, 1856), 354.

that biblical pasts should not be revered as exceptional golden ages but instead appreciated as luminous periods that pointed the way toward even brighter futures. This armed Parker for his engagement in the nation's most wrenching moral, political, and legal crisis. The issue of slavery would drive him to further historicize biblical pasts; it also led him to highlight the temporal distance between his time and America's founding.

3

"Texts ... Designed for Local and Temporary Use"

Discussions about slavery accelerated preexisting debates about the historical nature of the Bible and, in time, the Constitution. The worlds of the legal and the religious often overlapped in American thought, contributing to a deep Western intellectual tradition in which the language and concepts of religion and law informed each other. Theodore Parker contributed to the American iteration of this tradition in 1840 when he described biblical texts and legal statutes as particular historical forms of "the indestructible religious sentiment."[1] During the next two decades, the actions of slaves, fugitive slaves, and free blacks forced the nation to focus its attention on slavery.[2] The ensuing debate sparked conversations about reading the Bible and the Constitution as historical texts. In this period, the Constitution joined the Bible as a subject of deep historical inquiry and an object of substantial historicization.

Before spurring the historicization of the Constitution (a process detailed in subsequent chapters), the slavery debate had already contributed to the historicization of the Bible. In the biblical battles over interpretation, the historicizing process began with the most distant period in question, the Old Testament era, before encroaching on the era of the New Testament. As outlined in previous chapters, liberal Christian scholars, who identified with the God of the New Testament more than

---

[1] Parker, "Relation of the Bible to the Soul," (December 1840): 338.
[2] See Manisha Sinha, *The Slave's Cause: A History of Abolition* (New Haven, 2016), 381–585. See also, R. J. M. Blackett, *The Captives Quest for Freedom: Fugitive Slaves, the 1850s Fugitive Slave Law, and the Politics of Slavery* (New York, 2018); and Andrew Delbanco, *The War before the War: Fugitive Slaves and the Struggle for America's Soul from the Revolution to the Civil War* (New York, 2018).

that of the Old, found biblical criticism useful in upholding the New Testament as the premier canonical text. During the same period, the revivalist emphasis on Christ led a broader group of American Christians to favor the Greek over the Hebrew scriptures.

When antislavery immediatism pushed the issue of slavery onto the national stage in the 1830s, most biblical interpreters appealed to the New Testament. Some antislavery interpreters continued to use the Old Testament and argued that slavery did not exist among the Israelites. More frequently, however, these interpreters accepted slavery's nominal biblical existence but maintained that it differed in crucial respects from southern chattel slavery. This interpretation attested to the foreignness of the Israelite past and the inapplicability of patriarchal precedent, thus undermining the privileged place the Hebrew scriptures had enjoyed in the United States and leading American Protestants – orthodox and liberal, proslavery and antislavery – to train their focus on the Gospels and the Epistles.[3] The historicizing process did not end there but soon threatened to unveil the dissonance between the New Testament and the new republic to a degree that antebellum biblical criticism alone had not. Shifting the grounds of debate to the Greek scriptures carried frightening and heavily freighted implications.[4] Where would Americans look for religious guidance if even the most recent biblical past was too foreign for use?

Although most biblical scholars accepted the reasonableness of the proslavery interpretation that the Bible sanctioned slavery, a number of slavery's opponents developed alternative arguments.[5] When proslavery exegetes dictated that the issue was not whether slavery was wrong in certain circumstances (*malum prohibitum*) but whether it was wrong in itself (*malum in se*), some antislavery readers attempted to explain how slavery became a sin over time, formulating what Molly Oshatz describes as a theological innovation of moral progress. Most Americans believed in

---

[3] Shalev, *American Zion*, 151–84.
[4] See J. Albert Harrill, "The Use of the New Testament in the American Slave Controversy: A Case History in the Hermeneutical Tension between Biblical Criticism and Christian Moral Debate," *Religion and American Culture: A Journal of Interpretation* 10 (Summer 2000): 149–86. Harrill argues that radical abolitionists' appeals to moral sense undermined biblicism and encouraged biblical criticism. I contend that this was a dialectical development; experience with biblical criticism informed the development of liberal Christians' later antislavery arguments, and those arguments reinforced the acceptance and use of biblical criticism.
[5] See Mark A. Noll, "The Bible and Slavery," in *Religion and the American Civil War*, ed. Randall M. Miller, Harry S. Stout, and Charles Reagan Wilson (New York, 1988), 43–74; and Noll, *The Civil War as a Theological Crisis* (Chapel Hill, 2006), 31–74.

social progress but neither northern abolitionists nor proslavery southerners thought that moral law itself, viewed as unchanging, progressed. In juxtaposing moral law with the Bible's teachings, abolitionists either accepted the proslavery reading and then damned the Bible, as Parker was prepared to do, or posited a fundamental difference between ancient and modern slavery, as Theodore Dwight Weld did. Finding a path between these opposing approaches, moderate antislavery Protestants, including liberals like William Ellery Channing and conservatives like Moses Stuart, posited that the revelation of slavery's sin had evolved in relation to the varied conditions of human existence. This reading defined sin not as disobedience to immutable law but as disobedience to revealed immutable law. In other words, slavery became a sin over time in relation to moral progress. In a way, this was similar to Parker's belief in the progress of moral sentiment. Using a variant of the accommodation theory, which held that biblical figures had accommodated to the language and understanding of their audiences, moderates argued that the apostles did not condemn slavery openly and loudly so as to not upset the established social order of their day. Instead, the first Christian leaders opted to carefully sow the seeds of slavery's gradual destruction.

The question of slavery's morality brought together Channing and Stuart, erstwhile opponents, on this point.[6] Biblical criticism had introduced them to the idea that context shaped revelation, but it was slavery that led even conservative readers to accept that historical circumstances had constrained Christ and his apostles, at least in the sense that context demanded their expedient approach to slavery. This narrative suggested that although antislavery truths had been planted in the New Testament era, the promises they contained could only flower in a distant and different future. This kind of appeal to almost hidden universal truths buried in the New Testament soil indicated the general transience of that period and its teachings. While Stuart seemed to hold that even after nineteen centuries the time for abolition had not arrived, a number of antislavery biblical interpreters implied that they inhabited that future – and abolitionists said so outright.

These various antislavery readings indicated historical distance. When Parker allowed that slavery was prevalent in biblical times and that the Bible might, in fact, support proslavery claims, his view suggested that white southerners used an obsolete text to justify a barbaric practice. When other antislavery biblical interpreters argued that ancient servitude

[6] See Oshatz, *Slavery and Sin*, 81–109.

was profoundly different than modern slavery, they highlighted historical differences as well. In light of these differences, they argued that the Bible could not be used to justify the southern institution. When moderate antislavery proponents, such as Channing, insisted on moral progress and posited that neither the precedent of slavery in the Old Testament nor the presence of slavery in the New Testament could be used to condone the peculiar institution in the enlightened present, it signaled substantive historical change. And when abolitionists proposed that enough change had occurred to implement the antislavery principles that Christ and his apostles had taught, it pushed that New Testament period to which they appealed further into the past. In most cases, slavery did not lead its critics to abandon the Bible, but it did direct them to interpret the sacred canon in ways that exposed the foreign nature of biblical pasts.

This chapter outlines antislavery readings of the Bible during the 1830s and 1840s, highlighting their implications for historical awareness. It shows how words such as *context*, *circumstance*, and *accommodation* seeped into the readings of those who demonstrated little interest in or awareness of biblical criticism and suggests that even interpretations that did not privilege historical explication sometimes challenged the assumption of a close correspondence between biblical and modern times. As the next chapter indicates, something similar occurred in constitutional interpretation, where readers also used *context*, *circumstance*, and *accommodation* in their debates. Most biblical and constitutional interpreters did not set out to explore the historical particularities of their favored pasts nor did they consider the implications of their interpretations for realizing historical distance. Indeed, most desired to recover static original truths in hopes of using them to resolve the slavery crisis. Nevertheless, their efforts had the undeniable potential of instilling a sense of historical distance from favored pasts.

PATRIARCHS, PROPHETS, APOSTLES, AND THE SHIFTING GROUNDS OF THE BIBLICAL DEBATE

The different antislavery arguments received their clearest articulation during the 1830s, 1840s, and 1850s, though components of each appeared much earlier, including in the writings of black abolitionists such as Daniel Coker. Born enslaved in Maryland, Coker eventually escaped to New York and converted to Methodism. Francis Asbury, the indefatigable Methodist minister, ordained him a deacon. Coker was also familiar with the pioneering black clergyman Absalom Jones. Furthermore, Coker helped Richard Allen organize the African Methodist Episcopal Church. In 1820, Coker migrated to Liberia and then moved on to Sierra Leone. In the years before his move, he joined figures such as Jones and Allen in calling for the emancipation of enslaved peoples in the American South.[7] In 1810, he published a pamphlet describing a fictitious dialogue in which an African minister convinced a Virginian slaveholder of the sin of slavery and the virtue of gradual emancipation.[8]

Coker's pamphlet demonstrates the conflicted development of historical consciousness; traditional historical understandings intermingled with new historical awareness in his pamphlet. In the dialogue, Coker's imagined minister conceded that "ancient nations" practiced slavery while also contending that "it is a cruelty that the present practice of all civilized nations, bears testimony against."[9] This temporal distinction made modern slavery anachronistic. And yet, the minister believed that the Bible, an account about a favored ancient past, condemned the practice. This kind of reasoning added to the Christian tradition of excluding biblical times when dividing ancient and modern, barbaric and civilized. Coker's minister argued that Abraham's command to circumcise purchased servants gave them rights to "all the common privileges of citizens."[10] Ancient Abrahamic religion, according to the minister, offered universal freedom. Sharpening his gaze on the United States, the minister contended that the Atlantic slave trade, outlawed only two years before, lacked an Old Testament precedent.[11] If progress from ancient times had made slavery anachronistic, the abolished Atlantic slave trade and ongoing southern slavery demonstrated declension since the golden age of the Old Testament. Such narrations of progress and decline from favored pasts, which developed and expanded among antislavery thinkers in subsequent decades – especially in constitutional debates – revealed an ambivalence about historical change that further drew attention to temporal distance.

Although Coker's minister often used a proof-texting approach to both the Old and New Testaments, at times he also valued an attention to context. In dealing with Paul's teachings, in particular, he stated that "to understand rightly the matter, we should recollect the situation of the Christians at that time." Citing Roman rule, "a heathen" political system

---

[7] On black abolitionism in this period, see Sinha, *The Slave's Cause*, 130–59.
[8] Daniel Coker, *A Dialogue between a Virginian and an African Minister* (Baltimore, 1810).
[9] Ibid., 9.   [10] Ibid., 20.   [11] Ibid., 22.

that he contrasted with the new republic's "Christian government," the minister explained that "in such circumstances ... had the apostle proclaimed liberty to the slaves, it would probably have ... injured the cause he loved so well, and that without the prospect of freeing one single individual."[12] Seeming to take a cue from English theologian William Paley, the minister believed context had dictated that Paul use prudence, even though Christian teachings clearly opposed servitude. "Though the apostle acted with this prudent reserve," the minister noted, "it is very evident, that slavery is contrary to the spirit and nature of the Christian religion."[13] The golden rule stood in contrast to the South's slave codes, which would have better fit the world in which that rule originated. Although written without the scholarly insights available to later antislavery writers, Coker's pamphlet contained many of the central components of their arguments. The attention he gave to temporal distinctions and the recognition of historical differences expanded as the debate over slavery gained momentum.

Shifting the grounds of debate from the Old to the New Testament was a gradual process, one that was bound up in the emergence of antislavery immediatism. Coker's antislavery reading of the Old Testament found expression throughout the antebellum era, including in publications by white abolitionists with evangelical backgrounds, such as James G. Birney and Theodore Dwight Weld.[14] Birney, a Kentucky-born lawyer and politician, had owned slaves before adopting antislavery positions in the 1820s and early 1830s. His moves from colonization to gradual emancipation to immediatism in some ways mirrored broader antislavery developments. In 1834, the year he freed his slaves, Birney published two letters on the sin of slaveholding. Addressing biblical appeals, he argued that even if Abraham had held slaves, patriarchal precedent did not sanction southern slavery, for such reasoning would justify "concubinage" too.[15] He viewed Hebrew slavery as an exceptional allowance and asserted that Mosaic laws all but extinguished the practice. While he did not relinquish the Old Testament

---

[12] Ibid., 23. See William Paley, *The Principles of Moral and Political Philosophy*, 2 vols., 4th ed. (London, 1787), 1:238–40. First published in 1785, Paley's work had been reprinted in six American editions by 1810.

[13] Coker, *Dialogue*, 25.

[14] [Theodore Dwight Weld], *The Bible against Slavery: An Inquiry into the Patriarchal and Mosaic Systems on the Subject of Human Rights* (New York, 1837). See also the American Anti-Slavery Society's *Anti-Slavery Record*, vol. 1 (New York, 1835), in which contributors distinguished biblical slavery from American.

[15] James G. Birney, *Letter to Ministers and Elders, on the Sin of Holding Slaves, and the Duty of Immediate Emancipation* (New York, 1834), 3.

to proslavery exegetes, Birney's reading stressed the differences and progress from ancient times. His antislavery reading of the New Testament was more straightforward. He granted slavery's existence among the first Christians but rejected the idea that the apostles had countenanced it. The "enormities of Roman or Grecian slavery" made it clear to Birney that neither Peter nor Paul could possibly have sanctioned such an institution.[16] These readings rendered ancient slaveries peculiar and revealed historical differences from both Old and New Testament times.

Birney's immediatism had been cultivated in correspondence with Weld, a formidable antislavery lecturer. Weld himself received training and direction from some of the era's most prominent religious and reform personalities, including Charles Grandison Finney, Lewis and Arthur Tappan, and Sarah and Angelina Grimké. Weld and Angelina Grimké married in 1838. In 1834, while attending Lane Theological Seminary, a Presbyterian college in Cincinnati, Weld led debates on slavery, which incited opposition. While religion cultivated the seeds of abolitionism, slavery and abolitionism created deep divisions among coreligionists. In response to the school's efforts to curb further discussion, Weld left for New York, where he became an agent of the recently formed American Anti-Slavery Society (AASS). Anti-abolitionism followed Weld to New York, where mob violence brought his speaking career to an end in 1836, the same year anti-abolitionist violence also visited Birney in Cincinnati. In the face of opposition, Birney and Weld continued to use the power of the word. Weld's publications, which ranged from religious and legal attacks on slavery to exposés of the southern institution, show his interest in both biblical and constitutional interpretation.[17] In the 1840s and 1850s, as the slavery debate became a crisis, a growing number of national commentators would demonstrate this dual interest.

In an 1837 publication, Weld brought his interpretive powers to bear on the biblical debate, even as his reading anticipated national commentators' increasing focus on constitutional issues. Referencing legal differences between Abrahamic bondage and southern slavery, Weld noted that "Abraham had neither 'Constitution,' nor 'compact,' nor statutes, nor

---

[16] Ibid., 6.
[17] [Theodore Dwight Weld], *The Power of Congress over the District of Columbia* (New York, 1838); [Theodore Dwight Weld], [Angelina Grimké], and [Sarah Grimké], *American Slavery as It Is: Testimony of a Thousand Witnesses* (New York, 1839); [Theodore Dwight Weld], *Slavery and the Internal Slave Trade in the United States of North America* (London, 1841).

judicial officers to send back his fugitives."[18] Like Coker, Weld found declension when measuring American slavery against Abrahamic servitude. He highlighted differences not only between ancient past and modern present but also between distinct ancient pasts. Weld joined Birney in contrasting the Mosaic system of "Divine authority" with that of Moses's patriarchal predecessors, of whom he wrote, "God has not made them our exemplars."[19] Even as they used the Hebrew scriptures to condemn the practice of slavery, figures such as Birney and Weld suggested that the oldest portion of the Old Testament past had no claim on the present.

Slavery encouraged biblical interpreters to set aside the more distant for the more recent favored historical periods. In addressing the situation of the Israelites, Weld aimed to undermine the proslavery position by arguing that slavery did not exist among them. He made a semantic distinction between the words *servant* and *slave* to argue that the Israelites did not reduce men to "articles of property," as was the case with "American slavery."[20] Weld displayed a conventional belief in timeless appeals to a portion of the biblical past and tracked moral decline from that period, even as his reading cast aside an older dispensation as dated.

When further examination indicated that even Mosaic practices were peculiar, efforts to favorably compare the ancient past to the American present served to identify slavery as the great contradiction of modern civilization more than it did to uphold the Old Testament past as a golden age. Subsequently, antislavery writers who were more attentive to biblical scholarship and more open to its criticisms conceded that historical evidence showed that slavery had existed in Abrahamic, Mosaic, and Christian dispensations, which gave shape to their critiques of American slavery as an archaic practice. In 1844, Reverend William Wisner, a New York Congregationalist, appealed to the "facts of the case" to reject Weld's claim that slavery did not exist among the Israelites and proceeded to argue that existence did not indicate divine sanction.[21] Wisner observed that God had done what he could "in that *dark* age," for he "has always dealt with man according to his situation." This reading indicated God's accommodation to context while also stressing "a steady and continual increase" in the "light of truth" since ancient times.[22] While some would continue to argue that the southern system

---

[18] Ibid., 28.   [19] Ibid., 15.   [20] Ibid., 6, 7.
[21] William C. Wisner, "The Biblical Argument on Slavery," *The American Biblical Repository* 11 (April 1844): 302.
[22] Ibid., 336, emphasis in original.

differed in significant respects from what had existed in biblical times, others would develop the idea Coker's minister had voiced: context had constrained early Christians. In asserting that both God and humans had accommodated on this issue, these readings refocused the debate from a question of slavery's existence in favored pasts to a proposition that the progress in moral understanding since those times had revealed the sinfulness of slaveholding. In either case, such readings highlighted temporal incongruities.

"PRINCIPLES WHICH, HOWEVER SLOWLY, COULD NOT BUT WORK [SLAVERY'S] DESTRUCTION"

The spread of antislavery readings attentive to context corresponded with interpreters narrowing their focus onto the New Testament. Weld had intended to discuss "the teachings of the New Testament" in his 1837 publication but did not carry through on this plan.[23] Perhaps he felt the ground had been adequately covered by Christian liberals, who had already demonstrated their canonical partiality for the New Testament and their interpretive predilection for contextual readings. Both preferences were on display in Channing's *Slavery* (1835).

Channing advanced an antislavery reading that demanded attention to the constraints of ancient contexts. His own contexts, including an 1830 trip to the West Indies and a former student's (Samuel J. May) query about why he had not addressed slavery, inspired him to write on the issue. Channing trained his attention on the New Testament. A believer in God's accommodation, he granted that polygamy, like slavery, "was allowed to the Israelites ... and was common and licensed in the age of the Apostles."[24] Channing assumed that proslavery southerners agreed with his position that polygamy was an outdated practice, and thus, he emphasized its biblical sanction to call into question their reasoning, quipping, "Why may not Scripture be used to stock our houses with wives as well as with slaves?"[25] This reading, which echoed that of Birney and others, assumed the progress of moral understanding and highlighted historical differences.

Channing proceeded to make a historical comparison to further emphasize progress. He asserted that "slavery in the age of Paul," in contrast to modern slavery, included the enslavement of white men, of

---

[23] Weld, *Bible against Slavery*, 81.   [24] William E. Channing, *Slavery* (Boston, 1835), 108.
[25] Ibid., 109.

Greeks, of "the virtuous, educated, and refined."[26] More than Coker or Weld, Channing highlighted ancient slavery's unique peculiarities to argue that "such slavery" could not have been "sanctioned by the Apostles!"[27] This temporal comparison indicated moral progress, which he later used to draw attention to the irony of American slavery. At this point, though, Channing focused on slavery's relationship to primitive Christianity. Echoing Coker's contextual argument, he wrote that "slavery ... had so penetrated society ... that a religion, preaching freedom to its victims, would have shaken the social fabric to its foundations, and would have armed against itself the whole power of the State. Of consequence," he explained, "Paul did not assail it. He satisfied himself with spreading principles which, however slowly, could not but work its destruction."[28] This contextual reading drew readers' attention to the distinct historical situation of the first Christians.

The thrust of Channing's argument centered on the idea that Christ and his apostles had planted seeds of emancipation because their environment did not allow them to abolish the system outright. He also offered a different reading of Paul's letter to Philemon than the one Buckminster had provided, proposing that the apostle had instructed Philemon to receive Onesimus as a brother, "thus asserting for the slave the rights of a Christian and a Man." Channing was unwilling to concede historical grounds to proslavery interpreters of the Bible. And yet, while he interpreted the New Testament according to "the general tenor and spirit of Christianity," he focused on the ways in which Christ and his apostles expected that tenor and spirit to develop and grow over time.[29]

Channing's emphasis on the general over the specific led to an incendiary question with unsettling implications: "Of what avail are a few texts, which were designed for local and temporary use, when urged against the vital essential spirit, and the plainest precepts of our religion?"[30] Channing was still invested in a historical Jesus and the historicity of his Gospel miracles, but he concluded that certain New Testament books had short shelf lives.[31] This approach aligned with Parker's distinction between the transient and the permanent. Channing believed that historical constraints did not allow Christianity's founders to root out slavery, forcing them instead to plant the universal seeds of abolition.[32] In

---

[26] Ibid. [27] Ibid., 110. [28] Ibid., 111. [29] Ibid. [30] Ibid., 113.
[31] See Grodzins, *American Heretic*, 123–27.
[32] On these and similar antislavery arguments, see Harrill, "Use of the New Testament," 150–60.

outlining distinctions between ancient and modern slavery and in positing the apostolic expectation of slavery's demise, Channing's arguments drew attention to the temporal chasm separating the nineteenth century from the first century.

Channing's publication drew criticism from all corners. His description of prudent apostles could be read as a critique of his contemporaries who called for immediate abolition. In fact, here and elsewhere, Channing encouraged what he viewed as a more prudent approach and criticized abolitionists' grating language.[33] While William Lloyd Garrison and others dismissed Channing's publication as impotent, Massachusetts Attorney General James T. Austin damned it as insurrectionary. Channing had blamed abolitionists for making matters worse; now Austin laid the same charge at his feet.

Austin contrasted Channing's approach with that of both Christian and American founders. Rather than pursuing the prudent apostolic approach he himself had outlined, Channing had, in Austin's opinion, forbidden the practice, which threatened to produce "that deadly hostility which the wiser teachings of the gospel were intended to prevent."[34] In his hurry to chastise and correct, Austin ignored Channing's temporal distinctions and conflated past and present. Combining religious with legal censure, he wrote that interference with southern "domestic arrangements" constituted a "breach of our highest political contract," the Constitution.[35] Not only had Channing set aside the prudent approach of the apostles but, in Austin's mind, he had also ignored the practical example of "the first statesmen and jurists of the country." Mocking this "new light," Austin scorned Channing as an "inventor who assumed to be wiser than past ages."[36] This derision of innovation echoed far and wide among critics of abolitionism. In return, antislavery forces began to designate the Slave Power as an unforeseen anomaly. Charges of novelty were useful in a society that reverenced sacred texts from favored pasts.

Austin prescribed a course of action that ignored historical distance and prioritized political expediency. He described the relationship between slavery and the American republic in the same way Channing and others had explained the relationship between slavery and primitive

---

[33] See, for example, William E. Channing, *A Letter to the Abolitionists, with Comments* (Boston, 1837).
[34] [James T. Austin], *Remarks on Dr. Channing's Slavery. By a Citizen of Massachusetts* (Boston, 1835), 17.
[35] Ibid., 5.   [36] Ibid., 19.

Christianity. He wrote that the institution was "so intimately connected with civil society" that its removal would result in the nation's demise.[37] Seeming to hold that little had changed since the founding of the Christian religion or the American nation, Austin instructed his contemporaries to follow the cautious examples of the founding religious and political fathers. Austin's response demonstrates the persistence of traditional appeals to timeless religious and legal principles and indicates the uneven development of historical awareness. Even as the interpretive debates over slavery spread a sense of distance from favored pasts and led figures such as Channing to formulate interpretations in light of that distance, those on various sides of the argument continued to ignore distance in the application of sacred texts.[38]

Both Austin and Channing believed morality depended on present circumstances, but they disagreed about the nature of those circumstances. Austin held that when the public deemed slavery wrong, the law "will be changed," but he argued that until then calls for change could not "be tolerated."[39] He was willing to grant the legal right to condemn slavery but insisted that present conditions made it immoral to do so. "All that is legally right is not expedient," he wrote, "and whatever is clearly and palpably inexpedient, ceases for the time to be morally right."[40] In contrast, antislavery writers increasingly argued that moral progress in the form of rising antislavery sentiment made it a moral imperative to condemn slavery. Channing himself would later insist that the antislavery spirit of the times demanded a constitutional amendment. Participants on all sides of the debate cited present circumstances to support their positions. Some, like Austin, focused on the parallels between present and past circumstances, while others, like Channing, emphasized their differences.

Austin hoped his efforts would help curtail abolitionism, but his actions actually proved instrumental in its spread. When Austin and others tried to quiet abolitionists, antislavery advocates tied their cause to freedom of speech and freedom of the press. This tie became tighter in late 1837, when, after the repeated destruction of abolitionist Elijah Lovejoy's press, an Illinois mob killed him. In response to Lovejoy's

---

[37] Ibid., 24.

[38] For an example of an antislavery reading that made an easy conflation between favored pasts and the present, see La Roy Sunderland, *The Testimony of God against Slavery* (Boston, 1836).

[39] Austin, *Remarks*, 20.   [40] Ibid., 21.

murder, Channing called for a meeting in Boston to condemn the mob actions. Austin was at that meeting, which was held in Faneuil Hall, and there he offered an uninvited defense of the mob, whom he compared to the American Revolutionaries – Austin's proclivity to conflate past with present knew no bounds. Austin's statements spurred Wendell Phillips to arise and deliver an impromptu rejoinder that placed Lovejoy in the Revolutionaries' ranks and encouraged their descendants to complete the cause of freedom they had initiated. Phillips's unrehearsed account of the Revolution ignited his influential career of abolitionist activism.[41] Austin seemed to have misread his own context.

In another 1835 publication, Baptist pastor Francis Wayland, a New York City native who had become the president of Brown University, provided a contextual reading of the Bible similar to the one Channing presented. As a student of Stuart's at Andover, Wayland had been trained in new methods of biblical exegesis and no doubt knew that historical evidence attested to slavery's existence in biblical times. Wayland opposed slavery – his views on the subject influenced Channing's – but he disapproved of the abolitionists' approach even more than the Unitarian did and, like Austin, believed that immediate emancipation would bring about greater ill than good. In maintaining a moderate position, Wayland was somewhat representative of most Protestant northerners. As much as any of his northern contemporaries, he worked to retain fellowship with southerners even as he spoke and wrote of slavery as a moral evil.[42]

In *Elements of Moral Science*, Wayland's approach to slavery mirrored that of Channing and Coker, and of Paley before them. Wayland's book, which replaced Paley's *The Principles of Moral and Political Philosophy* as the most important textbook on moral science in antebellum America, built on the Englishman's reading of the New Testament on slavery.[43] Like Paley and Channing, Wayland addressed both slavery and polygamy. The tie between these practices grew stronger in succeeding years, placing southerners on the defensive.[44] Wayland

---

[41] See James Brewer Stewart, "Wendell Phillips Is the Subtlest, Stubbornest Fact of the Times: Abolition's Golden Trumpet and the Fall of the Slaveholders' Republic," in *Wendell Phillips, Social Justice, and the Power of the Past*, ed. A. J. Aiséirithe and Donald Yacovone (Baton Rouge, 2016), 36–39.

[42] On Wayland and his approach to slavery, see Matthew Hill, *Law, Morality, and Abolitionism: Francis Wayland and Antislavery in America* (Newcastle, UK, 2011).

[43] See Hill, *Law, Morality, and Abolitionism*, 53–60.

[44] See Elizabeth Fox-Genovese and Eugene D. Genovese, *The Mind of the Master Class: History and Faith in the Southern Slaveholders' Worldview* (New York, 2005), 513–15.

granted that slavery, like polygamy, was permitted anciently, but asserted that the gospel, a system "designed ... for all races, and for all times," was meant to bring about slavery's "universal abolition." While calling attention to historical "circumstances," he suggested the gospel acted to "quietly and peacefully ... work a revolution in the whole mass of mankind." If the gospel "had forbidden the *evil*, instead of subverting the *principle*," Wayland posited, "it would have arrayed the two parties in deadly hostility," resulting in Christianity's quick demise.[45] Like Channing, he believed Christ intended to rid the world of the sin of slavery by teaching universal principles that would flower in a future context.

At this point, Wayland did not believe that this future context had come. His reading drew the scorn of southerners, but also heavy criticism from abolitionists. Like Austin, Wayland maintained that the Constitution demanded that northerners respect the laws of southern states until the moral climate led to changes in those laws. His timidity bred abolitionist contempt.[46] Even still, Wayland's proposal that Christianity's founders had planted seeds of slavery's destruction, which time would nourish, foreshadowed influential antislavery legal and political arguments about the framers' expectations of abolition.[47]

Appeals to both Christian and American founders began to appear even in obscure places, as in a sermon Arthur Granger gave in Meriden, Connecticut, in 1837. In March 1836, after graduating from Princeton Theological Seminary and working as a Presbyterian pastor in Massachusetts and Delaware, Granger was installed as the reverend of the First Congregationalist Church in Meriden. (The Plan of Union of 1801 allowed Presbyterian and Congregationalist churches to hire ministers from either denomination.) The following year, the same year in which the Presbyterian Church divided between Old and New Schools over theology and other issues, including slavery, Granger, who aligned with the New School, accepted some of his congregants' request to invite Henry Ludlow to lecture on abolitionism. Ludlow's presence caused a stir; a mob, which included members of Granger's flock, interrupted Ludlow's lecture by throwing rocks and rotten eggs.[48] Angered at the "humiliating scene," which came in the same year as Lovejoy's murder,

---

[45] Francis Wayland, *The Elements of Moral Science* (London, 1835), 204, emphasis in original.
[46] Hill, *Law, Morality, and Abolitionism*, 60–68.
[47] On this and other antislavery arguments from the New Testament, see Harrill, "Use of the New Testament," 150–58.
[48] David Grimsted, *American Mobbing, 1828–1861: Toward Civil War* (New York, 1998), 47.

Granger preached a sermon to make his views clear.[49] Once again, another occasion of anti-abolitionist violence broadened the antislavery cause, fueled abolitionism, and inspired antislavery readings of sacred texts.

In his sermon, Granger addressed both historical context and historical differences, and joined other antislavery writers in positing historical progress. He granted slavery's presence in the apostles' time and noted that if the New Testament "did not admit the existence of slavery ... it would not be a faithful record of facts."[50] Like Wayland, Granger proceeded to argue that context constrained the apostles, who could not interfere in civil society without drastic results. He even cited Paley on this point.[51] But these facts are "matters of history," Granger noted, not "moral principles for the guidance of our conduct."[52] While observing a "striking resemblance" between Roman and American slavery, Granger insisted that "our circumstances are totally different.... We profess to be a Christian nation."[53] The apostles, he wrote, "had no hand in the formation of their laws," but in the United States, "the people are the sovereign rulers ... and if Christians find that they or their fathers have lent their influence to justify offensive law, it is not only their right, but their solemn duty, to use all lawful means ... to correct the bad influence."[54] While figures such as Austin and even Wayland urged northerners to await a change in climate and a change in laws, Granger called on them to work to make the change themselves. This emphasis on the right of the people to change law, along with the right of the people to interpret law, increased in subsequent decades.

In addressing the intentions of the nation's founders, Granger advanced a similar reading: context had limited them, but they had laid down principles to bring about slavery's eventual abolition. Granger taught that the founders had "permitted an incidental evil which they could not well avoid under the peculiar circumstances," and then he asked, "did they intend to bind their children to all generations to tolerate the evil"?[55] Granger stressed human progress, arguing that the "general influence of the age" and advances in "Science, Literature, Morals, Philosophy, Common Sense, and Poetry" allowed the Bible to pour

---

[49] Arthur Granger, *The Apostle Paul's Opinion of Slavery and Emancipation, A Sermon, Preached to the Congregational Church and Society in Meriden, at the Request of Several Respectable Anti-Abolitionists* (Middletown, CT, 1837), 3.
[50] Ibid., 13.   [51] Ibid., 9.   [52] Ibid., 13.   [53] Ibid., 7, 15.   [54] Ibid., 16–17.
[55] Ibid., 18.

"light on the dark system."[56] While positing progress, Granger echoed Coker and Weld in contrasting Mosaic servitude with American slavery to highlight the institution's paradoxical American existence. Antebellum thinkers' emphasis on progress from biblical times coexisted with the continued use of portions of that past. Granger's parallel contextual readings of the New Testament and the Constitution, both of which carried appeals to what I have termed an *original expectation* of abolition, grew in importance in the 1840s and 1850s.

"THE GRADUAL DEVELOPMENT OF THE TRUTHS OF REVELATION"

Granger's antislavery preaching led to his removal as pastor in Meriden, which signaled the denominational discord over slavery that increased in subsequent years. The discord that surfaced among northerner congregations soon broadened to become a sectional issue. In 1844, disagreement over whether or not bishops could hold slaves led to a division between northern and southern Methodists. Baptists split along sectional lines the following year when northern Baptists disapproved of slaveholding missionaries. The split came despite ongoing efforts by individuals such as Wayland, who worked to maintain ties with his southern colleagues.[57]

In the midst of this denominational strife, Wayland tried to model cordial dialogue with southerners, as evidenced in his exchange with Richard Fuller. In 1844, the *Christian Reflector*, a Baptist periodical published in Worcester, Massachusetts, invited Fuller, a slaveholder and Baptist minister from South Carolina, to outline the proslavery position. Fuller had graduated from Harvard and then studied and practiced law in South Carolina until a conversion experience led him to leave the bar for a career in the ministry. Beginning with its founding in 1844, Fuller became a prominent figure in the Southern Baptist movement. In the same year, he debated Wayland on slavery and the Bible.

Fuller's letter to the *Christian Reflector* displayed the tenor of the southern position by working to establish slavery's Old Testament presence and emphasizing New Testament continuity. He argued that "the Old Testament did sanction slavery" and cited a favorite proslavery passage from Leviticus, which refers to "bondmen" as "an inheritance...

---

[56] Ibid., 17.   [57] Hill, *Law, Morality, and Abolitionism*, 117–18.

"Texts ... Designed for Local and Temporary Use"

for ever."[58] Fuller proceeded to contend that "the institution is, to say the least, tolerated" in the New Testament.[59] Linking the Testaments supported the contention that, as another proslavery writer put it, slavery "was an early arrangement of the Almighty, to be perpetuated through all time."[60] Fuller responded with contempt to the idea that Christ and his apostles had refrained from a straightforward denunciation of slavery. Answering both Wayland and Channing, he wondered why Paul had "declined uttering a word" about slavery and allowed "millions on all sides" to sink "into hell through this crime," and instead settled with "spreading principles which would slowly work a cure," if "nothing but this unyielding, uncompromising, condemnation of every sin could content" Paul.[61] Context could not and did not constrain Fuller's fearless Paul.

Having established continuity between the Testaments on this issue, Fuller strove to untie the noxious knot between slavery – a divinely established institution – and polygamy – a human corruption of monogamy. To do so, he applied to polygamy the argument that many antislavery readers applied to slavery, arguing that "the gospel does forbid, and did at once abolish polygamy."[62] To the extent that proslavery writers proved this point, it undercut the authority of the Old Testament, which, in turn, troubled their appeal to continuity. And to the extent the argument from continuity retained force, the New Testament suffered from its association with the Old.

In his response to Fuller, Wayland broadened his argument from expediency to a claim about the progressive nature of revelation. His reading indicated that the sin of slavery had been revealed over time and in relationship to distinct contexts. Maintaining that slavery "is always and everywhere ... a moral wrong," he conceded its existence in the

---

[58] Richard Fuller and Francis Wayland, *Domestic Slavery Considered as a Scriptural Institution* (New York, 1845), 3. See Lev. 25:44–46.

[59] Fuller and Wayland, *Domestic Slavery*, 3–4.

[60] Alexander McCaine, *Slavery Defended from Scripture, against the Attacks of the Abolitionists* (Baltimore, 1842), 5. For earlier examples of similar readings, see Seth Lewis, *A Review of Abolitionism, Or the Question of Slavery, As It Exists in the United States, Considered* (New Orleans, 1830); Seth Lewis, *Abolitionism Reviewed, Being a Further Exposure of the False and Most Dangerous and Mischievous Doctrines and Proceedings of the Abolitionists* (New Orleans, 1837); and S. Taylor, *Relation of Master and Servant, as Exhibited in the New Testament* (Richmond, VA, 1836).

[61] Fuller and Wayland, *Domestic Slavery*, 6. On this and similar proslavery responses, see Harrill, "Use of the New Testament," 163–73.

[62] Fuller and Wayland, *Domestic Slavery*, 11.

patriarchal and Mosaic eras.[63] To explain this apparent inconsistency, he proposed that "God did not see fit to reveal his will on this subject ... to the ancient Hebrews."[64] Thus, Old Testament permissions were "peculiar," "anomalous," and "exclusive" allowances – the command to destroy the Canaanites, for example, did not "authorize American citizens ... to destroy, or to enslave, or to hold in slavery, the people of another continent."[65] God enlightens "our race progressively," Wayland explained, and thus "we cannot plead ... that what was permitted without rebuke in a darker age is permitted to us to whom greater light has been given."[66] In this passage, Wayland used dispensationalism, the idea that biblical peoples inhabited different eras, to advance a belief that moral understanding developed in relation to different contexts. This view, which Channing and Stuart adopted too, was not unlike Parker's idea of the progress of religion. While these figures pursued distinct antislavery positions, each of them held a belief in progress that rendered slavery archaic and emancipation modern.

This kind of reasoning encouraged attention to historical differences, which undermined easy conflation between ancient precepts and modern principles. Given the distinctions between past and present slaveries, Wayland did not see how the practice's sanction among the Hebrews "could justify slavery in the United States."[67] Emphasizing the progress of God's revelation and spotlighting differences between ancient servitude and modern slavery allowed Wayland to uphold Christianity's principles of freedom while also dismissing Old Testament precepts as particularities of a bygone past.

Wayland presumed that "the Scriptural argument in defence of slavery is narrowed down to the limits of the New Testament," a text given not "for one period, but for all time."[68] As in 1835, he again stressed "*a consideration of the circumstances*," arguing that "at the time of our Saviour and his apostles, slavery was universal."[69] Thus, Christ and his followers inculcated timeless principles such as the brotherhood of man, which, once "instilled into the public mind, must of necessity abolish slavery."[70] Wayland's stress on the "gradual development of the truths of revelation" took historical limitations into account.[71] He argued that God "promulgates truth of universal efficacy, but frequently allows long time [sic] to elapse before the effect of it appears."[72] While the gospel era

---

[63] Ibid., 48. [64] Ibid., 49–50. [65] Ibid., 50, 51, 59. [66] Ibid., 52, 53. [67] Ibid., 58.
[68] Ibid., 77, 78. [69] Ibid., 85, emphasis in original. [70] Ibid., 93. [71] Ibid., 70.
[72] Ibid., 103.

was a moral advancement over patriarchal and Mosaic dispensations, it emerged in a dark time, and "it was necessary that this darkness should be dispelled, before the moral light could shine upon slavery."[73] The gospel principles were timeless, Wayland believed, but the New Testament past obscured them. A new context would remove the darkness. Wayland found that context in a more recent favored past.

In a clear instance of biblical and legal interpretive overlap, which also signaled a gradual turn to the founding era as the most useful favored past, Wayland argued that gospel truths received "their fullest development in the principles of the Declaration."[74] He went so far as to posit that "the gospel of Christ, on the subject of human rights, falls infinitely below the Declaration," though he believed the flowering of the principles in that document relied on the cultivation of original gospel truths.[75] This view brought together biblical and Revolutionary pasts and marked a growing emphasis that founding-era texts were authoritative in the slavery debate. In comparing Roman past and American present, Wayland now sounded like Granger, arguing that "the case with us is different.... We, in our Declaration ... have already acknowledged the very principles now in question." To primitive Christians, he stated, "laws were nothing but the published will of a despot.... It is by no means the same with us. *We make our own laws.*"[76] Wayland emphasized the democratic nature of the American republic and the amendatory potential of its laws. This was a statement of historical fact as well as an indictment of Americans who lived in an age wherein the sin of slavery had become clear but who had not made the legal move to abolition. With change in the hands of the people, he implied, the time was ripe to pick the fruit born of gospel seeds.

This narrative and others like it contributed to a large chorus of American commentators heralding human progress. More often than not, their present and future focus had little chance of spreading more than a surface-level awareness of historical distance. The interpretive battles over slavery had far greater potential in this regard. Describing the contexts of favored eras and tracing progress since then drew attention to the relationship between past and present in ways that indicated temporal dislocation. And figures such as Wayland used that sense of dislocation to encourage legal change.

In his final responses, Fuller again made the argument for biblical continuity – "both Testaments constitute one entire canon" and "furnish a complete rule of faith and practice" – but also from biblical

---

[73] Ibid., 105. [74] Ibid., 74. [75] Ibid., 88. [76] Ibid., 105, emphasis in original.

circumstances. He did not conflate Abrahamic servitude with American slavery or Mosaic laws with southern slave codes. Like his opponents, he recognized historical differences, but used them to argue that slavery was similar to a "large number of actions whose moral character depends on the peculiar circumstances of each case."[77] And the biblical case, Fuller believed, demonstrated that "slavery is not necessarily, and always, and amidst all circumstances, a sin."[78] While individuals such as Wayland believed that certain acts might be morally wrong but not divinely prohibited "at a particular time," Fuller held that if a practice was divinely sanctioned at a particular time, it was not morally wrong in and of itself.[79] Its morality depended on the particulars of the case; he granted that some slave codes were immoral, but that did not mean that slaveholding itself was immoral. When antislavery writers pointed out differences between ancient and American slaveries to nullify biblical justification for the latter, proslavery writers cited biblical precedent to show that slavery's sin was circumstantial and then concluded that southern slavery was often, if not always, moral. Attention to context and circumstance could be used both to deny and to affirm slavery's biblical sanction.

While positing slavery's circumstantial morality, Fuller scoffed at the notion of progress in moral understanding. "The Bible operates *too slowly* for our reformers," he taunted, before insisting that "the moral character of [ancient] actions is immutable."[80] Fuller derided the idea that moral insight changed in relationship to human progress. "Nothing can be more utterly sophistical," he wrote, "than the idea that we have any light, as to matters of pure revelation, which the first Christians had not." While Fuller acknowledged "prodigious progress in all the arts and sciences," he did not agree with Wayland, Channing, and Stuart, much less Transcendentalists like Parker, that progress shed new light on original scriptural truths.[81] Southern writers would continue to mock the idea that "what was no sin at all with Abraham and Moses – with Paul and the Christian fathers ... has suddenly 'developed' itself into the most atrocious of human crimes" and to observe progress in "physical science" while doubting all improvements "in religion and morals ... not known to certain fishermen who lived some eighteen hundred years ago."[82] In

---

[77] Ibid., 166. [78] Ibid., 170. [79] Ibid., 246. [80] Ibid., 169, 180, emphasis in original.
[81] Ibid., 185.
[82] Ebenezer Boyden, *The Epidemic of the Nineteenth Century* (Richmond, VA, 1860), 18; and William F. Hutson, "Fictitious Literature," *Southern Presbyterian Review* 1 (September 1847): 78.

stark contrast to a figure such as Parker, these writers held that primitive Christians had access to the same gospel light as nineteenth-century Americans.

Unlike Parker, Fuller believed biblical scholarship had obscured rather than illuminated static gospel truths, blinding Americans to the fact that slavery was moral in the present just as it was in the past. Aiming to remove the occlusion, he cited scriptural passages, including Paul's instruction that Onesimus return to Philemon, to demonstrate that "in the days of the Saviour and the apostles, this institution existed everywhere," and to show that they "permitted it to continue."[83] Fuller had noted historical differences between Old Testament past and American present, but here he collapsed the distance from the more determinative New Testament era, positing that "should [the apostles] appear now, they would find the same institution.... And they would act just as they acted then; or rather, they are here in the gospel, and are now doing what they then did."[84] Fuller articulated a traditional sense of contemporaneity with the New Testament past, its peoples, institutions, and sentiments. Many readers continued to claim a clear connection to at least portions of the biblical past. And in the readings of figures such as Fuller, that connection sanctioned American slavery and condemned abolitionists.

This debate among leading Baptists inspired similar debates among figures in other denominations and drew southern and northern responses over the next decade, all of which promised to encourage attention to historical questions about the biblical past and its relationship to the American present.[85] While readings such as Fuller's insisted on a kind of fluid relationship with a favored ancient past, the growing focus on historical circumstances made it impossible to ignore historical differences from that era. In the face of the sense of distance that began to emerge, such clear correspondence with the biblical past became more of an assertion than an assumption. This opened up space for more biblical interpretations like Wayland's, which acknowledged this distance and suggested that new circumstances called for the realization of Christianity's highest aims.

One of those readings came from Albert Barnes, who made significant use of the published Wayland and Fuller debate. Another graduate of Princeton Theological Seminary, Barnes gained notoriety as a champion of New School Presbyterianism at Philadelphia's First Presbyterian

---

[83] Fuller and Wayland, *Domestic Slavery*, 187, 200.   [84] Ibid., 200–201.
[85] For more on this debate, see Hill, *Law, Morality, and Abolitionism*, 73–104.

Church. His writings on the New Testament, which drew the ire of Old School Presbyterian Charles Hodge, demonstrated his training in biblical criticism.

In an 1846 publication, Barnes offered a historical interpretation to determine southern slavery's morality. He first established that "all have a right to discuss" slavery.[86] This emphasis on popular participation in the slavery debate corresponded with the prevailing opinion that all could read and understand the Bible.[87] And the growing focus on historical reasoning in biblical and constitutional interpretation only bolstered the appeal to the people. Historical reasoning, many believed, was the province of all, and thus, all could interpret the nation's sacred texts. Using such historical reasoning, Barnes addressed Fuller's careful distinction between slaveholding and slave laws, a distinction that Barnes also found in a review of Channing's book that had appeared in Hodge's *Biblical Repertory*. This distinction aimed to show that slavery was not wrong in and of itself. In response, Barnes insisted that the determinative question was "whether slavery as it exists in the United States is ... in accordance with the principles and the spirit of Christianity."[88]

Barnes first addressed patriarchal and Mosaic servitude. His reading underscored the growing canonical distinction between the Testaments. To undermine appeals to the patriarchal past, he examined terms denoting servitude and concluded that "the mere use of the *word* in the time of the patriarchs, determines nothing in the issue before us."[89] In concurrent constitutional debates, some antislavery writers stressed a word's *absence*, but historical research highlighted the elision. In the case of the Old Testament, Barnes argued that even if slavery had existed among the patriarchs, that was no sign of divine approval. "It is perfectly clear," he wrote, presenting a familiar equation, "that, so far as the conduct of the patriarchs goes, it would be just as easy to construct an argument in favour of polygamy as in favour of slavery.... Considering their circumstances," he continued, they "were men eminent for piety. But they were imperfect ... they lived in the infancy of the world; they had comparatively little light on the subjects of morals and religion."[90] In other words, the patriarchs were relatively exceptional – they were luminaries in their own time who nevertheless did not transcend that time. Aware of the more

---

[86] Albert Barnes, *An Inquiry into the Scriptural Views of Slavery* (Philadelphia, 1846), 5.
[87] See Mark A. Noll, *America's God: From Jonathan Edwards to Abraham Lincoln* (New York: Oxford University Press, 2002), 367–85.
[88] Barnes, *Inquiry*, 12.   [89] Ibid., 70, emphasis in original.   [90] Ibid., 79.

frequent appeal to the Mosaic period, Barnes contrasted southern slave codes, which were "designed to perpetuate slavery," and "Mosaic statutes [that] were intended to modify the system, and ultimately abolish it."[91] On the one hand, Barnes asserted that historical differences resulting from moral progress undermined the relevance of outdated patriarchal precedents. On the other hand, like Weld, he suggested that present southern laws fell short in relation to enlightened Mosaic laws. Similar to the developing antislavery appeal to apostolic intentions, this reading imagined a biblical past in which slavery's abolition was expected.

In turning to the New Testament, Barnes followed Channing and Wayland in arguing that the principles of abolition had been planted in a constraining context and could now flourish in nineteenth-century America. He argued that "God has ... removed most of the evils of the world by a *gradual* development of principles."[92] Emphasizing historical "circumstances," he explained that "the apostles ... had no agency in making the laws; they had no power to change them. Slavery ... was interwoven with every custom and habit of social life.... What *would* have been the effect of denouncing it.... [The apostles] would have been banished at once from every slaveholding community – just as abolition agents are now at the South."[93] Unable to resist historical comparison, Barnes underscored the apostles' limiting context. Turning to the case of Onesimus, he again complicated the conflation of servant and slave and, like Channing, proposed that Paul had sent him back as a fellow Christian. Stretching the argument to the brink, Barnes posited that "the principles laid down in ... Philemon ... would lead to the universal abolition of slavery."[94] He concluded that the "fair application of the Christian religion would remove it from the world."[95] Such an application, though, depended on a new context, which he foresaw in light of "the progress towards universal freedom.... The spirit of the age," he insisted, would bring the institution to its knees.[96] Barnes joined other writers in positing moral progress, which again highlighted distance from the pasts to which he appealed. In his account, the antislavery seeds that had been sowed centuries ago soon would flower in the fertile grounds of a new age in which Americans, unlike the apostles, had the power to change their laws.

The issue of slavery deepened the growing commitment to historical readings of the Bible. And the back and forth about what kinds of slavery

---

[91] Ibid., 196.   [92] Ibid., 288, emphasis in original.   [93] Ibid., 291, emphasis in original.
[94] Ibid., 330.   [95] Ibid., 375.   [96] Ibid., 380.

prevailed in biblical times and what portions of the Christian canon justified or condemned the institution carried important implications for how Americans thought about their favored ancient pasts. Historical arguments about whether slavery existed in Old Testament times gave way to debates about whether or not patriarchal or Mosaic slavery had any relevance to the peculiar institution. The readings indicated historical differences and distance, which historicized the Old Testament past. Many writers persisted in appealing to Hebrew scripture, but even their readings demonstrated that the words and actions of past patriarchs and prophets had lost some relevance. Proslavery and antislavery polemicists agreed that the teachings and examples of less distant figures such as Jesus and Paul mattered more. The new Gospel trumped the old Law. This made the proslavery effort to fuse the Testaments counterproductive. Some antislavery readers conceded slavery's presence in both the Old and New Testaments but then cited the Gospels' universal teachings to condemn the practice. They also used historical arguments to separate ancient from southern slavery. In turn, this began the process of historicizing the New Testament.

In different ways, both proslavery and antislavery biblical appeals had the potential to highlight historical distance. Although proslavery appeals often collapsed time, their readings nonetheless attended to temporal difference. Despite Barnes's best efforts to refocus the discussion on whether or not the Bible sanctioned *southern* slavery, proslavery interpreters continued to insist that the question of consequence was whether or not slavery was always wrong, regardless of era and location.[97] Fuller's contextual readings indicated that God had sanctioned different forms of slavery at different times, which allowed him to argue that God could and did sanction it now. While white southerners used such readings to support a circumstantial defense of slavery, antislavery readers used contextual readings to attack the institution as archaic. Wayland, Channing, Granger, and Barnes accepted slavery's existence in New Testament times, but rather than join Parker in dismissing the Bible as outdated, they countered with interpretations focused on the *intentions* of Christianity's founders. Their readings, which assumed and advanced a progressive historical view, held that the seeds of universal antislavery principles would outlast and overcome particular sentiments and peculiar institutions, reaching full fruition in the more democratic and progressive American present.

[97] See Oshatz, *Slavery and Sin*, 61–69.

While also an appeal to a favored past, this was not an argument to return to or reclaim that past. The antislavery emphasis on submerged universal principles under a surface of outdated precepts highlighted the foreign nature of biblical times. As the number of the Bible's useful and permanent teachings shrunk to a few universal principles from a handful of texts, the remaining instructions and passages were relegated to the status of passing peculiarities from a distant past. The argument that the universal principles would find fulfillment in the future drew attention to the distance between the biblical past and the American present. This contention, which retained faith in sacred texts, held great potential to spread awareness of that distance.

As demonstrated in Wayland's and Granger's arguments, appeals to biblical pasts could overlap with appeals to the Revolutionary past and, as Wayland's discussion in particular showed, the recent American past could be valued as more enlightened than even the sacred Jewish and Christian pasts. The emphasis on using certain portions of a favored past and on uncovering universal principles that were expected to flower in time found a clear parallel in constitutional debates. This began the process of historicizing the favored founding era and raised questions about the relevance of another erstwhile timeless text.

4

"The Further We Recede from the Birth of the Constitution"

During the 1840s, participants in the slavery debates continued to discuss slavery's relation to the biblical and American pasts in tandem. Jonathan Blanchard was among those participants. A former student of Moses Stuart, Blanchard had left Andover soon after Andover's faculty denounced immediatism and, in response, most of the students agreed to focus on their studies rather than pursue antislavery reform. In 1836, Theodore Weld journeyed to Andover and recruited Blanchard to become a lecturer for the American Anti-Slavery Society (AASS).[1] The next year, Blanchard enrolled at Lane Seminary to finish his education, and soon after graduation in 1838, he was ordained as minister of Cincinnati's Sixth Presbyterian Church, a congregation associated with the New School and with abolitionism.[2]

Blanchard provided arguments familiar among biblical scholars during another mid-1840s intradenominational debate, this time between Presbyterians. In the debate, held in October 1845, Blanchard pitted the Bible against slavery and tied together biblical and American pasts while also arguing that morals had progressed since biblical times. In doing so, he criticized the learned readings of Stuart and others. Perhaps Blanchard shared the sentiment expressed by Albert Barnes that all had a right to discuss the issue. Blanchard asserted that slavery is always and

---

[1] On these and related developments at Andover, see J. Earl Thompson Jr., "Abolitionism and Theological Education at Andover," *The New England Quarterly* 47 (June 1974): 238–261.

[2] On Blanchard's abolitionism, see Richard S. Taylor, "Beyond Immediate Emancipation: Jonathan Blanchard, Abolitionism, and the Emergence of American Fundamentalism," *Civil War History* 27, no. 3 (1981): 260–74.

everywhere wrong and that it alone "has remained the same" while "every relation and department of civil society has been revolutionized and regenerated."³ He appealed to "the history of the times" to contrast Mosaic "bond service" and American slavery and dismissed what he described as "illogical inferences from just and necessary institutions of past ages."⁴ Blanchard highlighted distinctions between Old Testament servitude and southern slavery to condemn proslavery uses of the Hebrew scriptures. At the same time, he tied together New Testament and American pasts, suggesting that the "great principles of human rights, drawn from the New Testament," had been set forth in the Declaration of Independence.⁵ In making this claim, Blanchard voiced a belief in moral progress, observing that as "the light of liberty increases, the darkness of adjacent slavery grows more dense."⁶ Like other antislavery writers, he located an initial idea of slavery's sin in the New Testament past and observed that progress since then had made the enormity of southern slavery much clearer.

Blanchard also narrated moral change since the founding era, but rather than focusing on progress, he tracked decline. In his opening speech of the debate, Blanchard asserted that "in 1776, there was no sentiment so popular ... as that '*God hath created all men free and equal.*'" Blanchard suggested that the Declaration had borne the fruits of New Testament seeds. But "this fundamental idea," he observed, "has been running down for the last fifty years."⁷ While some commentators had narrated decline from biblical times, many more antislavery writers began to signal negative change following the founding era, particularly in the form of proslavery advances. These narratives sounded discordant against the chorus of commentators who tied national progress to the founding. And, in light of the antislavery insistence on the progress of moral sentiment, such narratives of decline indicated ambivalence about historical development. The short time between American past and present made it easy to track change, but the change Americans tracked, both positive and negative, complicated their historical views. In conjunction, contextual readings of the founding-era texts, an insistence on a founding-era expectation of abolition, and narrations of post-founding-era decline began to highlight substantive differences between the present and the favored political past.

---

³ Jonathan Blanchard and Nathan L. Rice, *A Debate on Slavery* (Cincinnati, 1846), 49.
⁴ Ibid., 335, 418.   ⁵ Ibid., 44.   ⁶ Ibid., 50.   ⁷ Ibid., 14, emphasis in original.

This chapter shifts the focus from the Bible to the Constitution by tracking the emergence of historical readings of the Constitution and showing how debates over slavery, such as the one with Blanchard, drew attention to the historical realities of distance from and contingent change since the founding era. An awareness of contingent change, or a recognition that history's course is unpredictable, constitutes a core assumption of modern historical thought. In antebellum constitutional interpretation, attention to contingent changes since the founding era as much as an emphasis on founding-era context accounted for a deepening perception of historical distance from that period. In complicated and sometimes counterintuitive ways, the discussion about slavery initiated a more direct confrontation with the foreign nature of the founding era. This debate produced innovative constitutional readings and accounts of profound historical change, which drew the curtain open on the period's pastness.

By the 1840s, a wide range of constitutional readers had joined biblical readers on the chosen historical grounds of interpretation. This constitutional development had more domestic origins than the transatlantic biblical one. Indeed, the very act of producing a written constitution had the potential to create a deep desire in future citizens to understand its original historical setting. The realization of that potential began to occur in the first decades after ratification, as congressional debates reimagined the Constitution as a document in need of historical excavation.[8] At first, the move to see the text as archival contributed to its status as a sacred document. However, seeing the Constitution as historical had the potential to rapidly desacralize it by revealing that its roots rested in a distinct temporal setting. The move from sacralization to historicization was swift in the constitutional conversation – it took place over decades instead of centuries – in part because it centered on a document from a recent past and in part because that document was politically contested from its creation. Furthermore, the constitutional debate commenced during a period when historical interpretation was already becoming fashionable.

While the first historical appeals in constitutional interpretation came soon after ratification, widespread emphasis on contextual readings and the corresponding recognition of historical distance only emerged after the founding generation's passing. In part, this was a function of later interpreters' relationship to the founding era; they revered it more than the founders did, which inspired greater interest in historical searches

[8] Gienapp, *The Second Creation*.

for original meaning. As soon as founding figures departed the scene, Americans started performing acts of resuscitation. The 1836 death of constitutional architect James Madison, in particular, encouraged excavation of the framer's writings. Distance from the founding era created an urgent desire to unlock the Constitution's original truths, and many believed Madison's notes of the Convention were the cipher to his creation.

As in the biblical debates, the growing crisis over slavery shaped much of the constitutional conversation that followed the publication of Madison's notes in 1840. While some abolitionists, such as William Lloyd Garrison, damned the Constitution, many of slavery's opponents produced narratives that paralleled antislavery biblical readings. Antislavery constitutionalists advanced interpretations that both highlighted slavery's founding-era presence and emphasized the framers' anticipation of eventual emancipation. Similar to antislavery views of apostles in the New Testament, this interpretation suggested that though limited by their historical setting, the framers had taught principles meant to gradually abolish slavery. Coupled with a stress on slavery's unexpected spread and the sudden rise of the Slave Power, these antislavery accounts of original expectation cultivated a new sense of temporal dislocation from America's most useful past. In light of such distance, the Constitution seemed more useful as a flexible set of guidelines rather than a strict set of rules constrained by a particular time and place.

The question of slavery also linked distinct biblical and constitutional interpretive traditions along the lines of historical argumentation, even if readers seldom made the connection explicit. Political uses of the nation's sacred texts produced interpretive overlap and led to new confrontations with history. To be sure, presentism continued to shape readings of the Bible and the Constitution, and interpreters voiced a kind of historicist confidence in their ability to extract original meanings from the past, but the interest in and use of historical information increased some antebellum Americans' awareness of the historical distance separating them from both biblical and founding eras. That awareness had the potential to trouble attempts to align the imperatives of those pasts with the present. And the process of historicizing these most favored pasts threatened to expose all experience as timebound.

"CONCURRENT EXPOSITIONS," THE CONSTITUTION, AND CHANGE IN THE EARLY REPUBLIC

The origins of historical readings of the Constitution date to before its creation. In a 1785 letter, Jefferson wrote that legislative intent should be gleaned "principally from the words of the law" but noted that in "ambiguous" cases one should look to "the history of the times."[9] This related to William Blackstone's instruction to discern a legislator's intentions from "*context*" whenever the words of the law "are ambiguous, equivocal, or intricate."[10] Participants in the constitutional debate over slavery would repeat this instruction in later decades.

The process of imagining the Constitution as a text fixed in time and in need of historical excavation began soon after ratification. This occurred in relation to congressional debates. In the first Congress, Madison and others opposed the essentialist argument that the Constitution did not allow for the removal of executive officers. They instead developed another kind of essentialism in referencing extraconstitutional historical information to contend that the removal power should reside with the president.[11] Subsequent debates about constitutional amendments led Madison to join some of his colleagues in viewing the Constitution not as a system of government but as a fixed and sacred text, which view inspired calls for historical readings.[12] In 1791, while arguing against the proposed national bank, Madison offered direction on constitutional interpretation that followed Blackstone's instruction. Madison suggested that "in controverted cases, the meaning of the parties to the instrument" should guide interpretation, which required the use of "contemporary and concurrent expositions."[13] He cited the ratification debates to combat Hamiltonian readings.[14] In such instances, Madison was just as interested in interpretive restraint as he was in constructive allowance, but this appeal and the historical appeals it garnered in response further contributed to the idea of the Constitution as an archival text.[15] In 1796, when George Washington referenced the Convention records in support of Jay's Treaty, Madison again called on the ratifiers' understanding to constrain Federalist actions. In his address to Congress, he stated that the framers' views "could never be regarded as the oracular guide in expounding the Constitution." While emphasizing that a search for "legitimate meaning"

---

[9] Thomas Jefferson to Philip Mazzei, November 1785, in *The Papers of Thomas Jefferson* (Princeton, NJ, 1950–), 9:67–72 (hereafter cited as *PTJ*).
[10] William Blackstone, *Commentaries on the Laws of England*, 9th ed. (London, 1783), 1:60, emphasis in original.
[11] Gienapp, *Second Creation*, 154–56.   [12] Ibid., 196–201.
[13] 2 Annals of Cong. 1946 (1791).
[14] On how the constitutional debates of the 1790s built on Federalist and Anti-Federalist positions, see Saul Cornell, *The Other Founders: Anti-Federalism and the Dissenting Tradition in America, 1788–1828* (Chapel Hill, 1999).
[15] Gienapp, *Second Creation*, 232–38.

must begin with the "text itself," Madison proposed that extratextual searches must focus on "the State Conventions."[16] More than an appeal to original understanding, this was an attempt to counter Federalist appeals to original intent.[17] And yet, while these congressional debates highlighted political differences, the politicians who engaged in them came to agree on the need to read the Constitution as historical.[18]

Madison's evolving view of the Constitution as a sacred text emerged in relation to Jefferson's ideas, which posed a threat to Madison's creation. In his *Notes on the State of Virginia*, published while Jefferson was acting as Minister to France in Paris, he applied his enlightenment critique to the authority of written constitutions. He hoped to "get rid of the magic supposed to be in the word *constitution*."[19] The sacralizing process, Jefferson believed, discouraged reasonable citizens from revising and replacing constitutions when circumstances demanded a change in laws. The constitution he had drafted for his unrealized 1783 Virginia convention included a mechanism that allowed for recurring conventions.[20] Jefferson's legal views held the potential to encourage historicization.

Across the Atlantic, Madison worried about the immediate implications of his friend's ideas. In Federalist nos. 37 and 38, published in January 1788, Madison acknowledged the Constitution's imperfections, but heralded its unique merits, and saw God's hand in its creation, which, Madison argued, gave the document a "chance for immortality."[21] In Federalist no. 49, he directly addressed Jefferson's proposal for periodic conventions. He feared that "frequent appeals would ... deprive the government of that veneration which time bestows on every thing."[22] Recurring conventions, he thought, would destabilize the government and undercut the sacralization brought about by time's passage.

---

[16] 5 Annals of Cong. 776 (1796).
[17] See Jack N. Rakove, "The Original Intention of Original Understanding," *Constitutional Commentary* 13 (1996): 159–86; and Rakove, *Original Meanings: Politics and Ideas in the Making of the Constitution* (New York, 1996), 2–22, 339–65. See also Paul Finkelman, "The Constitution and the Intentions of the Framers: The Limits of Historical Analysis," *University of Pittsburgh Law Review* 50 (Winter 1989): 349–98.
[18] Gienapp, *Second Creation*, 287–324.
[19] Thomas Jefferson, *Notes on the State of Virginia* (London, 1787), 202–203, emphasis in original.
[20] Ibid., 376.
[21] [James Madison], "The Federalist no. 37," and "The Federalist no. 38," *in The Federalist Papers*, ed. Ian Shapiro (New Haven, CT, 2009), 179–92, quotation on 190.
[22] [James Madison], "The Federalist no. 49," in *The Federalist Papers*, ed. Ian Shapiro (New Haven, CT, 2009), 256–59, quotation on 257.

Jefferson did not share Madison's fear of destabilization. Writing to him in the afterglow of France's revolutionary summer of 1789, Jefferson addressed the cloudy concern of public debt.[23] The debt of one generation, he suggested, should not encumber the next. Stretching the application, he insisted that "no society can make a perpetual constitution.... The earth belongs to the living generation." Combining an enlightenment calculus with a republican historical sense, Jefferson asserted that "every constitution ... naturally expires at the end of nineteen years."[24] Jefferson gave Madison this letter in early 1790, and Madison responded soon after. Having already moved toward the idea of the Constitution as a fixed sacred text, Madison could not let this idea of constitutional expiration stand.

Madison believed that if Jefferson's approach were to be applied to the United States Constitution, it would render government "too mutable to retain those prejudices in its favor which antiquity inspires." Both he and Jefferson understood the sacralizing power of time, but they disagreed about its merits. Addressing "the relation which one generation bears to another," Madison argued that "the *improvements* made by the dead form a debt against the living" that "cannot be otherwise discharged than by a proportionate obedience to the will of the Authors of the improvements." America's primary constitutional author agreed that debts against the latter generation should "not exceed the advances" of the former, but he held that the republic's endurance required the assent of a well-housed progeny to their fathers' construction.[25] Madison wanted later generations to look back to the founding era and thank the framers for their sacred creation, and they would oblige him.

Madison's approach shows how imagining the Constitution as both archival and sacred functioned in the early republic, while Jefferson's approach demonstrates the historicizing potential of what could happen when those imaginings diverged. In the short term, Madison's view, which emphasized reverence and continuity, won out over Jefferson's, which

---

[23] On public debt and the French Revolution, see Michael Sonenscher, *Before the Deluge: Public Debt, Inequality, and the Intellectual Origins of the French Revolution* (Princeton, NJ, 2007).

[24] Thomas Jefferson to James Madison, September 6, 1789, in *PTJ*, 15:396.

[25] James Madison to Thomas Jefferson, February 4, 1790, *Founders Online*, National Archives (hereafter NA), emphasis in original. On these conversations, see Lance Banning, *Jefferson and Madison: Three Conversations from the Founding* (Lanham, MD, 1995), 27–55; Dustin A. Gish and Daniel P. Klinghard, "Republican Constitutionalism in Thomas Jefferson's *Notes on the State of Virginia*," *The Journal of Politics* 74 (January 2012): 35–51; and Gienapp, *Second Creation*, 199–201.

insisted on change and revision. As later generations of Americans adopted and advanced Madison's view, it slowed the process by which they realized the historical imperfections and particularities of the founding era. However, even as Madison's vision gained new strength, the debates over slavery threatened to make real the historicizing potential in Jefferson's approach.

Although Madison never convinced Jefferson of the need to reverence the Constitution – in fact, the latter continued to privately lament that some viewed it as "too sacred to be touched" – Jefferson did find cause to make use of historical information to read it.[26] On March 5, 1801, the day after he was sworn into office, five men wrote Jefferson from Providence, Rhode Island, encouraging him to administer the Constitution according to "the plain understanding of the People ... at the time of its adoption."[27] In committing to do so, he noted that the people's understanding could be gleaned from "publications of the time."[28] While Jefferson offered this instruction to oppose Federalist constructions – and though these and subsequent uses of the ratifiers did not displace a focus on the text itself – it nonetheless indicates that the Constitution had been reimagined as something fixed in time and in need of historical attention.[29] These first historical appeals had little potential to create awareness of founding-era particularities, but they did set the stage for that development to occur once the founders left the scene.

These conversations related to the increasing sacralization of the Constitution that came in succeeding decades. While Madison had encouraged this development, the generation that followed the framers went much further than he and his contemporaries did in reading the Constitution as static, sacred, and timeless. Madison, who was aware of his own historical situatedness, promoted a qualified constitutional veneration; he did not grant his creation the same veneration as those who

---

[26] Thomas Jefferson to [Samuel Kercheval], July 12, 1816, in *The Papers of Thomas Jefferson*, Retirement Series, ed. J. Jefferson Looney, (Princeton, NJ, 2004), 10:226.

[27] Providence Citizens to Thomas Jefferson, March 5, 1801, in *PTJ*, 33:188.

[28] Thomas Jefferson to Providence Citizens, March 27, 1801, in *PTJ*, 33:476.

[29] See H. Jefferson Powell, "The Original Understanding of Original Intent," *Harvard Law Review* 98 (March 1985): 885–948. Charles Lofgren distinguishes between framers and ratifiers in contending that some early constitutional interpreters looked to the ratifiers for insight into original understanding. Charles A. Lofgren, "The Original Understanding of Original Intent?" *Constitutional Commentary* 5 (1988): 77–113. For examples of Jefferson's and Madison's later appeals to the ratifiers, see Thomas Jefferson to William Johnson, June 12, 1823, *Founders Online*, NA, and James Madison to Henry Lee, June 25, 1824, *Founders Online*, NA.

came after him.[30] Nor did his contemporaries. The framers had conceived their creation with the expectation of adaptation.[31] And while the debate over how to incorporate the first amendments into the Constitution had contributed to the idea of a fixed original, the fact that the members of the founding generation used the amendment process more in fifteen years than subsequent generations did in the next hundred and fifty indicates something about the founders' willingness to formally change the Constitution. The founding generation's appeals to a fixed and sacred text had as much to do with politics as reverence.

Second-generation sacralization was bound up with the passage of time and the passing of founding figures, which accelerated the mythologizing process. In an 1831 Fourth of July oration, Massachusetts representative John Quincy Adams voiced the prevailing view that the Constitution had "been in successful operation upwards of forty years" with only a "few ... unimportant alterations."[32] Rather than hold new conventions, produce new constitutions, or generate new constructions of the Constitution, later generations of Americans exalted the original Constitution and tied the republic's success to its endurance.

Observing post-founding-era change had the potential to draw attention to distance and contingent historical movement, though the ways in which early Americans viewed change mitigated the realization of that potential. The first generations of Americans often policed change. Federalists and Jeffersonians accused each other of betraying the principles of the Revolution, and national historians, such as Mercy Otis Warren and David Ramsay, faulted their contemporaries for replacing civic virtue with self-interest.[33] Madison and Jefferson hoped territorial acquisitions would arrest history's processes but soon realized that even a geographically expansive republic was bound by time.[34] Taking note of postrevolutionary disappointments could make it difficult to chart the

---

[30] See Jeremy D. Bailey, *James Madison and Constitutional Imperfection* (New York, 2015).

[31] In the preamble of the Committee of Detail's draft of the Constitution, Edmund Randolph instructed that they include "essential principles only; lest the operations of government should be clogged by rendering those provisions permanent and unalterable, which ought to be accommodated to times and events." Edmund Randolph, "Draft Sketch of Constitution," in *Supplement to Max Farrand's The Records of the Federal Convention of 1787*, ed. James H. Hutson (New Haven, CT, 1987), 183.

[32] John Quincy Adams, *An Oration Addressed to the Citizens of the Town of Quincy* (Boston, 1831), 28–29.

[33] On the historians' narratives of decline, see Shalev, *Rome Reborn*, 188–215.

[34] Drew R. McCoy, *The Elusive Republic: Political Economy in Jeffersonian America* (Chapel Hill, 1980).

nation's providential course toward an inevitable end.[35] And yet, while republican narratives signaled unexpected change, the temporal proximity to the founding era mitigated a sense of dislocation. Indeed, these early jeremiads carried a hope of restoration: the precepts of the past could be and, some Americans hoped, would be restored.

Narrations of national progress soon overwhelmed tales of decline. A chorus of commentators stressed the economic advances resulting from industrialization. As new modes of transportation linked more of the population with domestic and foreign markets, economic development lent credence to the liberal vision that redefined civic virtue as self-interest.[36] Economic change was often a tortured process – it came with financial panics and personal and regional setbacks – but many of the founders' sons and daughters embraced capitalism's advance as progress and assumed a natural bond between democratic government and economic growth.[37] Supreme Court decisions reaffirmed this sentiment.[38] Ties between material advance and territorial expansion further cemented ideas of the nation's forward movement.[39] Abraham Lincoln later captured this view in stating that "we look upon the change as exceedingly advantageous to us and to our posterity, and we fix upon something that happened away back, as in some way or other being connected with this rise of prosperity."[40] Highlighting material differences from the founding era could have produced a sense of distance, but such changes were often heralded as the predictable fruits of the founders' work, which linked rather than severed past and present. What might have been seen as unanticipated change was accepted as the natural result of political independence, thus blunting a sense of indeterminate historical movement and mitigating the perception of a temporal gap. To be sure, morally anxious

---

[35] On the founding- and post-founding-era challenges to the enduring historical providentialism that had been forged during the Revolution, see Nicholas Guyatt, *Providence and the Invention of the United States, 1607–1876* (New York, 2007), 137–72.

[36] See Joyce Appleby, *Capitalism and a New Social Order: The Republican Vision of the 1790s* (New York, 1984).

[37] See Joyce Appleby, *Inheriting the Revolution: The First Generation of Americans* (Cambridge, MA, 2000).

[38] In *Charles River Bridge v. Warren Bridge* (1837), for example, Chief Justice Roger Taney ruled against monopolies. To do otherwise, he contended, would throw Americans "back to the improvements of the last century, and [oblige them] to stand still." *Proprietors of Charles River Bridge v. Proprietors of Warren Bridge*, 36 U.S. 420, 553 (1837).

[39] See, for example, John L. O'Sullivan, "The Great Nation of Futurity," *The United States Democratic Review* 6 (November 1839): 426–30. O'Sullivan's expression of exceptionalism was extreme, but his general sense of the nation's progress was not.

[40] Abraham Lincoln, "Speech at Chicago, Illinois, July 10, 1858," in *CWAL*, 2:500.

Americans continued to call for repentance and restoration in response to war, injustice, and economic crisis, but their calls fell on deaf ears. In any case, neither narratives of decline nor narratives of progress since the founding era spread a deep sense of historical dissonance.

These narrations functioned to further sacralize the Constitution, which had varied implications for historical awareness. Viewing the document as timeless muted a sense of distance even as that distance increased. And yet, relying on a set historical era and text for answers to the nation's most pressing problems created an impetus for investigation that could inadvertently reveal historical differences. This pattern mirrored what occurred in biblical interpretation, where the effort to get at timeless original meanings also uncovered the particularities of original historical eras. Constitutional debates dealt with a much more recent, favored past, but examining its relative abundance of sources had the potential to highlight that past's foreignness. Although the most dominant antebellum-era approaches to the Constitution obscured the perception of distance from the founding era, the debate over slavery soon began to encourage the kind of historical interpretations that pushed that awareness of distance to the surface.

SLAVERY, THE CONSTITUTION, AND HISTORICAL CHANGE

Members of the Constitutional Convention understood slavery's potential to divide the new nation, but they may not have recognized how sanctioning slavery created the potential to divide time.[41] Giving written legal standing to slavery opened the door to a series of far-reaching political conversations about a historical text that was meant to endure. Much of recent scholarship concludes that the Constitution reflected the dominance of proslavery interests and functioned as a proslavery document.[42] Perhaps in response to the threat posed by *Somerset v. Stewart* (1772), wherein Lord Mansfield determined that only positive

---

[41] See Rakove, *Original Meanings*, 85–92.

[42] See, for example, Paul Finkelman, *Slavery and the Founders: Race and Liberty in the Age of Jefferson* (Armonk, NY, 1996); Leonard L. Richards, *The Slave Power: The Free North and Southern Domination, 1780–1860* (Baton Rouge, 2000); Garry Wills, "*Negro President*": *Jefferson and the Slave Power* (Boston, 2003); David Waldstreicher, *Slavery's Constitution: From Revolution to Ratification* (New York, 2009); and George William Van Cleve, *A Slaveholders' Union: Slavery, Politics, and the Constitution in the Early American Republic* (Chicago, 2010). For a recent alternative argument, see Sean Wilentz, *No Property in Man: Slavery and Antislavery at the Nation's Founding* (Cambridge, MA, 2018).

law, or statutes created by local governments, protected slavery, southern delegates ensured that the Constitution gave states power to regulate the institution.[43] However, ratification did not establish a consensus on slavery, which was constantly contested in the early republic.[44] During the War of 1812, for instance, Britain used southern slavery to claim the moral high ground, which contributed to the rise of sectional politics and energized the northern antislavery movement.[45]

Toward the end of the 1810s, a series of legal and political developments fueled the debate over slavery and inspired more use of history in constitutional interpretation, even as that use failed to draw much attention to historical distance. In March 1819, Chief Justice John Marshall, Jefferson's Federalist cousin and nemesis, confirmed Congress's power to establish the Bank of the United States. "The principle now contested," Marshall explained, "was introduced at a very early period of our history, [and] has been recognised by many successive legislatures."[46] In linking economic development to founding-era principles, Marshall's decision demonstrated continuity. He also attended to historical change, arguing that because the framers' textual creation "was intended to endure" and adapt "to the various crises of human affairs," Congress should "accommodate its legislation to circumstances."[47] Notably, this ruling came just two months before William Channing's ordination sermon on the need to attend to accommodation and circumstance in biblical interpretation. Such rhetorical overlap increased over the next few decades. Whereas Channing's reading had privileged the use of reason in biblical interpretation, Marshall's historically informed decision upheld the Supreme Court as the final arbiter of constitutional interpretation.[48]

While Jefferson agreed that historical change should inform legal development, he disagreed with Marshall about who should drive development and what that development should mean. In June 1819, Spencer

---

[43] *Somerset v. Stewart*, Lofft 1, 98 Eng. Rep., 499 (1772).
[44] See John Craig Hammond and Matthew Mason, eds., *Contesting Slavery: The Politics of Bondage and Freedom in the New American Nation* (Charlottesville, VA, 2011).
[45] Matthew Mason, *Slavery and Politics in the Early American Republic* (Chapel Hill, 2006), 42–74.
[46] *McCulloch v. Maryland* 17 U.S. 316, 401 (1819).   [47] Ibid., 415.
[48] On the Supreme Court's appeal to the founding-era in this early period, see Michael Bhargava, "The First Congress Canon and the Supreme Court's Use of History," *California Law Review* 94 (December 2006): 1745–90; and Aaron Hall, "'Plant Yourselves on Its Primal Granite': Slavery, History and the Antebellum Roots of Originalism," *Law and History Review* 37 (August 2019): 743–61. Hall argues that an authoritative founding began to emerge in this period and soon entered the courtroom.

Roane, a former classmate of Marshall's at William and Mary, attacked *McCulloch v. Maryland* in a series of articles in the *Richmond Enquirer*.[49] In September, after reading his attacks, Jefferson wrote Roane. Jefferson combatted the notion that the Constitution was "a mere thing of wax in the hands of the judiciary," insisting that each department "has an equal right to decide ... meaning."[50] This fear that the Supreme Court wielded too much interpretive power dated back to anti-Federalist resistance.[51] Debate over who should determine constitutional meaning continued to surface in discussions about federalism, including during the nullification crisis, when South Carolinians such as John C. Calhoun and Robert Hayne prioritized the views of the states, while Massachusetts's Daniel Webster and Joseph Story argued that ultimate interpretation rested in the Supreme Court.[52] In the meantime, Jefferson voiced his view in private on the topic of who had the right to interpret and again resigned "every thing cheerfully to the generation now in place," which he described as "wiser" due to the "progressive advance of science."[53] He held onto his view that new generations should be granted primacy in constitutional development and interpretation even as he lamented the changes he observed regarding the Supreme Court's rise to interpretive prominence.

Southerners like Roane believed Marshall's decisions might undermine state jurisdiction, which was a crucial issue in the concurrent congressional debates over Missouri's admission as a slave state. In those debates, a few northerners used the Declaration and historical readings of the Constitution's guarantee and necessary and proper clauses to argue that Congress had discretionary power over admittance.[54] In the Sixteenth Congress, Senator David Morril of New Hampshire cited the recently published Convention debates to indicate the framers' expectation of slavery's gradual abolition.[55] William Plumer Jr., a New Hampshire representative, contrasted those "expectations" with slavery's spread and accused his opponents of advancing "new and alarming doctrines."[56] And yet, even though most northerners wanted to prohibit slavery in Missouri,

---

[49] Gerald Gunther, ed., *John Marshall's Defense of McCulloch v. Maryland* (Redwood City, CA, 1969), 106–54.
[50] Thomas Jefferson to Spencer Roane, September 6, 1819, *Founders Online*, NA.
[51] See Gienapp, *Second Creation*, 92–95.
[52] David P. Currie, *The Constitution in Congress: Democrats and Whigs, 1829–1861* (Chicago, 2005), 88–119. For Story's views, see Joseph Story, *Commentaries on the Constitution of the United States*, 3 vols. (Boston, 1833), 1:344–81.
[53] Jefferson to Roane, September 6, 1819.
[54] 33 Annals of Cong. 1179–84 (1819); 35 Annals of Cong. 135–56, 149, 1033–42 (1820).
[55] 35 Annals of Cong. 138 (1820).   [56] 36 Annals of Cong. 1437 (1820).

they agreed that slavery's status in existing states should be determined at the state level.

Those arguing against restricting slavery observed that Americans had given allegiance to this view of state authority since at least 1787. In Nicholas Van Dyke's congressional speech on Missouri's statehood, which was published soon after he gave it, the Delaware senator asserted that American law and legislation "establish incontrovertibly that involuntary servitude ... has ever been universally acknowledged to be a subject of State jurisdiction."[57] He dismissed the precedential use of the Northwest Ordinance, noting that it was passed in "circumstances so entirely dissimilar" from the present situation.[58] Van Dyke further argued that the framers had not "anticipated that the Declaration ... would be resorted to, as furnishing a key to the construction of the Constitution," and dismissed such readings as "novel."[59] (A few southerners historicized the Declaration to limit its scope, though most set it aside.)[60] The argument from continuity – that slavery had always been a state matter – carried the day.[61]

Jefferson saw a rupture in the Missouri Compromise, which sounded to him like "a fire bell in the night."[62] In an 1821 letter to Roane, Jefferson restated his generational views but, perhaps recalling Madison's idea of generational indebtedness, wondered if the current generation would "preserve for their sons the political blessings delivered into their hands by their fathers." Jefferson was seeing change in a different light. "Time ... changes manners and notions," he stated, and "we must expect institutions to bend to them. but time produces also corruption."[63] In Jefferson's view, *McCulloch* v. *Maryland* and the Missouri crisis raised the specter of negative change in the form of growing sectionalism and the threat of expanding federal power. Increasingly, participants in the slavery debates began to track lamentable change, which could spread a sense of change as contingent. And a sense of contingency marked distance from the founding era.

Madison did not embrace Jefferson's alarmism, and neither did most white southerners. Even when they labeled abolitionism a contagious

---

[57] 35 Annals of Cong. 303 (1820). [58] 35 Annals of Cong. 309 (1820).
[59] 35 Annals of Cong. 301, 305 (1820).
[60] 35 Annals of Cong. 1004–5 (1820); 36 Annals of Cong. 405 (1820).
[61] On the historical implications of these debates, see also Gilhooley, *Antebellum Origins*, 23–41.
[62] Thomas Jefferson to John Holmes, April 22, 1820, *Founders Online*, NA.
[63] Thomas Jefferson to Spencer Roane, March 9, 1821, *Founders Online*, NA.

disease, their arguments did not rely on grand arcs of decline or progress. They desired to maintain the status quo. In his 1830 debate with Webster, Hayne noted that southerners had inherited the institution and ascribed slavery's presence to God's providences.[64] In the Virginia emancipation debates that followed Nat Turner's 1831 rebellion, historian Thomas Dew argued that slavery had been forced on the South and that God sanctioned the practice, as the Bible showed.[65] In the years that followed, white southerners began to prefer clear biblical arguments to vague providential narratives.[66] At the same time, antislavery writers started to offer sweeping providential accounts predicting slavery's certain death.

As proslavery providentialism narrowed, an argument from circumstance expanded, but it was one that its articulators married to the appeal to continuity. Dew believed slave labor was unfit for Virginia but had a natural place in the climate farther south.[67] Calhoun later added to this idea while condemning abolition petitions. In 1837, the same year Arthur Granger highlighted circumstantial differences to posit slavery's awkward place in contemporary America, Calhoun voiced the view that the "present state of civilization" made slavery a "positive good."[68] A year later, Calhoun juxtaposed not slavery and freedom but rather radical abolitionism and slavery, which he heralded as "the most safe and stable basis for free institutions in the world."[69] These ideas corresponded to the biblical argument that "American slavery is not only not a sin, but especially commanded" in the Old and New Testaments.[70] This argument also related to the enduring proslavery contention that slavery

---

[64] Robert Hayne, "Debate in the Senate on Mr. Foot's Resolution," in *Speeches of Hayne and Webster in the United States Senate, on the Resolution of Mr. Foot, January 1830* (Boston, 1853), 10–11.

[65] Thomas R. Dew, *Review of the Debate in the Virginia Legislature of 1831 and 1832* (Richmond, VA, 1832), 45–46, 106–108. On the constitutional and historical dimensions of these debates, see Gilhooley, *Antebellum Origins*, 87–115.

[66] Guyatt, *Providence and Invention*, 236–46. [67] Dew, *Review of the Debate*, 126.

[68] John C. Calhoun, "Speech on the Reception of Abolition Petitions," in *The Works of John C. Calhoun*, ed. Richard K. Crallé (New York, 1851–56), 2:625–33, quotation on 631 (hereafter cited as *WJCC*).

[69] John C. Calhoun, "Remarks on the State Rights' Resolutions in regard to Abolition," *WJCC*, 3:180.

[70] J. H. Hammond, "Slavery in the Light of Political Science," in *Cotton Is King, and Proslavery Arguments: Comprising the Writings of Hammond, Harper, Christy, Stringfellow, Hodge, Bledsoe, and Cartwright on This Important Subject*, ed. E. N. Elliott (Augusta, GA, 1860), 636.

"The Further We Recede from the Birth of the Constitution"   149

"is not always and everywhere wrong."[71] In both biblical and constitutional debates, proslavery proponents tied the appeal to legal continuity.

Even those who were marginally opposed to slavery tied its existence to continuous legal developments. Speaking about abolition petitions in 1839, Senator Henry Clay of Kentucky argued that "two hundred years of legislation have sanctioned and sanctified negro slaves as property." While blaming impatient and reckless abolitionists for throwing emancipation "back for a half century," he placed abolition in the hands of God and the states – just as, he believed, the framers had intended.[72] Clay also depicted slavery as "an exception ... resulting from a stern inexorable necessity."[73] Clay held that circumstance had required the framers to keep slavery planted in the nation's soil, and that their descendants needed to resist the urge to pluck it out and instead wait for God and circumstance to make the change. These narratives paid attention to context in a way that muted historical change. They did not threaten ideas of historical progress like later antislavery narratives did.

THE PUBLICATION AND USE OF FOUNDING-ERA SOURCES IN ANTEBELLUM AMERICA

Along with new conversations about change, debates over Missouri's admission inspired new discussions about history's interpretive role. In his 1820 speech in Congress, Van Dyke expressed relief that the American government was not one "whose origin is buried in the rubbish of antiquity." He was grateful legislators relied on a "written instrument" and he gloried that "its history is brief" and that the "circumstances" of its creation and "adoption are recent and familiar." As some of Van Dyke's contemporaries were learning, the same could not be said for the history, creation, and transmission of the nation's sacred religious text – the Bible. Van Dyke noted that many of the Constitution's "enlightened statesmen" still enjoyed the fruits of their labors. The fact that some founding figures were still alive and that many commentators tied their creation to current economic and political enjoyments made the founding era appear more present than past. The idea of a familiar founding era made interpretation

---

[71] Albert Taylor Bledsoe, *An Essay on Liberty and Slavery* (Philadelphia, 1856), 140.

[72] This argument, which aimed to recover and employ a founding-era spirit of compromise, had been present from the start of the congressional debates over antislavery petitions in 1836. Gilhooley, *Antebellum Origins*, 158–186.

[73] Henry Clay, *Speech of Mr. Clay, of Kentucky, on the Subject of Abolition Petitions* (Washington, DC, 1839), 11, 12, 16.

appear straightforward. It seemed easy to discover the framers' "intention," which was, Van Dyke argued, "the leading rule of construction." Voicing the dominant originalism of the period, he stressed the need to discern intent in the document's "language" and, if ambiguous, "from the situation of the parties at the time of the compact."[74] Van Dyke proceeded to cite the Constitution and *The Federalist* to show that Congress did not have power to regulate a state's domestic affairs. In comparison to biblical scholars, who had access to relatively few ancient sources, constitutional readers made greater use of extracanonical texts. Debates over slavery encouraged this development, as did the publication of founding-era sources.

In March 1818, Congress resolved to print the Convention records that George Washington had deposited in the State Department.[75] Within a year and a half, Adams had edited and published them.[76] Aside from newspaper notices, the volume received scant attention. In November 1828, six months after Congress passed the decried "Tariff of Abominations," Adams's volume of Convention records was discussed in Hugh Legaré's *Southern Review*. The writer cited the records to challenge Marshall's "unlimited construction" in *McCulloch* v. *Maryland* and to insist that the framers "preserved to the respective States the entire control of their domestic arrangements."[77] Writing a few weeks before Vice President Calhoun issued his "Exposition and Protest," the reviewer used the publication to argue that "the compact is one between States."[78] In the face of threats to their institutions, white southerners used founding-era sources to make founding-era appeals.

Americans soon had several publications to use in making such appeals. In 1821, Edmond-Charles Genet, France's former ambassador to the United States and a New York resident, published an altered copy of Robert Yates's Constitutional Convention notes.[79] While Genet appears to have hoped the publication would result in the revision of his state's

---

[74] 35 Annals of Cong. 304 (1820).
[75] See Mary Sarah Bilder, "How Bad Were the Official Records of the Federal Convention?" *The George Washington Law Review* 80, no. 6 (2012): 1620–82.
[76] [John Quincy Adams, ed.,] *Journal, Acts and Proceedings, of the Convention, Assembled at Philadelphia* ... (Boston, 1819).
[77] "The Federal Constitution," *The Southern Review* 2 (November 1828): 434.
[78] Ibid., 450.
[79] [Edmond-Charles Genet, ed.,] *Secret Proceedings and Debates of the Convention Assembled at Philadelphia* ... (Albany, NY, 1821). On Genet's role in the publication, see James H. Hutson, "The Creation of the Constitution: The Integrity of the Documentary Record," *Texas Law Review* 65 (November 1986): 9–12.

"The Further We Recede from the Birth of the Constitution" 151

constitution, the few newspapers that took notice expected the publication to illuminate the Convention's proceedings.[80] In the late 1820s, political journalist Jonathan Elliot republished the Convention records in four volumes.[81] He also included the partial and partisan record of ratification debates.[82] Neither Yates's notes nor Elliot's *Debates* produced robust interpretive discussions. Both, however, were republished during the 1830s and 1840s and were cited in writings that addressed states' rights and slavery's constitutionality.[83]

For example, both publications were used in a mid-1830s debate over Virginia's "right of instruction," which directed senators to obey their legislature's directions or resign.[84] In January 1836, after Virginia's legislature instructed its senators to introduce a vote to expunge the Senate's censure of President Andrew Jackson, the *Richmond Enquirer* quoted the ratification debates to answer the *National Intelligencer*'s claim that the right of instruction was unconstitutional.[85] The next month, Senator John Tyler's decision to resign rather than vote to expunge the censure added fuel to the fiery debate. In June, the *Southern Literary Messenger* published US District Judge Joseph Hopkinson's response to the *Enquirer*, in which he argued that the right of instruction "is not coeval with the Constitution."[86] While noting problems with the state convention records, Hopkinson used them, along with Madison's writings in *The Federalist*, to support his position. To lend further credence to his views. Hopkinson reported that shortly before Marshall's death, Marshall, a founding-era figure, had told him that the right of instruction was incompatible with good government.[87] Made within days of Madison's own death, Hopkinson's appeal spoke to an interest in dead founders.

---

[80] See, for example, *New-England Galaxy*, August 31, 1821.
[81] Jonathan Elliot, ed., *The Debates, Resolutions, and other Proceedings, in Convention, on the Adoption of the Federal Constitution*, 4 vols. (Washington, DC, 1827–30).
[82] Hutson, "Creation of the Constitution," 13–23.
[83] Beginning in the mid-1830s, Elliot published an expanded second edition of his collection. Jonathan Elliot, ed., *The Debates of the Several State Conventions on the Adoption of the Federal Constitution*, 5 vols. (Washington, DC, 1836–45).
[84] *Proceedings of the Legislature of Virginia, in Support of the Right of State Legislatures to Instruct Their Senators in Congress* (Lexington, KY, 1812).
[85] *Richmond Enquirer*, January 16, 1836; *Daily National Intelligencer*, January 12, 1836. The *Enquirer* did not cite but seemed to use Elliot's *Debates*.
[86] Joseph H[opkinson], "Right of Instruction," *Southern Literary Messenger* 2 (June 1836): 407.
[87] Ibid., 410. See also Joseph Hopkinson, "The Right of Instruction," *Southern Literary Messenger* 2 (August 1836): 530–35.

Though valued in life, death and distance gave the founders' words added weight.

Historical contestations ensued. In response to Hopkinson, someone with the signature of "Roane" wrote two articles containing views reminiscent of the late Spencer Roane. Citing Madison, Jefferson, and other founders, the writer contended that the right to instruction was not "new."[88] While questioning Hopkinson's use of Yates's "maimed and meagre skeleton of debates," "Roane" also cited the founders to pit the entire convention against Hopkinson "and his coadjutors."[89] The effort to link one's views to the framing while distancing an opponent's views from the same multiplied and took on added weight once the framers passed from the scene.

In closing, "Roane" identified the illuminative potential of Madison's unpublished record of the Convention as he memorialized the framer and his creation. "Roane" suggested that though the "Sun of Montpelier has sunk ... below the horizon," his glorious influence would shine on and "shed a brilliant but mellowed light" on obscured constitutional truths. In a final sentence, the writer signaled the sacralizing process that followed Madison's death. "If it be no profanity to quote the sacred founder of our religious faith in defence of our hallowed constitution," "Roane" noted, "I would say, 'If they hear not Moses and the prophets, neither will they be persuaded, though one rose from the dead.'"[90] The writer drew together the Bible and the Constitution and proposed that if contemporaries did not harken to the framers' words, neither would a miraculous act of resurrection convince them. "Roane" welcomed the use of Madison's record, but he did not account for the inconclusive meanings such use would produce. Conjuring the past and restoring the dead to life could have unpredictable consequences.

Like late eighteenth-century congressional debates, early nineteenth-century discussions about state and federal power encouraged some interpretive use of the first published records of the Convention. The tradition of using founding-era sources to understand the Constitution deepened and expanded in unprecedented ways after the publication of Madison's notes in 1840. Two developments in the 1830s were crucial to that development: the passing of the founding generation, symbolized by Madison's death in 1836, and the rise of radical abolitionism. The

---

[88] R[oane], "Right of Instruction," *Southern Literary Messenger* 2 (September 1836): 628.
[89] Roane, "Right of Instruction," *Southern Literary Messenger* 2 (October 1836): 684, 686.
[90] Ibid., 692.

former inspired an unprecedented interest in founding-era sources; the latter produced competing antislavery appeals to the founding era. In the process, the recent American past grew more distant. As in the biblical debate over slavery, the constitutional debate historicized a favored past and inspired new readings of its sacred text.

"WE PLANT OURSELVES UPON THE DECLARATION ... AND THE TRUTHS OF DIVINE REVELATION"

Radical abolitionists contributed to both the historicization of the founding era and the development of innovative constitutional readings. In calling for immediate emancipation, they sparked a rhetorical clash that soon took constitutional form. Most combatants concluded that the letter or spirit of the Constitution either supported or condemned slavery, and they wielded the document to defend those positions. A few, however, abandoned it altogether.

Garrison raised the level of debate in both biblical and constitutional interpretation.[91] He did not provide rigorous historical readings, but his early uses and abuses of the documents evoked new questions about favored pasts and sacred texts, especially about the founding era and the Constitution. In making himself heard on the public stage, Garrison spurred and spread conversations about reading the nation's sacred legal text as a historical production. In short, America's most determined abolitionist forced new confrontations with the founding era.

Garrison had a conflicted approach to the American past. His interest in the Revolution had nothing to do with past achievements and everything to do with revolutionizing present social relations.[92] Speaking at Boston's Park Street Church on July 4, 1829, the twenty-three-year-old reformer designated the day as one "of great lamentation."[93] Speaking of blacks born in the United States, he declared this "their country by birth" and insisted that "their children possess the same inherent and unalienable

---

[91] As David Brion Davis notes, "The framework of Scriptural arguments over slavery changed very little prior to the radical defiance of the Garrisonians and the gradual influence of German higher criticism." Davis, *The Problem of Slavery in the Age of Revolution, 1770–1823* (Ithaca, NY, 1975), 551.

[92] See Maier, *American Scripture*, 197–99.

[93] William Lloyd Garrison, "Address to the American Colonization Society, July 4, 1829," in *William Lloyd Garrison and the Fight Against Slavery: Selections from The Liberator*, ed. William E. Cain (Boston, 1994), 62.

rights as ours."[94] In his writings and speeches, Garrison essentially rewrote "the Declaration ... to include African-Americans."[95]

He also cited the golden rule injunction, which he mined from a second crucial source: the Bible.[96] Like his Quaker mentor Benjamin Lundy, whom he assisted in editing the *Genius of Universal Emancipation* from September 1829 to March 1830, Garrison rooted his antislavery ideas in the Declaration and in the Bible.[97] In the *Liberator*'s inaugural issue, published on the first day of 1831, he proposed to "lift up the standard of emancipation ... *within sight of Bunker Hill and in the birth place of liberty*." Laying claim to the Declaration's self-evident truths, he committed to "contend for the immediate enfranchisement of our slave population."[98] In his second issue, Garrison held out hope for the nation's redemption "as long as there remains a single copy of the Declaration ... or of the bible, in our land."[99] Garrison hoped to realize the universal gospel truths that Francis Wayland had found embodied in the Declaration. Notably, Garrison left the Constitution off his list of redeeming texts.

In the early 1830s, awakened by the southern intransigence resulting from Nat Turner's slave rebellion and the nullification crisis, immediatists won converts from the colonizationists. This included Boston's Samuel May, a Unitarian minister who had been a student of Norton's at Harvard. May abandoned colonization after meeting Garrison in 1830. In a speech given on July 3, 1831, May decried slavery as an outrage to the "fundamental doctrine of our Constitution" and "the first principles of our Holy Religion!"[100] While allowing that the framers had created a compromised Constitution that contradicted the Declaration, May noted that the "fathers" did not deem their creation "perfect," as indicated in a provision that allowed their "children" to "amend it."[101] While most Americans heralded the Constitution as sacred, some began to

---

[94] Ibid., 64–65. On prior black uses of the Declaration of Independence to claim citizenship, see Gilhooley, *Antebellum Origins*, 42–62.

[95] Henry Mayer, *All on Fire: William Lloyd Garrison and the Abolition of Slavery* (New York, 1998), 67. On antebellum Americans' different approaches to the Fourth of July and their varied uses of the Declaration of Independence, see Michael F. Conlin, *One Nation Divided by Slavery: Remembering the American Revolution While Marching toward the Civil War* (Kent, OH, 2015), 18–36, 53–64.

[96] Garrison, "Address," 65. See Matt. 7:12.   [97] Garrison, "Address," 52–53.

[98] *Liberator*, January 1, 1831, emphasis in original.   [99] *Liberator*, January 8, 1831.

[100] Samuel J. May, *A Discourse on Slavery in the United States, Delivered in Brooklyn, July 3, 1831* (Boston, 1832), 4.

[101] Ibid., 11.

challenge that idea with the views of the framers themselves. Arguing that prejudicial circumstances had not allowed blacks to progress, May contended that changing these circumstances would permit them to "attain an equal elevation with ourselves."[102] May's appeal to the first principles of favored pasts foreshadowed later appeals to the founders' original expectations of change.

Such an appeal came in the inaugural address of the New York Anti-Slavery Society (NYASS). The NYASS was founded in October 1833 by abolitionist brothers Arthur and Lewis Tappan, who had both abandoned the American Colonization Society. The speaker at the group's inauguration acknowledged that states must bring about slavery's abolition. However, he proposed that in crafting provisions thought "necessary to keep slavery in view, as an existing state of things, [the framers] acted under the expectation that it was only temporary, and would soon cease." This view implied that the framers had aimed to create the Constitution as a document meant to outlive their own limiting context. "Slavery has not polluted its pages," the speaker explained, thus demonstrating "that our fathers would not have that document go down to posterity, carrying the disgraceful record that free Americans once held their fellow men as slaves."[103] But their sons, the speaker continued, had departed "from the principles of [their] fathers," as shown by the slave trade in the District of Columbia.[104] These developments were not the ones the framers had expected. The members of the NYASS thus hoped to "restore the abolition principles of Franklin, Jefferson, Rush, Jay, and others, and do what we conceive those sages would do, if they were now on the stage of human life."[105] In pitting original antislavery expectation against proslavery success, this historical appeal sought a restoration not of the past but of a sentiment articulated in the past that would bring about a new state of existence. As this narrative expanded and spread in the next few decades, it signaled contingent change and laid bare founding-era peculiarities even while working to fulfill founding-era promises.

In December, Arthur Tappan and other immediatists established the AASS in Philadelphia. Garrison, another founding member, incorporated the Gospels' golden rule and the Declaration's egalitarian principles

---

[102] Ibid., 14.
[103] *Address of the New-York City Anti-Slavery Society, to the People of the City of New-York* (New York, 1833), 23.
[104] Ibid., 24. [105] Ibid., 26–27.

into the society's constitution.[106] In its "Declaration of Sentiments," he wrote, "we have met together for the achievement of an enterprise, without which, that of our fathers is incomplete; and which ... as far transcends theirs, as moral truth does physical force."[107] Garrison was not writing history; instead, he was harnessing the power of the revolutionary past to signal the momentousness of the revolutionary present.

The document's conclusion affirmed the twin pillars of Garrison's faith: the Bible and the Declaration of Independence. However, at the suggestion of Quaker minister Lucretia Mott, he changed their order: "We plant ourselves upon the Declaration ... and the truths of Divine Revelation."[108] Like Wayland's view of the Declaration as a clear articulation of inchoate New Testament truths, Mott's suggestion hinted at antebellum Americans' gradual reordering of favored pasts.

Garrison's use of favored pasts called for sustained historical examination. He himself did not provide close contextual readings of sacred texts; he drew out abstract ideas and put to work ready-made passages. But in a public conversation of growing significance, his uses turned constitutional debates into historical contestations. As in the biblical debates, even those who approached the Constitution as a static, sacred text provided contextual readings. While such approaches had reinforced each other just after ratification, as time wore on, contextual readings grew in their potential to historicize the document and set off the founding era from the present. Garrison's approach to the past promised that the Constitution's sacralization would not proceed unhindered.

Setting off past from present supported Garrison's anticonstitutionalism. The AASS's declaration conceded "that Congress, *under the present national compact*, has no right to interfere with any of the slave States." Garrison's emphasis indicated his belief in the Constitution's impermanence and anticipated his call for its abrogation. Even at this early stage he insisted that the three-fifths, fugitive slave, and insurrection clauses "MUST BE BROKEN UP." Still, Garrison encouraged "the people of the free States, to remove slavery by moral and political action, as prescribed in the Constitution."[109] AASS members held that the Constitution empowered Congress to abolish slavery in the District of Columbia and to

---

[106] *Proceedings of the Anti-Slavery Convention, Assembled at Philadelphia, December 4, 5, and 6, 1833* (New York, 1833), 5–6.

[107] Ibid., 12. On the abolitionists' idea of completing and transcending the founders' works, see Gilhooley, *Antebellum Origins*, 63–86.

[108] *Proceedings of the Anti-Slavery Convention*, 15.   [109] Ibid., emphasis in original.

forbid its presence in the territories.[110] They also used the due process clause to develop equal protection arguments. These ideas, which set the agenda for later antislavery constitutionalisms, began to spread through the efforts of AASS agents.

Garrison soon replaced his tepid constitutionalism with a fiery anticonstitutionalism. He shared these views with foreign audiences first. Back in August, just four months earlier, Garrison had sent a letter to the London *Patriot* in which he had challenged the Constitution's sacralization. In statements excised from the version he published in the *Liberator*, he disputed "the sacredness of the compact" and pronounced it "the most bloody and heaven-daring arrangement ever made by men." He faulted the framers, who "were men, like ourselves – as fallible, as sinful, as weak, as ourselves." Like Emerson and Parker, Garrison believed venerated prophets and politicians were just as susceptible to human foibles as other men. He argued that their Constitution's time-bound failures had undercut the Declaration's timeless, "solemn and heaven-attested" truths. Thus, the Constitution had no power to claim adherence: "It was not valid then – it is not valid now."[111] Garrison's attack on the Constitution was moral rather than historical, but it forced others to engage the expanding contextual contestations over constitutional meaning. In turn, the idea of the Constitution as archival began to diverge from the idea of the Constitution as sacred, and historical readings of the text threatened to unveil the text's historical peculiarities.

"THE FURTHER WE RECEDE FROM THE BIRTH OF THE CONSTITUTION, THE MORE PRECIOUS DO CONTEMPORARY EXPOSITIONS OF IT BECOME"

The effort to provide historical readings of the Constitution gained new momentum with the publication of Madison's notes. The passing of time had cultivated a deep interest in the words of dead framers, and none more so than those of Madison. Understanding the interpretive potential of his notes, he had revised them even as he had resisted invitations to publish. He hoped that practice would cement the Constitution's

---

[110] On the centrality of the debate over slavery in the District of Columbia during this period, see Gilhooley, *Antebellum Origins*, 125–157.

[111] William Lloyd Garrison, "To the Editor of the London *Patriot*, August 6, 1833," in *The Letters of William Lloyd Garrison*, ed. Walter M. Merrill and Louis Ruchames (Cambridge, MA, 1971–81), 1:249.

status and meaning, which might eliminate troubling uses of the Convention's controversial debates. Though Madison relied on time, he also did his own part to firm up the canon and soften discrepancies; his revisions depicted unified framers and a static Constitution. By the late 1820s, after his brother-in-law John C. Payne had created a fair copy, Madison was favoring posthumous publication, which had the chance to help immortalize him while also ensuring that he would not be around if his notes shed too much light on founding-era peculiarities.[112]

Increased sacralization preceded historicization. In the wake of Madison's death on June 28, 1836, politicians honored him and his work. When President Jackson's letter apprised Congress of Madison's passing, John Quincy Adams noted, "Of that band of benefactors ... Madison is the last who has gone to his reward. Their glorious work has survived them all."[113] The time-bound framers had left behind a timeless Constitution. In the Senate, William Rives of Virginia spoke of Madison as the one selected by "Providence, to witness for a longer period than any of his illustrious colleagues, the rich blessings which have resulted from" the creation "of that sacred instrument." Rives believed that Madison's death itself served to "canonize the works of his hands, and surround, with a new veneration, that precious relic of the wisdom of our departed patriots and sages."[114] The founders' deaths heightened a sense of generational indebtedness and made Americans anxious about their future. It was in this period that Lincoln, a young Illinois lawyer and politician, spoke of this "departed race of ancestors." Now that the founding generation had fallen victim to "the silent artillery of time," Lincoln wondered how Americans would preserve its dual legacy of liberty and equality.[115] He prescribed "*a reverence for the constitution and laws.*"[116] Death cemented the idea of the Constitution as the source of national endurance and continued success.

The deaths of the founders also inspired readers of the Constitution to use the founding fathers' writings to discover their original intent.

---

[112] Mary Sarah Bilder, *Madison's Hand: Revising the Constitutional Convention* (Cambridge, MA, 2015), especially 223–40. On the notes as part of Madison's bid for immortality, see Douglass Adair, "Fame and the Founding Fathers," in *Fame and the Founding Fathers: Essays by Douglass Adair*, ed. Trevor Colbourn (New York, 1974), 21.

[113] 12 Reg. Deb. 4563 (1836).   [114] 12 Reg. Deb. 1911–1912 (1836).

[115] Abraham Lincoln, "Address before the Young Men's Lyceum of Springfield, Illinois, January 27, 1838," in *CWAL*, 1:108, emphasis in original.

[116] Ibid., 115, emphasis in original.

A founding mother played a key role in this development. In August, Dolley Madison wrote to Jackson, notifying him that she was preparing to place "before Congress and the World, what [her husband's] pen had prepared for their use."[117] Writing to Senator Rives just over a week later, presidential candidate Martin Van Buren asserted that the notes in Dolley's possession "furnish the only full & authentic history" of the Convention. He also noted Dolley Madison's struggle to find a publisher and floated the idea that Congress could purchase the notes.[118] In November, after months of unsuccessful negotiations, Madison again wrote to Jackson, asking if Congress would foster publication.[119] She cited her husband's expectation that the notes "will be particularly gratifying to the people." Like her husband, she worried about the notes' potential to illuminate too much, referring to the deferential "restraint which veiled ... this record," but she believed "the grave" had created a protective barrier, effectively separating the framers' public acts from their private lives.[120] Burying bodies seemed to make it safe to unearth hidden words.

Congressional commentators shared none of the Madisons' concerns about the notes' historicizing potential but shared all of their expectations about their historical value. In his November message to Congress, Jackson expressed confidence that the notes would provide "accurate knowledge" of the Convention's "circumstances."[121] The next month, Rives motioned that Jackson's message be referred to the Committee on the Library, and in January the committee issued a joint resolution to purchase the notes for $30,000.[122] In mid-February, two days before the resolution received its third reading, Senator Ashur Robbins of Rhode Island compared Madison's notes to Francis Bacon's *Novum Organum*, stating that the work would "unfold to us all the steps of that diversified

---

[117] Dolley Madison to Andrew Jackson, August 20, 1836, in *The Selected Letters of Dolley Payne Madison*, ed. David B. Mattern and Holly C. Shulman (Charlottesville, VA, 2003), 331 (hereafter cited as *Selected Letters*).

[118] Martin Van Buren to William C. Rives, August 29, 1836, William C. Rives Papers, Library of Congress. On Van Buren's successful appeal to a founding-era spirit of compromise as a presidential candidate, see Gilhooley, *Antebellum Origins*, 187–213.

[119] Dolley Madison to Charles J. Ingersoll, August 29, 1836, in *Selected Letters*, 333. See also George Tucker to Dolley Madison, August 23, 1836; Dolley Madison to Ann Maury, September 7, 1836; Dolley Madison to Ann Maury, October 9, 1836; and Dolley Madison to Henry Clay, November 8, 1836, in *Selected Letters*, 331–335, 341.

[120] 13 Reg. Deb., Appendix, 98 (1837).   [121] 13 Reg. Deb., Appendix, 97 (1837).

[122] Senate Journal, 24th Cong., 2d Sess., December 14, 1836 and January 17, 1837, 36 and 128; see also House Journal, 24th Cong., 2d Sess., January 24, 1837, 280.

analysis ... which [led] to" the "happy and splendid result" of the Constitution's creation. Taking on adherents of an earlier interpretive tradition, Robbins noted that those few who still believed that the Constitution alone "was enough for the instruction of mankind on this subject [were] much mistaken."[123] The First Congress had imagined the Constitution as archival, and the Twenty-Fourth Congress worked toward ensuring that the archival text would be read in the light of newly available founding-era sources.

Slavery informed this discussion of using these sources to read the Constitution, which came in the midst of contentious debates about the right to consider abolition petitions. These debates resulted in an informal gag rule on antislavery petitions in the Senate and a formal gag rule on the same in the House.[124] The debates over the antislavery petitions shaped conversations about purchasing Madison's notes. Calhoun, a major figure in the debates, did not believe Congress had power to acquire the notes, much less purchase them. This shows the depth of southern anxieties about federal meddling. Calhoun did state that the notes "would throw a new and brilliant light upon our institutions."[125] His southern colleagues agreed with him about their interpretive value but did not see the danger he saw. Fellow South Carolinian William Preston "was by no means disposed to construe the Constitution merely by the words it contained" and "thought it exceedingly desirable to know the ... intentions of the framers, which must be regarded as the only true spirit of the instrument." Kentucky's John Crittenden held that no other source could offer "more light as to the [Constitution's] just interpretation," while Rives observed that the notes afforded them "important light towards its practical construction." After these and similar comments, the Senate approved the resolution.[126] In doing so, they sanctioned a robust interpretive emphasis on using founding-era sources such as Madison's notes to discern the framers' original intent.

Beyond the walls of Congress, newspaper writers observed the crucial role that time was playing in this development. In April 1837, Dolley Madison sent Payne's fair copy to the nation's capital, and about a year

---

[123] 13 Reg. Deb. 851 (1837).
[124] See William Lee Miller, *Arguing about Slavery: John Quincy Adams and the Great Battle in the United States Congress* (New York, 1996); and Stephen M. Feldman, *Free Expression and Democracy in America: A History* (Chicago, 2008), 133–139.
[125] Cong. Globe, 24th Cong., 2d Sess., Appendix, 252, 254 (1837).
[126] Cong. Globe, 24th Cong., 2d Sess., Appendix, 252–56 (1837).

and a half later, Congress decided to print the notes.[127] During the next two years, Attorney General Henry Gilpin prepared the notes for publication while an eager American press waited. Gilpin secured Samuel Langtree and John O'Sullivan as publishers. In a March 1839 notice of the pending publication, a writer for O'Sullivan's paper noted that the connection between a "continuance of these manifold blessings" and proper constitutional interpretation "united to give a value almost sacred to every authentic document calculated to throw light upon the history of the Constitution."[128] Newspapers with less of an investment in the publication also prized Madison's notes as the "only full" account of the Convention.[129] The *Boston Recorder* asserted that the "authentic information which they furnish of the feelings, the motives and the words of the illustrious men of those times, is becoming ... more and more valuable with the lapse of each successive year. The further we recede from the birth of the constitution," the paper observed, "the more precious do contemporary expositions of it become."[130] Time's passage imbued the records with great interpretive value and, as in biblical interpretation, inspired a historicist confidence in using them to understand a sacred text from a favored past. In the face of death and distance, Americans prized founding-era remainders, especially Madison's notes, as the cipher to the Constitution.

Belief that the notes had power to unlock the meaning of the sacred Constitution went hand in hand with the notes' own sacralization. In late 1839, a number of newspapers reprinted an anecdote in which congressmen Asher Robbins had suggested that the published notes would "become the political bible of the land."[131] The canonization of Madison's papers depended on the belief that they would provide unmediated access to the godlike framers and their inspired views. Gilpin contributed to this idea in downplaying his editorial role. In response to a book notice that had described his work on the volumes as extensive, he noted that the reporters had "mistaken the extent of [his] agency." He

---

[127] See Senate Journal, 25th Cong., 1st Sess., September 11, 1837, 29; Senate Journal, 25th Cong., 2d Sess., February 5, 1838 and July 9, 1838, 205, 580, and 583; House Journal, 25th Cong., 1st Sess., September 27, 1837, 105; and House Journal, 25th Cong., 2d Sess., July 9, 1838, 1246.

[128] "Madison, and the Madison Papers," *United States Magazine and Democratic Review* 5 (March 1839): 243.

[129] *Niles' National Register*, April 27, 1839. [130] *Boston Recorder*, October 23, 1840.

[131] *Niles' National Register*, September 7, 1839. See also *Boston Weekly Magazine*, September 28, 1839; and *Christian Register and Boston Observer*, October 5, 1839.

strongly corrected the idea that he "would suffer any commentary ... to accompany" the work. In light of the fact that the notes included obscure allusions to letters and facts, Gilpin had added "a few pages ... but in such a manner as not, in the slightest degree, or even in appearance, to connect them, or interfere with the text or work of Mr. Madison."[132] Such language echoed biblical passages about adding to or diminishing from the word of God and recalled the First Congress's decision to append amendments rather than alter the original text of the Constitution.[133] The sacralization of Madison's notes ushered in a new era of using founding-era sources to uncover original intent.

While Madison's notes obtained sacred status in some quarters, they had yet to be ratified through reading and use. In early 1840, Gilpin published the *Papers* in three volumes.[134] Alongside O'Sullivan's newspaper, which cited historian George Bancroft's endorsement, a number of other periodicals heralded the production.[135] A writer for the *Iris*, a New York literary magazine, described it as the "fountain-head of information" with respect to "the true opinions of some of the prominent" founders. "Great questions of constitutional power are here seen in their true form," the writer noted.[136] The reviewer only regretted that the price of the handsome volumes made them inaccessible to some. Accessibility had also been threatened in April, when a fire broke out in the office of Langtree and O'Sullivan and destroyed some of the stereotype plates.[137] Within a year, though, the New York publishers James and Henry G. Langley, who had taken over publication of O'Sullivan's paper, issued a new edition of the volumes. Once again, the press praised the publication for its power to illuminate the Constitution, though some reviews offered a more nuanced appraisal than earlier notices, which had reflected the excitement of anticipation more than the appreciation of analysis.[138] The earlier notices had shown no signs that the effort to conjure the past might summon undesirable ghosts.

---

[132] *Niles' National Register*, October 5, 1839.   [133] Deut. 4:2; Rev. 22:18–19.
[134] Henry D. Gilpin, ed. *The Papers of James Madison*, 3 vols. (Washington, DC, 1840; hereafter cited as *PJM*). See *Niles' National Register*, January 11, 1840; and *Niles' National Register*, March 14, 1840.
[135] "Political Portraits, with Pen and Pencil: Henry D. Gilpin (no. 23)," *The United States Magazine and Democratic Review* 8 (November/December 1840): 534.
[136] "Literary Notices: The Madison Papers," *The Iris, or Literary Messenger* 1 (November 1840): 43.
[137] *Boston Cultivator*, April 18, 1840.
[138] "Quarterly List of New Publications," *The New York Review* 8 (April 1841): 540.

More measured reviews indicated that the notes obliged some readers to grapple with the historical particularities of the era in which the Constitution was born. In July 1841, a writer for the *North American Review* disagreed with Senator Robbins's comparison of Madison's record of notes to Bacon's revolutionary work of genius, explaining that the value of the former "is of a peculiar and somewhat unique character. It is the record of an extraordinary coincidence."[139] The writer affirmed the public belief that the Constitution had generated national progress but argued that its creation was due to a "lucky accident" and observed that it had "worked in practice far better than was anticipated."[140] Along with these historical insights, the notes exposed constitutional imperfection. "One of the great merits of its framers," the reviewer explained, was "that they did not pretend that it was a perfect instrument."[141] Madison's notes drew this and other reviewers' attention to the historical nature of the framers' creation, making it clear that the "miracle" of the Constitution was more the result of a reasoned construction than an immaculate conception.[142]

Narratives of qualified sacralization came interlaced with traces of historicization. New efforts to shed light on the esteemed Constitution opened the door to the kind of scrutiny that undermines filiopietistic veneration. Digging into the past carried the risk of unearthing unfamiliar remains, and Madison was not around to touch them up. The dead author had given up control of his works.

MADISON'S PAPERS AND THE ARTICULATION OF MODERATE ANTISLAVERY CONSTITUTIONALISM

The process of historicization related to a developing popular constitutionalism. Politicians and politically authorized constitutional interpreters soon learned that Madison's *Papers* exacerbated rather than solved the question of interpretation. Part of the problem was the fact that the *Papers* gave the American public a tool to more fully participate in the debate. Indeed, while United States courts, including the Supreme Court, made some use of the *Papers* – most notably in *Prigg* v. *Pennsylvania* (1842) – Americans outside of courtrooms were just as responsible for making

---

[139] "The Papers of James Madison," *North American Review* 53 (July 1841): 42.
[140] Ibid., 43, 44. [141] Ibid., 44.
[142] E. L. C., "The Madison Papers," *American Jurist and Law Magazine* 26 (January 1842): 395.

them the go-to interpretive source.[143] Participants in the debate over slavery, and antislavery writers in particular, played a key role in this development.[144]

Historicizing features began to crowd out sacralizing elements in various antislavery readings of the Constitution. Antislavery constitutionalism evolved, expanded, and diverged in the 1830s and 1840s, finding embodiment in radical and moderate constitutionalists. Opposed to nonresistance and disunionism – two positions Garrison advanced in the late 1830s and early 1840s – members of each group of antislavery constitutionalists formed the Liberty Party in 1840. Although the party disbanded in the late 1840s, it shaped an enduring antislavery political effort focused on destroying the Slave Power.[145] Its dislocated moderates found a home in the Free Soil Party (1848) and, later, the Republican Party (1854). The influential moderates had powerful proponents in Senators Salmon P. Chase and William Seward. Moderates held that freedom was national and slavery local, leaving abolition to the states but insisting that the federal government could not protect or expand slavery. Radicals, meanwhile, believed that the Constitution itself opposed slavery. Figures such as Alvan Stewart, William Goodell, Lysander Spooner, and Gerrit Smith articulated this position. In contrast to Garrisonians, both moderates and radicals continued to pay allegiance to the nation's supreme legal canon.

It was no coincidence that radical and moderate positions received their clearest articulation in the years following the publication of Madison's *Papers*. In 1836, James Birney, who ran for president on the Liberty Party ticket in 1840 and 1844, established Cincinnati's *Philanthropist*, and Gamaliel Bailey took over editing duties the next year. Like Weld, Bailey had become an abolitionist during the Lane Seminary debates. While more politically moderate than Birney, Bailey cast the Constitution as a "shameful bargain" in an early 1841 editorial. He found "the details of this dark transaction" in Madison's *Papers*. Noting that "we have been taught to venerate the character of the framers," Bailey instructed readers "to discriminate in bestowing our respect." He did point out that Madison "thought it WRONG TO ADMIT IN THE CONSTITUTION

---

[143] See Hall, "'Plant Yourselves on Its Primal Granite,'" 752–54. In an 1850 letter to Theodore Parker, James Birney challenged the *Prigg* decision by "very carefully" examining Madison's *Papers*. James Birney to Theodore Parker, August 21, 1850, in Theodore Parker Parkers, MHS.

[144] See Gilhooley, *Antebellum Origins*, 225–33.

[145] Corey M. Brooks, *Liberty Power: Antislavery Third Parties and the Transformation of American Politics* (Chicago, 2016).

THE IDEA THAT THERE COULD BE PROPERTY IN MEN."[146] This statement, one of only two against slavery made by Madison in the notes, quickly became a favorite quotation among antislavery writers.[147] However, the article emphasized that an accursed compromising spirit had governed the Convention. Just as biblical criticism contributed to the desacralization of the Bible and its Christ – who some believed had held mistaken beliefs – the use of founding-era sources, and Madison's *Papers* in particular, qualified the conventional view of the framers as inspired and the view of their creation as sacred. The interpretive debate over slavery began to show that no favored past was beyond reproach.

Channing, a veteran in the biblical debate, found historical constraints in the founding era just as he had in New Testament times and again anticipated the realization of a sacred text's permanent principles. While he distrusted political abolitionism, including the Liberty Party, he toed the moderate line in an 1840 publication, wherein he suggested an amendment to remove "us from a participation in [slavery's] guilt."[148] Channing believed the fugitive slave clause was "virtually fading away" anyway, due to "a spirit spreading through the country ... which demands changes of the constitution."[149] An amendment, he proposed, would bring the Constitution "into harmony with the moral convictions" of the time.[150]

Channing continued the argument in 1842, when he deemed the fugitive slave clause a temporary law that had been forced on the free states by "circumstances." He also designated freedom as the Constitution's "great, living, all-pervading idea."[151] Noting that the framers had "carefully avoided" recognizing slaves as property, he quoted the go-to line from Madison's *Papers*.[152] In turning from past to present, Channing struggled to reconcile the spread of antislavery sentiment with slavery's continued existence: "Our country is free; this is its glory. How deeply to be lamented is it, that this glory is obscured by the presence of slavery."[153] In such accounts, the anachronism of slavery threatened to stall a progressive nation, and it challenged the belief in history's progressive

---

[146] *Philanthropist*, February 17, 1841, emphasis in original.
[147] See Bilder, *Madison's Hand*, 148–49, 188–89.
[148] William E. Channing, *Emancipation* (Boston, 1840), 94.   [149] Ibid., 96.
[150] Ibid., 98.
[151] William E. Channing, *The Duty of the Free States: Second Part* (Boston, 1842), 11.
[152] William E. Channing, *The Duty of the Free States, or Remarks Suggested by the Case of the Creole* (Boston, 1842), 24, 25. See also Channing, *Duty of the Free States: Second Part*, 19.
[153] Channing, *Duty of the Free States, or Remarks*, 50.

movement. Still, writing within months of his death, Channing held out hope for abolition, insisting that "no law, no constitution, can prevail against the moral convictions of the people."[154] The acts of emphasizing founding-era expectations and appealing to the people to realize them were becoming crucial features of antislavery writings. These moves often included an effort to link forebears and descendants but indicated a willingness to defer to the latter, signaling the founding era's historical limitations.

Some antislavery efforts to link forebears and descendants continued to collapse historical distance and to conflate temporal distinction. In January 1843, Bailey's *Philanthropist* published the Ohio Liberty Party's "Address to the People of Ohio," which Salmon Chase and other members of the party had presented at their state convention in late December. In the address, the authors bound themselves to the revolutionaries: "We wish to revive the old Liberty party of the times that tried men's souls. We stand where Hancock, Jefferson and other old patriots stood in 1776." The authors slighted the Slave Power while vindicating the founders, "who did not attempt, by subtle argumentation, to prove that slavery is the foundation of civil liberty," nor "torture the pages of Inspiration itself" to support the idea "that man can hold property in man." Neither did they intend, the authors argued, to limit "their grand and comprehensive declaration that 'all men are created equal.'" In answering proslavery readings, the authors posited the abuse of sacred texts and faulted the Slave Power for slavery's unexpectedly powerful presence in nineteenth-century America. While the authors quoted Madison's statement about not recognizing property in men, they were not concerned with context, which might undermine their appeal to universals. Instead, the authors emphasized the absence of certain words and the presence of egalitarian ideas.[155]

That emphasis can be seen in the authors' assertion that "the principle of the declaration was embodied in the Constitution," an idea which most antislavery writers embraced.[156] Slavery encouraged American interpreters to make canonical distinctions among the various founding documents used in this debate just as it did in the biblical one – where the New Testament achieved a higher status than the Old Testament – despite some proslavery interpreters' best efforts to hold the testaments together. In the constitutional debate, Garrisonians and some proslavery

[154] Channing, *Duty of the Free States: Second Part*, 38.
[155] *Philanthropist*, January 11, 1843.   [156] Ibid.

readers strove to sever the connection between the two main founding documents – the former to lay claim to the Declaration and damn the Constitution, the latter to damn the Declaration and lay claim to the Constitution – but the texts remained tied together in the antislavery imagination. Proximity assisted antislavery interpreters in this effort; some of the same figures that signed the Declaration drafted the Constitution. To the extent that the latter diverged from the former, antislavery advocates considered it retrogressive. To protect against the Constitution's transgressions, they read it in the prelapsarian light of the Declaration.

Madison's *Papers* troubled appeals to the favored founding era but still allowed for antislavery readings. The authors of the Liberty Party address granted that the framers "did not attempt to put an end to slavery in the states" and crafted "provisions ... subversive of justice and liberty," but the authors argued that the states had maintained slavery "in opposition to the principles of the Declaration and of the Constitution and in violation of the plain precepts of Revelation." The authors denied Garrisonians' sole claim to the Declaration and the Bible. The authors quoted Washington, Jefferson, and Madison to argue that the founders had anticipated that the states "would speedily and voluntarily abandon [slavery], when the clause ... having reference to it as existing under state authority, would become inoperative, while the sacred instrument itself would still remain a perfect and consistent expression of the National Will."[157] This kind of constitutional reading, which antislavery readers increasingly valued, assumed that the framers had thought historically; they had expected the fruition of universal seeds to overcome founding-era weeds. Like Channing, the authors of the address granted that the Constitution contained proslavery provisions but focused on the expectation of their removal and the states' failure to accomplish the task.[158] When Congress attempted to gag abolitionists, they ventriloquized the founders in a way that both allowed for slavery's place in the American past and laid bare its awkward presence in the American present. This narrative highlighted distance by positing moral dissonance.

---

[157] Ibid. On antebellum Americans' appeals to Jefferson and Washington in the slavery debates, see Conlin, *One Nation Divided*, 37–105.

[158] *Philanthropist*, January 11, 1843. For a similar view of the founding era from this period, see "Relations of the Federal Constitution to Slavery," *New Englander* 3 (October 1845): 595–600.

In a century characterized by a belief in progress and among a citizenry who often thought of their nation as the embodiment of civilization's advance, slavery introduced doubts. Identifying the founders' expectation of abolition and then tracing "how exactly the national policy has conformed to the interests of the slave-holder" challenged traditional assumptions about history's direction.[159] Digging into the recent past both highlighted the historical peculiarities of the founding era and made clear what had and had not changed since then. It revealed how America's historical peculiarities still haunted the present. In particular, the antislavery narration indicated declension: the Slave Power betrayed founding-era anticipation by exploiting the Constitution's proslavery provisions rather than allowing its antislavery spirit to flower. This dual stress on emancipatory promise and failure became a central component of many antislavery narratives, which posed a new challenge to notions of history's predictable movement.

In the shadow of emancipatory failure, the authors closed with a call to "enter into a second [revolutionary] contest." Hoping to deliver "the government ... from the corruptions fashioned upon it by slavery" and "make it what our fathers designed it to be," the authors concluded with a national appeal "to vindicate the true construction of the Constitution." Like biblical interpreters who appealed to the apostles, constitutional interpreters claimed the support of the chosen founders – "we have the example and spirits of our fathers on our side."[160] This kind of appeal tended to collapse temporal distance, but the call for another revolution did not simply represent a naïve desire to recreate a pure past. Instead, it carried a mandate to move beyond that past into a more egalitarian future.

These ideas spread beyond third-party politics. Some of the Whigs who opposed slavery, called "Conscience Whigs," voiced similar views. This included John Palfrey, who had learned historical interpretation from Norton, become a Unitarian minister, and then filled Norton's position as Professor of Biblical Literature at Harvard. In the early 1840s, Palfrey involved himself in politics as a Whig. In 1846, while serving as Massachusetts Secretary of the Commonwealth, he published a series of articles on the Slave Power, in which he contended that the three-fifths

---

[159] *Philanthropist*, January 11, 1843. For a similar narrative of proslavery advances, see Horace Bushnell, *Politics Under the Law of God: A Discourse, Delivered in the North Congregational Church, Hartford; On the Annual Fast of 1844* (Hartford, CT, 1844).

[160] *Philanthropist*, January 11, 1843.

clause had "reference to a merely temporary state of things" and only later became "the lodging-place of the leading policy of the Government."[161] In stressing temporary provisions, Palfrey echoed Channing and Bailey. He noted that the framers had not included slavery in the Constitution "because it was understood that the thing was soon to perish, and the Constitution ought not to enshrine its detestable memory."[162] In succeeding years, this reading continued to find adherents among politicians, including Abraham Lincoln. As expected, Palfrey cited Madison's *Papers* to buttress his contention. He used his historical understanding of the founding era in observing that the framers had erred in "supposing that Slavery was not to grow, and ... was soon to die," but he pointed out that they had "provided a peaceable method for introducing such emendation as time might show to be needful."[163] Palfrey explained that this resolution depended on *"the will of the voters."*[164] The people, he noted, "are the constitutional constitution-menders and law-makers."[165] Palfrey, who soon carried these views into the United States Congress, joined figures such as Channing in linking original expectation and popular will, a move that sanctioned and encouraged popular constitutionalism.

In granting slavery's founding-era presence and expressing a belief in the framers' expectations that time would make slavery obsolete, these narratives exposed the foreignness of that past. And while proslavery consolidation might complicate that characterization, antislavery commentators simply characterized the rise of the Slave Power as an anachronism that opposed the spirit of their age. Yes, their narratives implied, slavery had existed comfortably in the founding period, but it made an awkward presence in the nineteenth century. The belief in the framers' original expectations and the stark contrast antislavery observers found between those expectations and the present prominence of the Slave Power called attention to the distance separating Americans from their founding.

MADISON'S PAPERS AND THE ARTICULATION OF RADICAL ANTISLAVERY CONSTITUTIONALISM

While radical constitutionalists were less eager to resurrect the dead than the moderates were, they nonetheless dug up founding-era skeletons. By

---

[161] John G. Palfrey, *Papers on the Slave Power, First Published in the "Boston Whig"* (Boston, 1846), 6.
[162] Ibid., 7.   [163] Ibid., 88.   [164] Ibid., 99, emphasis in original.   [165] Ibid., 89.

insisting on a strict reading that revealed an antislavery Constitution, they inadvertently fixed attention on the historical realities that lay behind the text. Radical constitutionalism had emerged in the late 1830s but found its clearest expression in the publications of Smith, Goodell, and Spooner in the mid-1840s.[166] These authors appealed to the due process, privileges and immunities, habeas corpus, and guarantee clauses while challenging proslavery readings of the three-fifths, importation, labor, insurrection, and domestic violence clauses. Smith, Goodell, and Spooner all joined moderates in using the Declaration as a lens with which to read the Constitution. And even though these radical constitutionalists dismissed historical evidence as extraneous and condemned searches for original intent, they used historical arguments to uncover original antislavery sentiment and to posit that a perverted interpretation had hidden the framers' emancipationist expectations. Both the radicals' wariness of historical readings and their use of historical narration indicated that they did not assume an easy transference of ideas and beliefs from a particular revolutionary past.

At times, radical constitutionalists showed no reservations about using historical evidence or appealing to original intent. In 1840, five years after anti-abolitionist violence inspired Smith's conversion to abolitionism, the New York reformer helped form the Liberty Party. Smith subsequently joined the ranks of the radicals. In an 1844 publication, he insisted that the proslavery usage of the Constitution did not change original antislavery meanings. Appealing to extratextual indications of intent, he cited the Northwest Ordinance as proof of an expectation of abolition among those "who framed" and "adopted" the Constitution.[167] Like Channing, Smith emphasized the text's "general principles," which he tied to abolitionism, and argued that even if the fugitive from labor clause was proslavery, it must give way, through amendment, to the "tide of Northern anti-slavery sentiment."[168] However, he also used Madison's *Papers* to contend that the fugitive from labor clause did not apply to slaves.[169] Smith held that antislavery historical evidence overwhelmed proslavery historical evidence, but slavery had "bewitched" public sentiment, giving rise to the corrupt proslavery reading of the Constitution dominant in the courts. This and other proslavery advances signaled distance from the founding

---

[166] See William M. Wiecek, *The Sources of Antislavery Constitutionalism in America, 1760–1848* (Ithaca, NY, 1977), 119–20, 181–90, 252–56.
[167] Gerrit Smith, *Constitutional Argument, against American Slavery* (Utica, NY, 1844), 5.
[168] Ibid., 6, 11.   [169] Ibid., 13.

era and challenged the belief in antislavery progress. But with Palfrey, Smith held out hope that "in the hands of the People" the Constitution could be used as an "anti-slavery instrument" as originally intended.[170] Turning to the public was symptomatic of the antislavery belief that slavery could not keep pace with the times.

Goodell, another reform veteran, also appealed to the people, including those of the present and those of the favored past. Goodell had been involved in founding the NYASS and the AASS, and he also helped form the Liberty Party. He opened an 1844 publication with a call to "the people ... the divinely appointed arbiters of their own destinies." Even more than Channing, Palfrey, and Smith, Goodell looked to the "public voice" in constitutional interpretation.[171] Such appeals, which paralleled Barnes's insistence on the people's right to interpret the Bible, often carried with them an acceptance of historical argumentation; the people, it was believed, could engage in historical debate.

At the outset, Goodell made clear his interest in a broad historical examination, criticizing proslavery interpreters for their unwillingness to venture "beyond the Constitution ... and the attendant circumstances of its formation and adoption." He observed that those providing proslavery readings neglected the Articles of Confederation, the Declaration, and common law.[172] To be sure, Goodell preferred a strict reading of the Constitution. Challenging the label of the "fugitive slave clause," he asked, "Who, unacquainted with the ... daily passing history of this country, would ever have conceived" it referred to escaped slaves? "No one!" he protested. Goodell held that proper interpretation "rules the Historian ... out of the witness box."[173] He thus purged clauses of their proslavery power or baptized them with antislavery meaning. But Goodell also looked beyond the text. He sought to recover "the intentions of THE PEOPLE" to help discern the spirit of the Constitution, and in doing so, he investigated "external evidences."[174]

Goodell stitched together the Constitution and Declaration and tied both to common law and the "ANTI-SLAVERY 'SPIRIT OF THE AGE.'"[175] He wrote that the Declaration used language "almost to plagiarism – of the popular and widely current anti-slavery literature of those

---

[170] Ibid., 16.
[171] William Goodell, *Views of American Constitutional Law, in Its Bearing upon American Slavery* (Utica, NY, 1844),5.
[172] Ibid., 19.   [173] Ibid., 21.   [174] Ibid., 82, 83, emphasis in original.
[175] Ibid., 105 emphasis in original.

times."[176] Jefferson's text, Goodell argued, indicated that "the claims of LIBERTY and EMANCIPATION" "are of older date."[177] Unlike in the biblical debate, antislavery participants in the constitutional debate often focused on the older of the two canonical documents (the Declaration rather than the Constitution). In comparison to the procedural Constitution, the brevity and makeup of the Declaration made it much easier to mine for antislavery principles.

Advancing a case for continuity, Goodell argued that the Constitution comprised the "outward form, the minutely detailed *provisions* ... the *instruments*, of which [the Declaration's] principles are the living spirit and substance."[178] Positing such congruence allowed him to conclude there had been "no legal slavery in the United States, since the 4th of July, 1776."[179] Just as some proslavery interpreters bound together the Testaments to claim slavery's divine sanction, antislavery interpreters tied together the founding-era texts to protest its legality. Goodell wrote that "even without the amendments," these texts, "considered as a *whole* ... are amply sufficient in their provisions, for either the legislative or judicial abolition of slavery."[180] This historical account demonstrated the Constitution's power – which became clear in light of the Declaration's promises – to cleanse the nation from slavery's stain.

While focused on the Declaration, Goodell did appeal to the framers' expectations of slavery's demise. Although Madison's *Papers* was not in Goodell's bibliography – he thought that the *Papers* housed ghosts that were better left alone – Goodell did use Madison's words. He also presented a list of "the most prominent statesmen," including Madison, Jefferson, Rush, Hamilton, Franklin, and Jay, who believed "SLAVERY was a fast waning system."[181] Both moderate and radical antislavery constitutionalists viewed the recent American past in the same way that a number of antislavery biblical interpreters viewed the primitive Christian past: like the apostles, the founders worked to secure slavery's demise and believed that the cultivation and spread of egalitarian principles would realize that expectation. In both scenarios, emphasizing emancipationist expectations highlighted the reality of slavery's presence in biblical and revolutionary pasts, signaling to slavery's opponents that the favored pasts were not golden ages to restore but troubled eras with universal promises to fulfill. And, in the view of antislavery

---

[176] Ibid., 104.   [177] Ibid., 134, emphasis in original.
[178] Ibid., 138, emphasis in original.   [179] Ibid., 141.
[180] Ibid., 155, emphasis in original.   [181] Ibid., 105, emphasis in original.

constitutionalists, the failure of these promises' fulfillment was attributable to the unexpected rise of the Slave Power. The dual assertion of founding-era expectation and post-founding-era failure laid bare historical difference and change. The founding era was still usable, but only in terms of realizing its expectation rather than recreating its setting.

Spooner provided a similar argument to Goodell's, but one grounded in natural law, which was understood to consist of universal moral principles discerned in the natural world and in human nature. Spooner had given up his career as a Massachusetts lawyer, which he began in defiance of state regulations, and had set up a private mail delivery service in violation of federal statutes. In his 1845 publication, he insisted that there was *"no law but natural law,"* and thus declared American slavery illegal.[182] Spooner narrated the history of slavery's illegality since the colonial period. Like antislavery biblical interpreters who argued that slavery's ancient presence did not signify divine sanction, Spooner wrote that "the fact, that slavery was *tolerated* in the colonies, is no evidence of its legality."[183] Believing *Somerset* had "settled the law both for England and the colonies," he thus held that "there was no *constitutional* slavery" after that decision.[184] Like Goodell, Spooner proposed that the Declaration was "the constitutional law ... for certain purposes" and further contended that neither the Articles of Confederation nor the 1789 state constitutions *"established, or recognized slavery."*[185] State endorsements *"inserted"* since then were deviations, he argued.[186] In short, Spooner posited slavery's continuous unconstitutionality before, and its corrupt presence after, the framing.

In discussing the Constitution, Spooner challenged the interpretive use of historical evidence. He believed that the appeal to original intent belied a proslavery anxiousness about a text that lacked the terms *slave* and *slavery*. Only "by the aid of exterior, circumstantial and historical evidence," he argued, had readers concluded that sanctioning slavery "was the intention of those who *drafted* the constitution."[187] Implying that evidence could be manipulated, Spooner instructed interpreters to focus

---

[182] Lysander Spooner, *The Unconstitutionality of Slavery* (Boston, 1845), 8, emphasis in original. On appeals to natural law in antislavery constitutionalism, see Justin Buckley Dyer, *Natural Law and the Antislavery Constitutional Tradition* (New York, 2012). See also Parker, *Common Law*, 168–218.
[183] Spooner, *Unconstitutionality of Slavery*, 26–27, emphasis in original.
[184] Ibid., 35, emphasis in original. [185] Ibid., 42, 46, emphasis in original.
[186] Ibid., 61, emphasis in original. [187] Ibid., 69, emphasis in original.

on *"words alone."*[188] Pitting one conventional interpretive approach against another, he wrote that no *"historical evidence* shall be admitted to fix upon a statute an unjust or immoral meaning, when the words ... are susceptible of an innocent one."[189] Rather than use context to resolve ambiguities, he measured them against natural law. Spooner believed historical evidence could uphold but not contradict natural law, writing that "no one would have ever dreamed" the labor, three-fifths, importation, and domestic violence clauses "contained so much as an allusion to slavery, had it not been for circumstances extraneous to the constitution."[190] While in the biblical debate some antislavery readers focused on the presence of the word *servant* in the scriptures to suggest that slavery did not exist in more advanced biblical times, in the constitutional debate other antislavery readers focused on the absence of the word *slavery* in the Constitution to posit an original expectation of abolition. Spooner went much further. He believed the word's omission made slaveholding illegal. Like Goodell, he thought proslavery interpreters used historical evidence to twist antislavery meanings.

Rather than avoid Madison's *Papers*, Spooner tried to disqualify them from use. He referenced them to illustrate the nuisance of historical evidence, proposing that "the partizans of slavery resort to the debates ... because the words of the instrument do not sanction [slavery]." He depicted the framers as "mere scriveners of the constitution" and dismissed the idea that their opinions, "then uttered in secret cabal, though now revealed," could shed light on the more determinative "intentions" of the American people.[191] Spooner valued the framers' intent to the extent that it aligned with the ratifiers' intent, and he argued that the people would have burned the Constitution if it had sanctioned slavery.[192] Regardless, he thought the quest to determine framers' intent was a "matter of conjecture and history, and not of law."[193] As in biblical debates, constitutional interpreters signaled the speculative nature of historical investigation when it benefited them. Spooner outlined the problem: "No two of the members of the convention would probably have agreed in their representations of what the constitution really was. No two of the people would have agreed in their understanding."[194] This idea, later vocalized by Frederick Douglass and Theodore Parker, challenged the assumption of founding-era consensus and presented the past as unrecoverable. Early commentators believed Madison's *Papers*

---

[188] Ibid., 71, emphasis in original. [189] Ibid., 74, emphasis in original. [190] Ibid., 105.
[191] Ibid., 139. [192] Ibid., 140. [193] Ibid., 142. [194] Ibid., 143.

would make the founding era more knowable, but the notes' usage often obscured as much as it clarified. Historical investigations, Spooner emphasized, unnecessarily complicated the otherwise straightforward examination of words alone.

Though Spooner decried historical investigation in this publication, he still used a historical narrative, this time of post-founding-era decline, to support the recovery of original antislavery meanings. "Such was the character of the constitution when it was offered to the people," he wrote, and "such is its character still. It cannot have been changed by all the errors and perversions ... of which the government may have since been guilty."[195] Spooner valued developments that aligned with his view of natural law and cast aside continuous practices that did not. Characterizing the latter as decline confirmed that the Constitution was "designed to destroy slavery, whenever its principles should be carried into full effect."[196]

These varied antislavery readings focused attention on the historical realities of contingent change and historical distance. Both moderate and radical constitutionalists observed that unfortunate developments had derailed the nation from the emancipationist course mapped by the founders. Yes, moderates acknowledged, the Constitution included exceptional proslavery provisions, but the framers had expected its general ideas to bring about slavery's end. Radicals granted nothing, arguing that the Constitution implemented the Declaration's antislavery principles and encapsulated common and natural law. While these readers differed in their approach to historical evidence, most insisted that the founding canon contained universal egalitarian ideas. Such efforts seemed to partake of a traditional proclivity to collapse the time separating a corrupted present from a virtuous past. However, these antislavery tales of declension did not demand a return to the founding era. The moderates' acknowledgement of the Constitution's proslavery provisions and the radicals' criticism of the interpretive use of historical sources made it clear that the favored past was a time to learn from rather than live in. And by positing the original expectation of slavery's demise and tracing the contingent rise of the Slave Power, these readings honored a past that anticipated change and lamented a present that unexpected developments had created. In short, these complicated historical understandings combined to register historical distance and signal contingent historical change.

[195] Ibid., 146. [196] Ibid., 149.

MADISON'S PAPERS AND THE CONSTITUTION AS A PROSLAVERY COMPACT

In the mid-1840s, Garrisonians used Madison's *Papers* to dismiss antislavery readings of the Constitution; rather than ignore the ghosts of the past or attempt to repurpose historical apparitions, they brought them out into the open to finally and fully exorcise them. Instead of finding their desired meaning in the Constitution, these abolitionists rejected this sacred text altogether. Garrisonian anticonstitutionalism had developed in relation to perfectionism, nonresistance, and disunionism.[197] Madison's *Papers* buttressed the anticonstitutional stance, facilitating contextual interpretations that confirmed proslavery readings. In short, the *Papers* assisted radical abolitionists' efforts to damn the Constitution as a proslavery compact conceived in a time since past by men now dead.

Wendell Phillips, another Massachusetts man with legal background, led the effort in using Madison's *Papers* to "prove the melancholy fact that willingly, with deliberate purpose, our fathers bartered honesty for gain."[198] Watching one mob try to lynch Garrison and hearing that another mob had murdered Elijah Lovejoy inspired him to sound the call of abolition, as did his wife Ann Terry Greene's reformist passion. Phillips held respect for the rule of law, but Story's decision in the George Latimer case (1842) led Phillips to take an anticonstitutionalist stand, which he maintained until the Civil War.[199] In 1844, he published *The Constitution a Pro-slavery Compact: Or, Selections from the Madison Papers*, which included extracts from the Convention's discussions and the ratification debates. In clear contrast to Spooner, Phillips wrote of the three-fifths, militia, slave trade, fugitive slave, and guarantee clauses: if "they were ambiguous in their terms, a resort to the history of those times would set the matter at rest for ever."[200] Voicing the dominant interpretive view among a range of both biblical and constitutional interpreters, Phillips suggested that a historical explication proved determinative.

Taking direct aim at radical constitutionalists, he proposed to correct those who had "tried to prove that the Constitution makes no compromise

---

[197] On Garrison's use of perfectionism, see Papke, *Heretics in the Temple*, 38–43.
[198] [Wendell Phillips, ed.,] *The Constitution a Pro-slavery Compact: Or, Selections from the Madison Papers, etc.* (New York, 1844), 6.
[199] See Dean Grodzins, "Wendell Phillips, the Rule of Law, and Antislavery Violence," in *Wendell Phillips*, 89–110; and Michael Les Benedict, "Wendell Phillips, the Constitution, and Constitutional Politics before the Civil War," in *Wendell Phillips*, 133–154.
[200] [Phillips], *Constitution a Proslavery Compact*, 5.

with slavery." Such a reading, he argued, required shutting one's eyes to the "clear light of history."[201] Phillips insisted that "*all* that these Debates have to say on the subject" demonstrated "that the Constitution was meant to be, what it has always been esteemed, a compromise between slavery and freedom."[202] The "unbroken practice of every department of the Government" confirmed its status as a "pro-slavery instrument."[203] Phillips stressed continuity, as had Goodell and Spooner, but rather than outline slavery's continuous illegality, he traced its legal sanction since the framing. And regardless of what it "may become a century hence," he wrote, the fact of what "*it is*" required immediate annulment and necessitated the stance, "NO UNION WITH SLAVEHOLDERS!"[204] The current climate of affairs made it difficult for Phillips to envision an antislavery Constitution. Not unlike the radical constitutionalists they opposed, "Garrisonians denied the possibility of legal flexibility."[205] The times called for constitutional revolution rather than evolution.

In an 1847 review of Spooner's work, Phillips again looked to "extraneous and historical evidence" – including Madison's *Papers* – to unveil the Constitution's original proslavery nature.[206] And, in examining relevant clauses, he again made a conventional appeal to the idea that "words, when doubtful and ambiguous, are to be interpreted by the context, by the object sought, and by contemporaneous usage."[207] Phillips continued to tie "the understanding of the nation at the time" of the founding to the government's "uniform practice" since.[208] This extended into the present moment. Phillips noted that "no one has ever denied that the Supreme Court now construes the Constitution in a pro-slavery sense."[209] Deference to the Court's interpretation, which ignored developing popular constitutionalisms, continued to spread during the next decade when politicians looked to the Court's members to solve the crisis over slavery. Phillips's review indicated that historical development confirmed what historical evidence made clear: both the framers and the ratifiers understood the proslavery nature of the Constitution. This reading revealed a past much more foreign than the one depicted by antislavery constitutionalists.

---

[201] Ibid. [202] Ibid., 7, emphasis in original. [203] Ibid., 6.
[204] Ibid., 6, 7, emphases in original.
[205] Wiecek, *Sources of Antislavery Constitutionalism*, 247.
[206] Wendell Phillips, *Review of Lysander Spooner's Essay on the Unconstitutionality of Slavery* (Boston, 1847), 54.
[207] Ibid., 29. [208] Ibid., 31. [209] Ibid., 6.

Phillips granted that the founding generation believed the abolition of the slave trade "would *ultimately* put an end to Slavery," but he found "no evidence of any general expectation that the constitution would have any influence *otherwise* in producing such a result."[210] Furthermore, he observed, "time has shown they were mistaken" and, because the sin remained, "the only way their sons can free themselves, is to disown their fathers' act."[211] Barnes had traced the gradual decline of slavery between the time of Moses and Christ, and Spooner outlined its quick undoing from Mansfield to Madison. Phillips provided an alternative narrative, showing that slavery was so engrained in English and colonial common law that it was taken for granted by the founding generation.

Phillips still cherished the Declaration and used republican language, but he felt no allegiance otherwise to the founding era.[212] In a move reminiscent of liberal Christians who unbound the antiquated Old Testament from the anticipatory New Testament, Phillips severed the tie between the corrupt Constitution and the divine Declaration, which he insisted "had nothing to do with Slavery."[213] In making this kind of canonical division between founding-era texts, Garrisonians like Phillips aimed to rescue timeless truths from a time-bound period that was moving further and further into the past. They stood ready to relinquish the founding era instead of striving to recover it. Let the dead bury the dead, their readings implied.

While providing a narrow Garrisonian reading, Phillips articulated an idea growing in popularity when he stated that the Constitution "is not so much a statute as a great national event, and is to be interpreted not by technical rules, but by liberal reference to the history of the times."[214] At this juncture, most constitutional interpreters agreed with the premise that a proper reading required the use of context. Even those who rejected contextual readings nonetheless strung together "historical fact[s]" to "rebut the historical presumption that the founders ... would desire or even consent legally to recognize ... slavery."[215] Reading the Constitution as a historical creation posed a challenge to Americans, many of whom assumed cultural, societal, and ideological sameness across time. In turn,

---

[210] Ibid., 34, emphasis in original.   [211] Ibid., 34, 35.
[212] See James Brewer Stewart, "Wendell Phillips Is the Subtlest, Stubbornest Fact of the Times," in *Wendell Phillips*, 27–49.
[213] Phillips, *Review*, 87.   [214] Ibid., 35.
[215] Joel Tiffany, *A Treatise on the Unconstitutionality of American Slavery* ... (Cleveland, 1849), 5–6, 20.

reading the Constitution as a historical text inspired clear dismissals but also creative readings of the Constitution.

Constitutional interpretation increased some Americans' perception of historical distance, though this process followed a complicated path, full of divergences and reversals. Disparate antislavery readings of the Constitution relentlessly and consistently drew attention to slavery's clear founding-era presence. One short text's silence spoke volumes.

And yet, as with antislavery biblical readers, constitutional readers' attention to original expectations implied that the crucial issue was not determining whether slavery existed in the favored past but whether that past's luminaries intended the institution to endure. Antislavery interpreters envisioned framers who anticipated a slavery-free future from within a slavery-filled past. Despite their different emphases, both constitutionalists and anticonstitutionalists conceded slavery's presence at the founding, posited an original expectation of change in the form of slavery's abolition, and then identified either corrupt deviation in the spread of slavery and the rise of the Slave Power or irresponsible innovation in the form of antislavery constitutionalism. Opposing arguments about what constituted expected and unexpected change forced new considerations about the nature of historical development. By conjuring a host of competing narratives about the founding era and declension from that time, slavery pushed the specters of historical particularity and contingency beyond mere apparition.

As constitutional debates challenged conventional views of the founding era and traditional ideas of historical movement, biblical debates also continued to draw attention to historical distance. In 1845, Garrison applied his constitutional approach to the Bible. He had once accepted the reigning reading that refused to see temporal dissonance between the biblical past and American present. In 1831, he wrote of God's "Statute Book": "It is immutable; the vicissitudes of time, the waves of revolution, the explosions of empires, cannot abrogate or change one of its acts.... It is of universal application."[216] Over a decade later, the Bible still inspired Garrison, but he had come to appreciate Thomas Paine's interpretive use of reason. Writing that the Bible was "to be examined with the same freedom as any other book," Garrison rejected the idea that "every thing contained within the lids of the Bible is divinely inspired." Instead, he proposed that it "must stand or fall by the test of just criticism, by its reasonableness and utility, by the probabilities of the case, by historical

[216] *Liberator*, April 2, 1831.

confirmation, by human experience and observation, by the facts of science, by the intuition of the spirit." After all, Garrison wrote, echoing Parker, "Truth is older than any parchment, and would still exist, though a universal conflagration should consume all the books in the world." How, he wondered, could the Bible be the people's "master" when it sanctioned the right "to enslave human beings!"[217] Slavery, much more than biblical criticism or even a late reading of *Age of Reason*, shaped Garrison's contention that the Bible must be examined according to reason and historical research. And when historical research exposed its failures and flaws, the Bible, like the Constitution, had to bow before unflinching intuition.

As historical readings spread, some adopted Garrison's radical approach to the Constitution, including America's most famous fugitive slave. Immediately after publishing his autobiography in 1845, Douglass set sail for a speaking tour in the British Isles. In a series of speeches, he spoke his mind before a foreign audience, highlighting the hypocrisy of his home nation, which "proclaimed to the world that all mankind were created freeborn" while also sanctioning slavery.[218] Douglass believed in the Declaration's egalitarian principles, principles for which black revolutionaries had died – "for it was a negro who shed the first blood" – but, like Garrison, he found treachery in uniting under a Constitution that "protected and supported slavery."[219]

Unlike Garrison, Douglass did not apply his critique of the Constitution to the Bible. Faulting a corrupt interpretation of that sacred text, he criticized his so-called Christian nation, where "Bibles and slaveholders go hand in hand," and he discouraged the Free Church of Scotland from accepting funds from their false brethren in the American South.[220]

---

[217] *Liberator*, November 21, 1845.
[218] Frederick Douglass, "Slavery Corrupts American Society and Religion: An Address Delivered in Cork, Ireland, on 17 October 1845," in *The Frederick Douglass Papers, Series One: Speeches, Debates, and Interviews*, ed. John W. Blassingame (New Haven, 1979–1992), 1:46 (hereafter cited as *FDP, Series One*).
[219] Frederick Douglass, "Slavery and America's Bastard Republicanism: An Address Delivered in Limerick, Ireland, on 10 November 1845," in *FDP, Series One*, 1:79, 80. See also, David W. Blight, *Frederick Douglass: Prophet of Freedom* (New York, 2018), 175–176.
[220] Frederick Douglass, "I Am Here to Spread Light on American Slavery: An Address Delivered in Cork, Ireland, on 14 October 1845," in *FDP, Series One*, 1:44. See also Douglass, "Slavery Corrupts," 1:49.

Whereas proslavery readers fused together the Testaments to defend slavery, Douglass united them to condemn it. In one speech, he cited a letter from Stuart wherein the Andover divine instructed his correspondent that Paul had sent back Onesimus "into slavery for life." Douglass referenced a passage in Deuteronomy to argue that because "there was no such thing known among the Jews as slavery for life," Paul must have sent back Onesimus "not as a slave ... but as a beloved brother."[221] He made the same argument in a subsequent speech. "I do not agree ... that the apostle Paul recognised Onesimus as the property of Philemon.... I do not think, that if, under Moses and the prophets, it would have been wrong to return me back to bondage, that in the nineteenth century of the Christian era it would be right to send me back."[222] Even as Douglass collapsed time in his use of the Bible, he appealed to the vast temporal gap separating the biblical past from his American present. The slavery debates cultivated a sense of distance even among those who still assumed contemporaneity with the past.

With other antislavery writers, Douglass believed that although "there never was so great a determination among large numbers to get rid of [slavery] as at the present time," the southern institution had a stranglehold on the United States.[223] In his mind, Douglass's nation was the last great defender of slavery, and slavery was the last great barrier to human progress. In his speeches and writings, along with those of other antislavery thinkers, slavery stood in strange juxtaposition to the apparent spread of antislavery sentiment. He explained slavery's endurance by referencing a "slave-holding religion in the south and a pro-slavery religion in the north." He also referred to a Constitution that "had been prostituted to uphold" slavery. Douglass and other antislavery writers drew attention to "one clause" in particular, "which made it the duty of the several states to return the slave to his master when he escaped from bondage."[224] The nation's lawmakers

---

[221] Frederick Douglass, "Baptists, Congregationalists, the Free Church, and Slavery: An Address Delivered in Belfast, Ireland, on 23 December 1845," *FDP, Series One*, 1:115, 116; Deut. 23:15. See also Douglass, "Slavery and America's Bastard Republicanism," 1:79.
[222] Frederick Douglass, "Emancipation Is an Individual, a National, and an International Responsibility: An Address Delivered in London, England, on 18 May 1846," *FDP, Series One*, 1:260.
[223] Ibid., 1:261.
[224] Frederick Douglass, "American Slavery and Britain's Rebuke of Man-Stealers: An Address Delivered in Bridgwater, England, on 31 August 1846," *FDP, Series One*, 1:364.

soon gave this clause a major renovation, which ignited a new series of interpretive debates. Slavery had brought together constitutional and biblical interpretation, and rhetorical overlap became real overlap as discussants appealed to both the Bible and the Constitution in discussing and debating the Fugitive Slave Law.

5

"The Culture of Cotton Has Healed Its Deadly Wound"

When, in 1850, Moses Stuart echoed Joseph Buckminster in muting historical distance to assert a correspondence between Paul's letter to Philemon and the Fugitive Slave Law, Theodore Parker accepted the reading as historically accurate and then dismissed it as historically dated.[1] Over a decade before, he had cast as past what he perceived to be the historical Jesus's false ideas. Damning Paul's directive seemed a small thing in comparison. Parker had lamented that "men justify slavery out of the New Testament, because Paul had not his eye open to the evil, but sent back a fugitive. It is dangerous," he warned, "to rely on a troubled fountain for the water of life."[2] In the wake of perceived proslavery consolidations, including the Fugitive Slave Law, Parker's reference to Paul's error picked up a new punctuation mark: "Paul had not his eye open to the evil, but sent back a fugitive!"[3] As slavery captured the nation's attention during the 1850s, it raised new questions about the relationship between the imperatives of sacred pasts and the duties of the pressing present. Slavery heightened the historical stakes.

Fellow Transcendentalist Henry David Thoreau addressed these issues in his 1847 speech against a government that warred with Mexico and defended slavery. "What is [the government] but a tradition," he asked, "endeavoring to transmit itself unimpaired to posterity, but each instant

---

[1] See M[oses] Stuart, *Conscience and the Constitution: With Remarks on the Recent Speech of the Hon. Daniel Webster in the Senate of the United States on the Subject of Slavery* (Boston, 1850), 60–61.
[2] Parker, *Discourse of Matters*, 1st ed., 375.
[3] Parker, *Discourse of Matters*, 4th ed., 353.

losing some of its integrity?"⁴ This question captured James Madison's hopes and his fears regarding sacralization. Thoreau criticized individuals such as Daniel Webster, a Cotton Whig, who endlessly deferred to the "men of '87."⁵ Thoreau noted that while those "who know of no purer sources of truth ... stand, and wisely stand, by the Bible and the Constitution," more enlightened souls "gird up their loins ... and continue their pilgrimage towards its fountain-head."⁶ Although Thoreau did not ground his critique in historical facts, his reasoning assumed historical distance, which placed sacred texts and favored pasts beyond the pale of present relevance.

In early 1848, on the heels of the final battles of the Mexican–American War, Unitarian minister Henry Whitney Bellows, another graduate of Harvard Divinity School, demonstrated an almost Garrisonian willingness to slough off the nation's supreme legal source. In an editorial response to an unsuccessful motion to again table abolitionist petitions, Bellows noted that "intelligent and conscientious foes of [slavery], know that its consideration is its condemnation; its trial, its doom." While critical of disunionists, Bellows wrote that "if it be proved that slavery *is* constitutional ... we will cut ourselves loose from that abomination, and take the consequences of dissolution." As with Parker, who had graduated a year ahead of him at Harvard, Bellows proved willing to accept the proslavery interpretation and then leave the Constitution and the South behind.⁷

This opinion reflected a growing realization of temporal distance from the founding era. If, in fact, the Declaration and the Constitution "recognized the lawfulness of negro-slavery ... would it follow," Bellows asked, that "fifty years afterwards, we had no right to see our duty any more clearly than at the time we adopted it?" Pushing such reasoning further back in time, he also queried, "Do we attempt to defend polygamy because it was practiced by the Patriarchs, or to adopt a monarchical form of government because the Gospel instructs us to honor the king[?]" Here, where the overlap between biblical and constitutional debate was both real and rhetorical, Bellows joined other narrators of moral progress in suggesting that "increased light" carried an "obligation to act up to its illumination."⁸

---

⁴ H[enry] D. Thoreau, "Resistance to Civil Government: A Lecture Delivered in 1847," in *Æsthetic Papers*, ed. Elizabeth P. Peabody (Boston, 1849), 189.
⁵ Ibid., 209. ⁶ Ibid., 210. ⁷ *Christian Inquirer*, January 8, 1848, emphasis in original.
⁸ Ibid.

Parker believed this obligation might require scrapping the nation's sacred religious and legal texts. But at the brink of relegating the benighted Constitution to a past that was quickly losing favor among radical abolitionists, Bellows suggested an alternative solution: "we did not make the Constitution and ... we have not sworn not to see its defects, not to awaken to its immoral concessions and compromises, not to labor to have it changed and improved!" Putting distance between the framers and their descendants, he wrote, "We seek to amend the Constitution."[9] Instead of calling for interpretations that aligned with original antislavery expectations, a reading that gained powerful adherents over the next decade, Bellows asserted that historical distance itself justified amendment.

As evident in these and other speeches and writings, the rise of a modern historical consciousness often saw a conviction of progress grow alongside an awareness of historical difference. While some thinkers used that awareness to sanction past actions and beliefs, as did Buckminster and Stuart, others used it to condemn them, as did Parker, Thoreau, and Bellows. Historical consciousness functioned as both a conservative and a progressive force in antebellum America, but whether one used historical insight to defend or damn past actions, the attention to contextual distinctions reified the sense of historical distance.

In this and other antislavery narratives, emphasis on the progress of moral insight, which antislavery thinkers viewed as embodied in the rise of antislavery sentiment, clashed with their fear of the Slave Power's growing strength, which antislavery thinkers traced in the Fugitive Slave Law, fugitive slave cases, and the Kansas–Nebraska Act. These developments checked antislavery hopes of emancipation. In their attempts to reconcile perceptions of general moral progress and peculiar moral decline, antislavery writers increasingly characterized proslavery advances as anachronistic deviations from founding-era expectations and slavery's unexpected spread as antithetical to the egalitarian spirit of the age. All of this indicated just how different the revolutionary past was from the present, signaling it was time to realize the permanent truths that had been enunciated in that transient period. By expressing both their hopes and fears, antislavery writers promoted a historical consciousness attentive to historical distance: sometimes they narrated the growth of moral opposition to slavery since the founding, and sometimes they narrated the Slave

[9] Ibid.

Power's rise since the founding, but in both cases, they pointed to the reality of change over time.

The 1850s debates brought together decades of biblical and constitutional interpretation, turning once-isolated theological uses of the biblical past into an important identifier of political posture, even as they also fueled slavery's constitutionalization. Increasingly, politicians, judges, and ministers turned to the nation's founding era to resolve the slavery crisis. If distance from ancient favored pasts had created historical gaps that were too great to close, and thus those pasts could no longer answer the nation's most pressing problems, then perhaps distance from the more recent golden age could be bridged. Biblical debates did not subside, but ministers joined other Americans in seeking resolutions to the crisis over slavery from their legal, rather than their religious, tradition. As one sarcastic observer noted, "It is a most marvelous thing, what a number of clergymen ... have, all of a sudden, become such great *Constitutional lawyers!*"[10] These developments fixed attention on the Constitution. Around midcentury, as popular constitutionalism spread and the Supreme Court sought to confirm its role as the final arbiter of constitutional meaning, American history became more relevant than biblical history in determining slavery's fate.

The growing focus on the Constitution raised the stakes on debates about sacred texts from favored pasts. In making an argument about founding-era expediency and original expectation, antislavery thinkers indicated both that slavery had loomed large at the founding and that the framers had crafted the Constitution with its eventual abolition in mind. Many antislavery writers and speakers suggested that while enough time had passed to realize that expectation, proslavery advances had quashed these founding-era hopes. Tracking unexpected departures from original expectations revealed contingent change, making it clear that temporal distance separated even the recent, favored founding era from the present. In turn, the historicizing process neared completion. An awareness that all existence bore the marks of time became a real possibility. The antebellum slavery debates shrunk the sphere of the timeless and expanded the realm of the temporal.

---

[10] Ichabod S. Spencer, *Fugitive Slave Law: The Religious Duty of Obedience to Law* (New York, 1850), 26, emphasis in original.

PARKER'S DOUBLE HELIX OF AMERICAN PROGRESS AND CORRUPTION

The dual tracking of the nation's progress and decline was most apparent in the writings Parker began to produce after enduring the ups and downs of a turbulent decade. The furor over *A Discourse on the Transient and Permanent in Christianity* and *A Discourse of Matters Pertaining to Religion* hounded him during the 1840s as Unitarian ministers, including erstwhile friends such as Convers Francis, declined to share the pulpit with him. In 1843, and again in 1844, the Boston Association of Congregational Ministers, an organization of Unitarians with whom Parker had been long affiliated, asked him to resign. Parker refused, despite being emotionally wrenched, and he continued to advance his radical views. After a sojourn in Europe where he met with German biblical critics, including de Wette, Parker returned even more secure in his beliefs. What he observed in Europe also encouraged him to consider issues of social and political reform. And soon enough, Parker had a new pulpit from which to promote his ideas. In January 1845, a group of supportive Unitarians secured Boston's Melodeon for his preaching on Sunday mornings. A year later, they formally organized as the Twenty-Eighth Congregational Society of Boston and installed Parker as pastor. In his first sermon, he mingled past with present, preaching that Jesus exemplified how all should approach God and that Boston churches were behind the times. He had long urged his contemporaries to abandon antiquated beliefs and practices, and now he was ready to train his attention on ridding American society of its archaic system of slavery.[11]

The Mexican–American War served as an impetus for Parker's prolonged engagement in the antislavery cause and encouraged his attention to a kind of double helix of American progress and decline. In February 1848, when American and Mexican representatives signed the Treaty of Guadalupe Hidalgo, it ended a conflict between two nations while fomenting discord between two sections. Territorial gains stirred northern fears of slavery's spread. In March, Parker acknowledged that "at the making of the Constitution, the South out-talked the North" but argued that in the process the framers violated "the ideas of the Revolution," or the "American idea," as he called it, "the idea that each man has unalienable rights." He praised the late John Quincy Adams, the subject of his speech, for going back "to the Declaration ... for the ideas of

---

[11] See Grodzins, *American Heretic*, 295–316, 333–40, 352–481.

the Constitution; yes, back to the Declaration to Human Nature and the Laws of God."[12] As Parker put it in another 1848 speech, "Our national idea out-travels our experience, and all experience. We began our national career by setting all history at defiance.... Our progress since has shown that we were right in refusing to be limited by the past. The political ideas of the nation are transcendant [sic], not empirical." In looking "behind human history ... to human nature," Parker's words echoed those of William Goodell and Lysander Spooner, but he would not explain away proslavery provisions.[13] Adams, he noted, "saw that the Constitution is 'not the work of eternal justice, ruling through the people,' but the work 'of man; frail, fallen, imperfect man.'"[14] By this point, Parker's approach to the Constitution mirrored his approach to the Bible; he highlighted the text's temporal nature and divided its transient teachings from its permanent truths. He set aside proslavery clauses to read the Constitution "as an instrument for the defence of the Rights of man."[15] Slavery, then, was "a lion who rent the Constitution, trampled under foot the Declaration ... and tore the Bible to pieces."[16]

Parker's speech drew the attention of ailing Liberty Party veteran James Birney, whose 1848 letters to Parker show how the slavery crisis encouraged historical research and creative constitutional interpretation. In late March, Birney commended Parker for "wading through the dull historical details" to offer the "first honest attempt to benefit the living by a public impartial account of the dead." He appreciated Parker's measured appraisal of Adams's relationship to slavery and relayed the results of his own historical research on the topic.[17] In October, Birney wrote again, offering to author an article on slavery and the Constitution. During the prior month, Parker's *Massachusetts Quarterly Review* had published a piece by William Bowditch, who cited historical context and continuity to reject Spooner's antislavery reading while also tracking decline in slavery's spread and finding hope that public sentiment "will disregard

---

[12] Theodore Parker, "A Discourse Occasioned by the Death of John Quincy Adams," in *Speeches, Addresses, and Occasional Sermons*, 3 vols. (Boston, 1861–67), 2:266, 271 (hereafter cited as *Speeches*). On the centrality of the revolutionary tradition to Parker's sense of moral self-reliance, see Paul E. Teed, *A Revolutionary Conscience: Theodore Parker and Antebellum America* (Lanham, MD, 2012).

[13] Theodore Parker, "The Political Destination of America, and the Signs of the Times," in *The Collected Works of Theodore Parker*, ed. Frances Power Cobbe, 14 vols. (London, 1863–71), 4:95.

[14] Parker, "Discourse Occasioned by the Death of John Quincy," 2:272.   [15] Ibid., 2:276.

[16] Ibid., 2:278.

[17] James Birney to Theodore Parker, March 27, 1848, Theodore Parker Papers, MHS.

all dead paper barriers."[18] Taking a middle path between radical constitutionalists and Garrisonians, Birney's article would show that the framers, "under a strong persuasion that Slavery would, at once, be on the wane and in the end die out, did not suppose there would be any necessity for abolishing it by *law*." Birney explained that they worked "as if Slavery did not exist" and "engrafted into the Constitution principles of freedom incompatible with it" while at the same time adopting "measures to keep the peace ... during its temporary existence and gradual extinction."[19] This particular argument based on original expectation, which had been made by William Channing, John Palfrey, Gamaliel Bailey, and others, began to find strong favor among many antislavery constitutionalists, who accepted and advanced historical readings of the Constitution.

But far from being rooted out, slavery had been nurtured. In stating that egalitarian ideas "shine out in all our history – I should say, our early history," Parker implied that something had changed.[20] In a December 1848 discourse, he described the change as an unexpected divergence from founding-era expectations. Perhaps with Birney's words in mind, he linked the Free Soil Party's attack on slavery's extension to founders who never "contemplated the extension of slavery beyond the limits of the United States at that time." Indeed, Parker insisted, "in 1787, the best and the most celebrated statesmen were publicly active on the side of freedom. Some thought slavery a sin, others a mistake, but nearly all in the Convention thought it an error." Tracing declension since that time, he argued that pecuniary interests had sapped Americans' moral stamina and muffled antislavery voices. As a result, Parker stated, the original political parties had devolved into groups "their fathers would scarcely recognize."[21] As a writer for the *Christian Register* put it a year later, Madison's *Papers* showed that the framers were not "perpetualists."[22] Parker's narrative, and others like it, made it clear that antebellum America was not the republic of the ancestors.

---

[18] [William I. Bowditch], "Constitutionality of Slavery," *Massachusetts Quarterly Review* 1 (September 1848): 508. See also William I. Bowditch, *The Constitutionality of Slavery* (Boston, 1848).
[19] James Birney to Theodore Parker, October 27, 1848, Theodore Parker Papers, MHS, emphasis in original.
[20] Parker, "Discourse Occasioned by the Death of John Quincy," 2:272.
[21] Theodore Parker, "Some Thoughts on the Free Soil Party, and the Election of General Taylor," in *Speeches*, 2:370.
[22] "The Fathers of the Constitution Not Perpetualists," *Christian Register*, March 24, 1849.

Simply tracing the nation's decline did not signal a new awareness of historical distance, but this was not a standard declension narrative. While the jeremiad had been an American tradition for centuries and narrations of decline from the founding era were coeval with the founding itself, Parker was not nostalgic; he was not hoping to recover the past. He traced decline but also posited the progress of antislavery sentiment. "Where sin abounded," he stated, "grace doth much more abound. There rose up one man," meaning William Lloyd Garrison, "who would not compromise, nor be silent, – who would be heard."[23] Parker anticipated that such new Christs would, like the first, have "some influence on the history of the world."[24] Like Francis Wayland, he linked Christianity to the Declaration but located fulfillment not in founding-era texts but in present ideas and actions. While finding abolitionism's origins in the past, Parker aligned it with his own era, describing it as the "idea of the time" and as consistent with "the spirit of the age."[25] He agreed with Garrison that the current crisis outmatched that of the Revolution. "The revolution in ideas is not over," he asserted, until the "motto 'No more slave territory'" gives way to "'No slavery in America,' nor the corresponding revolution in deeds," he continued, "while a single slave remains in America." He proposed that the "day is not far off" when the natural spread of antislavery sentiment would overcome the unnatural rise of the Slave Power.[26] "What slavery is in the middle of the nineteenth century is quite plain," he observed, "what it will be at the beginning of the twentieth it is not difficult to foresee." Parker implied that slavery belonged to a ruder era. He conceded that "the slave power ha[d] gained a great victory" in the election of Zachary Taylor but declared that "one more such will cost its life."[27] The scalpel of abolitionism would soon cut out the cancerous tumor of slavery.

While anticipating eventual triumph, slavery qualified Parker's view of America as exceptional. "Men will be astonished in the next century to learn that the 'model republic,' had such an affection for slaveholders," he stated.[28] America sometimes seemed more ancient than modern to him. Citing a deed of sale in which a slave had been sold to President Taylor, Parker demonstrated a keen sense of historical distance: "If this document had been discovered among some Egyptian papyri, with the date 1848 before Christ, it would have been remarkable as a sign of the times. In a republic, nearly four thousand years later, it has a meaning which some

---

[23] Parker, "Some Thoughts on the Free Soil Party," 2:375.   [24] Ibid., 2:378.
[25] Ibid., 2:377, 383.   [26] Ibid., 2:385.   [27] Ibid., 2:386.   [28] Ibid., 2:390.

future historian will appreciate."[29] Parker's statement captures the antislavery move to mark slavery as an anachronistic institution, a move that further demarcated the past, both ancient and recent, from the present. This antislavery dialectic antiquated and historicized the peculiar institution and whatever supported it, including favored pasts and sacred texts.

Parker's narrative suggests a profound ambivalence about change since the founding era. He believed that the lamentable rise of the Slave Power was only matched by the glorious spread of antislavery sentiment. On the one hand, he depicted the sale of slaves as a barbaric archaic practice. On the other hand, he described abolitionism as in step with the spirit of his age. This double helix imposed an order onto history, but one that allowed for change. Coupled with the idea that slavery undermined the exalted status of the American republic, it created a sense of the contingent nature of historical movement. In Parker's rendering, the Slave Power fought an uphill battle. By granting slavery a comfortable place in the biblical and revolutionary pasts, and then stressing its awkward existence in the present, he drew attention to historical distance and used it to damn the peculiar institution. Parker expressed concern about "another compromise," but remained certain of the ultimate triumph of the American idea.[30]

WEBSTER'S "JUDGMENT THAT THE SOUTH IS RIGHT, AND THE NORTH IS WRONG"

But then came the Compromise of 1850 and its Fugitive Slave Law, and the double helix of national progress and decline continued. The new law gave federal teeth to the Fugitive Slave Act of 1793, which was meant to enlist free-state authorities in the effort to return fugitives to their slave-state masters. While *Prigg* v. *Pennsylvania* (1842) had privileged the 1793 act over a contradicting antislavery state law, it also opened the door for northern states to create personal liberty laws that undermined the same. In turn, the new 1850 law undercut the state laws by imposing a fine and reward system that encouraged federal marshals and local officers to assist in returning fugitives to their masters. The new law also stipulated fines and imprisonment for those caught assisting fugitives. Some northerners interpreted this as a move to nationalize slavery. The fugitive slave cases that followed further fanned the flames of antislavery discontent while also giving rise to apologists. The 1850 law's apologists and its opponents

[29] Ibid., 2:392. [30] Ibid., 2:396–98, quotation on 396.

both authored accounts that drew attention to historical distance from biblical and American pasts.

In the midst of senatorial debates about the law, Daniel Webster spoke on its behalf. In the 1830s, he had warred against nullification and slavery before adopting a more conciliatory stance with the South and its institution during the 1840s. Then, on March 7, 1850, while proclaiming allegiance to union over section, the Massachusetts senator delivered a speech in support of the new compromise and its attendant law.[31] He outlined a position that accorded well with the views of moderate antislavery constitutionalists, who conceded slavery's legality as a state institution while emphasizing federal restrictions against its spread.

Webster explained his position through biblical and constitutional explication, which was symptomatic of the interpretive convergence that accompanied debate over the new law. He located slavery "among the Jews," Greeks, and Romans, and "found no injunction against" the practice "in the teachings of the Gospel of Jesus Christ, or of any of his apostles."[32] Seeing correspondence between the biblical past and the southern present, he noted that slaveholders "take things as they are."[33] Webster likely had in mind the circumstantial argument that slavery's very existence manifested its propriety as a southern institution. In contrast to antislavery readers who argued that ancient allowance did not imply divine sanction, many of slavery's defenders equated the institution's endurance with providential approval.[34] The difference between these positions hinged on whether circumstances shaped and even obscured God's revelation, or whether they simply reflected God's will. In holding the former position, some antislavery writers began to emphasize the role of human actors in bringing about emancipation. Webster, like other northern moderates, thought abolitionists went too far in this regard.

---

[31] Daniel Webster, *Speech of Hon. Daniel Webster, on Mr. Clay's Resolutions, in the Senate of the United States, March 7, 1850* (Washington, DC, 1850), 6. On the sectional nature of Webster's unionist appeals, see Harlow Sheidley, *Sectional Nationalism: Massachusetts Conservative Leaders and the Transformation of America, 1815–1836* (Boston, 1998), 141–47; and Christopher Apap, "The Genius of Latitude: Daniel Webster and the Geographical Imagination in Early America," *Journal of the Early Republic* 30 (Spring 2010): 201–23.

[32] Webster, *Speech*, 11, 13.   [33] Ibid., 14.

[34] In the 1850s, white southerners followed John C. Calhoun and Richard Fuller in developing this argument. See, for example, Bledsoe, *Essay on Liberty and Slavery*; and E. N. Elliott, ed., *Cotton Is King, and Pro-slavery Arguments: Comprising the Writings of Hammond, Harper, Christy, Stringfellow, Hodge, Bledsoe, and Cartwright, on This Important Subject* (Augusta, GA, 1860).

He found them "too impatient to wait for the slow progress of moral causes in the improvement of mankind."[35] If Christ and his apostles had planted the seeds of slavery's destruction, the harvest season had not yet arrived. Humans could not force God's hand.

While Webster's proof-texting approach to the Bible bore the markers of traditional thinking, he showed more historical awareness in turning attention to "the state of sentiment ... at the time this Constitution was adopted."[36] His "historical research" of "authentic records" indicated that "slavery did exist," but his examination of statements "from all the eminent men of the time" also demonstrated "the clearest expression of their opinion that slavery was an evil."[37] Webster believed "Mr. Madison" included the slave trade clause because the founders "thought that slavery could not be continued ... if the importation of slaves were made to cease." He further proposed that Madison's contempt for the idea of property in man explained why the word "slave, or slavery, is not used in the Constitution."[38] In apparent contradiction of his central argument, Webster even noted that "the Constitution does not require that 'fugitive slaves' shall be delivered up" and pointed to Congress's "contemporaneous" passage of the Northwest Ordinance to support this point.[39] In describing as "historical truths" the framers' original expectation of emancipation, Congress's power to prevent slavery's spread, and the Convention's intent to "leave slavery, in the States, as they found it," Webster produced an account containing the basic elements of moderate antislavery constitutionalism.[40] He seemed to suggest that the framers had both sowed the seeds of slavery's demise into the Constitution and expected the slow nurturing of historical change to bring them to fruition.

In tracing changes in sentiment since the founding era, however, Webster's narrative departed from the antislavery view of historical development. He described southerners' growing support for slavery as natural, while characterizing northerners' increasing disdain for slavery as dangerous. Because of their "disinclination to perform, fully, their constitutional duties in regard to the return of persons bound to service," Webster judged "that the South is right, and the North is wrong."[41] Webster had provided a strict reading of the importation clause in his previous mention of Madison's careful word choice, but here he left no doubt that it referred to fugitive slaves. He was ready to support the

---

[35] Webster, *Speech*, 16. [36] Ibid., 17. [37] Ibid., 17, 18. [38] Ibid., 19. [39] Ibid., 20.
[40] Ibid., 22, 23. [41] Ibid., 47.

Fugitive Slave Law "to the fullest extent."[42] While he agreed that present circumstances placed the North in a situation in which "it never did expect to find itself when they agreed to the compact," Webster blamed the present crisis on the contingent development of northern agitation instead of that of southern intransigence.[43] He illuminated the founding era through historical explication, and although he discovered an expectation of slavery's dissolution, he argued that the North had to recognize the proslavery provisions that post-founding-era events bolstered rather than banished. In conclusion, Webster outlined the blessings resulting from the "great, popular, constitutional Government," blessings, his narrative implied, that abolitionist actions threatened to spoil.[44]

Webster's speech showed that antislavery writers were not the only ones lamenting change since the founding era. He observed the unexpected advances of the Slave Power but agreed with proslavery southerners and other moderate northerners who viewed abolitionist sentiment as a more dangerous threat to the original compromise. Divergent accounts of change signaled to each section that at least a portion of the nation had turned from its promising path. In emphasizing change from the founding era, narratives such as Webster's drew attention to contingent development and highlighted the historical distance that historical changes produce.

STUART'S DIRECTIVE TO KEEP THE "BAD BARGAIN"

During the dark days surrounding Webster's speech, Parker's optimism seemed to waver. In a speech given on March 25, 1850, at Boston's Faneuil Hall, he described the conflict of the age as one between "the party of Slavery" and "the party of Freedom."[45] Webster had struck a blow in favor of the former with his speech, which Parker compared to "the act of Benedict Arnold!"[46] In Parker's updated historical narration, support for the Fugitive Slave Law followed a string of proslavery victories. The Constitution was neutral in this account. Parker traced proslavery advances in 1803 (the Louisiana Purchase), 1819 (the acquisition of Florida), 1820 (the western expansion of slavery), 1845 (the Texas annexation), and 1848 (the Mexican cession).[47] But 1850 marked a new

---

[42] Ibid., 48. [43] Ibid., 55. [44] Ibid., 64.
[45] Theodore Parker, "A Speech at a Meeting of the Citizens of Boston in Faneuil Hall," in *Speeches*, 3:2.
[46] Ibid., 3:33. [47] Ibid., 3:6–7.

low point. Even Wendell Phillips, in his response to Webster's speech, noted that after slavery's "seeming death of 1787," it "was resuscitated by Cotton and Compromises."[48] Parker outlined the slave population's rise from two hundred thousand in 1750 to "three millions" in 1850 and then projected possible retrogression in the future: "In 1950, let Mr. Webster's counsels be followed, there will be thirty millions."[49] Parker knew how to create a useful past in order to forecast a useful future, and that future looked bleak. Perhaps the proslavery compromise would not translate into antislavery success after all.

Near his speech's conclusion, Parker turned to the Constitution, not to condemn its creators but to warn their political descendants. While attentive to the sacred text's errors, he attributed the framers' failures to the limitations of their age. While explaining that they "did a wrong," he also asked, "Was it an error in our fathers; not barely a wrong – was it a sin? No, not in them; they knew it not. But what in them to establish was only an error, in us to extend or to fester is a sin!"[50] This sense of historical progress – by which errors became sins – could encourage a sympathetic approach to the past, though it also placed it on a lower moral standing in relation to the present. While Parker believed that, like Paul, the framers' eyes were not open to evil, developments in moral insight made his contemporaries culpable. Webster merited greater condemnation than Paul or Madison.

Presbyterian minister Sylvester Graham responded to Webster with a similar historical narrative. Referencing the "logic of historical facts," he bound the Declaration and Constitution to the "common ideas ... of the whole people," who, he wrote, "*regarded slavery as an evil.*"[51] He also cited Madison to argue that the fugitive slave clause itself indicated the "intent of the framers and adopters" to prohibit slavery's extension, "with an ulterior view to its final extermination."[52] Adding to an increasingly popular view, Graham suggested the clause was intended as a "temporary expedient," which aligned with his idea that slavery was a "*conditional moral necessity,*" an "*accommodated institution*" that "*must* pass away."[53] In contrast to the framers' expectations, he noted, new slave territories and states had been admitted. These proslavery victories

---

[48] Wendell Phillips, *Review of Webster's Speech on Slavery* (Boston, 1850), 5. Parker's copy of this pamphlet is housed at the Boston Public Library.
[49] Parker, "Speech at a Meeting of the Citizens of Boston," 3:35. [50] Ibid.
[51] S[ylvester] Graham, *Letter to the Hon. Daniel Webster, on the Compromises of the Constitution* (Northampton, MA, 1850), 4, 5, 9, emphasis in original.
[52] Ibid., 8. [53] Ibid., 9, 16, 17, emphasis in original.

opposed what Graham observed as the "progress of the human mind." In an appendix, he quoted Thomas Jefferson on the need for laws to match that progress, which, he argued, made it "*a moral impossibility*" for New Englanders to execute the fugitive slave clause. Graham saw in southern proslavery hostility a sharp departure from founding-era expectations while he found perfect "harmony" between those expectations and present northern antislavery sentiment.[54] The morality of that sentiment gave the people the right to "alter, and even abolish the Constitution, whenever it shall fail to accomplish the objects for which it was framed."[55] With Parker, Graham's narrative stressed historical limitation *and* expectation, as well as historical decline *and* progress, which supported his stance that the common people should be constitutional arbiters.

After these attacks on Webster's speech, some sprang to the senator's defense, including Stuart, America's most eminent biblical scholar, who had continued to train students in biblical exegesis at Andover until his resignation in 1848. In *Conscience and the Constitution* (1850), the Congregationalist made clear his intention "to support every shade of sentiment" in Webster's speech.[56] Following the senator's lead, Stuart provided readings of the nation's religious *and* legal texts.

First, Stuart established "the great *antiquity* of slavery."[57] While this appeal had become precarious in light of findings that made ancient words and deeds seem immoral rather than immortal, Stuart remained committed to the Bible as a whole. He framed ancient actions in a positive light, noting that slaves in Abrahamic times were "generally treated ... more as human beings."[58] He granted that their bondwomen often served as concubines but, like proslavery interpreters, separated slavery from polygamy, arguing that the latter "[does] not concern us ... . Every man's conduct," he noted "is to be judged ... by the light he has, and by the age and circumstances in which he lived."[59] The debate over slavery was pushing Stuart closer to the view that over time, humans gained greater understanding of God's revelation. Stuart began to recognize the peculiarities of a biblical past, and his readings drew attention to its estrangement from the current era.

---

[54] Ibid., 16–17, quotation on 17, emphasis in original. See also Charles Dickinson, *A Discourse Delivered Fast Day, March 27th, 1850, on the Compromise Question* (Birmingham, CT, 1850), 6–7.
[55] Graham, *Letter to the Hon. Daniel Webster*, 14.
[56] Stuart, *Conscience and the Constitution*, 7.   [57] Ibid., 23, emphasis in original.
[58] Ibid., 24.   [59] Ibid., 25.

In the face of a growing sense of distance from biblical times, Stuart tried to recover permanent principles for present use, and he did so with historical reasoning. This produced a somewhat confused reading. Stuart did not believe the Old Testament sanctioned American slavery. As Molly Oshatz argues, slavery forced him to recognize its archaic nature.[60] He wrote that "none can now ... purchase slaves ... on the ground of Mosaic permission."[61] But Stuart still used the Bible to defend the Fugitive Slave Law. He applied the argument of expediency to Moses's actions, writing that the ancient figure recognized "legislation could not change the established internal structure of a nation ... in a day."[62] While Stuart highlighted historical particularities to undermine antislavery uses of Deuteronomy 23, he also collapsed time by writing that "if Abolitionists are right in their position, then Moses is greatly in the wrong."[63] In his attempt to demonstrate that slavery was not always and everywhere a sin, Stuart suggested that despite significant temporal differences and vast historical distances, the Old Testament stood on the side of fugitive-seeking slaveholders. He argued that the "*moral* and *spiritual*" aspects of the Mosaic Law "are unrepealed and irrepealable," and he seemed to think this law had relevance in the mid-nineteenth-century debate over slavery.[64]

Stuart also applied the argument of expediency to the New Testament. While he believed "the Saviour uttered sentiments, which, in their ultimate effects, must abolish ... all slavery," he found no evidence that Christ or his apostles had meddled "with then existing relations."[65] This argument paralleled those of Wayland, his one-time student, and Channing, his erstwhile Unitarian correspondent. But Channing had concluded that enough time had passed to cultivate antislavery seeds sowed in New Testament times. Even Wayland, who opposed the Fugitive Slave Law, was slowly moving toward that conclusion. Stuart, on the other hand, ignored historical distance and instead contrasted Christ's "policy ... from that of the immediate Emancipationists." He granted that Christ had left "the completion of the work to time," but Stuart did not believe that eighteen hundred years was sufficient to nourish the antislavery seeds Christ had planted.[66] Despite a keen awareness of historical difference, Stuart seemed to suggest that little, with regard to slavery, had changed since Jesus introduced the gospel.

---

[60] Oshatz, *Slavery and Sin*, 108.   [61] Stuart, *Conscience and the Constitution*, 36.
[62] Ibid., 29.   [63] Ibid., 31, 35.   [64] Ibid., 43, emphasis in original.   [65] Ibid., 45.
[66] Ibid., 46.

Stuart made a similar argument in regard to Paul.[67] He used de Wette to build a contextual case showing that the apostle did not believe conversion changed the status of servants.[68] He also returned to the oft-debated New Testament passage wherein Paul sends Onesimus, an escaped slave and recent Christian convert, back to his master, Philemon. Using historical reasoning, Stuart dismantled the claim, put forth by figures such as Channing and Frederick Douglass, that Onesimus was something other than a slave. He then asserted that unlike the abolitionists, "Paul's Christian *conscience* would not permit him to injure the vested rights of Philemon."[69] While Stuart was attentive to context, his orthodoxy demanded a literal reading of the text and a unilateral application of its moral lessons. His comparisons conflated time: "if the great apostle himself were to reappear on earth ... he would unquestionably incur the danger of being mobbed."[70] Stuart failed to notice how his historical distinctions might undermine his historical analogies. As those distinctions became increasingly important in interpretive debates, they drove a sense of distance further into participants' consciousness.

While slavery encouraged Stuart's attention to historical difference, the institution's clear presence in the ancient past and American present seemed to blind him from seeing how changes in governance might allow Americans to do what the apostles could not: agitate for laws to abolish slavery. He emphasized that the political situation of the early Christians was "entirely different ... from our own," but whereas figures such as Wayland contrasted ancient and American governance to assert the possibility of popular legislation – "*we make our own laws*" – Stuart urged Americans to follow the example of the apostles, who "thought it best to wait."[71] The lesson of history, in his view, was a call to inaction rather than action. Traditional interpretive assumptions about the applicability of biblical ideas across time persisted among participants in these debates even as those participants highlighted historical distance and change.

While offering a detailed biblical exegesis, Stuart looked to a different canonical text to settle the debate. In what might have been a surprising concession, he stated that "even if the Bible had neither said nor implied

---

[67] Stuart cited a number of New Testament passages, including Eph. 6:5–9; Col. 4:1, 8:22–25; 1 Tim. 6:1–4; Titus 2:9, 10; and 1 Pet. 2:18.
[68] Stuart, *Conscience and the Constitution*, 52. See 1 Cor. 7:20–24.
[69] Stuart, *Conscience and the Constitution*, 61, emphasis in original.   [70] Ibid., 54.
[71] Ibid., 55, 56; Fuller and Wayland, *Domestic Slavery*, 105, emphasis in original.

anything in relation to this whole matter, the solemn *compact* which we have made... to deliver up fugitives... is enough to settle the question of *legal* right."⁷² Even orthodox biblical scholars grasped that the constitutional debate mattered most in the 1850s political climate.

Stuart emphasized the constitutionality of state sovereignty and dismissed those, such as Parker, who valued conscience over Constitution. He used historical investigation to recover the relevant views of past politicians, just as he had with past apostles, and then collapsed temporal distance to claim their consent on the matter. Stuart wrote that if Paul "were now among us," his life would be in danger. Stuart further noted that if John Jay could see the actions of his antislavery son, William Jay, the founding father would look on "with a mixture of sorrow and of frowning."⁷³ One pseudonymous reviewer of Stuart's publication went even further in suggesting that the framers would suffer alongside Paul if "they were to come again in the flesh."⁷⁴ These controlled conjurings collapsed time and space, implying that disparate groups from distinct pasts sanctioned the new law on fugitive slaves. Stuart accepted historical discourse as determinative, but while Parker's religious beliefs and political motivations encouraged historical sensibility to the determinations of change over time, Stuart's views sought to constrain the same.

In an awkward conclusion, Stuart described slavery as "a glaring contradiction of the first and fundamental principle, not only of the Bible ... but of our Declaration."⁷⁵ Earlier in the text, the practitioner of the grammatical-historical method had referenced the phrasing of the fugitive slave clause to soften the dissonance between the Declaration and the Constitution.⁷⁶ Now, he tied the New Testament and the Declaration to the spirit of the revolutionary age, writing that the golden rule was "the unquestionable index of all but universal American feeling in 1776." Stuart held that it was "universally understood among all the States who formed [the Constitution], that slavery was to be got rid of," but only "as soon as it could be done peaceably."⁷⁷ With Webster, Stuart argued that the time had not arrived in large part because abolitionism had delayed emancipation by "at least half a century."⁷⁸ Such narratives of the nation's history suggested that abolitionism, not the so-called Slave

---

⁷² Ibid., 32, emphasis in original. ⁷³ Ibid., 63, 64. See also 71 and 98.
⁷⁴ Amicus, *Slavery among the Puritans. A Letter to the Rev. Moses Stuart* (Boston, 1850), 35.
⁷⁵ Stuart, *Conscience and the Constitution*, 103–04. In his argument against slavery from the New Testament, he relied on Matt. 22:39, 7:12; Acts 17:26; Rom. 3:29; and Eph. 2:14.
⁷⁶ Stuart, *Conscience and the Constitution*, 57. ⁷⁷ Ibid., 110. ⁷⁸ Ibid., 109.

Power, had upset original antislavery expectations.[79] Like Parker, Stuart believed "the spirit of freedom is waking the world to new life" but maintained that the North remained bound "so long as the Article in the Constitution remains," for, he insisted, "even a *bad* bargain must be kept."[80]

PARKER'S "'SHORT AND EASY METHOD'"

The interpretive debate over the Fugitive Slave Law incited further discussion. Some discussants offered a more simplistic version of Stuart's argument. For example, in a late 1850 discourse given after the law was passed in September, Episcopalian Nathaniel Wheaton of Connecticut used the language – but not the method – of historical interpretation. Insisting that the circumstances surrounding Paul's epistle to Philemon exactly paralleled the situation in modern America, Wheaton wondered if God might have had Paul write in anticipation of the present crisis. In this and similar accounts, the apostle's message transcended time. Whereas Parker believed new light obliged Americans to free slaves, the only historical difference Wheaton identified – a compact to return fugitives – made Americans' obligation to the enslavers even greater. Wheaton echoed Stuart: put "faith in *time and progress*" and, in the meantime, keep the "sacred" compact.[81] In these accounts, progress pitted God's providences against abolitionist actions.

In a January 1851 editorial, the venerable Charles Hodge also appealed to Providence – "all events depending on human agency are under [God's] control" – to sanction slavery's presence.[82] In 1820, Hodge had traveled to New England to consult with Stuart about the Unitarian threat. Now, over thirty years later, he voiced his agreement with the Congregationalist in the *Biblical Repertory and Princeton Review*. Hodge rejected claims that slavery was sinful and argued that the Fugitive Slave Law was neither unconstitutional nor unscriptural. The bulk of his editorial focused on obedience to government as a scriptural injunction, though he did find

---

[79] See also B. R. Allen, *The Responsibilities and Duties of American Citizens* (Boston, 1851), 24.

[80] Stuart, *Conscience and the Constitution*, 71, 81, 113, emphasis in original.

[81] N[athaniel] S. Wheaton, *A Discourse on St. Paul's Epistle to Philemon: Exhibiting the Duty of Citizens of the Northern States in Regard to the Institution of Slavery* (Hartford, CT, 1851), quotations on 27 and 28, emphasis in original.

[82] Charles Hodge, "Conscience and the Constitution," *The Princeton Review* 23 (January 1851): 138.

room for those who felt the law conflicted with their conscience to peacefully pursue its repeal.[83] While indicating that he would leave the question of the law's constitutionality "in the hands of the constituted authorities," he could not resist asserting that the principle in question had remained the same since 1793. Turning to the biblical question, Hodge agreed with both Stuart's argument that "the law of Deuteronomy has no application to the present case," and his insistence that Old Testament precedent conflicted with abolitionist demands.[84] Hodge, who had had long ago accepted historical readings as crucial, continued to apply scripture in ways that set aside the historical distance that those readings revealed.

While most accepted Stuart's reasoning, a number of antislavery writers did not. Some of their accounts, like Wheaton's, offered surface-level historical readings to argue that differing circumstances disqualified biblical precedents, while at the same time insisting that the Bible's universal moral principles condemned slavery.[85] William Jay provided a nominal historical reading to reject Old Testament precedent and to tie abolitionists to biblical figures such as Paul and to founding figures such as his father, John Jay.[86] More seasoned participants offered more sophisticated interpretations. Even though Spooner again condemned the historical conversation, which seemed to make the Constitution a text of "historians, and not the people," he made a historical case that the fugitive slave clause did not apply to slaves.[87] He even used Madison's *Papers* to show that Americans only later applied the clause to slavery. Once again, Spooner's constitutional reading emphasized original antislavery meanings, traced national decline in the form of proslavery progress, and insisted on the right of the people to "decide all constitutional questions."[88]

William Bowditch, although he still disagreed with Spooner on the nature of the Constitution, also continued to appeal to public sentiment. In a speech-turned-pamphlet, he answered the question of whether "slaveholding is *always* wrong" in the affirmative, regardless of

---

[83] Ibid., 132–56.   [84] Ibid., 129.
[85] See, for example, G[eorge] W[illiam] Perkins, *Prof. Stuart and Slave Catching* (West Meriden, CT, 1850); A[bijah] P[erkins] Marvin, *Fugitive Slaves: A Sermon* (Boston, 1850); and K[azlitt] Arvine, *Our Duty to the Fugitive Slave: A Discourse* (Boston, 1850).
[86] William Jay, *Reply to Remarks of Rev. Moses Stuart* (New York, 1850).
[87] Lysander Spooner, *A Defence for Fugitive Slaves, against the Acts of Congress of February 12, 1793, and September 18, 1850* (Boston, 1850), 55.
[88] Ibid., 39.

"circumstances."[89] This raised the inevitable issue of biblical sanction, which Bowditch addressed with a rather unsettling idea that underlay the Protestant position that all could read the Bible: "we admit that there is no existing authority capable of telling us with certainty which of these conflicting interpretations of Scripture is the true one."[90] As occurred in constitutional interpretation, Bowditch questioned the quest to determine original meanings. He proceeded to mock Stuart's temporally conflating view that "Jesus Christ, if now on earth, would be willing ... to act as United States Commissioner, and St. Paul as United States Marshal."[91] Bowditch placed his faith neither in sacred texts nor in the government or political parties, but in changing public sentiment, which could make proslavery laws "dead, though living on a statute book."[92] While Spooner encouraged popular constitutionalism as a means of making the Constitution antislavery, Bowditch anticipated a change in popular sentiment that would render the Constitution, or at least its proslavery clauses, obsolete.

Parker seemed to be moving in Bowditch's direction on this matter. In his view, the Bible and the Constitution had been written by good men who could not escape the erroneous notions of their times. In a speech delivered in late May at a convention of the New England Anti-Slavery Society (NEASS), Parker somberly retraced the advances of the Slave Power in the conflict between the "idea of Freedom" and the "idea of Slavery."[93] Growing ever more ambivalent about change, Parker found "much to discourage a man who believes in the progress of his race." He lamented that "since the adoption of the Constitution, protected by that shield, mastering the energies of the nation, and fighting with that weapon, slavery has been continually aggressive."[94] Parker no longer viewed the Constitution as neutral. Instead, it signaled a fatal first step in the proslavery rise to political prominence. He still held that slavery and its spread was out of step with the general sentiment of the nineteenth century. The current state of affairs reminded him of "the spirit which prevailed in the Roman Senate, A. D. 62, when about four hundred slaves were crucified."[95] Unlike Stuart's historical comparisons, Parker's were not meant to condemn the actions of a particular group or confirm the

---

[89] William I. Bowditch, *The Anti-Slavery Reform, Its Principle and Method* (Boston, 1850), 4–5, emphasis in original.
[90] Ibid., 8. [91] Ibid., 9. [92] Ibid., 17.
[93] Theodore Parker, "A Speech at the New England Anti-Slavery Society Convention in Boston," in *Speeches*, 3:41–42.
[94] Ibid., 3:46. [95] Ibid., 3:43.

relevance of ancient deeds but rather to evidence the regressed and aberrant state of the American nation.

Parker held out hope that the people of Massachusetts would condemn Webster's act, which he again compared to "the treachery of Benedict Arnold."[96] He did not believe that the Bay State would "efface Lexington and Bunker Hill from her memory."[97] Parker, who grew up in Lexington as the grandson of a commander who had fought the British there, still knew how to use the Revolutionary past.[98]

He continued to make use of favored pasts but had given up any necessary allegiance to their sacred texts. Proposing "a 'short and easy method' with Professor Stuart, and all other men who defend slavery out of the Bible," he noted that "if the Bible defends slavery, it is not so much better for slavery, but so much the worse for the Bible."[99] Parker did not discriminate among biblical texts or between patriarchs, prophets, and apostles. "If Christianity supports American slavery, so much the worse for Christianity," he declared. "We all know it does not .... But if Paul was an apologist for slavery, so much the worse for Paul."[100] Parker's wry comment carried awful weight; if and when the traditional canon contradicted conscience, conscience trumped canon. Rather than argue, as Albert Barnes had, that Paul had instructed Philemon to receive Onesimus as a freeman in Christ, or, as Channing and Wayland had, that Paul had inculcated principles meant to abolish slavery, Parker was willing to grant the accuracy of Stuart's reading and then reject its relevance as a moral guide in the present.

What, though, of Stuart's enlistment of the Constitution? Parker made it clear that he was no respecter of founding documents. While he honored Salmon Chase and William Seward, he also called on them to go further in putting an end to slavery, warning that "if the Constitution ... will not allow it, there is another Constitution that will."[101] Instead of struggling to salvage the nation's founding religious and legal texts through creative interpretations, Parker stood ready to admit that these documents had worn out their welcome in the antislavery nineteenth century. When historical awareness functioned to maintain the status quo, Parker set aside historical insight in favor of conscience.

---

[96] Ibid., 3:58.   [97] Ibid., 3:64.
[98] On Parker's ties to Lexington, and his appeals to that legacy, see Teed, *A Revolutionary Conscience*, xv, 1–13, 123–24, 133–58, 182–83, 200.
[99] Parker, "Speech at the New England Anti-Slavery Society," 3:68.   [100] Ibid., 3:79.
[101] Ibid., 3:85.

While reaching different conclusions, Stuart and Parker each provided historical readings of the Bible and the Constitution that drew attention to real temporal distances dividing biblical times from modern and also highlighted real historical changes separating the founding era from the present. Although Stuart set aside historical distinctions to condemn the abolitionists, he highlighted these distinctions in defending Moses's and the apostles' actions as expedient. As debates over slavery uniquely forced new kinds of confrontations with the past, those debates also induced Stuart to conclude that sacred writers and actors, and not just God, had accommodated in their teachings. Stuart, and even Webster, granted that Christ and his apostles had inculcated principles meant to extinguish slavery's searing flames and that the framers had expected the clanging of chains to eventually cease. However, newfangled abolitionism had thwarted these emancipationist expectations. But even in negating the applicative importance of historical distance, such narratives inevitably drew attention to the realities of historical difference and change.

Parker made more direct use of temporal distance. Historical criticism had nourished his understanding of religious and moral progress, which allowed him to concurrently accept Stuart's reading as historically sound and dismiss recovered biblical teachings and constitutional imperatives that sanctioned proslavery laws as dated. In Parker's view, the sin of slavery was not in the unenlightened Christian and founding fathers whose eyes were shut to evil. Instead, it was in their illuminated descendants, who knew better. His narration of proslavery progress conflicted with his emphasis on the spread of antislavery sentiment, suggesting that historical movement was a contingent process. Parker resolved the contrasting developments by depicting proslavery actions as anachronistic. All of this suggested that substantial historical changes had created a gulf between Americans and their favored biblical and revolutionary pasts. While his observations cast a shadow on America's exceptional status, Parker remained convinced that the nineteenth century was an age of freedom, an age in which he and his contemporaries could fulfill the promises of the fathers. So did Frederick Douglass.

DOUGLASS AND THE "PRO-SLAVERY INSTRUMENT"

In the spring of 1847, months after obtaining his freedom, Douglass returned from a speaking tour and began to explore new means of spreading his antislavery message. Before the close of the year, the same English friends who had purchased his freedom helped him establish the *North*

Star. T. Gregory Garvey argues that Douglass created the paper as a strategic move to claim structural equality on the public stage and to shift the center of attention from himself to the Constitution. In other words, Garvey suggests, Douglass wanted to be a participant in, rather than just an object of, debate. Garrison, Douglass's mentor, had elected to "come out" from traditional religious and political institutions, but that was not a choice Douglass could make. In order to embrace come-outerism, one had to be firmly situated within American society and Douglass, a free black man, was not. He thus turned away from his erstwhile guide in an ongoing struggle to situate himself within American political culture. This move, which was emblematic of a broader defection from come-outerism and disunionism in the 1850s, had a constitutional component.[102]

The constitutional question started to weigh heavily on Douglass's mind in the late 1840s. Writing in the *North Star* in early 1849, he stated, "I now hold, as I have ever done, that the original intent and meaning of the Constitution (the one given to it by the men who framed it, those who adopted, and the one given to it by the Supreme Court of the United States) makes it a pro-slavery instrument."[103] This echoed Phillips's narrative of proslavery continuity. When Gerrit Smith, the recent Liberty Party candidate, challenged his statement, Douglass granted that "the Constitution ... standing alone, and construed *only* in the light of its letter ... is not a pro-slavery instrument."[104]

But, like Parker and Garrison, Douglass viewed the Constitution as a temporal text, an indication of historicization working against sacralization. "It is human," he noted, "and must be explained in the light of those maxims and principles which human beings have laid down as guides to the understanding of all written instruments."[105] An appeal to "facts" cast the Constitution as a creation of time-bound beings and made it one text among many others. As such, Douglass argued that the Constitution could be read without legal expertise. "Having a terrestrial ... origin," Douglass wrote, "we find no difficulty in

---

[102] T. Gregory Garvey, *Creating the Culture of Reform in Antebellum America* (Athens, GA, 2006), 121–60. On these developments, see also Blight, *Frederick Douglass*, 178–227.
[103] Frederick Douglass, "The Constitution and Slavery," *North Star*, February 9, 1849, in *The Life and Writings of Frederick Douglass*, ed. Philip S. Foner, 5 vols. (New York, 1950–75), 1:353 (hereafter cited as *LWFD*).
[104] Frederick Douglass, "The Constitution and Slavery," *North Star*, March 16, 1849, in *LWFD*, 1:362, emphasis in original.
[105] Ibid.

ascertaining its meaning .... It was made in view of the existence of slavery, and in a manner well calculated to aid and strengthen that heaven-daring crime."[106] Over the next decade, many others also interpreted the Constitution under the assumption that, as a historical text, it could be understood without legal expertise, which further encouraged popular constitutionalism.

Douglass's constitutional reading indicated not only that slavery was part of the framers' original intent but that its continued existence was part of their original expectation. Like Phillips, he dismissed the strict constitutional interpretations of Goodell and Spooner and instead interpreted the three-fifths, insurrection, slave trade, fugitive slave, and domestic violence clauses in light of the framers' statements. This manifested the document's corruptions, which demanded "immediate disannulment."[107] Douglass's reading implied that because the Constitution was a human document, created in time and subject to temporal vicissitude, it was not immutable and could be and should be replaced with a more suitable guide.

Douglass invited Smith to use the *North Star* to further explain his constitutional interpretation, noting he would "gladly and zealously" accept Smith's reading if he could "satisfy us of the fact."[108] Douglass debated constitutional interpretation on various occasions. In May 1849, he sparred with Samuel Ringgold Ward, an African American Congregationalist minister, in New York City. In familiar fashion, Ward focused on the Constitution's words and disregarded the "intentions and sentiments of the framers."[109] In response, Douglass used "the *Madison Papers*" to show that "the North bowed to the mandates of Slavery."[110]

In early 1850, at a multiday conference in Syracuse, New York, Douglass again debated Ward, Smith, and other abolitionists. He outlined the anticonstitutional position – "We want to say to the slaveholders, we admit your views of the Constitution, but we war on that and on you" – and emphasized the hypocrisy of the framers, who "attempted to unite Liberty in holy wedlock with the dead body of Slavery." Countering the era's prevalent filiopietism, Douglass declared, "They wrote of Liberty in the Declaration ... with one hand, and with the other clutched their brother by the throat!"[111] While most participants in the slavery debates

---

[106] Ibid., 1:363.   [107] Ibid., 1:366.   [108] Ibid.
[109] *New York Daily Tribune*, May 14, 1849, in *FDP*, Series One, 2:195.
[110] Ibid., 2:196, 197.   [111] *National Anti-Slavery Standard*, January 31, 1850.

claimed affinity with the founders, anticonstitutionalists distanced themselves from them, their proslavery compact, and, by association, their era.

After Ward again responded with an appeal to "*plain* language" and an assertion that "Truth in the Declaration, and Good in the Constitution, are one," the discussants began debating the Liberty Party. Sensing a distraction, Douglass returned their focus to constitutional interpretation, which he called "THE QUESTION OF THE DAY." It soon became the question of the decade. In the meantime, Douglass again said he might be persuaded to accept "an Anti-Slavery interpretation" but, like Phillips, believed that because politicians defer "to the Supreme Court," their interpretation "is LAW to all intents and purposes." At this point, Smith asked Douglass to "suppose a Justice in this city bring in a false or corrupt judgment; would you overturn the government? No! turn out the Justice .... You may have the wisest and purest Constitution," he stated, "and have it perverted. Your only security is in the sentiment of the country." Though Douglass, like Parker, would eventually place faith in the people's antislavery interpretation and popular constitutionalism would challenge increasing assent to the Court, at this point, Douglass remained unmoved. The "overwhelming array of testimony" created too large a chasm to bridge.[112]

"WE ARE IN THE PRESENCE OF NO ORDINARY ASSEMBLY"

The Fugitive Slave Law and the cases that followed provided the impetus Douglass needed to bridge that chasm. The cases incited white northerners to stake their grounds. Even as a preoccupation with the Slave Power displaced the slave's plight in the northern consciousness, fugitive slave cases and the presence of former fugitives such as Douglass made the human element undeniable. Whether preoccupied with their own liberties or the slaves' suffering, people in positions of power felt compelled to verbalize and defend their constitutional views as conflict over the issue seemed more inevitable. Even before 1850, fugitive slave cases had deepened existing divisions. Garrisonians believed the arrest of George Latimer in 1842 validated their constitutional interpretation.[113] Cases in the 1850s brought the constitutional issue closer to the fore, leading some northerners to dig in their heels in defense of slaveholders' legal rights and inciting others to denounce slaveholding. The actions of fugitive slaves

---

[112] Ibid., emphases in original.   [113] See, for example, *Liberator*, November 4, 1842.

turned the intricate arguments of once-isolated constitutional debates into national talking points.[114]

Parker dramatically depicted the volatile climate in a September 1850 speech. Finding a loophole in the American people's contractual obligation to uphold the Constitution, he contrasted God's constant laws, which "never change," with man's changing laws, which "depend ... on the finite will of man."[115] He explained that though God's laws reside within man as conscience, conscience "is often immature in the young, who have not had time for the growth ... and in the old, who have checked and hindered its development."[116] "The young," in Parker's framework, included eminent historical figures who had sanctioned slavery in their ignorance, while "the old" included present proslavery supporters who justified slavery in spite of illumination. Between these groups existed contemporaries who acknowledged slavery's sin and cast aside the Constitution. "Suppose," Parker directed, that "a man has sworn to keep the Constitution ... and the Constitution is found to be wrong in certain particulars: then his oath is not morally binding, for ... he is morally bound to keep the law of God as fast as he learns it."[117] Parker's learning taught him that "the man who attacks me to reduce me to slavery ... alienates his right to life, and if I were the fugitive, and could escape in no other way, I would kill him with as little compunction as I would drive a mosquito from my face."[118] Historical understanding underlay Parker's violent rhetoric. He found moral blindness – but not sin – in Paul or Madison. However, he could not hold nineteenth-century Americans guiltless, including Stuart, the "eminent theologian of New England," who bound himself to a corrupt compact.[119] As for himself, Parker preferred "conscience to cotton," the Bible, and the Constitution.[120]

A number of Boston's residents answered Parker's call "to rescue every fugitive slave" in assisting William and Ellen Craft.[121] Successfully escaping from Georgia to Boston in late 1848, the Crafts had publicly recounted their harrowing getaway to great effect. In October 1850, bounty hunters tried to use their popularity to track them, but the

---

[114] See Michael F. Conlin, *The Constitutional Origins of the American Civil War* (New York, 2019), 40–80.
[115] Theodore Parker, "The Function and Place of Conscience, in Relation to the Laws of Men: A Sermon for the Times," in *Speeches*, 3:133, 133–34.
[116] Ibid., 3:138.   [117] Ibid., 3:170.   [118] Ibid., 3:154.   [119] Ibid., 3:171.
[120] Parker, "Speech at the New England Anti-Slavery Society," 3:86.
[121] Parker, "Function and Place of Conscience," 3:153.

Boston Vigilance Committee hid the Crafts in various dwellings, including the homes of Bowditch and Parker. Parker married them in his home in early November. The Crafts eventually escaped to Canada and then England, but not before Harvard graduate and Massachusetts lawyer Benjamin Robbins Curtis prepared a legal opinion for US Marshal Charles Devens, who was charged to apprehend the Crafts. Around the same time that they set sail in late November, Curtis outlined his defense of the Fugitive Slave Law in a "constitutional meeting," which was organized with the help of his younger brother George Ticknor Curtis.

On November 26, "the Citizens of Boston ... who reverence the Constitution" met in the famed Faneuil Hall, a virtual battleground in the fight to claim the revolutionary legacy.[122] Speakers at Constitution meetings, which were common during this time, often mimicked Webster: they tied national progress to the Constitution's creation, traced slavery's continuous constitutionality, and observed decline in the form of dangerous abolitionist agitation.[123] In his speech at the Boston meeting, Benjamin Robbins Curtis, who had helped organize a reception for Webster following his speech, echoed the senator's pledge to "the whole CONSTITUTION and the whole UNION."[124] Referencing higher-law propositions abolitionists had made earlier at Faneuil Hall and Parker's violent statements in his September sermon, Curtis damned anticonstitutionalism as deserving of "the rebuke of every good citizen."[125] He also criticized Free Soilers, who acknowledged the fugitive slave clause but could not consent to uphold it "in any particular way, or by any particular means, or in any *modern* instance."[126] Annoyed at antislavery assertions of moral progress and appeals to temporal distinctions, Curtis sought to close the gap between past and present.

Curtis carried his listeners back to the Massachusetts ratification debates. His speech was not simply a history lesson, but an experiment in time travel. "We are in the presence of no ordinary assembly," he observed, perhaps drawing attention to the portraits on the walls. Awakening the imagination of his audience, he stated, "In the chair is John Hancock .... There is Theophilus Parsons .... There is Samuel Adams."[127] Surely such illustrious men had not made "a compact so

---

[122] *Proceedings of the Constitutional Meeting at Faneuil Hall, November 26th, 1850* (Boston, 1850), 3.
[123] See, for example, *The Proceedings of the Union Meeting, Held at Castle Garden, October 30, 1850* (New York, 1850).
[124] *Constitutional Meeting at Faneuil Hall*, 5, emphasis in original. [125] Ibid., 9.
[126] Ibid., 11, emphasis mine. [127] Ibid., 13.

grossly immoral, that their children ... must now overthrow and destroy the work of their hands." Parker believed the founders had expected time to save their children the trouble, and he had used distance from the founding to implicate his own generation. But Curtis conflated time to damn figures like Parker. "It is but the other day," he noted, "we were shedding our blood to obtain the Constitutions under which we live – Constitutions of our own choice and making – and now we are unsheathing the sword to overturn them."[128] In conflating the generations, Curtis made the abolitionists' position seem violently equivocal. "May the State make a promise to-day," he railed on, "and to-morrow say, 'On the whole, our interest did not require that promise, and it is not to be kept?'"[129] Curtis's speech is a striking example of the ways in which conventional ideas about continuity between the present and the favored founding era maintained their hold on the American imagination. Sometimes the debate over slavery reinforced the proclivity to conflate distinct historical contexts.

In positing his own version of original expectation, Curtis collapsed time in ways that might leave twenty-first-century readers dizzy. Subtly closing the gap between past and present, he stated that "men of forecast must then have foreseen, and subsequent events have demonstrated," the need for a fugitive slave clause.[130] This appeal to the framers' expectations carried an assumption of change, but the original expectation Curtis found aligned with an era-specific intent that proscribed new readings or, rather, prescribed old readings in new conditions. The framers, Curtis reasoned, had articulated the fugitive slave clause in their own era to be used in a future era. In contrast to figures such as Channing, Palfrey, Graham, and others who emphasized the Constitution's silences and looked outside it to find an original expectation of antislavery readings in new conditions, Curtis found original expectation by providing a strict reading of a text that he bound to an old context. And his appeal to original expectation emphasized continuity in slavery's protection rather than change in its eventual abolition.

Just as Stuart had stressed the prophets' and apostles' expedient approach to ancient servitude in an effort to condemn abolitionism, Curtis highlighted the framers' reasoned handling of American slavery to condemn disunionism. "History proves" that the nation cannot endure without the Constitution, he wrote, which "comes as near to perfection as the lot of humanity permits."[131] With these words, Curtis was working to

[128] Ibid., 14.   [129] Ibid., 15–16.   [130] Ibid., 16.   [131] Ibid., 16, 17.

stem the tide of the antislavery figures who undercut the text's sacred status. Breaking the sacred compact, he concluded, would produce fatal results. Curtis recognized laws were man-made. For that very reason, he thought it unreasonable to measure them according to a standard of natural or divine justice. And although he believed some of the Constitution's clauses must be adapted to changing circumstances, he held that clear provisions, such as the fugitive slave clause, did not allow for change. While he proposed that the founding generation had thought historically, he did not seem to think their sons and daughters should. Positing contemporaneity with the past allowed Curtis to reject the idea that the time since the founding era had created new imperatives with respect to fugitive slaves.

On the same day that Curtis insisted time could not annul the fugitive slave clause, Andrews Norton, liberal Christianity's experienced defender, made the opposite assertion. In an anonymous article, he disconnected slavery, which he granted was moral "under certain circumstances," from the new law, which he abhorred. His distinction rested on beliefs about human agency and progress, along with a clear failure of imagination. Norton assumed that enslaved blacks had acquiesced to servitude, while the "fugitive slave" had elected to throw "himself upon the universal rights of our nature for his safeguard." Norton failed to grasp the nature of slavery's repressive circumstances, not to mention blacks' individual and collective actions in such settings, but the link he made between black agency and freedom made returning fugitives reprehensible.[132]

Norton also articulated a view of moral progress not unlike that of Parker, his longtime foe, which spoke to how much Unitarians and Transcendentalists had in common – but also how slavery could bring thinkers into alignment as well as push them apart. Rejecting the very argument Curtis was making in Faneuil Hall, Norton applied the contextual approach he had advanced in biblical interpretation to the Constitution, arguing that at its creation "the moral feeling respecting slavery and its attendant evils was very different from what it is at present. Those evils had not been brought home to men's minds." Like Parker, Norton traced both the general "progress of public opinion" as well as the present "downward progress of degradation," indicated by the fact that

---

[132] *Boston Daily Atlas*, November 26, 1850. A copy of this anonymous article exists among Andrews Norton's compositions in the Andrews Norton Papers at Harvard's Houghton Library.

some southern congressman "pretend that slavery is a great good ... and that all free States should rest on a basis of slaves, like the republic of antiquity." Spurning the proslavery conflation of epochs, Norton followed Channing, his late Unitarian colleague, and others in his instructions to repeal the law and allow the fugitive slave clause to "lie inoperative, as something obsolete and unsuited to the times in which we live." Norton's argument assumed historical distance and signaled contingent change.[133]

So did Parker's response to both Stuart and Curtis, made in a speech given two days later. While he never embraced the Garrisonian contention that the Constitution must be scrapped for slavery to be abolished, he proved willing to cast it aside if other means fell short. Still believing that the people of 1787 expected slavery to "die 'of a rapid consumption,'" Parker mourned that "the culture of cotton has healed its deadly wound."[134] Given the nation's direction, he believed the only solution soon might rest in replacing the Constitution. Speaking of Curtis and his ilk, Parker noted, "Men say there is danger of disunion, of our losing fealty for the Constitution. I do not believe it yet!" he announced. "Suppose it be so," he continued, "the Constitution is the machinery of the national mill; and suppose we agree to take it out and put in new; we might get worse, very true, but we might get better. There have been some modern improvements; we might introduce them to the State as well as the mill."[135] Once again, Parker narrated both the corrupt rise of the Slave Power and the progress and spread of antislavery sentiment: "the spirit of the age, which is the public opinion of the nations, is against slavery."[136] As Webster and Curtis endlessly deferred to the founders, antislavery thinkers turned to their contemporaries. And while figures such as Norton believed public sentiment would make a single clause obsolete, Parker held that it might require an entirely new Constitution.

"THE STATESMEN OF THAT EARLY PERIOD HELD SLAVERY TO BE AN EXPIRING INSTITUTION"

While the controversy over fugitive slaves pushed some abolitionists toward a Garrisonian reading, it led more to move in the other direction.

---

[133] *Boston Daily Atlas*, November 26, 1850.
[134] Theodore Parker, "The State of the Nation, Considered in a Sermon for Thanksgiving Day," in *Speeches*, 3:203–04.
[135] Ibid., 3:216.   [136] Ibid., 3:206.

In January 1851, Douglass notified Smith that he had convinced Douglass "to let Slaveholders and their Northern abettors have the Laboring *oar* in putting a proslavery interpretation upon the Constitution." Douglass's break from Garrison had freed him to read the text in a new light. He still believed slaveholders "are doubtless right so far as the intentions of the framers ... are concerned," but the escalating furor over fugitive slaves seems to have pushed him toward Smith's radical constitutionalism.[137] And yet, while Douglass adopted Smith's interpretive focus on the text itself, America's most famous former fugitive slave remained interested in the framers' intentions and expectations. In other words, his historical investment survived his interpretive transformation.

The case of Thomas Sims, another fugitive from Georgia, reverberated throughout the North. In April 1851, George Curtis issued a certificate for Sims's removal. As Boston's US commissioner, Curtis had also issued arrest warrants for the Crafts and for Virginia native Shadrach Minkins. To the chagrin of the Curtis brothers, the Boston Vigilance Committee had saved Shadrach from his would-be captors. In his journal, Parker placed this rescue on par with famous revolutionary acts, estimating the event to be "the most noble deed done in Boston since the destruction of the tea."[138] Sims was less fortunate. Beginning on April 4, his lawyers, including prominent attorneys Richard Henry Dana Jr. and Charles Sumner, made arguments to free him in a courtroom that doubled as a federal prison. A week later, Curtis's certificate of removal placed three hundred deputies in position to march Sims back to bondage. Millard Fillmore sent 250 federal soldiers to assist. Days later, Sumner wrote to Parker, "My appeal is to the people, and my hope is to create in Massachusetts such a Public Opinion as will render the law a dead

---

[137] Frederick Douglass to Gerrit Smith, January 21, 1851, in *LWFD*, 2:149, emphasis in original. John Stauffer pinpoints Douglass's conversion to Smith's reading of the Constitution at the "Fugitive Slave Law Convention" held in August. John Stauffer, *The Black Hearts of Men: Radical Abolitionists and the Transformation of Race* (Cambridge, MA, 2002), 163–64. See also David W. Blight, *Frederick Douglass' Civil War: Keeping Faith in Jubilee* (Baton Rouge, 1989), 26–35; Eric Foner, *The Fiery Trial: Abraham Lincoln and American Slavery* (New York, 2010), 43–44; and Blight, *Frederick Douglass*, 213–16. On Douglass's antislavery constitutionalism more generally, see Damon Root, *A Glorious Liberty: Frederick Douglass and the Fight for an Antislavery Constitution* (Lincoln, 2020).

[138] Theodore Parker, Journal, February 16, 1851, in *Life and Correspondence*, 2:103. Parker described the rescue of Jerry M. Henry, another fugitive slave, in similar terms. Theodore Parker to Samuel May, September 23, 1853, Theodore Parker Papers, MHS.

letter."[139] As some looked to the federal government to uphold proslavery laws, others looked to the people to render those laws inoperative.

In this tense setting, Douglass made his transition public. On May 21, he informed Smith that he had adopted antislavery constitutionalism months before. Two days later, he announced in the *North Star* his "firm conviction that the Constitution, construed in the light of well-established rules of legal interpretation, might be made consistent in its details with the noble purposes avowed in its preamble; and that hereafter we should ... demand that it be wielded in behalf of emancipation."[140] Douglass had been blinded by "the history and practice of the nation," but a "careful study of the writings of Lysander Spooner, of Gerrit Smith, and of William Goodell" had given him sight.[141] Recent events gave new force to their arguments. As the rise of abolitionism had incited white southerners to craft proslavery defenses, proslavery incursions encouraged more and more black and white northerners to adopt antislavery readings of the Constitution. While Parker, proved willing to accept a Garrisonian reading, Douglass opted for a Smithian one.

Douglass retained an interest in the framer's intent, however, perhaps in part because he wanted to answer those who continued "to see slavery in the Constitution."[142] Granted new vision by Smith and others, Douglass began to read extraconstitutional sources in a new light. In a July 1851 editorial published in his newly formed eponymous paper, which resulted from the merger of the *North Star* and Smith's *Liberty Party Paper*, Douglass responded to an article in the *Pennsylvania Freeman* that had taken umbrage with his new constitutionalist stance. The article's author could "'hardly conceive of a fact in law or history being proved more conclusively, than is the fact that the Constitution was intended to protect slavery.'"[143] Douglass had once promoted this very position, but now he proceeded along a new line of inquiry, asking "who the persons were who intended that the Constitution should protect slavery?"[144] His playful point had a serious edge. In terms of "traditional history," Douglass wrote, "we shall find many conflicting versions about

---

[139] Charles Sumner to Theodore Parker, April 19, 1851, Theodore Parker Papers, MHS.

[140] Frederick Douglass to Gerrit Smith, May 21, 1851, in *LWFD*, 2:157; and Frederick Douglass, "Change of Opinion Announced," *North Star*, May 23, 1851, in *LWFD*, 2:155.

[141] Douglass to Smith, May 21, 1851, 2:155–56, 156.

[142] Frederick Douglass, "Is the United States Constitution for or against Slavery?," *Frederick Douglass' Paper*, July 24, 1851, in *LWFD*, 5:192.

[143] Ibid., 5:193.   [144] Ibid., 5:194.

the very point which is so conclusively proved."[145] Like Spooner, Douglass introduced historical skepticism into the debate. In doing so, he challenged the idea of founding-era consensus. His statements also called into question all historical accounts, but at the same time they opened the door to alternative narratives.

Douglass outlined a range of prominent constitutional readings, including the Calhounian version that viewed slavery as "co-extensive with the Constitution," along with the widely accepted version that designated slavery as a state institution. He then expounded a third reading, prominent among antislavery interpreters, which held that "the extension and perpetuity of slavery was never dreamed of by the men of the Revolution ... but that, on the contrary, the fathers of the Revolution sought to limit, circumscribe, and to hasten the extinction of slavery."[146] Douglass's own reading followed from the third.

Just as Parker had used a sympathetic approach to dismiss the framers' views, Douglass used a similar method to advance the prevalent antislavery emphasis on the framers' original expectations of slavery's demise. He urged taking "the most favorable possible view of the motives and intentions of men ... who lived in the stormy and trying time in which the Constitution was originated."[147] Reading accounts of their sentiments made it clear "that slavery was looked upon as a great evil" and "that the statesmen of that early period held slavery to be an expiring institution." Douglass believed these facts were "no slight testimony in proof of the intention to make the Constitution a permanent liberty document."[148] Historical evidence could be used to develop a range of accounts, even one that countered the proslavery reading Douglass himself had accepted.

Ultimately, Douglass considered an analysis of the Constitution's actual words to be most determinative. If historical investigation showed that the framers sought to protect slavery, then, he wrote, "their intention was wicked, and contrary to the spirit and letter of the Constitution."[149] Following Smith, Goodell, and Spooner in this regard, Douglass's emphasis on spirit would support a growing interest in the interpretive role of the people. He remained concerned with the framers' intentions, but if those fell short, other means existed to read the Constitution as "a permanent liberty document."

In closing, Douglass again drew attention to the difficulty of discovering the framers' true intentions. "How are we to know now, or a century

[145] Ibid., 5:195. [146] Ibid. [147] Ibid., 5:192. [148] Ibid., 5:196. [149] Ibid., 5:198.

hence, what were the motives and intentions of the various parties to the Constitution?" he asked. Emphasizing the messiness of the past placed Douglass more in line with Spooner than Phillips. The problem was further complicated by proslavery incursions in American society and politics since the founding era. "Nothing is more evident," Douglass wrote, "than that as slavery becomes strong," slaveholders' "claims to be protected under the Constitution become more and more unreasonable and audacious."[150] Like Spooner, Douglass believed proslavery gains obscured the Constitution's original intent and meaning. Ambiguity about the framers' intentions authorized him to introduce his own historical narrative, one that attributed antislavery sentiments and expectations to the writing and ratification of the Constitution and then traced slavery's corrupting and obscuring influence since that time.

Despite signs of proslavery progress, Douglass, like Parker, still believed the nineteenth century was an age of freedom and insisted that this should be most true in the United States. He voiced that belief in his 1852 speech "What to the Slave Is the Fourth of July?" In this, his most powerful jeremiad – which Douglass deliberately delivered on the Fifth – he started by praising the American revolutionaries and then proceeded to conjure Old Testament prophets to damn slavery as the great contradiction of American freedom and Christianity. Douglass used both biblical and founding favored pasts but approached them differently; he did not provide a historical reading of the Bible. Instead, he wrested the words of ancient prophets and brought them to bear forcefully on his American moment. As biographer David Blight put it, "Douglass not only used the Hebrew prophets; he joined them."[151] While approaching the Bible and Constitution differently, Douglass sought to rescue both from proslavery readings. In doing so, he was not simply pointing out the nation's most glaring flaw; he was also laying claim to its most glowing promises.[152] Similar to the antislavery constitutionalists whom he again named in this speech, Douglass saw the best chance for realizing these promises in the people. He cast aside the biblical readings of "eloquent Divines" and dismissed the notion that slavery's constitutionality "is not a question for the people.... Every American citizen," he stated, "has a right to form an opinion of the constitution, and to propagate that opinion, and to use

---

[150] Ibid.   [151] See Blight, *Frederick Douglass*, 228–36, quotation on 228.
[152] See James Oakes, *The Radical and the Republican: Frederick Douglass, Abraham Lincoln, and the Triumph of Antislavery Politics* (New York, 2007), 3–38.

"The Culture of Cotton Has Healed Its Deadly Wound" 217

all honorable means to make his opinion the prevailing one."[153] In contrast to his earlier emphasis on the framers' proslavery intentions and the Supreme Court's construction, Douglass now pointed to the framers' egalitarian expectations and the people's interpretation.

Douglass still had occasion to refer to the founding generation's failures. Indeed, their conflicting opinions permitted him to join the growing chorus of antislavery figures who argued that the evolving views of the people mattered most in constitutional interpretation.[154] In a speech on the Fugitive Slave Law given in August 1852, the proud disciple "of Gerrit Smith" divided his enlightened listeners from their shortsighted forefathers and severed past from present imperatives. "It has been said that our fathers entered into a covenant for this slave-catching," Douglass told his audience. "Who were your daddies?" he asked, drawing laughter. "I take it they were men, and so are you .... If they have made a covenant that you should do that which they have no right to do themselves ... surely it is not binding on you."[155] While Douglass had transitioned from a Garrisonian to a Smithian position, in practical terms he was still willing, like Parker, to set aside constitutional commitments. The transient laws of illustrious ancestors held no claim on their illuminated descendants. Douglass believed that "he who has God and conscience on his side, has a majority against the universe .... He represents the future state."[156] A few months earlier, while writing about progress from biblical times in his notebook, Parker had noted, "The past golden age is a fable; the true one lies in the future."[157] As hell extended its borders, abolitionists anticipated a glorious millennium.

The fugitive slave cases led some northerners to adopt antislavery readings at a time when constitutional interpretation became supremely determinative in the slavery debates. Garrisonian and Smithian approaches each carried implications for how their adherents thought about the relationship between the founding era and the present. At times, Douglass drew attention to the nation's failure to realize the founders' expectations, and at other times, he exposed the failures of the

---

[153] Frederick Douglass, "What to the Slave Is the Fourth of July?: An Address Delivered in Rochester, New York, on 5 July 1852," in *FDP, Series One*, 2:377, 385.

[154] See Garvey, *Creating the Culture of Reform*, 156–60; and Mark E. Neely Jr., *Lincoln and the Triumph of the Nation: Constitutional Conflict in the American Civil War* (Chapel Hill, 2011), 53–55.

[155] Frederick Douglass, "The Fugitive Slave Law," in *LWFD*, 2:208.   [156] Ibid., 2:209.

[157] Theodore Parker, February 15, 1852, Notebook, 1851–53, in Theodore Parker Papers, MHS.

founders themselves. This dual emphasis indicated historical distance by highlighting original context and in sounding the discord between original expectations and existing circumstances. As antislavery thinkers continued to contrast slavery's corrupting presence with the current era's call for freedom, their narratives signaled an increasing ambivalence about historical development and further suggested that change was contingent.

AMERICAN DESPOTISM IN THE AGE OF ABOLITION

In a mid-April 1854 discourse, Hartford pastor Horace Bushnell observed "that our government, although ... starting into being with a strong bent toward abolition ... afterward so changed its policy that its action ... has fostered the slaveholding interest."[158] Bushnell was among the few biblical scholars of the period who did not embrace historical exegesis, but he did track post-founding-era changes.[159] Recent events shaped the Connecticut Congregationalist's narration. In January, Illinois Senator Stephen A. Douglas had submitted the Kansas–Nebraska Bill, which drew immediate criticism and a response from prominent antislavery politicians, including Chase, Sumner, Smith, and Joshua R. Giddings. Their widely distributed *Appeal of the Independent Democrats* convinced many northerners that the Slave Power was plotting to overrun the union with slavery.[160] A few months later, a concerned Bushnell described Douglas's bill as the most recent indication that "the model republic of the world, the people of Washington, are left almost alone, in this nineteenth century, in the maintenance of chattel slavery!"[161] Like Channing, Parker, Douglass, and others, Bushnell retained faith in general moral progress and believed that the spirit of the age and God would soon bring about abolition, but the perceived advance of the Slave Power clouded this optimism.[162]

About a month after Bushnell gave his discourse in Hartford, Parker warned a New York City audience that while moral sentiment had

---

[158] Horace Bushnell, *The Northern Iron: A Discourse Delivered in the North Church, Hartford, on the Annual State Fast*, April 14, 1854 (Hartford, CT, 1854), 13.

[159] On Bushnell's figurative approach to the Bible, see James O. Duke, *Horace Bushnell: On the Vitality of Biblical Language* (Chico, CA, 1984).

[160] Salmon P. Chase et al., *Appeal of the Independent Democrats in Congress, to the People of the United States. Shall Slavery Be Permitted in Nebraska?* (Washington, DC, 1854).

[161] Bushnell, *The Northern Iron*, 14.

[162] On the development of Bushnell's views on slavery, see Robert Bruce Mullin, *The Puritan as Yankee: A Life of Horace Bushnell* (Grand Rapids, MI, 2002), 211–26.

"The Culture of Cotton Has Healed Its Deadly Wound"

matured among "the human race as a whole.... A nation may go back as well as forward."[163] In the United States, he argued, the North had "yielded continually" to "the Slave Power."[164] Bruised by upset expectations, Parker anticipated the confusion awaiting a nation blind to trouble. And yet, even when his dark forecasting suggested he was teetering on the precipice of disillusionment, he again fell back on his teleological convictions, maintaining that "every triumph of Slavery is a day's march towards its ruin."[165] Parker envisioned an "America" without tyrants and slaves, where "the Anglo-Saxon Family" filled "a whole hemisphere, with industry, freedom, religion. The fulfillment of this vision is our province," he stated, "we are the involuntary instruments of God."[166] Revealing his commitment to a romantic racial theory, Parker believed Anglo-Americans, in particular, ineluctably acted as God's hands to realize divine plans for a free and flourishing nation.[167] Subsequent events again challenged this faith.

These events included fugitive slave cases. These cases served as an important representation of both black agency and southern slavery, especially as white northerners often failed to remember the enslaved past of struggling free blacks in their presence or, as Parker's speech demonstrated, to envision them in the American future.[168] The figure of Frederick Douglass served as a constant reminder that behind the high-level debates in which he participated stood suffering men, women, and children anxious to embrace the promises of American freedom. At times, as with Weld's *American Slavery As It Is: Testimony of a Thousand Witnesses* (1839), abolitionists drew sympathetic attention to the sad situation of blacks in bondage, but antislavery readings of the Constitution and the founding era often remained at the level of abstraction.[169] However, slaves and former slaves forced themselves into the national spotlight through heroic escapes and efforts to remain

---

[163] Theodore Parker, *An Address Delivered by the Rev. Theodore Parker, before the New York City Anti-Slavery Society* (New York, 1854), 9–10.
[164] Ibid., 43.   [165] Ibid., 44.   [166] Ibid., 45–46.
[167] On Parker's romanticism, including his racial theory, and its relationship to his abolitionism, see Ethan J. Kytle, *Romantic Reformers and the Antislavery Struggle in the Civil War Era* (New York, 2014), 29–71.
[168] See Joanne Pope Melish, *Disowning Slavery: Gradual Emancipation and "Race" in New England, 1780–1860* (Ithaca, NY, 1998).
[169] See Elizabeth B. Clark, "'The Sacred Rights of the Weak': Pain, Sympathy, and the Culture of Individual Rights in Antebellum America," *Journal of American History* 82, no. 2 (1995): 463–93.

free, making it harder for northerners to forget the human lives at stake. Black action continued to fuel abolitionism.[170]

Anthony Burns, who had escaped from Richmond in early 1854, was arrested and jailed in Boston's federal courthouse in late May. When abolitionist resistance to his imprisonment led to the death of a US marshal, President Franklin Pierce sent federal troops to maintain order. On June 2, when US Commissioner Edward G. Loring directed these troops to escort Burns to a ship bound for slavery, New England burst into a panic. An enraged Garrison declared that Loring had pronounced Burns "no man, but a thing ... the Declaration ... to be a lie, George Washington and his associates traitors and cutthroats, the Golden Rule an absurdity, and Jesus of Nazareth an impostor."[171] Amos Lawrence of Groton, Massachusetts, observed "a revolution of sentiment," writing that "we went to bed one night old fashioned, conservative, Compromise, Union Whigs & waked up stark mad Abolitionists." Like most Bostonians, Lawrence intended to "stand by the laws until they are repealed," even as he rhetorically moved toward radicalism by insisting that "Massachusetts never can be made hunting grounds" for slaveholders.[172] Perceived proslavery advances were met by the spread of antislavery sentiment.

In the midst of Burns's case, Pierce signed into law the Kansas–Nebraska Act, which fueled the tug-of-war between conciliatory government action and antagonistic abolitionist response. The law repealed the Missouri Compromise and instituted popular sovereignty. This permitted settlers to decide whether or not to introduce slavery into territories formerly designated as free. In the wake of southern despotism's apparent encroachment, abolitionists increasingly narrated decline.

In speeches and sermons given during this period, Parker became even more insistent that since ratification, slavery "has advanced, and Freedom declined."[173] He still believed global events trended toward liberty but had learned that progress was not unilateral. Perhaps this understanding led him to argue that as God's instruments, humans drove historical development. In a June 4 sermon, he conflated Providence and his audience. "The remedy is in our hearts and hands. God works no miracles. There is power in human nature to end this wickedness. God appointed the purpose, provided the means – a divine purpose, human

---

[170] Sinha, *The Slave's Cause*, 381–460, 500–42.   [171] *Liberator*, June 9, 1854.
[172] Amos Lawrence to Giles Richard, June 1, 1854, Amos Adams Lawrence Papers, MHS.
[173] Theodore Parker, *The New Crime against Humanity: A Sermon* (Boston, 1854), 21.

means.... We are His instruments. Let us faithfully do the appointed work! Darkness is about us! Journey forward! Light is before us!"[174] Parker responded to uncertainty by placing hope in his contemporaries.

When Benjamin Curtis, now a Supreme Court justice, issued an indictment against Parker and Phillips for their role in the attempt to free Burns, Parker's faith in the nation's future faltered once again. "No fate holds us up," he stated in an early July sermon, counting "only two national steps" against slavery since 1776.[175] "I know not what is before us," he noted a few months later.[176] Now more than ever, doubts hampered Parker's hope in general progress toward freedom. "I seldom take counsel of my fears, often of my hopes," he stated, "but now I must say that since '76 our success was never so doubtful as at this time."[177] By the mid-1850s, even those with the firmest convictions of history's forward movement began to falter at the emerging specter of historical contingency.

Two days later, the Massachusetts Anti-Slavery Society formalized the lament. They declared the Fourth of July a day of public mourning and gathered in Framingham to mark the occasion. Thoreau spoke on a familiar theme, instructing Americans to obey "that eternal and only just CONSTITUTION, which He, and not any Jefferson or Adams, has written in your being." While referencing the divine, Thoreau grounded his higher-law appeal in the people. "The law will never make men free," he explained, "it is men who have got to make the law free."[178] Dramatizing the point, Garrison held up a copy of the Fugitive Slave Law and set it aflame. Next, he torched Loring's decision. Then came Curtis's indictment. Finally, the unrelenting abolitionist set fire to a copy of the Constitution. Only the Declaration escaped the conflagration. Garrison's symbolic act made visual what he had been preaching for over a decade. Now he had razed a corrupt Constitution in both word and deed.[179]

While Garrisonians responded to despotism's spread with oratorical fury and staged pyrotechnics, many more antislavery proponents

---

[174] Ibid., 72.
[175] Theodore Parker, *A Sermon of the Dangers Which Threaten the Rights of Man in America* (Boston, 1854), 11, 38. The indictment, which failed to produce convictions, provided more fodder for Parker to attack Curtis as a Slave Power pawn in *The Trial of Theodore Parker, for the "Misdemeanor" of a Speech in Faneuil Hall against Kidnapping* (Boston, 1855).
[176] Theodore Parker, *A Sermon of the Moral Dangers Incident to Prosperity* (Boston, 1855), 27.
[177] Parker, *Sermon of the Dangers Which Threaten*, 11.
[178] *Liberator*, July 21, 1854, emphasis in original. [179] *Liberator*, July 7, 1854.

considered different kinds of responses. Some contemplated the use of violence. In the wake of Europe's revolutions, slavery's American enemies more readily called on the martial legacy of their own Revolution, which undermined Garrison's particular claim to the Declaration and his concentrated push for a revolution in sentiments.[180] In a March 1855 letter to Gerrit Smith, James McCune Smith wrote, "please preserve this note as a sort of Madison Paper." The African American physician was reporting on the formation of the New York City Abolition Society and the construction of its founding resolution to "abolish Slavery by means of the Constitution; or *otherwise*." James Smith noted that he had "squeezed" the last two words into the resolution. While the Society's organizers had made an antislavery interpretation central to its aims, Smith insisted that they remain open to extraconstitutional approaches. In using the phrase, "or otherwise," he had something specific in mind: "should there be any quarrel in the future as to the meaning of" the words, he told his correspondent, "I mean *fight*." Smith's supplemental letter revealed his original intent. Hence his instruction to "preserve this note as a sort of Madison Paper."[181]

A few months later, the two Smiths met with Douglass, Goodell, and other abolitionists to form the Radical Abolition Party. This interracial group cherished the Constitution and the Bible as sacred creeds. Millenarian in their mindset, they launched a holy crusade against slavery, the last great obstacle to establishing heaven on earth. Such ideas later informed John Brown's violent foray into the belly of the beast even as they also continued to inspire constitutional and political measures.[182] The proliferation of antislavery approaches during the 1850s was tied to a growing realization that human initiative played a determinative role in history, which fugitive slaves had made abundantly clear. In drawing attention to historical contingency, then, antislavery narratives of decline also indicated the romantic possibility of redeeming human action.

"GIVING UP THE OLD FOR THE NEW FAITH"

Decline in the form of the Slave Power's rise became the focus of Illinois lawyer Abraham Lincoln in the mid-1850s. He had served in the US

---

[180] See Mayer, *All on Fire*, 450.
[181] James McCune Smith to Gerrit Smith, March 31, 1855, in *The Black Abolitionist Papers*, ed. C. Peter Ripley, 5 vols. (Chapel Hill, 1985–92), 4:275, emphasis in original.
[182] On the Radical Abolition Party, see Stauffer, *Black Hearts of Men*.

"The Culture of Cotton Has Healed Its Deadly Wound"   223

House of Representatives from 1847 to 1849 before returning to practice law in Springfield. The Kansas–Nebraska Act, which Stephen A. Douglas sponsored, helped give rise to the Republican Party and led Lincoln back to politics. It also trained Lincoln's focus on the issue of slavery. He ran for but did not fill a seat in the US Senate in late 1854. In 1856, he was runner-up in the bid for the vice presidential candidate of the newly formed Republican Party. In 1858, after the Lincoln-Douglas debates, Douglas defeated him in a race for the US Senate. Finally, in 1860, Lincoln won election as the Republican Party's presidential candidate. An antislavery reading of the founding era was key to his political rise.

Lincoln voiced that reading in 1854, which marked the beginning of his standoff with Douglas. Lincoln, still a Whig, followed Douglas, a Democrat, around Illinois and debated him as Douglas campaigned for the incumbent James Shields. Lincoln's speech in Peoria, in particular, signaled the rise of slavery as the central issue in his political thought. In late May, he had holed himself up in the state library in Springfield to study the history of the peculiar institution.[183] When he rose to engage Douglas in Peoria on the evening of October 16, he was armed with historical evidence.

Lincoln made clear the distinction between slavery as an "EXISTING institution" and its "EXTENSION," which allowed him to posit continuity with and assent to founding-era expectations.[184] He began with pre-ratification legislation in hopes of shedding light on the time "away back of the constitution, in the pure fresh, free breath of the revolution." "For sixty-one years," he argued, "all parties acted in quiet obedience to" the Northwest Ordinance, bringing about the prosperous state "Jefferson foresaw and intended."[185] In contrast to Garrisonians, who found continuity between a proslavery Constitution and the Fugitive Slave Law, or antislavery constitutionalists, who outlined decline from 1787 to 1850, Lincoln narrated beneficial efforts to contain slavery from before the founding to the present. The Kansas–Nebraska Act interrupted the sequence. "*Now* new light breaks upon us," he scoffed. Of slaveholders' desire to take slaves into Nebraska, he stated, "That *perfect* liberty they sigh for – the liberty of making slaves of other people – Jefferson never thought of."[186] Over the next decade, Lincoln's position came to rest on

---

[183] Oakes, *The Radical and the Republican*, 53.
[184] Abraham Lincoln, "Speech at Peoria, October 16, 1854," in *CWAL*, 2:248, emphasis in original.
[185] Ibid., 2:249.   [186] Ibid., 2:250, emphasis in original.

what he believed the founders did and did not intend, which further gave life to the idea that contingent changes separated past from present.

Continuing his speech, he contrasted founding-era principles with the "covert *real* zeal for the spread of slavery," which he believed had motivated the repeal of the Missouri Compromise. Lincoln acknowledged slaveholders' "constitutional rights," emphasized that he was not seeking equality for blacks, and said that he "would consent to the extension of [slavery] rather than see the Union dissolved."[187] While voicing this preservationist position, which guided his politics throughout the rest of his life, Lincoln also indicted the South for betraying the principle that "no man is good enough to govern another man, *without that other's consent*." Tracing this idea to the Declaration, he upheld it as "the sheet anchor of American republicanism."[188] This shaped Lincoln's attack on slavery's extension, which he described as "the great Behemoth of danger."[189]

Glad that Douglas, in a speech given before his own, had called on the examples of the "revolutionary fathers," Lincoln looked to them to answer the question of whether the Constitution had "any reference to the carrying of slavery into NEW COUNTRIES." Holding it to be "a question of discrimination between" the founders and Douglas, Lincoln objected to the idea of a moral right to enslave fellow humans "because the fathers of the republic ... rejected it. The argument of 'Necessity' was the only argument they ever admitted in favor of slavery."[190] This supported Lincoln's own expedient approach to slavery and placed geographical and chronological limits on the Constitution's proslavery provisions.

Lincoln also deployed the common antislavery argument that the framers had crafted the Constitution within one context with an eye toward a future, more egalitarian, context. Similar to Palfrey, Bailey, Birney, and others, he argued that the founders "hid away" those provisions "just as an afflicted man hides away a wen or a cancer, which he dares not cut out at once, lest he bleed to death; with the promise, nevertheless, that the cutting may begin at the end of a given time."[191] This idea assumed that the framers had written with historical change in mind. Lincoln referenced an original expectation of slavery's removal and recounted post-founding-era acts aimed at realizing this expectation,

---

[187] Ibid., 2:255, 256, 270, emphasis in original.   [188] Ibid., 2:266, emphasis in original.
[189] Ibid., 2:270.   [190] Ibid., 2:267, 274, emphasis in original.   [191] Ibid., 2:274.

including laws limiting and prohibiting the nondomestic slave trade and plans for gradual emancipation in slave states. The nation had been on track to fulfill founding promises.

"The institution was rapidly becoming extinct within these limits," Lincoln proposed, "but NOW it is to be transformed into a 'sacred right.'" The Kansas–Nebraska Act was an innovation that deviated from founding-era ideals, a "giving up [of] the OLD for the NEW faith. Near eighty years ago," he stated, Americans declared "that all men are created equal; but now from that beginning we have run down to the other declaration, that for SOME men to enslave OTHERS is a 'sacred right of self-government.'" Not unlike Benjamin Curtis had done in 1850, Lincoln brought together past and present generations, but his approach emphasized a founding-era expectation of change. Much separated Parker's and Douglass's positions from Lincoln's, but like them, the aspirant for an Illinois senatorial seat also observed profound deviations from founding-era ideals, though his focus on expansion led him to see signs of national decline as new. Lincoln proposed that if someone had called the Declaration "'a self-evident lie'" in "old Independence Hall," as it recently had been by Indiana Senator John Pettit, "the very door-keeper would have throttled the man, and thrust him into the street." Lincoln did not assert that the founders would support or attack the Kansas–Nebraska Bill, as Stuart had in reference to the Fugitive Slave Law, but he did argue that "the spirit of seventy-six and the spirit of Nebraska, are utter antagonisms."[192] Lincoln's narrative indicated that times had changed and not for the better.

Lincoln understood recent developments as having distinctly temporal implications. Quoting an article from London's *Daily News*, he noted the apprehension of "the liberal party throughout the world ... 'that the one retrograde institution in America, [was] undermining the principles of progress, and fatally violating the noblest political system the world ever saw.'"[193] Singing a new antislavery song, Lincoln intoned that an anachronistic institution placed America behind the times. While he agreed with Douglas that, "in point of mere fact," the "government was made for the white people and not for the negroes," he voiced the growing fear that turning from the "first precept of our ancient faith" would

---

[192] Ibid., 2:275, emphasis in original.
[193] The *Daily News* article was reprinted in the *New York Times*. See *New York Times*, September 29, 1854.

threaten "even the white man's charter of freedom."[194] Lincoln never went as far as some in reading the Constitution as antislavery, and in certain respects, he was closer to promoting the unionisms of Webster, Stuart, and Curtis than the abolitionisms of Douglass or Parker. Even still, he viewed slavery's spread, not abolitionism, as the cause of the current crisis. While his narrow focus led him to see alarming proslavery intrusions as a new development, Lincoln's historical reading of the Constitution also highlighted the temporal implications of failed founding-era expectations. His tale of expected and unexpected changes suggested that historical development had a reasoning all its own, a reasoning that divided past from present in ways that could not be bridged.

These sustained historical, and increasingly political, debates highlighted historical distance. More than ever before, a wide range of antislavery writers and speakers granted slavery's legal presence in the founding era. In emphasizing original expectations, they acknowledged the fact that proslavery forces had successfully exerted their influence at the framing. They went on to suggest that the framers, realizing that times would change, had crafted the nation's sacred legal creed with that historical change in mind. In other words, they implied that the framers had thought historically when writing slavery into the Constitution. In asserting that enough time had passed to abolish slavery, these antislavery writers and speakers assumed distance from the founding era. Unlike earlier narratives of decline, which often signaled a desire to return to the favored past, these readings displayed a hope that Americans would finally move forward and fulfill that era's best and highest ideals, ideals that could not have been realized before. Such appeals to the Constitution demanded more sustained historical attention than the Garrisonian effort to set it aside. As more and more antislavery figures provided these kinds of constitutional readings, the readings drew added attention to the idea of historical distance. Their dissemination in high-profile and widely printed speeches like Lincoln's increased the potential for more Americans to view the founding era as a discrete historical period.

These sorts of readings also drew new attention to historical contingency and the role of human agency in contributing to history's movement. Emerson's writings on slavery highlight this development. In an

---

[194] Lincoln, "Speech at Peoria," 2:276, 281. On this and similar later Republican responses to popular sovereignty, see Jeremy J. Tewell, *A Self-Evident Lie: Southern Slavery and the Threat to American Freedom* (Kent, OH, 2013).

1844 speech, which marked his first full-throated denunciation of slavery, he described slavery as "incidental and exceptional" and suggested that the "genius of the Saxon race" would bring about its demise.[195] He was thus alarmed seven years later when men like Webster and Curtis relied on "a past Adams and Jefferson" rather than a "present Adams and Jefferson."[196] Like Thoreau and Parker, Emerson attacked hero-worship and sought new Christs and new Madisons, but he did not find them. In a March 1854 speech in Concord, he articulated his concern with the mutable nature of written forms, stating that "neither Constitutions nor laws nor covenants nor churches nor bibles, are of any use in themselves; the devil nestles comfortably into them all."[197] Emerson believed the Fugitive Slave Law and Kansas–Nebraska Act proved his point. In an early 1855 address, he damned what he described as the "Party of Property" for resisting "every progressive step" and continually looking "over their shoulders" to "their ancestors, the framers of the Constitution." In wishing "their age should be absolutely like the last," he stated, the nation's politicians failed both to recognize and realize change.[198] Old devils rather than new Christs were directing the nation's course. But Emerson still found redemptive possibilities in historical contingency, which he viewed as bound up with human agency. Ever focused on individuals, he had told his Concord audience, "you must be ... yourselves Declarations of Independence."[199] While some, believing that God himself would bring about the slaves' emancipation in his own due time, continued to see slavery as "subordinate and incidental," Emerson informed his listeners that "there is Divine Providence in the world which will not save us but through our own co-operation."[200]

Parker had reached a similar conclusion. In two speeches given in New York on the same day in May 1856, he offered his bleakest narration of events to date, stating that "for the last seventy years Congress has not

---

[195] Ralph Waldo Emerson, "An Address ... on ... the Emancipation of the Negroes in the British West Indies," in *Emerson's Antislavery Writings*, ed. Len Gougeon and Joel Myerson (New Haven, CT, 1995), 32, 33.
[196] Ralph Waldo Emerson, "Address to the Citizens of Concord," in *Emerson's Antislavery Writings*, 66–67.
[197] Ralph Waldo Emerson, "The Fugitive Slave Law," in *Emerson's Antislavery Writings*, 83.
[198] Ralph Waldo Emerson, "American Slavery," in *The Later Lectures of Ralph Waldo Emerson, 1843–1871*, ed. Ronald A. Bosco and Joel Myerson, 2 vols. (Athens, GA, 2001), 2:5.
[199] Emerson, "Address to the Citizens of Concord," 83.
[200] James H. Perry, *The Man for the Times: A Thanksgiving Discourse* (New York, 1855), 22; Emerson, "Address to the Citizens of Concord," 89.

taken one single step towards abolishing slavery" while slavery "took nine great steps towards absolute rule over the United States."[201] Worried that he and his contemporaries, who were "so confident of destined triumph and so wonted to success, forecast only victory, and so heed none of all this danger," Parker asked his hearers, "Who knows what is before us?"[202] But even on the brink of resignation, he continued to trust in the "Spirit of the Age."[203] He observed that spirit at work in the North, which he described as "progressively Christian and democratic," and under attack in the South, which he portrayed as "progressively anti-Christian and undemocratic."[204] Parker rested his faith in the "Anglo-Saxon" and predicted that America "will show the nations how divine a thing a People can be made."[205] As politicians started to look to the Supreme Court to solve the national crisis, Parker rested his hope in the people to read the Constitution in light of the framers' emancipationist expectations. A few years before, in September 1853, he wrote to Samuel May, "I hope nothing from the Court, only from the Jury."[206]

Although Parker had shown a willingness to abandon the Constitution during the first half of the decade, by 1855 he was writing to individuals such as Sumner that "the Constitution is not so proslavery as the administration has always made it."[207] Once again, Parker used a historical argument to buttress this claim. During the 1840s, readers of the Constitution had advanced historical investigation as the proper mode of interpretation. By the 1850s, this approach was axiomatic. In January 1855, for example, Sumner instructed Parker on how to respond to Curtis's indictment, noting that "whoever you have to speak at any stage should be able to do something *historical*; for the time will belong to history."[208] And *Dred Scott* (1857) proved Sumner right; the time did belong to history. The question remained as to who could decide its meaning.

---

[201] Theodore Parker, *The Great Battle between Slavery and Freedom, Considered in Two Speeches* (Boston, 1856), 11–12, 67–68.
[202] Ibid., 37. [203] Ibid., 33. [204] Ibid., 56. [205] Ibid., 91, 93.
[206] Theodore Parker to Samuel May, September 23, 1853, Theodore Parker Papers, MHS.
[207] Theodore Parker to Charles Sumner, February 2, 1855, Theodore Parker Papers, MHS.
[208] Charles Sumner to Theodore Parker, January 9, 1855, Theodore Parker Papers, MHS, emphasis in original.

6

"Times Now Are Not as They Were"

One respondent to *Dred Scott* contended that Chief Justice Roger B. Taney's deciding opinion "does not rest so much upon any interpretation of the law as it does upon a construction of the facts of history."[1] Indeed, Taney had accepted the historical grounds of debate that had been prepared through decades of interpretive emphasis on the historical explication of sacred texts.[2] His decision and the response it garnered are best understood against the backdrop of a climactic constitutional debate, a debate that followed lines of historical argumentation similar to those of protracted biblical disputes.

In his decision, Taney insisted that slavery's constitutional viability in the present depended on an understanding of its place in the revolutionary past. In the syllabus, written by the chief justice himself, he asserted that "when the Constitution was adopted, they [black people] were not regarded in any of the States as members of the community which constituted the State, and were not numbered among its 'people or citizens.'" Based on this observation, he concluded that "the special rights and immunities guarantied [sic] to citizens do not apply to them," and, consequently, "they are not entitled to sue ... in a court of the United States." Taney conflated blacks at the founding with blacks in the present through his fluid use of pronouns – from "they" to "them" and back to "they." He designated blacks as noncitizens in 1787 and thus, given his assumption of

---

[1] "History, as Expounded by the Supreme Court," 541.
[2] On the constitutional component of this development, see also Gilhooley, *Antebellum Origins*, 237–42.

the Constitution's timelessness, in 1857 he rendered "African American" a misnomer.³

Like Daniel Webster, Moses Stuart, and Benjamin Curtis, Taney observed changes in northern sentiment and, even more forcefully than they, asserted that those changes had no place in constitutional interpretation: "The change in public opinion and feeling in relation to the African race which has taken place since the adoption of the Constitution cannot change its construction and meaning." Times had changed, Taney allowed, but the meaning of the nation's sacred legal text had not. In his effort to administer it "according to its true meaning and intention when it was formed and adopted," a stance which reflected the originalism that had become dominant since the publication of Madison's *Papers*, Taney categorically rejected readings informed by historical distance and change.⁴

The *Dred Scott* decision struck at the antislavery idea that the progress of moral insight demanded new constitutional readings. Originalism seemed to preclude these readings, but many antislavery proponents had uncovered an original expectation of abolition, which suggested that the framers had bequeathed their political descendants with an interpretive approach open to historical change – that their original intent was adaptability. This idea informed the *Dred Scott* dissenting opinions of John McLean and Benjamin Curtis, who reasoned that the framers had foreseen the institution's eventual demise and had written with that vision in mind. This gave official credence to a kind of originalist living constitutionalism that had first emerged in antislavery readings during the 1840s and 1850s.⁵ While the Garrisonian reading of the Constitution as a static proslavery document received the chief justice's stamp of approval, the antislavery interpretation of original expectations also achieved federal prominence in McLean's and Curtis's dissenting opinions, bringing increased attention to the idea that the Constitution was meant to adapt to new circumstances.

In contrast to antislavery accounts, which lamented the Slave Power's rise, Taney depicted new antislavery feeling as unfortunate, which

---

³ *Scott v. Sandford*, 393. The published version of the decision, used here, includes additions that Taney incorporated after the ruling to buttress his argument.
⁴ *Scott v. Sandford*, 393.
⁵ The first full articulation of a living US Constitution emerged much later among legal realists, including Oliver Wendell Holmes Jr. and Louis D. Brandeis. See H. L. Pohlman, *Justice Oliver Wendell Holmes: Free Speech and the Living Constitution* (New York, 1991); and Philippa Strum, "Brandeis and the Living Constitution," in *Brandeis and America*, ed. Nelson L. Dawson (Lexington, Kentucky, 1989), 118–32.

justified his attempt to collapse the historical distance his reading revealed. If distance came from unwanted change, then few could protest restorative appeals to a pure founding-era past. Similar to the arguments Webster, Stuart, and even Curtis had made, Taney used synchronic components of the revolutionary golden age (i.e., late eighteenth-century ideas of black inferiority) to combat diachronic components of corrupted American history (i.e., the rise of abolitionist-informed egalitarian sentiment). Fearful of unwanted change, he asserted that the Constitution "must be construed now as it was understood at the time of its adoption." The founding document, Taney urged, continued to speak "not only in the same words, but with the same meaning and intent with which it spoke when it came from the hands of its framers and was voted on and adopted by the people."[6] While figures such as Frederick Douglass had identified the problem with attempting to uncover founding-era consensus, Taney ventriloquized and unified the framers, making them speak as one on the present crisis. He collapsed time just as Stuart had when Stuart asserted that Paul supported the Fugitive Slave Law or as Curtis had when he insisted that the anticonstitutionalists betrayed the legacy of those who had died to obtain a constitution "but the other day."[7]

An irony was built into this debate. Like most of America's biblical interpreters, Taney made the following hermeneutical assertion: times change, but the meaning and authority of sacred texts do not. In emphasizing the latter point, he brought new attention to the first. Taney's efforts to brush aside new ideas to recover the original ideas they masked inevitably designated those original ideas as old. In this way, the tendency to depict change as corruption indicated historical distance more than the effort to depict change as progress. Change cast as continuous with founding-era sentiment muted the dissonance resulting from distance, while change deemed to diverge with that era's sentiment amplified it.

Interpretations such as Taney's, which rejected change as distracting and unconstructive, nonetheless highlighted differences between the revolutionary past and antebellum present. Alone, Taney's interpretation had limited potential to indicate those differences. After all, when a consensus views changes as negative, collapsing historical distance to reclaim a golden age obscures the reality of historical differences. But in the 1850s, when antislavery readers asserted that the founding figures had expected abolition and thus characterized as progress what Taney

---

[6] *Scott v. Sandford*, 426.   [7] *Constitutional Meeting at Faneuil Hall*, 14.

identified as decline, they raised awareness of temporal distance in an unprecedented way.

While scholars have examined Taney's historical arguments, they have not explained how the case drew attention to historical change and distance.[8] *Dred Scott* embodied how the debates over slavery held unique potential to deepen Americans' awareness of distance from the founding era. The deciding and dissenting opinions, along with political and popular responses to the decision, accelerated a growing sense that more than just chronological difference separated nineteenth-century Americans from their revolutionary predecessors. In their appeals to the founding era, the justices and the respondents to the decision highlighted unmistakable historical differences between that past and their present.

A realization of such distance seemed impossible, given how close and useful the sacralized founding era appeared, but the historical interpretations and narrations produced by the slavery debates suggested that no historical era transcended time. As these official and popular readings of the Constitution spotlighted contingent changes since the founding era and disclosed the context thereof, more and more Americans began to recognize the discreteness of each historical moment. In a time and place that measured progress in terms of a nation's move toward a millennial existence, historical awareness of the favored founding era suggested that even the present was bound by temporal constraints.

THE CONTROLLING CIRCUMSTANCE OF A "DARK AND FELL SPIRIT"

Once again, black bodies in motion induced conversations about historical development. Dred Scott, who had been born into Virginia slavery near the turn of the century, toiled under multiple owners, including John Emerson, a doctor in the US Army who took Scott with him on assignments to Illinois and the Wisconsin Territory in the 1830s. Scott asserted agency in certain regards, including in his marriage to Harriet Robinson.

---

[8] See, for example, David M. Potter, *The Impending Crisis: America before the Civil War, 1848–1861*, ed. Don E. Fehrenbacher (1976; repr., New York, 2011), 267–96; Don E. Fehrenbacher, *The Dred Scott Case: Its Significance in American Law and Politics* (New York, 1978); Austin Allen, *Origins of the Dred Scott Case: Jacksonian Jurisprudence and the Supreme Court, 1837–1857* (Athens, GA, 2006); Mark A. Graber, *Dred Scott and the Problem of Constitutional Evil* (New York, 2006); and Robert Pierce Forbes, *The Missouri Compromise and Its Aftermath: Slavery and the Meaning of America* (Chapel Hill, 2007), 286–90.

However, Emerson rented out both of them while he answered the army's call to Missouri and Louisiana and then called on them to rejoin him after Emerson's marriage to Eliza Irene Sanford in early 1838. The movements continued with a move back to the Wisconsin Territory and then to Missouri, where Eliza took ownership of the Scotts after Emerson's death in 1843.[9] Slaves became all too familiar with uncertainty and contingency.

Perhaps in the face of the fact that his slave status transcended the mortality of his owner, Scott sought liberation. In 1846, he attempted to purchase his family's freedom, but Eliza refused. Taking legal action, Scott sued for his freedom in the St. Louis County Circuit Court, where his lawyers argued that Emerson had relinquished ownership of Scott by taking him into free regions. The court ruled against Scott and his family, which now included two girls, Eliza and Lizzie, before the judge ordered a retrial due to hearsay. In *Scott v. Emerson* (1850), the jury found that Emerson had illegally held Dred and Harriet in Illinois and the Wisconsin Territory, and they awarded the Scotts their freedom. However, Eliza Emerson won an appeal before Missouri's supreme court, which reversed the decision in November 1852. Circumstances, Scott learned, rewarded the legal actions of white slaveholders over those of enslaved blacks.

In his decision, Judge William Scott made an argument grounded in circumstance. He lamented northerners' changing views on slavery, but rather than dismiss them as blinding and irrelevant as Taney later would, Scott cited those changes as the basis of his ruling.[10] While acknowledging that in similar cases individuals had been "adjudged to be entitled to their freedom," he proceeded to use Taney's recent ruling in *Strader v. Graham* (1851) to depart from precedent.[11] In *Strader*, a case dealing with slaves who had been taken from Kentucky to Ohio, Taney had dismissed the case for lack of jurisdiction, placing the fate of the escaped slaves in the hands of Kentucky judges. This showed, Scott argued, "that the comity extended to the laws of other States, is a matter of discretion, to be determined by the courts of that State in which the laws are proposed to be enforced." He continued, "If it is a matter of discretion, that discretion must be controlled by circumstances." Scott designated the spread of

---

[9] For more on the Scott family biography, see Lea VanderVelde, *Mrs. Dred Scott: A Life on Slavery's Frontier* (New York, 2009).

[10] *Scott v. Emerson*, 15 Mo. 576, 582–87 (1852). For more on the legal developments in Scott's cases, see Ethan Greenberg, *Dred Scott and the Dangers of a Political Court* (Lanham, MD, 2009).

[11] *Scott v. Emerson*, 583.

antislavery sentiment as the controlling circumstance in this case: "Times now are not as they were when the former decisions on this subject were made. Since then not only individuals but States have been possessed with a dark and fell spirit in relation to slavery." Consequently, Scott concluded, "it does not behoove the State of Missouri to show the least countenance to any measure which might gratify this spirit."[12] Like many antislavery readers of the Constitution, Judge Scott believed change should inform law, but in viewing the spread of antislavery sentiment as negative, his decision aimed to counter rather than embrace that change.

In dissent, Judge Hamilton Rowan Gamble criticized Scott's approach, seeing "nothing in the law relating to slavery, which distinguishes it from the law on any other subject, or allows any more accommodation to the temporary public excitements."[13] Fearing reactive decisions, Gamble argued that "the judicial mind, calm and self balanced, should adhere to principles established when there was no feeling to disturb the view of the legal questions upon which the rights of parties depend."[14] He indicted the court for wavering in the midst of a public maelstrom, arguing that "times may have changed, public feeling may have changed, but principles have not and do not change."[15] Curtis would make a similar point in his dissent in *Dred Scott*, condemning as political Taney's ruling that Congress had no power to regulate slavery. At the same time, Curtis would suggest that when original expectations matched current sentiment, a new construction was acceptable. In *Scott* v. *Emerson*, both sides acknowledged change, but while one delivered an opinion in response to it, the other contended that law must function independent of change. Slavery had again drawn attention to change and forced new conversations about the relationship between law and historical developments.

A subsequent ruling focused Scott's case on historical readings of the founding era. Around the time of Judge Scott's decision, Eliza Emerson remarried and moved to Massachusetts, leaving Dred Scott in the ownership of her brother, John Sanford (misspelled as Sandford in the court records), a resident of New York. On the basis of diverse jurisdiction, wherein a case involves citizens from different states, Scott's lawyers obtained a hearing before a federal district court. This made the question of Scott's citizenship paramount. The district court judge directed the jury to rely on Missouri law and decide in favor of Sanford, who rejected Scott's citizenship claims on the basis that "his ancestors were of pure

---

[12] Ibid., 586.   [13] Ibid., 589.   [14] Ibid., 590.   [15] Ibid., 591–92.

African blood, and were brought into this country and sold as negro slaves."[16] On a writ of error, Scott's attorneys appealed to the US Supreme Court. In the events that followed, slavery's politicization merged with its constitutionalization.

The political nature of the *Dred Scott* case centered on the Court's choice to deliver a broad ruling on slavery in the territories. President-elect James Buchanan, who believed such a ruling would dissolve rising sectional tensions, took steps to ensure bipartisan support. In February 1857, within weeks of taking up residence in the White House, he wrote to Justice John Catron and pointed out the benefits of a broad decision. Catron promised little in his first few responses. Initially, the Court decided to have Justice Samuel Nelson of New York write a narrow opinion that would return the case's jurisdiction to Missouri courts. However, the threat of extensive dissenting opinions from McLean and Curtis, along with political interest in a broad proslavery decision, led the Court to take the pen from Nelson and place it in the hand of Taney. Catron apprised Buchanan of this pleasing development but noted that the decision needed northern support. He suggested that Buchanan implore fellow Pennsylvanian Justice Robert Cooper Grier to join the majority. Buchanan did so and succeeded, which allowed Taney to address the question of congressional power in the territories. In short order, Republicans attacked Buchanan and Taney as co-conspirators with the Slave Power, and a decision meant to unite the nation left it further divided. Far from providing a lasting resolution, Taney's pronouncements thrust the nation toward sectional conflict.[17]

Dred Scott also deepened America's confrontation with history. Scott's initial cases focused on the question of his freedom, and the early rulings either used or dismissed precedential decisions to decide his family's fate. The nature of the case changed when Scott's lawyers obtained a hearing before a federal court and the court based its ruling on a historical assertion about Scott's ancestors. This highlighted the question of Scott's citizenship and focused attention on the Constitution, binding the case to decades of debate. In an effort to conclude the debate, Taney delivered a landmark decision grounded in assertions about the revolutionary past. In doing so, he responded not only to immediate concerns but also to

---

[16] *Dred Scott, Plaintiff in Error, v. John F.A. Sandford*, in *Southern Slaves in Free State Courts: The Pamphlet Literature*, ed. Paul Finkelman, 3 vols. (New York, 1988), 3: 5–6.

[17] See Fehrenbacher, *Dred Scott Case*, 305–14; Potter, *Impending Crisis*, 272–74, 287–89; and Greenberg, *Dangers of a Political Court*, 65–85.

a culture in which interpreters had come to view contextual readings of the nation's sacred legal text as definitive. Taney accepted that conclusion and hoped to end the slavery debates with a decisive ruling.

THE TANEY COURT AND "THE FIXED OPINIONS CONCERNING THAT RACE"

Dred Scott marked the culmination of Taney's evolving stance on slavery, which was representative of white southerners generally. In 1818, as a slaveholding attorney from Maryland, he condemned slavery as an institution in need of gradual removal while defending abolitionist minister Jacob Gruber. That same year, he began manumitting his own slaves. During this period, Taney supported colonization and, as a state senator, voted to limit slavery's spread. These were his last antislavery deeds. In the 1820s and 1830s, he argued in favor of slaveholders and, as US attorney general, defended South Carolina's statute allowing for the arrest of black seamen. In partial response to the rise of abolitionism and Nat Turner's rebellion, Taney embraced and implemented proslavery tenets, as exhibited in some of his decisions as chief justice, including *Groves v. Slaughter* (1841), *Prigg v. Pennsylvania* (1842), and *Strader v. Graham* (1851). His broad decision in *Scott v. Sandford* indicated that he had fully moved from viewing slavery as a domestic blot in need of eventual removal to a civilizing blessing in need of vigilant protection.[18] While change in public sentiment contributed to his personal change of heart, Taney resolved to not allow the former to cloud constitutional construction.[19]

While claiming to set aside contemporary circumstances, Taney grounded his decision in a particular understanding of the founding era. He set out to show that "a negro whose ancestors were imported to this country and sold as slaves" could not obtain citizenship because those ancestors "were at that time considered as a subordinate and inferior class of beings."[20] This understanding allowed him to use legal formalism and absolve the Court of moral failing: "It is not the province of the court to decide upon the justice or injustice ... of these laws." He maintained that "the duty of the court is to interpret the instrument they have framed with

---

[18] On Taney's consistently proslavery decisions, see Paul Finkelman, *Supreme Injustice: Slavery in the Nation's Highest Court* (Cambridge, MA, 2018), 172–218.
[19] See Timothy S. Huebner, "Roger B. Taney and the Slavery Issue: Looking beyond – and before – Dred Scott," *Journal of American History* 97 (June 2010): 17–38.
[20] *Scott v. Sandford*, 403, 404–05.

the best lights we can obtain ... and to administer it ... according to its true intent and meaning when it was adopted."[21] To that end, Taney used the slave trade and fugitive slave clauses to show that blacks were property according to the prevailing "opinion of the time."[22] They were not, he argued, citizens of states: though states retained the power to grant citizenship, this status was distinct from federal citizenship. Taney thus used what he determined to be "historical facts for the purpose of showing the fixed opinions concerning that race upon which the statesmen of that day spoke and acted."[23] Like contemporary biblical scholars, he claimed to use "the best lights" to illuminate the founding generation's position on slavery, which he recovered to show that "indelible marks" separated "the unhappy black race ... from the white."[24]

As had become common in historical interpretation, Taney's constitutional reading featured the use of extraconstitutional and post-founding-era sources. He cited the Articles of Confederation, "the legislation and histories of the times," and the Declaration of Independence to "show that neither the class of persons who had been imported as slaves nor their descendants, whether they had become free or not, were then acknowledged as part of the people, nor intended to be included in the general words used in that memorable instrument."[25] Taney also referenced state legislation forbidding interracial marriage from before ratification up to 1844.[26] His reading emphasized continuity: just as the tie between Euro-Americans and their founding-era predecessors allowed them to claim promised constitutional privileges, so the link between African Americans and their enslaved ancestors made them ineligible for such privileges. Forming a new nation signaled a sharp break from the past, but in Taney's view, it also froze the era's inequities for all succeeding time: At the framing, blacks could not be citizens, but could be property; therefore, seventy years later, Dred Scott could not sue in court, but he could be held as property. Denying his ancestors citizenship in the past held him hostage in the present.

In a striking acknowledgment, Taney cited the phrase "all men are created equal" and granted that "the general words ... would seem to embrace the whole human family, and if they were used in a similar instrument at this day [they] would be so understood." Drawing attention to these memorable words with seemingly universal applicability, Taney admitted that recent developments in moral sentiment gave them a more

[21] Ibid., 405. [22] Ibid., 408. [23] Ibid., 409. [24] Ibid., 410. [25] Ibid., 407.
[26] Ibid., 412–16.

egalitarian meaning. He went on to argue that because these inclusive significations rested on postratification developments, they must be set aside in favor of original exclusive meanings. He asserted that "the enslaved African race were not intended to be included, and formed no part of the people who framed and adopted this declaration." The founders had used "the ordinary language of the day, and no one misunderstood."[27] Aware of changing perceptions and sympathies that gave old words new meanings, Taney rendered these new meanings irrelevant when interpreting the Constitution.[28] While many antislavery constitutional readers, like their antislavery biblical counterparts, posited that the founders had discreetly undermined slavery in their slavery sanctioned context, Taney rejected such explanations as dangerously naïve.

The chief justice highlighted such change, but only to warn that it could obscure the founding moment. Precisely because he believed "it is difficult at this day to realize the state of public opinion" in the founding era, Taney stressed the clarifying value of his historical lesson about blacks.[29] Wishfully, he again presumed, "No one ... supposes that any change in public opinion ... should induce the court to give the words of the Constitution a more liberal construction in their [blacks'] favor than they were intended to bear when the instrument was framed and adopted." In this clash of historical modes, the synchronic trumped the diachronic, unless the diachronic revealed continuity: present views either gave way to founding-era opinions or confirmed them, in which case the eras complemented rather than contradicted each other. Taney insisted readers should not force current ideas about blacks into the text, for "it is obvious," he repeated, "that they were not even in the minds of the framers ... when they [the framers] were conferring special rights and privileges on citizens."[30] Like an archaeologist in search of a precious relic, Taney brushed aside the accruing dirt and dross that threatened to hide original truths. His historical excavation showed that Scott would

---

[27] Ibid., 410.
[28] See Streichler, *Justice Curtis*, 122–25. Taney had issued decisions grounded in historical change. In *Charles River Bridge* (1837), he famously ruled in favor of commercial progress, arguing that to do otherwise would throw the nation "back to the improvements of the last century." On that occasion, he claimed continuity with the founding era even as he prescribed progress, *Proprietors of Charles River Bridge* v. *Proprietors of Warren Bridge*, 36 U.S. 420, 423 (1837). Though a good candidate to evidence historical change and distance, the issue of commerce did not draw as much attention to the founding era nor introduce near as much division and disagreement as did the slavery issue. See Parker, *Common Law*, 128–58.
[29] *Scott v. Sandford*, 403, 407.   [30] Ibid., 411–12.

have been a noncitizen when the document was written, and so Scott could not now sue in federal court.

Once again, interpretive debates over slavery threatened to historicize an entire canon. While Taney insisted on the continued relevance of the Constitution and the Declaration, he aimed to constrain their meanings by binding them to a particular moment. Refuting both Garrisonians, who held onto the Declaration's ostensibly universal ideas, and antislavery constitutionalists, who bound the Constitution to the Declaration and the perceived antislavery spirit of the founding era, Taney subjected the Declaration to the Constitution and to the proslavery spirit he ascribed to that period.

After taking the time to teach a lengthy historical lesson, Taney concluded that the *Dred Scott* case rested outside federal jurisdiction. He thus relied on the ruling of the Missouri Supreme Court, which wielded state law to cast Scott as a slave. For all intents and purposes, Taney had ruled on the matter at hand and might have closed his decision. Instead, he continued to write, delivering an executive-backed pronouncement on the territorial question, which the dissenters dismissed as lacking authority and the press attacked as *obiter dictum*.[31]

Almost in passing, Taney declared the Missouri Compromise unconstitutional, and he did so by uncovering original intent through historical explication. Appealing to the "history of the times," he issued a narrow reading of the clause granting Congress territorial power, arguing that it referred strictly to land held in common at ratification. He thus declared that it had "no bearing on the present controversy."[32] Throughout this portion of his decision, Taney used words such as "specific," "particular," and "local" in an effort to "put aside ... any argument, drawn from precedents, showing the extent of the power which the General Government exercised over slavery in this Territory."[33] Taney's excavation uncovered both permanent axioms and transient powers, and in both instances his historical findings further bound slaves to their masters.

While some of the justices offered little more than their general assent in their opinions, others built on Taney's historical arguments.[34] In his separate opinion, Peter Daniel asserted that "the following are truths

---

[31] Fehrenbacher points out that Taney's ruling was consistent with the Court's actions in prior cases involving judicial review, thus discounting the view that it was an anomaly in this respect. Fehrenbacher, *Dred Scott Case*, 209–35 and 330–32.
[32] *Scott v. Sandford*, 432.   [33] Ibid., 436, 438, 442.
[34] Not all of the justices addressed each issue. Catron, Campbell, and Nelson did not discuss the status of free African Americans. But, despite some distinctions, Fehrenbacher shows

which a knowledge of the history of the world, and particularly of that of our own country, compels us to know – that the African negro race never have been acknowledged as belonging to the family of nations."[35] When John Campbell delivered his concurring opinion, he might have had in mind the recent revolutions in Europe. He insisted that "the American Revolution was not a social revolution" and aimed to interpret the Constitution "by the light of the circumstances in which the Convention was placed."[36] This Alabama native, who later served as assistant secretary of war for the Confederacy, determined that the call to grant Congress power in the territories was "not supported by historical evidence."[37] In his separate opinion, John Catron, a Tennessee slaveholder, also emphasized that "every provision in that instrument has a history that must be understood before" the Constitution "can be comprehended in the relations its authors intended." Using Madison's *Papers*, Catron argued that "historical facts" evidenced the specific and limited nature of congressional power.[38] While officially sanctioning the use of contextual interpretation, the Taney court discarded as temporary those powers that threatened slavery and upheld as timeless those that endorsed the institution.

These justices claimed that public sentiment and legal decisions that they deemed continuous from the framing moment – including fixed racist ideas about blacks and set laws against miscegenation – illuminated original intent. They also claimed that contemporary public sentiment and legal decisions that they determined have deviated from that moment – including evolving egalitarian ideas about blacks, new legislation regarding congressional power in the territories, and precedent granting former slaves freedom – obscured original intent. The consistency of this interpretive position rested on discerning specific intent. If the founders intended that a certain provision should endure as a universal rule, then any departure from it must be deemed unconstitutional. If they intended that a precept should only answer specific questions in specific contexts, then continuing to apply it in new contexts must be unconstitutional. Change appeared to be a double-edged sword, but in wielding that sword Taney left blunt the side that deviated from narrow original meaning and intent.

And yet, while Taney used history in a way that ignored unexpected changes and collapsed historical distance, his attack still signaled that such

---

that "none of the major rulings in Taney's opinion can be pushed aside as unauthoritative." Fehrenbacher, *Dred Scott Case*, 333.
[35] *Scott v. Sandford*, 475.   [36] Ibid., 502, 504.   [37] Ibid., 512.
[38] Ibid., 520–21, quotation on 520.

changes had in fact created a temporal division. Implicitly, he used distance to dismiss meanings that contradicted his position, but, as in biblical debates, such usage made clear the challenge of separating transient from permanent and of determining what distance had or had not made obsolete. Taney aimed to avoid the messiness by trying to make simple assertions about what was timeless and what was timely, arguing, for example, that the framers' government "is pledged to protect [a slaveholder's right to traffic property] in all future time."[39] Such brazen declarations harkened back to earlier interpreters' assumptions about the timeless teachings of sacred texts. But the move from easy assumption to strained assertion indicated that something had changed in historical awareness; Taney's rhetoric belied an anxiousness born of a new kind of confrontation with history.

Taney tried to paint with bold and indelible strokes, but his focal point was obscured against an emerging background of historical distance that even his narrative illuminated. This had important interpretive implications. While Taney had bound meaning to the past, he never considered how the framers' original expectations might demand new meanings in light of new contexts. In recognizing that temporal differences separated the revolutionary past from his mid-nineteenth-century present, Taney characterized those differences as an interpretive problem to be overcome. But the dissenters' deeper and more precise historical excavations gave further credence to the idea that a realization of distance might warrant new readings inspired by change.

"ITS TENDENCIES WOULD GREATLY AMELIORATE THEIR CONDITION"

Dissent from northern justices was not a foregone conclusion. Grier had his marching orders from the president. Nelson was a northern "doughface" Democrat. McLean, a Republican from Ohio, had been associated with nearly every party on the political spectrum. Finally, Boston's Curtis had been fairly stable in his political ties and had tended to side with slaveholders on slavery-related issues: he had served as counsel for the defense in *Commonwealth* v. *Aves* (1836), which addressed whether a northern defendant could hold his southern son-in-law's six-year-old slave, and he had also upheld the constitutionality of the Fugitive Slave Law and issued indictments against some of its detractors.

[39] Ibid., 451–52.

Whatever their political motivations, Curtis and McLean believed that history conflicted with Taney's understanding of original intent. They argued that in a number of states, blacks had, in fact, voted at the time of ratification, and they described voting as an outward sign of citizenship. Curtis and McLean also cited the framers' expectation that future developments would expand constitutional rights and protections to free blacks. They further contended that the framers had created the clause granting Congress territorial power with an eye toward present *and* future concerns.

In contrast to Taney's constitutional reading, these opinions implied that because the framers had expected certain changes, change should be used rather than dismissed in constitutional interpretation. Rather than bind constitutional meaning to the past or dictate that old meanings hold sway, this kind of appeal opened up space for new meanings in new settings. To be sure, appeals to an original expectation of change can mute awareness of the contingent nature of change and mitigate a sense of historical distance: expecting change removes the unpredictability of change and when expected changes do in fact occur, this suggests that the changes were inevitable. This apparent inevitability draws together the time in which those changes occurred and the predictive moment in the past. Nevertheless, much like Douglass and Lincoln, while McLean and Curtis uncovered an original expectation of change, they also pointed out developments that undermined the framers' expectations. Such narratives highlighted the contingent nature of change and the reality of unanticipated temporal difference.

Covering thirty-five pages, McLean's opinion was more extensive than any single concurring or separate opinion.[40] He began by declaring defective the plaintiff's plea that a free black who descended from slaves could not be a citizen. Then, he argued that Scott, as a person born under the Constitution and a resident of a state different from Sanford, could claim access to the privileges and immunities clause and sue in federal court. Before proceeding further, McLean questioned the relevance of the Court's claim "that a colored citizen would not be an agreeable member of society." By ascribing this view to the framers and their audience, Taney had attempted to make this a constitutional position. Although McLean considered this "more a matter of taste than of law," he indicated that African Americans had, in fact, voted as members of states.[41] Having

---

[40] Ibid., 529–64. [41] Ibid., 533.

dispatched Taney's extralegal assertion, McLean proceeded to take apart the central components of Taney's decision.

McLean used Madison's *Papers* to historicize slavery and the idea of slave property, arguing that "slavery is emphatically a State institution" and, following a long line of antislavery writers, cited the "historical fact that James Madison ... was solicitous to guard the language of that instrument so as not to convey the idea that there could be property in man."[42] McLean viewed slavery and slave property, like the slave trade and slave trafficking, as archaisms. He valued "the lights of Madison, Hamilton, and Jay as a means of construing the Constitution" and opposed efforts to look "behind that period into a traffic which is now declared to be piracy."[43] McLean characterized slavery as an institution of a dark, prefounding past, and disregarded that era's interpretive power.

McLean had his eye on the founding era and on the founding generation's view of the future. With many of his contemporaries, he saw the Constitution as an epochal divider that initiated a more egalitarian age. He wrote that "our independence was a great epoch in the history of freedom, and while I admit the Government was not made especially for the colored race, yet many of them were citizens of the New England States, and exercised, the rights of suffrage when the Constitution was adopted, and it was not doubted by any intelligent person that its tendencies would greatly ameliorate their condition."[44] McLean held that the Constitution divided time, but also that it was made to change over time. He explained how several of the new states abolished slavery in their jurisdictions, which confirmed the "well known fact that a belief was cherished by the leading men, South as well as North, that the institution of slavery would gradually decline until it would become extinct."[45] McLean historicized and localized slavery, in some ways working to rebury the relic Taney had uncovered even while participating in an effort to resurrect and mobilize the framers' occluded original expectations of abolition.

McLean observed that new contingencies, including the "increased value of slave labor" and "the culture of cotton and sugar, prevented the realization of this expectation."[46] He blamed corrupt interests and the "degradation of negro slavery" – the same sources presented by Parker and Abraham Lincoln – for hindering expected advances in egalitarian sentiment and commensurate legislation.[47] McLean agreed with Taney that change could obscure original intent or, in McLean's case, original

[42] Ibid., 536, 537.   [43] Ibid., 537.   [44] Ibid.   [45] Ibid., 538.   [46] Ibid.   [47] Ibid., 537.

expectation. However, what McLean found obscuring was the decline rather than the rise of egalitarian sentiment. And yet, he also held that historical change, as an interpretive lens gifted by the founders themselves, might reveal as much as it might conceal. Brushing aside the unexpected change in the form of proslavery consolidation illuminated the original expectation of slavery's demise. As with narratives like Parker's, which traced both general progress and particular decline, McLean's juxtaposition of anticipated and actual developments drew attention to contingent changes and the distance that those changes placed between the present and the founding past.

In discussing congressional power in the territories, McLean again appealed to the framers' future-oriented intentions but also endorsed legal departure from original intent if that departure proved beneficial. He first appealed to future-oriented intentions in arguing that because "the Constitution was formed for our whole country," "expansion or contraction" need not alter "fundamental law." He then noted that Congress had, in fact, established temporary governments and, using rhetoric reminiscent of Lincoln's attack on the Kansas–Nebraska Act, scoffed at the "extraordinary" finding that Congress did not have such power.[48] Pausing on this point, McLean asked, "What do the lessons of wisdom and experience teach ... if the new light, which has so suddenly and unexpectedly burst upon us, be true?" McLean insisted that even if the framers had intended to restrict congressional power, the "advancement and prosperity" that came from "acquiescence under a settled construction" that Congress *did* have power in the territories made this "construction" more valuable than the framers' supposedly original intent. He tied this "practical wisdom" of assenting to beneficial precedent to the examples of founding figures such as Madison and wondered if "this impressive lesson" had been "lost to the present generation."[49] Once again, McLean appealed to the framers to endorse legal change.

In addressing laws related to slavery in the territories, McLean grounded his reasoning in historical evidence, noting that "it is refreshing to turn to the early incidents of our history and learn wisdom from the acts of the great men who have gone to their account."[50] Along with Madison's *Papers*, he used the *Somerset* decision to contend that masters lost local rights over their slaves when they carried them into free states and territories. He also argued that the Missouri Compromise was consistent with the Northwest Ordinance, the enactment of which rested on

[48] Ibid., 545.   [49] Ibid., 546.   [50] Ibid., 545.

an act of Congress under the Constitution. Continuing his argument from continuity, he used the decisions of state supreme courts, including the Supreme Court of Missouri, to show that the common law that had made Scott free in free regions protected his freedom when he was in slave regions. In tracing these legal continuities, McLean concluded that *Dred Scott v. Emerson* had "overruled the settled law for near thirty years."[51] In his account, context and continuity favored Scott's freedom.

Like Taney, McLean valued legislative actions seen as continuous with founding-era sentiment and damned departures from precedent, but, unlike Taney, he was comfortable with legal evolution. He implied that law, instead of imposing change, should respond to it. More specifically, McLean believed law should develop not only in relation to original expectations of change, including the framers' antislavery anticipation, but also in accordance with the practical needs of the nation. He thus appealed to the past to encourage legal development; he used both sides of the double-edged sword of history, including the side Taney left blunt. Drawing on the interpretive power of history's diachronic mode, McLean suggested the time had come for a new construction.

"THE GREAT TRUTHS ... THEY WERE READY AND ANXIOUS TO MAKE EFFECTUAL"

Reaching sixty-nine pages and comparable in length only to Taney's fifty-four-page decision, Curtis's dissenting opinion covered much of the same material as McLean's. Curtis also began by setting aside as irrelevant the plea's link between Scott's enslavement and "the fact that his parents were sold as slaves."[52] He undermined the conflation between black slaves of the revolutionary past and their living descendants and proceeded to address the actual question raised by the plea of whether one's ancestral tie to enslaved blacks invalidated claims to citizenship. Curtis argued that states retained the right to determine citizenship under the Constitution and that state citizenship constituted federal citizenship: if citizens of states became federal citizens at ratification, then in a number of states, free blacks had gained US citizenship at birth. Curtis concluded that "in some of the original thirteen states, free colored persons" who were descended from slaves "were citizens of those States," voted at the time of ratification, and had the right to sue, thus proving the plea was incorrect.[53] Rather than conflate Scott with his

---

[51] Ibid., 555. [52] Ibid., 564–633, quotation on 569. [53] Ibid., 575.

enslaved ancestors, Curtis linked him to the contingent potential that blacks at the founding could be either slave or free. In stark contrast to the way in which he had brought together past and present when defending the Fugitive Slave Law in 1850, Curtis's reasoning in *Dred Scott* marked change and distance from the founding era.

In focusing on Dred Scott and his ancestors, the Court's decision placed an unprecedented amount of attention on blacks and the revolutionary era. The nature of the debate over slavery, which Taney had ratified in his decision, allowed Curtis to consider the place of blacks in the past and the framers' original expectations about their place in America's future. His historical findings led him to conclude that the framers had anticipated beneficial changes for blacks. Curtis worked to shift the focus of the debate from proslavery clauses and proslavery intent to black actors, African American citizenship, and the founding-era expectation of abolition. This shift corresponded with his apparent turn from proslavery pawn to antislavery ally.

Curtis historicized the Declaration even as he posited that the founders had expected that eventually it would apply to blacks. While noting, in passing, that he would not examine founding-era opinions of blacks or discuss the intent "of those who asserted ... that all men are created equal," Curtis nonetheless drew attention to the Declaration's famous phrases.[54] Although Curtis conceded that, had Jefferson meant to include blacks in the designation "all men" in 1776, it might have produced "more evil than good," he also opined that historical investigation would show "that the great truths they [the founders] asserted on that solemn occasion, they were ready and anxious to make effectual, wherever a necessary regard to circumstances ... would allow." Curtis believed that the founders expected blacks to benefit from the Declaration's egalitarian principles in the right circumstances.[55]

Curtis's "opinion" on this matter approached those of antislavery biblical and constitutional interpreters who emphasized the expediency of Christian and American founders. In a way, he contradicted Taney's interpretive directive to dismiss changes in popular sentiment, particularly when it could be shown that the founders had expected the changes. In other words, Curtis intimated that it was precisely because the founding fathers had anticipated change that their descendants should be allowed to adapt the meaning of the Constitution's language to the circumstances of their own time. He remained committed to the framers' intent, but instead

[54] Ibid., 574. [55] Ibid., 575.

of insisting that their intent demanded strict allegiance to old interpretations, as he had in 1850, he now implied that their intent required new interpretations. Curtis applied his understanding of common law to the Constitution, holding that in general terms construction should evolve in relation to historical development.[56] Like McLean's, Curtis's rhetoric pointed toward a constitutional reading that internalized historical change.

Turning attention to the territorial clause, Curtis grounded his discussion in context and continuity. Noting that "some facts" of the Constitution's framing and ratification would "shed much light" on the issue, Curtis, like McLean, emphasized the Convention's familiarity with the Northwest Ordinance.[57] He allowed that the clause referred to immediate concerns but argued that the framers had meant for it to apply to later land acquisitions as well. He found nothing "which restricts its operation to territory owned ... when the Constitution was adopted."[58] The framers, he insisted, had made provisions for both their own circumstances and for future developments.

Continuing the contextual argument, Curtis noted that "the allowance and the prohibition of negro slavery were recognised subjects of municipal legislation."[59] To substantiate this claim, he traced eight instances in which Congress had prohibited slavery and six in which it had allowed slavery, lining up examples from the presidency of Washington to that of John Quincy Adams. Curtis valued the continuity indicated in "the practical construction of the Constitution contemporaneously with its going into effect, by men intimately acquainted with its history from their personal participation in framing and adopting it, and continued by them through a long series of acts."[60] He thus contended that the framers intended to have the territorial clause be applied to slavery in future territories and that postratification legislation had corresponded with this intent. Even in this appeal to continuity, Curtis's reading indicated distance from the framing by ascribing forward-looking intentions to the framers, especially as he tracked the Court's deviations from continuous practice.

Curtis censured what he viewed as new constitutional readings resulting from political passion. Because political reasons differ "in different men" and "in the same men at different times," and because the framers had been clear on the territorial clause's present and future purpose,

---

[56] See Streichler, *Justice Curtis*, 6, 125–34, 209–10. [57] *Scott v. Sandford*, 605.
[58] Ibid., 612. [59] Ibid., 616. [60] Ibid., 619.

Curtis demanded a "strict interpretation."[61] If "the history of this provision" showed that the framers and ratifiers intended to introduce an exception, Curtis would carefully weigh "such considerations." However, he required something other than volatile "abstract political reasoning" to alter his interpretation "where the Constitution has said *all* needful rules and regulations."[62] Curtis faulted the Court not only for being politically motivated but also for issuing a ruling that deviated from original meanings and subsequent practices consistent with those meanings.

CHANGE, CONSTITUTIONAL CONSTRUCTION, AND HISTORICAL DISTANCE

In both the decision and the dissent, the justices recognized the reality of historical change and distance, but the two sides valued these realities differently. Taney argued that some constitutional passages referred strictly to temporary and local concerns – such as the clause granting Congress territorial power – thus rendering subsequent legislative use of those clauses unconstitutional. By implying that the framers had not made provisions for new land acquisitions, this reading proscribed interpretive changes related to such acquisitions. In essence, the clause still applied, but in the negative: because the passage did not positively grant Congress power over slavery in future territories, subsequent use of that power was unconstitutional. In such cases, provisions that the framers had made for all time, including the protection of individual property rights, came into play. In short, the Court's majority held that historical changes must yield to static meanings.

In contrast, McLean and Curtis opined that the framers had crafted the Constitution with an awareness that the future might, owing to historical changes – such as expected land acquisitions or shifts in public opinion – require new constructions. Like Taney, Curtis and McLean aimed to recover timeless constitutional meanings, but they held that some of those timeless meanings allowed for and even required the Constitution to evolve with historical development. While theirs was not the full-blown living constitutionalism that emerged much later, they did conceive of a constitution that was meant to accommodate new circumstances. In general, antebellum historical consciousness constrained interpreters to search out and either reject or accept original meanings, but developments in this historical consciousness encouraged a third path: appealing to an

---

[61] Ibid., 621.   [62] Ibid., 621, 623, emphasis in original.

original intent wherein the framers conceived of a constitution that could adapt to temporal changes and new circumstances.

According to this formulation, the Constitution's endurance depended on adaptability. While the amendment mechanism, which Taney had referenced, spoke to the future-oriented nature of the framers' project, the prospect of emendation called for interpretive restraint. In other words, precisely because a mechanism existed for official changes in the form of amendments, informal changes in the form of new interpretations and constructions seemed illegitimate.[63] But there had not been an amendment since 1804, and the two that followed the 1789 Bill of Rights seemed more like administrative fine-tunings than drastic constitutional transformations, which suggested that weighty formal emendations were a thing of the past. Perhaps the growing temporal gap since such changes, like the distance from the founding era, opened up space for interpretive freedom. The dissenters' opinions implied that if the framers created a document with an expectation of change, then the main text of the Constitution could and should, of necessity, be molded to the exigencies of the times in which it persisted. This kind of an originalist appeal countenanced and even required a Constitution amenable to change.

As in prior interpretive debates over slavery, the deciding and dissenting opinions in *Dred Scott* uncovered change by tracing deviations from original intent and original expectation. Taney earnestly attempted to set aside what he perceived to be a deviation from original ideas (e.g., shifts in public opinion to more egalitarian views about blacks) and to collapse the time between 1857 and the founding era to reclaim those ideas; these attempts attested to the realities of historical change and distance. Similarly, when McLean and Curtis identified original expectations of change that seemed to contradict the circumstances of the 1850s (i.e., when slavery became more entrenched instead of fading away and when the Court ruled according to new proslavery political stances), their narratives also drew attention to temporal vicissitude and historical dislocation. Regardless of how the various justices viewed and used change, their opinions exposed the reality of the historical distance separating the founding era from the present. The relatively short time between the

---

[63] See Donald S. Lutz, "Toward a Theory of Constitutional Amendment," in *Responding to Imperfection: The Theory and Practice of Constitutional Amendment*, ed. Sanford Levinson (Princeton, NJ, 1995), 237–74. David Holland applied this theory to antebellum biblicism in "Sovereign Silences and the Voice of War in the American Conflict over Slavery," *Law and History Review* 26 (Fall 2008): 571–94.

two periods protected the revered Constitution from widespread cries of obsolescence, but such discussions did raise questions about its relationship to temporal evolution, leading some Americans to sense that historical changes since the founding era had created a vast temporal gap between the present and this particular favored past.

While the dissenters grounded their positions in historical arguments, they also appealed to the kind of extralegal reasoning that some antislavery thinkers used to supplement or supplant traditional sources of religious, moral, political, and legal reasoning. McLean in particular contended that a slave "bears the impress of his Maker, and is amenable to the laws of God and man, and he is destined to an endless existence."[64] Appeals to abstract truths had found their way into official settings. McLean's statement aligned with the dissenters' idea that blacks' legal rights should change over time in relation to new contexts. He seemed to suggest not only that Scott and his fellow African Americans, free and enslaved, possessed the potential for citizenship, which both historical and extrahistorical sources revealed, but also that the requisite circumstances were now, or soon would be, in place to realize that potential.

"AN INCONSISTENCY ... WHICH IT WAS SUPPOSED THE PROGRESS OF EVENTS WOULD REMOVE"

Creating the circumstances for abolition and black citizenship partly depended on the public response to *Dred Scott*, which came quickly. The Republican press, which had learned that the ruling would not favor Scott, began denouncing the Court even before Taney issued his decision. While the debate between Taney and Curtis continued as the dissenting opinions were published and the chief justice's decision was then revised and published, most detractors did not address the decision's specifics but instead attacked the Court as overreaching and conspiratorial.[65] Rather than attend to the question of citizenship or the authority of precedent, they insisted that Taney's ruling on the territorial question was unwarranted.[66] In contrast to these detractors, a number of southern and northern Democratic newspapers heralded the opinion and,

---

[64] *Scott v. Sandford*, 550.
[65] See, for example, *New York Daily Tribune*, March 9, 1857. On the postdecision back-and-forth, see Fehrenbacher, *Dred Scott Case*, 315–21; and Allen, *Origins of the Dred Scott Case*, 203–08.
[66] Potter, *The Impending Crisis*, 281–85.

to the chagrin of the Republicans, tied criticism of the Court to that of the Constitution. One northern newspaper writer concluded that the Republicans "hate the Constitution, the Bible, and God."[67] Despite the polemical and political nature of the response to the decision, many critical observers took notice of its historical components and responded in kind.

The stark distinctions in historical understanding and argumentation between the chief justice and Curtis opened the door to alternative constitutional readings. While proslavery southerners upheld Taney's decision as historically sound, their opponents dismissed it as historically faulty. Most respondents centered their discussions on the founding era, its documents, and developments since that time. They did so, in part, due to the belief that while few could follow legal reasoning, almost all could understand American history, and, as congressman Joshua Giddings wrote in a published letter to Taney, "the inquiry into the views of those who framed the Declaration ... is more properly a matter of history than of law."[68] Taney accepted that constitutional interpretation was a matter of history, and most respondents felt comfortable meeting him on those grounds. New Haven's *New Englander* noted, "If the case were one simply of technical and subtle law, the 'lay' public would leave such examination to the lawyers," but the decision entered "into a field where the student of history" could contribute, and thus, the people felt authorized to voice their views.[69] In the 1840s and 1850s, a range of antislavery writers had called for popular constitutionalisms, and now newspapers voiced the popular opinion that Taney's decision was "a falsification of history" and that it contradicted "the notorious facts of history."[70] In noting that the Court had "exceeded itself" in *Dred Scott*, the *Chicago Tribune* declared that it was "time the people resumed the law making prerogative."[71] The roles of the people and the historian merged in the response to *Dred Scott*.

Most of those with legal training focused their responses on jurisdictional and territorial questions. Thomas Hart Benton, a rare antislavery Democrat, addressed these concerns in his lengthy *Historical and Legal Examination* (1857). While he agreed with Taney that the territorial

---

[67] See *Daily Iowa State Democrat*, March 17, 1857.   [68] *Liberator*, April 3, 1857.
[69] "Opinion of Judge Daniel, in the Case of Dred Scott," *New Englander* 15 (August 1857): 345.
[70] *Chicago Daily Tribune*, September 18, 1857; *Boston Independent*, March 19, 1857.
[71] *Chicago Daily Tribune*, September 18, 1857.

clause referred specifically to the disposal of public lands held at the time of ratification, he used historical evidence to show Congress's repeated use of power in the territories, which, he argued, sanctioned future use. The aged Benton's emphasis on precedential congressional action was out of step with the constitutionalization of the slavery debate. Against the backdrop of that debate, his focus on post-founding-era developments inadvertently called into question the Constitution's reach and contributed to a sense of distance from the founding era.[72]

Capitalizing on their access to newspapers with small and large readerships, a host of antislavery writers published critiques of the *Dred Scott* decision, collectively setting off the founding era as distant. Abolitionists whose reliance on abstract truths stretched far beyond McLean's more openly questioned the relevance of a dated document in the new nineteenth century. John Humphrey Noyes's *Circular* responded to the decision by casting aside the Constitution in favor of a higher guide. In a March 1857 article, one writer perceived "an instinct for broader freedom growing" beyond "that which became embodied in the Constitution." The writer explained, "musty precedent and time-honored institutions have not stood, and in the long run cannot stand, against the instinct of freedom."[73] Voicing a common belief in the spread of antislavery sentiment, the article's author held that the outdated Constitution and the antiquated institution of slavery must give way to the voice of the people and the progress of freedom. In the same issue of the *Circular*, another writer observed, "All profess to venerate that instrument, and worship the same long list of saints of the American calendar who made it. And yet that same instrument ... binds each State, through all time, to respect all the laws that every other State may make to hold men to service." Rather than proposing formal or informal constitutional emendation, the writer suggested that "if the 'Expounders' of the Constitution would cease their quarrel about its meaning, and begin to criticize the instrument itself, and the virtues and talents of the men who made it, there would be more hope of progress, if not of peace."[74] A growing number of higher-law idealists were ready to accept as historically sound proslavery interpretations and then dismiss the Constitution, its creators, and their views as outdated.

---

[72] [Thomas Hart Benton], *Historical and Legal Examination of that Part of the Decision of the Supreme Court of the United States in the Dred Scott Case Which Declares the Unconstitutionality of the Missouri Compromise Act* (New York, 1857).
[73] *Circular*, March 19, 1857.   [74] Ibid.

As expected, the *Liberator* gave voice to similar critiques. In May, it published the proceedings of the AASS's annual meeting in New York City, which featured speakers such as William Lloyd Garrison, Wendell Phillips, Thomas Wentworth Higginson, and Robert Purvis. Swept up by the interpretive currents, Garrison in his opening speech decried Taney's decision as "marked by ... a daring disregard of all historical verity" and labeled it "a wanton perversion of the Constitution," though he still described the document as "'a covenant with death and an agreement with hell.'" Higginson showed little deference to the Constitution and instead endorsed an interpretive relativism: "Give us a Supreme Court that is favorable to liberty, and the Constitution is an anti-slavery document to-morrow." Although he believed the era's antislavery demands should dictate the text's meaning, he valued the facts of slave resistances much more than theories about a "dead letter." Higginson approved of any and all methods to achieve emancipation, "Constitution or no Constitution."[75] Purvis, an African American abolitionist who had helped Garrison found the AASS, described the Smithian interpretation as "contrary to history and common sense," and Phillips aimed to "exercise" the "timidity" of antislavery constitutionalists, "who [were] exceedingly tender of the flower-pot – the Constitution."[76] The evening speakers offered similar views. Reformed Presbyterian minister J. R. W. Sloane lamented that some men recognized "no higher law" and felt a need to either "obey the Constitution and disregard [their] conscience, or obey [their] conscience and forsake the Constitution."[77] This group left no doubt about which source held its allegiance. In his speech given on the second day of the meeting, Phillips declared, "I know no Constitution; success to the strongest arm; might makes right to-day."[78] Patience had worn thin among many radical abolitionists.

Some speakers used religious rhetoric in ways that continued to bring together constitutional and biblical interpretation. During the first day's evening session, William Furness had lamented that "the reverence ... for the Constitution and the Union is like that of the ancient Jews for the Temple."[79] The Unitarian minister, who had voiced his Transcendentalist views during the miracles controversy two decades earlier, continued to value an internal moral sense over dated written documents. As with Parker, Furness transferred his reading of the Bible to the Constitution.

---

[75] *Liberator*, May 22, 1857.   [76] Ibid.   [77] Ibid.   [78] *Liberator*, May 29, 1857.
[79] Ibid.

And while Furness referenced the Constitution's status as a sacred text, his comments and others like them placed that status in question.

Some respondents to *Dred Scott* made more explicit use of developments in biblical criticism to comment on the Court's constitutional construction. Weeks before the AASS's meeting, a sarcastic antislavery writer for the AASS's *National Anti-Slavery Standard* observed that while the Constitution had been viewed as an inspired document since the Compromise of 1850, "the political scribes have not been disposed to receive the Declaration ... as entitled to a place in the *canon* of political inspiration." The writer, who had in mind those who thought the text's universal statements were either too abstract or clearly wrong, observed that the Declaration was now "looked upon as a sort of *old* and *repealed* dispensation, the *Andrews Norton* theory prevailing with reference to its authority."[80] The writer, who knew enough about developments in biblical scholarship to know that Norton had privileged the New over the Old Testament, observed that the Court had valued the newer Constitution above the older Declaration. Most antislavery writers and thinkers rejected this valuation, either prizing the Declaration while damning the Constitution, or using the Declaration to interpret the Constitution.

Garrisonians opted for the former approach, and in doing so, they framed the current struggle for abolition in revolutionary terms. At the AASS's annual meeting in May, Baptist minister Andrew T. Foss followed Garrison and Phillips in describing the current crisis as a revolution. He deemed the "present revolution as of more importance than" all former revolutions, including that of 1776. Foss viewed the crisis, which centered on "the rights of man," as the "legitimate fruit of the government which our fathers made." Foss knew he was "treading on dangerous ground" in criticizing "the fathers," but he insisted that they "did a very wrong and wicked work." The minister believed that "if their spirits" were present, they would not be displeased with his remarks, reasoning that "our fathers would have no objection to their sons being better men than they were." Foss noted that they had "believed that slavery would in a few years come to an end," but he saw this founding view as naïve, stating that "they cast the seed of slavery into the soil, and it was in vain for them to expect to reap liberty."[81] Rather than appeal to an original expectation of abolition to argue for an antislavery reading of the Constitution, Foss

---

[80] *National Anti-Slavery Standard*, April 11, 1857, emphasis in original.
[81] *National Anti-Slavery Standard*, May 23, 1857.

condemned the framers' original sin, which had resulted in slavery's advance. All of these discussions demarcated the revolutionary era and the founding period as temporally distant.

Although the Garrisonian reading rang out louder than ever before, it sounded from ever more isolated sources. Most antislavery respondents to *Dred Scott* followed Curtis in contending that free blacks were citizens at the founding and also followed McLean in proposing that the founding era had initiated an evolution in public sentiment. The dissenters' carefully packaged explications made them easy for others to use. Above all, Taney's critics reiterated earlier antislavery accounts that appealed to the framers' expectation of abolition, which obviated the choice between conscience and Constitution.

Some respondents countered Taney's static proslavery portrayal of the founding era with a static antislavery depiction of the same. A May 1857 article published in New York's *Putnam's* traced the development of antislavery sentiment from the sixteenth century to 1776, which the article's writer designated as an egalitarian "epoch for all coming time."[82] Other abolitionist newspapers, like Gamaliel Bailey's *National Era*, labeled the period "an Antislavery era."[83] The writer for *Putnam's* complained that Taney "post-dates the period of the black-plague which ravaged human conscience by a half century at least; just as the spirit of his decision is a whole century behind his own times."[84] Some of Taney's Catholic coreligionists felt the need to designate the decision as even more archaic. In April, Orestes Brownson's *Quarterly Review*, which generally agreed with the Court's decision, had relegated the claim that blacks were not citizens "to an epoch prior to the introduction of Christianity," finding it "more in accordance with the teaching of Aristotle than with that of the Gospel."[85] The paper wanted to dissociate Taney's claim from Catholicism, which Protestant contemporaries viewed as outdated. While not going as far as other antislavery publications, Brownson's *Review* cited a founding-era "opinion against the justice of negro slavery."[86] Designating the founding era as an epoch of freedom contradicted many antislavery writers' growing recognition of slavery's presence in the American past and their increasing emphasis on the framers' expediency.

---

[82] "History, as Expounded by the Supreme Court," 543.
[83] *National Era*, March 19, 1857.
[84] "History, as Expounded by the Supreme Court," 543.
[85] "The Slavery Question Once More," *Brownson's Quarterly Review* 2 (April 1857): 276.
[86] Ibid., 275.

But, as with the writer for *Putnam's*, many depicted proslavery developments, including Taney's decision, as an anachronism that opposed the expectations of the founders, who "looked towards a speedy and universal freedom."[87] These persistent efforts to read the Constitution in light of the Declaration's universal promises and to reclaim the founding era as a transcendent epoch again indicated unexpected changes. Resuscitative attempts to revive the past signaled that the past was indeed dead.

In a later edition of *Putnam's*, a writer attempted to resurrect Jefferson and Adams and place them alongside Taney's antislavery critics. The author asked, "Were they with us to-day, is there a doubt that they would unite in the most determined resistance to the effort ... to establish ... a custom which they considered to be wholly an evil, and for a speedy extirpation of which their hope was coördinate with their faith in the progressive civilization of mankind?"[88] A careful redaction of the framers' writings allowed the writer to claim continuity in antislavery sentiment. The founding fathers could be called on to support abolitionism just as easily as they were called on to support proslavery laws. Again, the tradition of conflating distance from the favored past persisted despite, and sometimes because of, a growing sense of its presence. And yet, this writer also voiced the common argument of original expectation, claiming that the founders believed that slavery's gradual extinction would parallel humanity's advance. This insistence suggested that the author did not hope for a return to an era in which the sin of slavery was countenanced. Further, the fact that slavery's demise remained a potentiality rather than a reality called into question the nation's direction since the founding era and signaled distance from that past.

That historical dissonance reverberated as respondents continued to engage the justices' use of historical facts and the justices' sense of historical development. In August, a writer for the *New Englander* followed Curtis in using historical evidence to establish that free blacks had held state and federal citizenship under both the Confederation and the Constitution, and to contend that "the children of the original citizens were born citizens, and the same is true of their descendants down to the present time."[89] While Taney had conflated Dred Scott with enslaved

---

[87] "History, as Expounded by the Supreme Court," 546.
[88] "A Short Exercise for the Fourth of July," *Putnam's Monthly Magazine of American Literature, Science, and Art* 10 (July 1857): 108.
[89] "Negro Citizenship," *New Englander* 15 (August 1857): 489. The fact that Garrison's *Liberator* and Brownson's *Review* pointed out that free blacks had been citizens at the framing shows that even papers with opposing stances called out Taney on this point. See

blacks at the founding, this writer backed Curtis in using "historical facts" to link free blacks in the past with those in the present and to assert their right to sue as citizens under the privileges and immunities clause.[90]

Like many prior antislavery readings, this latest articulation of founding-era expediency and expectation suggested that the framers themselves had ratified a sense of historical awareness. The writer acknowledged black degradation in the founding era but argued that blacks were citizens despite such views. This highlighted the framers' foresight. They "were inconsistent," the writer explained, but "their inconsistency ... was precisely the inconsistency of all great, philosophical statesmen, whose views are in advance of the age in which they live, and the circumstances which surround them. Moreover, it was an inconsistency which was acknowledged at the time, but which it was supposed the progress of events would remove."[91] In heralding the framers as hopeful prophets, this view required adherence to an interpretation that was open to historical change.

But this writer, like the others, found declension instead of progress: Taney "speaks as if there had been a great change in this country in favor of the blacks, since the Revolution .... But we believe the reverse is nearer the reality." The writer traced "a great apostasy ... from the opinions of the Revolutionary era," noting the disenfranchisement of blacks in several states.[92] Once again, an antislavery writer lamented the spread of prejudicial feeling, which obscured more inclusive original expectations.

In discussing Taney's appeal to state laws, the writer found an even greater "misapprehension of historical facts."[93] Finding the chief justice to be a better politician than a historian or a judge, this critic argued that Taney had measured "the Virginia of the Revolution, and of the other slave states of that period, by the Virginia of to-day."[94] Anticipating a central modernist critique, the writer questioned, "Is it not obvious that Judge Taney is interpreting past history with the feelings of the present?"[95] If the issue of slavery often encouraged presentism, it also created greater awareness of presentist readings and even inspired critiques of the same. The availability of this critique depended on an awareness – and even an assumption – of historical distance.

Liberator, April 24, 1857, and March 26, 1858; and "The Slavery Question Once More," 274–75.
[90] "Negro Citizenship," 495.   [91] Ibid., 508.   [92] Ibid., 510.   [93] Ibid., 514.
[94] Ibid., 513.   [95] Ibid., 518.

Depicting Taney's historical argument as presentist and portraying the framers as forward-thinking allowed the writer to suggest that contemporaries should "take into view the new emergencies which have arisen, and act as we are sure *they* would have acted if these circumstances had existed then."[96] The writer stressed the differences between 1787 and 1857 and implied that if the framers had predicted the emergence of the Slave Power rather than the spread of egalitarian sentiment, they would have taken greater measures to ensure slavery's demise. Consequently, this reading suggested, northerners should feel secure in taking measures to abolish slavery themselves. In arguing that historical figures had planted the seeds of egalitarian principles, and in tracing the seeds' failure rather than their fruition, this account (and the many others like it) drew attention to the historical distance from the favored founding era that resulted not only from rot but also from the inevitable passage of time.

Dred Scott marked the high point in an ongoing historical conversation about America's favored past: it directed participants, observers, and commentators to fixate on the founding era in an attempt to discern the framers' original intent, the Constitution's original meaning, and the people's original understanding. Justices and respondents on all sides of the widening sectional divide met on a historical battleground that had been prepared through nearly three decades of interpretation. In wielding history on the public stage, participants amplified the historical overtones of the debate. The decidedly historical nature of Taney's decision encouraged more people to articulate what a number of antislavery writers had been championing: popular readings of the Constitution. Most of those who responded agreed with the Court's assumption that if one could rightly read the supreme legal text in light of historical context, one could resolve the slavery crisis now and for all time. As in biblical interpretation, most respondents found what they were looking for in the past – and they continued to extract permanent proslavery and antislavery truths for present use. And once again, while the historical approach allowed for a rich range of constitutional interpretations, each reading unmistakably drew attention to the presence of historical distance from the founding era. In the nineteenth century, a range of developments cultivated new kinds of confrontations with the past, and in the United States, these confrontations revolved around interpretive debates that historicized America's favored eras and sacred texts.

---

[96] Ibid., emphasis in the original.

The constitutional debate had less to do with the fact of historical change and distance than with whether and how change and distance should shape construction. According to Taney, static and original meanings trumped the new meanings imposed on the Constitution by shifting public opinion and new legislation. Taney recognized and then dismissed historical distance in the name of legal truth. Meeting Taney on the chosen historical grounds, McLean and Curtis also sought to recover original meaning, intent, and understanding, but they left room for original expectation as well. In their effort to rescue the permanent from the transient, they recovered the framers' openness to change, implying that the Constitution should be construed in the light of expected developments. The dissenters' opinions endorsed an emerging view of the Constitution as a document that endured because it adapted to the needs of different people in different times.

While members of the Court offered differing interpretations in light of distance, the sense of distance itself encouraged popular readings. As figures such as Douglass insisted, the passage of time empowered the people as interpreters. And once again, respondents used historical change in different ways. Oneida perfectionists and Garrisonian abolitionists grew louder in dismissing the Constitution as an outdated creed. They insisted that the document was created as – and functioned as – a proslavery text standing in the way of freedom. In their judgment, timeless conscience trumped a time-bound Constitution. Their appeal to the Declaration's universal assertions and the Revolution's immediacy was an attempt to snatch a few universal truths from the clutches of an otherwise defunct era, the pastness of which seemed more clear by the year. In their case, recognizing change and distance did not inform constitutional interpretation as much as it made the interpreted text irrelevant.

Most antislavery respondents, however, opted to follow the dissenters in attacking Taney's narrative of the revolutionary era. Some argued that the framers had crafted an antislavery Declaration and Constitution in an increasingly antislavery Western world. Like Taney, they appealed to static original meanings, but ones critical of the proslavery position. Their creative revisions resurrected the founders as contemporary northern abolitionists just as Taney had resurrected them as proslavery southerners. But although these antislavery writers conflated historical distance, they also posited an original expectation of abolition and damned Taney's decision as dated. In doing so, they implied that reversals had taken place since the founding era. Like Taney, these antislavery constitutional interpreters did not value historical change as an interpretative lens, but their narratives made that change apparent.

Rather than paint with such broad strokes, other antislavery respondents depicted the founding fathers as forward-thinking in their antislavery positions: the founders had created an antislavery Constitution in spite of their proslavery constituents and audiences. Respondents proceeded to posit that the founders' original expectation that their egalitarian principles would spread in future generations had failed. Historical progress, these critics suggested, should have nurtured modern sentiments, but instead they observed that moral and political decline had reinvigorated the ancient power relation of master and slave. Consequently, the founders' exceptional ideas remained hidden behind the corrupted views of their contemporaries and descendants. These interpreters suggested it was time for Americans to recover and use the founders' ideas to bring about changes in the present. This view aimed less at reviving the founders to prescribe static axioms than at allowing their ghosts to guide their descendants toward new constitutional meanings. Similar to the opinions of McLean and Curtis, this interpretation valued changes that were consistent with original expectations and condemned those that deviated from those expectations. In their effort to reclaim pure principles from the founding era, these respondents attended to both expected and unexpected changes and insisted that the resulting historical distance should inform antislavery readings.

While none of these approaches fully valued change as a viable interpretive tool, they nonetheless spoke to its unmistakable presence. Binding change to expectations undermines an appreciation of its contingent nature, while depicting change as positive or negative and measuring it according to historically articulated ideals qualifies the interpretive value of change. However, even attempts to dismiss change as irrelevant or value it only in relation to original expectations nonetheless bring attention to its existence as a historical reality. Americans endeavored to control their historical conjurings, but those conjurings took on lives of their own when the public and political nature of the debate over slavery spread historical awareness in a way that other antebellum developments did not. In this debate, participants offered contrasting narrations of deviations from the original intent of a group of people from a set historical period. These narrations spotlighted change and highlighted its contingent nature. When discussants tracked divergences from the founding era, which they described either as antislavery innovation or proslavery consolidation, they drew more attention to the reality of change than when they outlined perceived continuities from the same period. And their calls to disregard unwanted and unexpected change only spotlighted its presence and signaled its power to divide the present from the past.

Even as constitutional interpreters attempted to set aside change, it became all the more impossible to ignore historical distance. The focus on negative change in the *Dred Scott* decision and the subsequent response seemed to signal a renewed hope of returning to the favored founding era and a fresh belief in recreating that historical context. Inherent in this hope and belief, however, was the idea that the American people remained constrained by the interpretive assumptions of their ancestors. With that constraint came opposing narratives about deviations from the framers' intent, which belied the assumption that one could collapse time. As *Dred Scott* fueled a public forum of historical debate, antislavery writers positing the framers' expectations of abolition gradually overwhelmed others who continued to ignore historical differences or insisted on reading the Constitution as a static text. In acknowledging slavery's presence in the founding era and calling on contemporaries to fulfill the framers' egalitarian expectations, these antislavery constitutionalists gave historical distance a central role in constitutional interpretation. While historicism took hold in Western thought, antebellum biblical and constitutional debates over slavery shed new light on historical change and drew unprecedented attention to historical distance. In the process, this new historical awareness began to shape the ways in which Americans read their sacred legal text.

7

"We Have to Do Not ... with the Past, but the Living Present"

The historical nature of Taney's decision moved the interpretive conversation regarding the Constitution further into the public sphere, expanding the audiences of those intent on winning over large sections of the American public to their interpretations. Prominent speakers and politicians took advantage of the setting to either affirm or challenge the federal judiciary's interpretation, a process that introduced more and more of the public to the idea that the past was profoundly different from the present. In private and public responses to *Dred Scott*, Theodore Parker, Abraham Lincoln, and Frederick Douglass reiterated antislavery readings of the founding era and its texts. These readings not only spread a sense of historical distance but also demonstrated the ways in which that sense gained power as an interpretive force.

Each of these three figures advanced antislavery readings of the Constitution in the wake of *Dred Scott*. At this stage, some might have expected Parker to use distance to abandon the Constitution once and for all, but he had always found ways to alchemize proslavery successes into freedom's advance. By 1857, he was using distance to advance a popular reading that stressed the framers' careful phrasing and the founding generation's expectations of change. Similarly, Lincoln drew on a sense of distance to confront Taney's decision. Using historical facts and the Constitution's specific wording, he emphasized the framers' technical precision to show that the text was meant to outlive the framers' context. Douglass, too, grounded his response in the antislavery expectations of the founders, distinguishing those expectations from the government's subsequent proslavery practices. Although he admitted the Slave Power's rise made him uncertain about the future, he drew attention to the unsettled nature of those proslavery advances to inspire faith in his contemporaries' moral progress. With a hope in founding-era expectations and a faith in public sentiment, these public figures advanced readings that drew attention to historical distance.

Their readings signaled historical distance in complicated ways. The focus on founding-era expediency and expectation inadvertently revealed slavery's firm place in America's favored past, and the narration of the Slave Power's rise demonstrated that slavery was still a prominent feature of the national landscape. On the surface, this narrative suggested little had changed. However, in calling attention to the dissonance between a general founding-era expectation of abolition and a sectional mid-nineteenth-century insistence on slavery's expansion, these readings indicated that the southern institution had gained power as a determinative social and political force in America. Much had changed after all.

Parker, Douglass, and Lincoln did not just signal distance; they used it in interpretation. They argued that the results of negative changes in the form of proslavery progress required progressive antislavery readings tied to the founding generation's abolitionist expectations. This argument aligned with the kind of belief in moral progress that had shaped Parker's view: the framers' error had become their descendants' sin. This belief made the Slave Power's rise all the more obvious and damnable. While many of those who perceived lamentable changes since the favored framing still called for restoration, as in Taney's effort to dismiss abolitionist advances in favor of a static meaning, Parker, Douglass, and Lincoln were not interested in setting aside the changes in order to apply set meanings from a time when slavery was culturally embedded. Decline (in the form of the Slave Power's rise) and progress (in the form of the spread of antislavery sentiment) indicated historical distance and authorized new constitutional readings.

While these readings promised to spread a sense of historical distance, they also demonstrate just how determinative historical distance and change became in antislavery constitutional interpretation. Even though the historical record does not permit a precise measure of the spread of historical awareness in this period, Lincoln's uneven rise in national politics brought these constitutional readings further into the open, expanding the group of Americans who might perceive historical differences from and changes since the founding era. However, the real significance of Douglass, Lincoln, and Parker's post–*Dred Scott* arguments rested in the fact that these individuals used a sense of change and distance to read the Constitution as an antislavery text and to insist that public sentiment endorsed this reading. In their public appeals, they argued the Constitution was not a static document, the meaning of which depended on its original proslavery context, but rather it was a flexible text, the meaning of which rested on a predicted antislavery context and actual antislavery sentiment.

The constitutional debates that culminated in *Dred Scott* and the response this decision elicited manifested the shape of American historical awareness. In conjunction with broader intellectual developments at home and abroad, decades of interpretive argumentation about the Constitution and the Bible had both permitted and constrained what could be said and written about the relationship between the present and the favored religious and legal pasts. The constitutional debates over slavery, having become the arena of the most pressing and determinative interpretive questions, had evolved in such a way as to demand new approaches to founding-era texts. An awareness of historical distance from the founding era became an interpretive problem that all parties had to address in their readings and uses of the Constitution. While some acknowledged change and then set it aside to offer strict interpretations, figures such as Douglass, Lincoln, and Parker used distance to encourage more egalitarian and progressive readings. Antebellum historical awareness allowed for a range of interpretations, but it forced interpreters to craft their readings in light of a growing perception of and attention to historical distance.

"IN A PROGRESSIVE PEOPLE THERE MUST BE A PROGRESSIVE INTERPRETATION"

Parker responded to *Dred Scott* in private letters and, when health permitted, in public speeches. Diagnosed with tuberculosis in March 1857, he ceased lecturing for much of the spring and summer, but he still voiced his opinions and considered others' views in correspondence.

In a letter written to Parker days after the decision, Lincoln's law partner, William Herndon, listed *Dred Scott* among other proslavery victories. A few months later Herndon, an antislavery Republican, noted, "I have been among our people a great deal, and I can say to you that none like it."[1] In Justice Benjamin Curtis, Herndon found a connection between proslavery progress and the rise of antislavery

---

[1] William H. Herndon to Theodore Parker, March 10, 1857 and May 14, 1857, Theodore Parker Papers, MHS.

sentiment, writing that the "nigger-driving court, and the persecutions of the Southern press will drive Curtis to be an abolitionist."² Once again, a commentator was suggesting that a proslavery development fueled antislavery sentiment.

Parker was less certain of progress, as indicated in an August letter to Herndon. Writing with characteristic anti-Catholic prejudice, he asserted that the Democratic Party "bears the same relation to Progress in America that the Roman Catholic Church does in Europe."³ Parker viewed certain parties and churches as he did certain sacred texts. As he wrote in a letter a year later, "At this day the Bible is to Protestantism what the Roman Church was then to all Christendom."⁴ Combining a Protestant anti-Catholicism with his Transcendentalist critique of Protestantism, Parker suggested that an overreliance on the Bible had hindered the progress of Christianity in the same way that Catholicism had. He believed the Democratic Party functioned in US politics like Catholicism and the Bible functioned in Christianity. To Parker, that comparison was made clear by the party's support of the recent *Dred Scott* decision, which decision he described as a "falsification of history."⁵ He no longer considered the accuracy of proslavery constitutional readings. He had transitioned from using historical awareness to set aside the Constitution to using distance to read it as a text that anticipated change.

In his public responses, Parker continued to focus on the historical flaws of the chief justice's decision. Speaking at the Massachusetts Anti-Slavery Convention in January 1858, he praised "Judge Curtis," who "in the name of History which they falsified, of Law which they profaned, of Justice which they mocked at ... pronounced his sentence against the wicked Court."⁶ Parker saw signs of a converted Curtis, who "DEFENDED ONCE THE HIGHER LAW OF RIGHT."⁷ He lamented, however, the justice's subsequent resignation. Unconvinced that Curtis had vacated the Court for financial reasons, Parker worried that the move signaled the Slave Power's growing political prowess.

Parker's narrations of decline and progress centered on whites. Peddling his romantic racial theory, he asserted that "civilization hitherto

---

² Herndon to Parker, May 14, 1857, Theodore Parker Papers.
³ Theodore Parker to William H. Herndon, August 9, 1857, Theodore Parker Papers, MHS.
⁴ Theodore Parker to Sarah B. White, May 22, 1858, Theodore Parker Papers, MHS.
⁵ Parker to Herndon, August 9, 1857, Theodore Parker Papers.
⁶ Theodore Parker, *The Present Aspect of Slavery in America and the Immediate Duty of the North* (Boston, 1858), 14–15.
⁷ Ibid., 15, emphasis in original.

has belonged only to the Caucasian race" and that "Africans have remained strangers to it in all times past."[8] Parker imposed a temporal cartography on present human experience; he cast Africans and other nonwhites, including Native Americans, as anachronistic beings, uncivilized savages in a civilized world. The point of his temporal mapping was to encourage Anglo-Americans to align their nation with other civilized countries and with the course of historical development by bringing an end to the US government's long and sordid relationship with the slave institution. Pointing to recent examples of freedom spreading abroad, he insisted that "the teachings of universal human history" are on our side.[9] Parker's sense of progress informed his call for abolition but also shaped his belief that black slaves needed white saviors. His call for new Christs was a call for white Christs.[10] White devils stood in their way.

In March, Ohio governor Salmon Chase also wrote to Parker about dark forces and the course of progress. A moderate antislavery constitutionalist, Chase had popularized the narrative about the Slave Power and had shaped the Republican Party's platform. In his letter to Parker he perceived light in the mist of darkness. "The future to me looks very hopeful," Chase wrote. "The Devil certainly has come down in great wrath these last few years, but he knows that his time is short." He argued that the Slave Power's open triumphs laid bare its true "nature." Once the light exposed the Slave Power's dark visage, the people would banish it from their presence. Then, he believed, "when we have the power it will be easy to turn all currents, even that Acherontian [sic] one of the Judiciary, into channels of Freedom."[11] The advance of antislavery sentiment gave Chase hope in the face of proslavery progress. Armed with an antislavery reading of the Constitution, he believed the northern people would rise to slay the dragon that had arisen from below.

Parker also exchanged letters on progress with Charles Sumner, who was still recovering from the congressional caning Preston Brooks had given him. In a mid-March letter to Sumner, Parker hid his belief in progress behind a statement on the outdated thinking of slavery's defenders. Citing proslavery biblical and classical appeals, he noted that "men say Slavery was consistent with a *Republican* Form of Government in Athens and Rome. No doubt of it – with their meaning of *Republican* at

---

[8] Ibid., 4.　[9] Ibid., 14.
[10] On the chauvinism of white abolitionists, see Margot Minardi, *Making Slavery History: Abolitionism and the Politics of Memory in Massachusetts* (New York, 2010), 92–94.
[11] Salmon P. Chase to Theodore Parker, March 3, 1858, Theodore Parker Papers, MHS.

that time. So Abraham's sacrifice of Isaac was 'imputed to him for Righteousness.'"[12] Parker implied that progress had altered the meaning of *Republican* and *righteousness*, rendering obsolete their prior significations. The persistence of the older usages, however, challenged his efforts to cast them as anachronistic. He remained ambivalent about his nation's historical direction.

Concerns about a lack of moral progress led Parker to consider other options. In 1857, in a reception in his home, Parker had sided with John Brown rather than William Lloyd Garrison in their debate over the means of emancipation. During the next few years, Parker joined Thomas Wentworth Higginson, Samuel Gridley Howe, Gerrit Smith, George Luther Stearns, and Franklin Benjamin Sanborn in providing Brown financial and moral support as he planned an attack on the South.[13] In March 1858, Brown met with Parker in Boston to discuss strategy.[14] Surfacing complications led Parker and other members of the Secret Six to convince Brown and an equally eager Higginson to postpone the insurrection until the following spring. While open to Brown's approach, Parker had doubts about its success. He continued to consider a constitutional avenue that depended on the progress of antislavery sentiment and faith in the people.

In late May, around the time he encouraged Brown to hold off, Parker gave a speech at the 1858 NEASS Convention, where he again described Taney's decision "as false in history as unjust in law." This statement came in a long narrative that once again laid out America's great contradiction between freedom and slavery. Parker restated his general belief in human progress, again placed "Caucasians" in the vanguard, and continued to argue that sometimes nations "stand still, or even go back." His American contemporaries thought their republic was "foremost in the world," but to Parker it resembled Turkish despotism, "the most rearword government in Europe." Slavery was to blame. Parker observed that because "what was once a transient exception in the history of the North, is becoming a typical institution" in the South, the region suffered retrogression in politics, law, commerce, and religion. Parker viewed the South

---

[12] Theodore Parker to Charles Sumner, March 15, 1858, Theodore Parker Papers, MHS, emphasis in original. On white southerners' use of classical and medieval pasts during this period, see Fox-Genovese and Genovese, *Mind of the Master Class*, 247–406.

[13] On Brown and the Secret Six, see David S. Reynolds, *John Brown, Abolitionist: The Man Who Killed Slavery, Sparked the Civil War, and Seeded Civil Rights* (New York, 2005). On Parker's involvement in particular, see Teed, *A Revolutionary Conscience*, 205–35.

[14] See John Brown to Theodore Parker, March 4, 1858, in *Life and Correspondence*, 2:163.

as a moral backwater that threatened to pollute the nation's otherwise salubrious moral climate. He asserted that "under [the Slave Power's] control, the Federal Government also retrogrades," as indicated by a clear "striding backward for five and sixty years!"[15]

Parker painted a somber picture, but he still held that the backward slide into the "Dark Ages" could be reversed. He insisted that the power rested in the broader progress of freedom and in the rule of the people. "The decision of the majority of the People is declaratory and final," he stated. Like other antislavery writers, Parker had in mind a popular reading of the Constitution.[16]

Parker's newer reading did not prize the "private opinions" of the framers, who "differed very widely on this ideal government." Instead, he focused on "the Purpose which the People had in view of making" the Constitution.[17] Parker's move mirrored an argument of Douglass, who had questioned the possibility of discerning consensus among the framers. It also imitated the argument of antislavery constitutionalists such as William Goodell, who had insisted that the framers' "intentions are *not* to be substituted for the intentions of THE PEOPLE."[18] Parker echoed Goodell in stating that the framers (some of whom, history showed, were slaveholders) "were simply the scriveners of the People."[19] While falling in line with those placing emphasis on the Constitution's words and the ratifiers' intent, Parker remained concerned with historical facts. Knowing of "no act of [the people], at that time, which intimates an intention to keep slavery," he insisted that "the Declaration affords light to read the Constitution" and that both documents uniquely embodied "the act of the People."[20] *Dred Scott* taught Parker what the fugitive slave cases had taught Douglass: the nation's prolonged affair with the sin of slavery did not originate in the Constitution but in a government that assented to an injudicious proslavery reading. Parker now looked to the people for redemption.

Parker's late push for a popular constitutionalism was grounded in his view of the founding era. The historical nature of the debate compelled interpreters to look to the past; that compulsion opened up a range of views, including one that saw the Constitution as amenable to and even generative of change. Slavery's presence in the past placed interpretive

---

[15] *Liberator*, June 4, 1858.   [16] Ibid.   [17] Ibid.
[18] Goodell, *Views of American Constitutional Law*, 83, emphases in original.
[19] *Liberator*, June 4, 1858. See Goodell, *Views of American Constitutional Law*, 139.
[20] *Liberator*, June 4, 1858.

constraints on readers, but a sense of historical distance and change allowed figures such as Parker to mine eternal principles – such as freedom for all people – from historical settings.

Parker still found the Constitution to be flawed, but now he was arguing that the framers themselves had "confessed that it had great defects." He explained that they had viewed certain passages as "exceptional" and had accepted the Constitution "as 'good for the present distress.'" He thus believed the framers would discountenance the common "talk now about the 'sacredness of the Constitution.'"[21] Parker continued to use temporal terms to highlight transient features, but now he desacralized and historicized the Constitution to rescue it. Just a few days before, Parker had written to Sarah B. White on the Bible's defects, including the mistaken teachings of Jesus. He had noted that he took "neither [Jesus] nor the New Testament for my master." But Parker still used "what is good in both ... with thankfulness of heart" and insisted that his approach to the Bible was "seven parts constructive – only the *eighth* is otherwise."[22] This interpretive approach had become even more true in Parker's reading of the nation's sacred legal text. Just as he endeavored to separate transient from permanent in the Bible, he applied the same approach to the Constitution; but rather than threaten to discard the texts because most of their teachings were transient, he used them because he believed their central truths were permanent.

Even still, Parker felt a need to cure the Constitution of its core contradictions. He looked to the founding generation for assistance, aligning the framers' expectation "that slavery would soon end in all the States" with the ratifiers' opinion that "Slavery would soon end if left alone."[23] Since the late 1840s and early 1850s, Parker had referenced a founding-era expectation of abolition, but it had never been a major factor in his interpretation.[24] In that period, he was willing to let the Constitution's proslavery features sink this historical document into the abyss of a dark past. However, after *Dred Scott*, Parker joined other interpreters in citing original antislavery expectations to buoy up the Constitution. He recovered permanent antislavery truths and put them to use in the project of creating a brighter future.

Although prior interpreters had contended the framers had crafted a document that would signify a new antislavery meaning in a new

---

[21] Ibid. [22] Parker to White, May 22, 1858, emphasis in original.
[23] *Liberator*, June 4, 1858.
[24] See Theodore Parker, "The State of the Nation," in *Speeches*, 3:203–04.

political context, Parker made this argument more explicitly. He claimed that the framers included "a clause ... which would ultimately destroy [slavery], and that without amending the Constitution itself." He had in mind the guarantee clause in particular, which he thought the framers had "enacted ... to meet the emergency [of states' rights] when it should happen."[25] In binding change to a specific expectation, Parker diminished its interpretive power. At the same time, though, his interpretation of the guarantee clause unhinged constitutional meaning from the past: his reading demanded a new application in a new setting. In other words, Parker believed the framers had constructed this clause in anticipation; he implied that its ideas were more characteristic of his era than of theirs.

Parker contrasted the clause with views he depicted as anachronistic. Echoing his letter to Sumner, he grieved over southern appeals to classical and medieval republics. He also lamented biblical readings that showed "Abraham was a slaveholder" and that "Moses authorized bondage," and that translated Paul's words as "'Slaves, obey your master!'" The Bible taught permanent truths, Parker believed, but these were not among them. Historical interpretation encouraged him to separate the eternal from the temporal. These efforts unveiled historical distance, which strengthened his belief in the progress of religious sentiment. Once, Parker had wondered if such progress made sacred historical texts unfit for the present era, but the tie he now made between a general belief in the progress of religious sentiment and the framers' and ratifiers' expectation of freedom's progress reoriented his approach. He now settled on a profound insight: "In a progressive People there must be a progressive interpretation of many institutions and statutes."[26] In light of historical distance and change, Parker prescribed informal and publicly driven constitutional emendations. Though he previously considered the Constitution dark and obsolete when looking at it through a transcendental lens, that lens now helped him read the document as a light-bearing, living text.

Parker found an illuminating example of a people's progressive reading of law in England, where "slavery perished by interpretation." There, injustice could not "withstand the demand for natural Justice made by the increased knowledge, virtue[,] and humanity of the progressive People." Writing in an early Jeffersonian mode, the experienced Parker insisted that laws must evolve to "suit the humane spirit of an enlightened age." He also used an example from US constitutionalism in his speech, noting that

---

[25] *Liberator*, June 4, 1858.   [26] *Liberator*, June 11, 1858.

certain punishments once viewed as "usual" were now considered "cruel."[27] By comparison, he presumed that no one would think to provide a child as a burnt offering and justify the practice with either the example of Abraham or the Eighth Amendment.

During the course of his speech, Parker brought together biblical and constitutional examples to highlight historical change, which he then used to read the sacred texts. He identified foreign components of both the Bible and the Constitution, not to dismiss these texts but rather to suggest that certain portions of them must be emphasized and read in light of subsequent developments. By the late 1850s, the currents of American constitutional interpretive debate had pushed many readers to recognize rather than dismiss change and to use change to embrace rather than reject the founding legal text. In doing so, such readers often combined the framers' expectations of change with the fact of change itself. Parker's mature constitutional reading, in particular, captured Jefferson's idea of generational change *and* Madison's idea of generational deference. This allowed him to interpret the Constitution as a dynamic document.

While seeing the Constitution as a progressive text, Parker still viewed human progress as a white endeavor. Speaking of the Anglo-Saxon race, he asserted that "a nation, a great tribe of men, does not lose its historic continuity of action." Parker's Anglocentric idea of human progress made him confident that whites would use the Constitution to abolish slavery. Now more than ever, he saw proslavery advances as somehow contributing to the inevitable march toward freedom for the enslaved. "It will not be long before slavery is abolished," he predicted. "When the Declaration ... is read on the Fourth of July, 1876, there will not be a slave in the United States."[28]

Perhaps encouraged by the observances of correspondents such as William Herndon, Salmon Chase, and Charles Sumner, Parker's trust in the people – however narrowly defined – had expanded in the aftermath of *Dred Scott*. In this speech, he incorporated the ideas of radical antislavery constitutionalists and emphasized the Constitution's words and the ratifiers' intentions. He also contended that the founding generation expected slavery's demise. This appeal to founding-era expectations supported Parker's assertion that the progress of abolitionism demanded a new interpretation of the Constitution. He asserted that original

[27] Ibid. [28] Ibid.

expectations matched present sentiment. In making a rhetorical link between the ratifiers' expectations and his contemporaries' advanced antislavery sentiments, which he saw as symptomatic of freedom's progress, Parker privileged a popular reading of the Constitution.

Parker's confrontation with historical distance had shaped this development. When he first perceived historical distance from the favored founding era, he was inclined to abandon the Constitution. Transcendentalist belief had encouraged him to sever the link between timeless religious and legal truths and transient historical texts. That severance cultivated a sense of historical distance from favored pasts and that sense of distance confirmed his Transcendentalist belief. By the late 1850s, however, he realized distance could be used to support a progressive popular reading of the nation's sacred legal text. Now, he insisted that the people's interpretation mattered most in deciding slavery's constitutionality.

Near the end of his speech, Parker criticized the Republican Party's narrow focus on slavery's extension and called for a party that embodied the people's desire for immediate emancipation. Believing that the people needed someone to champion their reading of the Constitution, Parker desired a new political leader. "Already the People look that way," he stated. "What they want is a LEADER, who is not only intellectually sharp, but also morally just."[29] Although Parker did not know it, Lincoln was developing into that role.

Since giving his Peoria speech, Lincoln had begun to focus on the framers' original expectation that slavery would gradually expire. To be sure, Lincoln argued that necessity had informed the framers' decision to temporarily sanction slavery, and this argument supported his own expedient approach in focusing on slavery's extension. But Lincoln also believed that the framers' expectation of slavery's eventual demise warranted informal constitutional alterations, and he argued that proslavery consolidations had obscured it. While he did not call for slavery's immediate abolition – and though Parker and other abolitionists criticized him for failing to attack slavery more directly – Lincoln did adopt key components of the antislavery reading of the Constitution, and those components formed the basis of his later emancipationist policy.[30]

---

[29] Ibid, emphasis in original.
[30] See Theodore Parker to William H. Herndon, September 9, 1858, Theodore Parker Papers, MHS.

THE FOUNDING-ERA "BELIEF THAT SLAVERY WAS IN COURSE OF ULTIMATE EXTINCTION"

In 1854, when Stephen Douglas's Kansas–Nebraska Act brought Lincoln back into politics, Lincoln followed antislavery interpreters in using the Declaration to read the Constitution. After the *Dred Scott* decision, he expanded that reading and communicated it to a broad audience during his well-publicized and widely published 1858 debates with Douglas in their fight for a seat in the US Senate.[31] Lincoln accepted decades of interpretive discussion rooted in historical arguments, agreeing with Taney that the constitutional conflict over slavery – which was accepted as the central and, it was hoped, last battle left to fight – was to be won or lost on historical grounds.

While Lincoln focused on arresting slavery's spread rather than extinguishing its flames, his narrative placed the framers' hopes in direct opposition to the southern institution. He tracked recent proslavery deviations from original antislavery expectations and this tracking heightened a sense of temporal dislocation. Lincoln authorized the interpretive use of that dislocation. If the republic was to endure in its intended form, his reading implied, then it must begin to conform to the framers' antislavery projections rather than continue to bend to the will of the Slave Power. This mature antislavery narrative gradually achieved greater prominence with Lincoln's rising political star, further spreading an awareness of perceived historical distance from the founding era while also offering a resolution to the problem such awareness created for the Constitution.[32]

The sparring between Lincoln and Douglas, which had begun years before their official debates in 1858, again showed that figures on all sides of the slavery issue felt compelled to use historical reasoning and rhetoric. In a speech delivered on June 12, 1857, in Springfield, Illinois, Douglas declared that Taney's recent "decision will stand in all future time a proud monument of [the court's] greatness." In making this statement – which time has shown to be profoundly wrong – he suggested that the "highest tribunal" had spoken with a weight that history would uphold.[33] In his later debates with Lincoln, however, Douglas himself would undermine

---

[31] On the national reach and importance of these debates, see Allen C. Guelzo, *Lincoln and Douglas: The Debates That Defined America* (New York, 2008).

[32] On the antislavery movement as a key source of Lincoln's constitutional ideas during this period, see Neely, *Lincoln and the Triumph*, 31–38.

[33] Stephen A. Douglas, *Kansas – Utah – Dred Scott Decision. Speech Delivered at Springfield, Illinois, June 12, 1857* (Springfield, 1857), 4–5.

the Court's verdict when he articulated the Freeport Doctrine, which held that the people of a territory had the right to determine whether or not to permit slavery. Popular sovereignty, along with popular constitutionalism, threatened to undercut the Court's ruling.

In his June 1857 speech, Douglas upheld Taney's use of the Declaration. Striking at the notion that it required slavery's abolition, he warned his audience that such a view would produce laws that made no "distinction whatever on account of race or color."[34] Drawing cheers from the crowd, he called their attention "to a few historical facts," including slavery's near-ubiquitous presence at ratification and the idea that "negroes were regarded as an inferior race."[35] Like the biblical interpreters who rejected antislavery arguments from expediency, Douglas contended that if the bold founders had wanted to abolish slavery, they certainly would have. In his view, "the whole history of our country" demonstrated that they had no intention to emancipate blacks.[36] Like Taney, Douglas historicized the revolutionary era to show that the Declaration addressed the rights of British subjects, not African slaves. True to his political precepts, he designated the issue of blacks' rights as a state matter and argued that changes in that regard should reflect local needs. Although Douglas acknowledged the power of present and future circumstances in shaping state laws and even pointed out how past conditions had informed the creation of federal laws, he failed to see how his emphasis on the determinative power of new contexts might demand new readings of the Constitution.

In Springfield a few weeks later, Lincoln delivered a response that challenged the authority of *Dred Scott*. He agreed that the Court's rulings "when fully settled, should control ... the general policy of the country," but, knowing that the Court "has often over-ruled its own decision," he moved to "do what we can to have it over-rule this." Lincoln's use of "we" was similar to Parker's use of "the people"; both optimistically aligned a vague referent with the perceived antislavery spirit of the times. "We offer no *resistance*" to the ruling, Lincoln stated, while noting that "judicial decisions are of greater or less [sic] authority as precedents, according to circumstances."[37] Lincoln believed that the present situation – shaped by antislavery sentiment in the North and proslavery overreach in the South – left the constitutional issue of slavery unsettled.

---

[34] Ibid., 7. [35] Ibid., 8–9. [36] Ibid., 9.
[37] Lincoln, "Speech at Springfield, Illinois, June 26, 1857," 2:401, emphasis in original.

Lincoln also called attention to the partisan nature of the ruling and the discrepancies between the justices' opinions. In doing so, he challenged Douglas's assertion that the decision would stand the test of time and created space to insert what he claimed to be the views of the people. Holding that the decision deviated from "legal public expectation," Lincoln drew a clear connection between founding-era anticipation and present popular expectation. This "public confidence," he contended, was supported by past decisions.[38] While this was an originalist position, it was one that posited an original expectation of historical change and encouraged interpreters to read the Constitution as a dynamic text.

Lincoln's focus on proslavery expansion made it easier for him to claim more of America's past than Parker had. He contended that "all that there ever was, in the way of precedent up to the Dred Scott decision ... had been against that decision."[39] Even more than John McLean and Benjamin Curtis, Lincoln saw *Dred Scott* as a legal deviation that unveiled the inner workings of the Slave Power. He could not accept such a decision as "settled doctrine."[40] Like Parker, Lincoln responded to unexpected developments by emphasizing the contingent nature of constitutional law.

Throughout the remainder of this speech, Lincoln coupled an emphasis on shocking proslavery innovations with a deep historical critique of Taney's central contention – that "negroes were no part of the people who made, or for whom was made, the Declaration ... or the Constitution."[41] As America's biblical scholars had agreed to use the historical mode of interpretation that biblical criticism had provided, so Lincoln used the historical mode of constitutional interpretation that the chief justice had authorized as normative. As much as anyone, Lincoln challenged Taney's historical claims.

Once again, the discussion fell along both synchronic and diachronic lines; Lincoln discerned the founders' intentions and expectations and gauged their fulfillment or failure. Quickly accepting Curtis's contention that free blacks "had the same part in making the Constitution that white people had," Lincoln turned his focus to the original meaning of the Declaration.[42] By discussing that text, Taney had unwittingly authorized efforts to read the Constitution in its light. With other respondents, Lincoln rejected Taney's assumption that "the public estimate of the black man is more favorable *now* than it was in the days of the Revolution." Citing new voting restrictions placed on free blacks and

[38] Ibid. [39] Ibid., 2:402. [40] Ibid., 2:401. [41] Ibid., 2:403. [42] Ibid., 2:403.

innovative restraints on emancipation, Lincoln argued that "the change between then and now is decidedly the other way."[43] Once, he claimed, the Declaration "was held sacred by all, and thought to include all."[44] Lincoln granted that the founders "did not mean to assert the obvious untruth, that all were then actually enjoying that equality, nor yet, that they were about to confer it immediately upon them." Instead, he contended, "They meant simply to declare the *right*, so that the *enforcement* of it might follow as fast as circumstances should permit. They meant to set up a standard maxim for free society, which should be familiar to all, and revered by all; constantly looked to, constantly labored for, and even though never perfectly attained, constantly approximated, and thereby constantly spreading and deepening its influence, and augmenting the happiness and value of life to all people of all colors everywhere."[45]

Lincoln insisted that circumstances had constrained the founders: understanding that they could not destroy slavery at the time of the framing, the framers wrote a Constitution that allowed for its later abolition. Arguing that the phrase "'All men are created equal' ... was placed in the Declaration ... for future use," Lincoln built on antislavery efforts to locate within the Constitution an expectation that these egalitarian ideals would later flourish.[46] In contrast to Douglas, he explained that past circumstances shaped federal laws; thus, present circumstances required new interpretations. Lincoln's historical appeal was an effort not to recover and apply static meanings but to highlight founding-era ideas that seemed to call for new readings.

Like Parker, who had argued that the framers looked to a future context when crafting the Constitution's guarantee clause, Lincoln believed they had envisioned that change would transform the Constitution into a more inclusive text. In other words, both figures identified historical awareness in the founders. Lincoln argued that if the Declaration had not "contemplated the progressive improvement in the condition of all men everywhere" and instead had referred strictly to the colonists' rights as British subjects, then that document "is of no practical use now" and exists only as "an interesting memorial of the dead past."[47] Lincoln insisted that the Declaration was not simply a historical relic. In doing so, he called attention to historical differences. As Taney's and Douglas's readings had historicized the founding era by binding the Declaration and the Constitution to past proslavery sentiment, Lincoln's

---

[43] Ibid., emphasis in original.   [44] Ibid., 2:404.   [45] Ibid., 2:406, emphasis in original.
[46] Ibid.   [47] Ibid., 2:407.

readings of the same documents drew attention to the discreteness of those contexts by characterizing the texts as living works that transcended their own time. But while Taney's and Douglas's readings conflated time, Lincoln's reading valued the interpretive importance of change over time. In his interpretation, distance made the past different but not dead. Indeed, an awareness of that difference created new kinds of historical appeals.

Lincoln continued to promote this reading in 1858. In his "House Divided" speech, delivered within hours of being named the Republican Party candidate for Illinois senator, Lincoln followed up one of his famous opening phrases – "The government cannot endure, permanently half *slave* and half *free*" – with a recitation of novel proslavery advances, including the Kansas–Nebraska Act, the election of James Buchanan, and the *Dred Scott* decision.[48] At the same time, Lincoln also tracked continuity between the founders' intentions and the public belief that slavery "is in course of ultimate extinction."[49] He contrasted these antislavery expectations with proslavery desires to grant "*permanency* to the institution through all the future."[50] Using "historical facts" to show signs of "preconcert" between Douglas and other politicians, Lincoln posited the possibility of a subsequent judicial decision that would nationalize slavery.[51]

Lincoln and his colleagues feared that a second *Dred Scott* decision would extend masters' rights to their slaves in free states. Some Republicans believed that this road, if taken, would lead to white servitude.[52] For example, in July 1858, Herndon wrote to Parker, expressing his concern that the Slave Power might "enslave the white man."[53] A useful political tactic, this dark forecasting also demonstrated a growing attention to the reality of contingent historical developments. Tracking post-founding-era changes had made it clear to at least some observers that the nation's course was far from determined.

Lincoln continued to ring warning bells in a speech on July 10. Proclaiming himself "tolerably well acquainted with the history of the country," he attributed national progress and endurance to the idea that "the public mind did rest, all the time, in the belief that slavery was in

---

[48] Abraham Lincoln, "'A House Divided': Speech at Springfield, Illinois, June 16, 1858," in CWAL, 2:461–64, quotation on 461, emphasis in original.
[49] Ibid., 2:461.   [50] Ibid., 2:464, emphasis in original.   [51] Ibid., 2:465.
[52] See Jeremy J. Tewell, *A Self-Evident Lie: Southern Slavery and the Threat to American Freedom* (Kent, OH, 2014).
[53] William H. Herndon to Theodore Parker, July 28, 1858, Theodore Parker Papers, MHS.

course of ultimate extinction." This idea, he argued, originated in the framers, whose efforts to constrain slavery and end the slave trade demonstrated that "they intended and expected the ultimate extinction of that institution."[54] Like Parker, Lincoln linked this expectation with those of the people at and since ratification. One week later, he noted that even the late Preston Brooks once admitted that the framers had placed slavery on the road to extinction. But Brooks, Lincoln explained, had gone on to argue that experience and technological advances, including the invention of the cotton gin, had made "men of the present age ... wiser than the framers." Lincoln quoted Brooks to show a "change of sentiment ... in the direction of making [slavery] perpetual and national," and he contrasted that sentiment with the framers' expectations.[55] Both Brooks and Lincoln observed contingent historical change, but narratives like Brooks's inverted the antislavery tale of moral progress: an awareness of slavery's blessing, rather than its sin, demonstrated moral maturity in the founders' descendants. In the slavery debates, an awareness of contingent developments yielded vastly different lessons about historical progress.

Lincoln thought southerners such as Brooks had learned the wrong historical lesson. Like Parker, Lincoln spent as much time identifying recent proslavery encroachments as he did outlining original antislavery expectations. Lincoln believed that innovations, especially the recent Kansas–Nebraska Act but also a new southern insistence on slavery's positive good, had arrested those expectations and ushered in a "new era" of proslavery dominance.[56] He scoffed at the "sacredness" Douglas had granted *Dred Scott*, which decision Lincoln characterized as "the first of its kind; it is an astonisher in legal history ... based upon falsehood in the main as to the facts."[57] The "extraordinary decision," he believed, had created "extraordinary circumstances," and those circumstances required a new constitutional reading.[58]

Lincoln and other antislavery writers argued that the framers had anticipated that a more egalitarian context would permit a more egalitarian constitutional reading. Precisely because a very different context had emerged, one that was less rather than more egalitarian than the founding era, these writers called for the American people to demand an egalitarian

---

[54] Abraham Lincoln, "Speech at Chicago, Illinois, July 10, 1858," in *CWAL*, 2:492.
[55] Abraham Lincoln, "Speech at Springfield, Illinois, July 17, 1858," in *CWAL*, 2:515. See also Lincoln, "Third Debate with Stephen A. Douglas at Jonesboro, Illinois, September 15, 1858," in *CWAL*, 3:117.
[56] Lincoln, "Speech at Chicago," 2:492.   [57] Ibid., 2:495.   [58] Ibid., 2:496.

construction from the Court. In other words, Lincoln argued, the founders thought historically, and so should their nineteenth-century progeny. The audacious and reckless nature of recent actions created new political conditions and justified the call for a construction that fulfilled founding-era promises. As in antislavery readings of the New Testament, this push to fulfill historical hopes rather than revive a dead past placed distance between the present and the favored founding. In the face of unexpected proslavery progress, the claim to continuity with the past was one that called for the realization of original antislavery expectations in the new context that existed in mid-nineteenth-century America.

Like Parker's account of American history, Lincoln's narrative highlighted an ambivalence about change. His focus on expected progress clashed with his fixation on unexpected decline. His historical appeals drew attention to developments that had resulted from the failure of founding-era hopes and the fruition of founding-era actions. Speaking only days after July 4, Lincoln observed the growth of the US population and of "everything we deem desirable among men" and noted, "We look upon the change as exceedingly advantageous to us and to our posterity, and we fix upon something that happened away back, as in some way or other being connected with this rise of prosperity." He supposed that "we hold [Fourth of July] to remind ourselves of all the good done in this process of time ... and how we are historically connected with it ... In every way we are better men in the age, and race, and country in which we live."[59] Characterizing national progress as the fruits of the founders' work recast change as continuity.

The problem of historical distance in antebellum America did not arise due to people simply realizing that change had occurred since the founding era, especially when the changes were registered as either positive or negative. Many Americans believed that beneficial changes, including technological advances and economic progress, flowed from the fount of the colonists' Revolution and the framers' and ratifiers' Constitution. In these Americans' view, change came in the form of evolution rather than rupture. Many agreed with Lincoln that they lived in a better world than their founding mothers and fathers, whom they thanked for the blessing. Such a view muted the determinative force of change. Simply tracking negative change since the founding did not inevitably indicate distance either. Even though Americans' narrations of decline highlighted contingent change more than their narrations of progress, narrations of decline

[59] Ibid., 2:500.

did not automatically induce the kind of awareness of historical distance that troubled appeals to the past. When people perceive unwanted change, they often call for a restoration, as with puritan jeremiads or republican lamentations. The Republican Party platform of 1856 seemed to promise just such a return in aiming to "restor[e] the action of the Federal Government to the principles of Washington and Jefferson."[60]

But the kinds of narratives advanced by Parker, Lincoln, and Douglass, each of whom tracked both progress and decline, aimed not to bridge past and present but to use past principles to guide forward movement. While highlighting various forms of progress since the founding, Lincoln observed that his audience inhabited a world that the founders had not expected. Unforeseen proslavery advances had arrested expected egalitarian progress. So Lincoln's restoration rhetoric signified something more along the lines of fulfillment rather than return.

The Declaration's universal promises had "not yet reached the whole." That would require a more inclusive understanding of "descendants." Lincoln explained that since the founders had made provisions for European immigrants "to claim" the founders' egalitarian ideas "as though they were blood of the blood, and flesh of the flesh of the men who wrote the Declaration," the same should be true of African Americans.[61] Denying them that claim cut them from "the electric cord in the Declaration" that was meant to tie "the hearts of patriotic and liberty-loving men together."[62] Not wanting to be seen as encouraging equal rights, the politician later pandered to those insisting on qualitative racial differences, noting that what he desired most was "the separation of the white and black races."[63] Although Lincoln's political stance placed severe restrictions on his concept of African American freedom, his reading of sacred founding-era texts nonetheless demanded a new and more egalitarian legal framework.[64]

Lincoln's belief that black contemporaries could claim the ideals of a document that was written and signed while many of their ancestors were in bondage demonstrates that his historical appeal was not a call for a return to, or an assertion of similitude with, the founding era. As scholar John Burt explains, "What Lincoln sought to restore was a legal order that did not actually exist but that had been promised, and what he described

---

[60] Kirk H. Porter, ed., *National Party Platforms* (New York, 1924), 47.
[61] Lincoln, "Speech at Chicago," 2:499–500.   [62] Ibid., 2:500.
[63] Lincoln, "Springfield, July 17, 1858," 2:520–21.
[64] See Guelzo, *Lincoln and Douglas*, 191–93.

as restoration is better seen as evolution."[65] Similar to a number of antislavery interpreters of the Bible, Lincoln called for the realization of universal ideas that had been seeded in limiting circumstances, meant for flowering in the more nourishing environment of a later time. The time had arrived, but some rather noxious weeds stood in the way of full fruition.

While some still proposed a slash-and-burn method aimed at both slavery and the text that sanctioned its existence, Lincoln encouraged further cultivation along constitutional lines. Rather than demand that his contemporaries reject the nation's founding texts or insist that the application of those texts rest on an unquestioning allegiance to founding-era sentiments, he urged his contemporaries to read the nation's sacred legal text in light of both expected and unexpected change. In other words, Lincoln held that the distance between past and present should mediate the meaning of sacred texts and thus preserve them for continued use.

THE CONSTITUTION'S "COVERT LANGUAGE," THE FOUNDERS' HISTORICAL AWARENESS, AND COMPETING APPEALS TO HISTORICAL CONTINGENCY

On the public stage offered by the official Lincoln–Douglas debates held from August to October 1858, Lincoln continued to promote his narrative about original promises that had been made and broken.[66] In the process, he also developed the argument from necessity that he had outlined in his Peoria speech. On that occasion, Lincoln had described the proslavery clauses as a cancer that the framers had temporarily hid away with the idea that future generations would cut it from the national body. Four years later, in his seventh and last debate with Douglas, Lincoln noted that the framers used "covert language" when crafting the importation, three-fifths, and fugitive slave clauses. He drew attention to the absence of "slavery" in the Constitution not to deny its prominence at the founding but rather to emphasize the framers' expectation of its eventual abolition. Calling on "the contemporaneous history of those times," he argued "that covert language was used" so that when the "Constitution, which it was hoped and is still hoped will endure forever ... should be read by intelligent and patriotic men, after the institution of slavery had passed ... there should be nothing on the face of the great charter of liberty suggesting that

---

[65] John Burt, *Lincoln's Tragic Pragmatism: Lincoln, Douglas, and Moral Conflict* (Cambridge, MA, 2013), 483.
[66] For example, see Lincoln, "Third Debate with Douglas," 3:116–18.

such a thing as negro slavery had ever existed among us."[67] This reading combined Jefferson's sense of legal development with Madison's idea of legal deference. Along with many antislavery readers, Lincoln believed the framers had written the Constitution with change in mind; they had used precise language to make it easier for their enlightened descendants to erase the peculiar institution from the American past and present. He thus ascribed historical awareness to the framers. In light of that awareness, the relic that Taney had recovered through historical excavation was a "relic of barbarism," a relic that was better off buried and concealed rather than unearthed and polished for preservation.[68]

Because the institution of slavery had been preserved and recent events had strengthened its presence, Lincoln had to grant slavery's existence at the founding. Slavery's persistence as an institution made it difficult for Lincoln to counter the idea that "our fathers, as Judge Douglas assumes, made this government part slave and part free." To resolve the problem, Lincoln demonstrated that the southern institution preceded the framing, which allowed him to posit the "absolute impossibility of [slavery's] immediate removal" at the time of the government's formation.[69] A number of southerners and their northern sympathizers had also made this claim, but Lincoln turned this to his advantage. Pushing slavery's existence further into the past indicated that it was contemporaries like Douglas, rather than the framers, who sought to establish a nation half free and half slave.

In this debate, Lincoln's historical narrative consisted of multiple components, which together combined to attune his listeners to the dissonance between the founding era and the present. His account addressed the framers' own limiting context and their original expectation that a more egalitarian context would emerge, while also describing deviations from that expectation and the unexpected context they had created. He used the sense of distance that his narrative helped generate to read the Constitution as a text meant to conform to new circumstances. In doing so, he did not join abolitionists in demanding immediate abolition but instead dramatized the dissonance between original expectations and present realities to curb slavery's extension.

Because the framers' expectations had not been met – recent developments had stunted rather than realized the anticipated transformation –

---

[67] Abraham Lincoln, "Seventh and Last Debate with Stephen A. Douglas at Alton, Illinois, October 15, 1858," in *CWAL*, 3:307.
[68] Porter, *National Party Platforms*, 48.   [69] Lincoln, "Seventh and Last Debate," 3:308.

Lincoln read the Constitution in light of expected changes and despite actual changes. He seemed to believe that Americans should bring the words of the Constitution into closer alignment with the transformation the framers had expected time to enact. In illuminating the founding era and its relationship to the present, he asked listeners to focus on historical differences. He highlighted these differences not only to warn Americans of the nation's direction but also to advance what might be viewed as a progressive reading of the Constitution. In short, his reading implied that historical change authorized new interpretations and new constructions of sacred texts.

The introduction of readings attentive to change exposed the static nature of more conventional readings and added to an environment in which interpreters increasingly had to confront distance as an interpretive problem. With Lincoln, Douglas followed American legal commentators and practitioners in accepting the historical terms of the debate. He agreed that the framers "did not establish slavery in any of the States," but he argued that his opponent sidestepped the fact that the framers had knowingly joined slave and free states and guaranteed "forever to each State the right to do as it pleased" on the issue. Planting popular sovereignty in founding-era soil, Douglas asserted that "this government can exist as they made it, divided into free and slaves States," even if circumstances had changed.[70] "Mr. Lincoln says that when our fathers made this government they did not look forward to the state of things now existing.... Suppose they did not," he said. "Does that change the principles of government?"[71] Broadening Lincoln's focus from the framers' expectations about the future status of slavery to their lack of foresight about "the state of things now existing" allowed Douglas to critique his challenger's position as inflexible. Whereas Lincoln had found the essential principles of government inseparable from the framers' original expectations, Douglas distinguished between the permanent principles of government set forth in the Constitution and the framers' transient expectations about the republic's future. Just as a number of biblical interpreters had done, these two figures attempted to separate out precious truths from particular favored-era dross. In doing this work on a national stage, both Lincoln and Douglas drew Americans' attention to the distance separating America's past from the present.

---

[70] Stephen A. Douglas, "Seventh and Last Debate with Stephen A. Douglas at Alton, Illinois, October 15, 1858," in *CWAL*, 3:322.
[71] Ibid., 3:322–23.

In a sense, both candidates' readings allowed for change. Lincoln identified permanent antislavery principles meant to check slavery's spread, and Douglas outlined states' native right to either abolish slavery or secure its existence. However, whereas the principles Lincoln highlighted endorsed expected changes in terms of slavery's confinement and ultimate collapse, the precepts Douglas stressed allowed for unexpected changes resulting from the contingent choices of each state. Broadening his focus on change, Douglas noted that the framers "did not probably foresee" the telegraph, railroads, "or the thousand mechanical inventions that have elevated mankind." Then he asked, "But do these things change the principles of the government?" Whereas Lincoln had emphasized that beneficial developments were the fruits of founding seeds to support his argument about the progressive nature of original expectations, Douglas stressed the unpredictable nature of mechanical developments to support his argument about the permanence of original meanings. He insisted that the framers had "made this government on the principle of the right of each State to do as it pleases in its own domestic affairs, subject to the constitution, and allowed the people of each to apply to every new change of circumstance such remedy as they may see fit to improve their condition. This right they have for all time to come."[72] Douglas bound constitutional meaning to the past in suggesting that the framers had outlined guiding principles that states could adapt to new circumstances, but he went further than most antebellum interpreters in valuing contingent changes.[73]

And yet, what if the guiding principles only functioned in relation to a particular historical trajectory? Lincoln's narrative posed the question: did the framers establish the principle of popular sovereignty with the expectation of slavery's eventual abolition? If so, then slavery's continued existence undermined the permanence of popular sovereignty as it applied to the southern institution. In this scenario, Douglas's assertion that states retained the right to abolish or establish slavery made *his* position, which failed to take into account the framers' expectations, inflexible.

---

[72] Ibid., 3:323.
[73] Harry Jaffa aligns Douglas's position with historicism, while situating Lincoln's approach, especially as articulated at Gettysburg, within the tradition of natural law. Harry V. Jaffa, *A New Birth of Freedom: Abraham Lincoln and the Coming of the Civil War* (Lanham, MD, 2000), 73–152.

"I DO NOT MEAN TO SAY WE ARE BOUND TO FOLLOW ... WHATEVER OUR FATHERS DID"

Lincoln later made clear that his view of the founding era allowed for changes on a broader scale than Douglas had implied. Although he lost the senatorial seat to Douglas in the 1858 election, he rose to political prominence in the process. Under the sponsorship of the Young Men's Republican Union, he addressed an audience at Cooper Union on February 27, 1860. Lincoln had initially agreed to speak at the New York City venue when Henry Ward Beecher, a formidable Congregationalist preacher and an abolitionist, extended an invitation the prior October. In the period between the invitation and the speech, Lincoln dedicated himself to a deep examination of the recent American past. He aimed to damn slavery's spread, and he wanted the framers on his side when he did so.

To begin his address, Lincoln noted that "the facts with which I shall deal this evening are mainly old and familiar." He proffered, "If there shall be any novelty, it will be in the mode of presenting the facts, and the inferences and observations following that presentation."[74] Agreeing with Douglas that the founding fathers understood, "even better, than we do now," the issue of territorial power, Lincoln used historical evidence to outline the relevant judgments of the thirty-nine framers, who, in his estimation, "fairly represented the opinion and sentiment of the whole nation."[75] While paying lip service to a popular reading of the Constitution, Lincoln focused on the framers' pre- and post-founding-era decisions. His research yielded six instances between 1784 and 1820 – "the only acts ... of any of them, upon the direct issue, which I have been able to discover" – in which, when taken together, twenty-one of twenty-three framers voted in such a manner as to suggest that nothing "in the Constitution, properly forbade Congress to prohibit slavery in the federal territory."[76] Based on his historical investigation, Lincoln suggested that the sixteen other framers, some of whom were "the most noted anti-slavery men of those times," would "probably have acted just as the twenty-three did."[77] This research led him to confidently posit that in the minds of the framers and of the "whole nation," the Constitution did not proscribe the federal regulation of slavery in the territories.[78]

---

[74] Abraham Lincoln, "Address at the Cooper Institute, New York City, February 27, 1860," in *CWAL*, 3:522.
[75] Ibid., 3:522–23.   [76] Ibid., 3:527, 530.   [77] Ibid., 3:531.   [78] Ibid., 3:532.

Establishing consensus and continuity among the founding generation allowed Lincoln to assert that it was contemporaries like Douglas who were proposing a national change in course. He defied "any one to show that any living man ... ever did, prior to the beginning of the present century, (and I might almost say prior to the beginning of the last half of the present century,) declare that ... any part of the Constitution, forbade the Federal Government to control as to slavery in the federal territories."[79] Since the 1820s, both northern and southern constitutional interpreters had dismissed innovative antislavery interpretations as deviations from a founding-era consensus. Lincoln reversed the narrative, pitting the founding generation's expectations against new proslavery readings. Lincoln's account suggested that unexpected decline rather than anticipated progress divided American present from American past.

On the surface, Lincoln's efforts to bind his position to the framers indicated, as Douglas had suggested, a reading resistant to change. But far from desiring a return to the world of the founders, Lincoln envisioned a use of the Constitution that fulfilled their most glowing promises. He conceptualized change as a problem of kind rather than of fact and posited that the answer to that problem was in further change toward fulfillment rather than restoration.

At Cooper Union, Lincoln made it clear that he did not believe that the founders' examples had an infinite claim on their descendants. While working hard to separate the founders' views from those of his opponents, Lincoln noted, "Let me guard a little against being misunderstood. I do not mean to say we are bound to follow implicitly in whatever our fathers did. To do so, would be to discard all the lights of current experience – to reject all progress – all improvement."[80] Rather than link progress to the founders' project, as he had on prior occasions, Lincoln placed distance between their actions and subsequent developments. He did not want listeners to think he was encouraging blind obedience to past figures. Indeed, he went further than Douglas in reminding his audience that if his interpretation failed, another method existed to make the Constitution accord with the public hope of abolition. Even Lincoln's use of passive voice – "a mode was provided for amending it" – omitted the framers as actors.[81] While granting the value of their views, he argued that in new circumstances the American people must privilege new illumination. In line with the interpretive effort to divide permanent principles from transient precepts, Lincoln laid claim to the framers' expectations but

[79] Ibid., 3:534.   [80] Ibid., 3:534–35.   [81] Ibid., 3:532.

left room to leave behind their directions when a new context made other options more practical.

On the question of territorial power, however, Lincoln believed original intent matched present needs and thus castigated Douglas for presuming that "he understands their principles better than they did."[82] In summarizing the framers' view of slavery as *"an evil not to be extended, but to be tolerated and protected only because of and so far as its actual presence among us makes that toleration and protection a necessity,"* Lincoln depicted Douglas's reading as a heretical deviation.[83] In response to Douglas, Lincoln asked, "Could Washington himself speak, would he cast the blame of that sectionalism upon us, who sustain his policy, or upon you who repudiate it?" Attempting to wrest the conservative argument from white southerners, he asserted that "we stick to, contend for, the identical old policy ... which was adopted by 'our fathers who framed the Government under which we live;' while you ... spit upon that old policy, and insist upon substituting something new."[84] Lincoln argued that the legal authorization of slavery's extension, the desire to revive the slave trade and institute territorial slave codes, and the insistence that slavery was morally right all lacked founding-era sanction. He contended that in light of southern "innovation," Republicans must follow the framers' expedient example.[85] Lincoln concluded, "Wrong as we think slavery is, we can yet afford to let it alone where it is, because that much is due to the necessity arising from its actual presence."[86]

By taking contingencies into account, Lincoln could promote a moderate political stance even as his reading pointed toward radical change. He could theorize that circumstances might require leaving behind the framers' opinions, while his practical approach allowed him to claim allegiance to their policies. In a sense, he adopted the southern argument from circumstance; he believed the current situation required expedient measures, just as at the founding. However, Lincoln did not characterize present circumstances as the result of progress or ascribe slavery's existence or its eventual abolition to Providence. Instead, he tracked negative change as he anticipated and – when circumstances made it expedient – tried to bring about new conditions in which descendants could fulfill the founding fathers' promises.

Lincoln's antislavery narrative placed historical distance within the purview of more Americans than ever before. What had been articulated

---

[82] Ibid., 3:535. [83] Ibid., emphasis in original. [84] Ibid., 3:537. [85] Ibid., 3:538.
[86] Ibid., 3:550.

among a marginalized subsection of the northern population became a consistent feature of a prominent political platform that promised to expose attentive listeners and readers to the temporal limitations of the founding era. It also attuned them to both expected and unexpected changes since that time. By emphasizing the failure of original antislavery expectations and the success of later proslavery consolidations, Lincoln's words had the potential to make politically observant Americans aware of contingent historical change. Available sources do not indicate how much of the American population gained a new historical awareness during this time, but the public nature of the debate over slavery made this moment singular in its potential to drive such awareness deep into the nation's collective consciousness. As Parker wrote to Herndon regarding the Lincoln–Douglas debates, "It is admirable Education for the masses."[87]

Regardless of how many Americans became more historically aware, Lincoln used historical distance to promote an antislavery reading of the Constitution, which helped him win the presidency and guided him as president. While holding fast to the framers' ideals – and even citing their expedient approach to sanction his own – he applied the insight of temporal dislocation to suggest that Americans needed to reinterpret the nation's sacred legal text to push forward into a new era. As Burt notes, according to Lincoln, the "meaning of the Founders' commitments is not to be sought in their documents and laws in an unmediated way, but in the future in which those commitments unfold consequences they could not have anticipated."[88] In other words, distance and change had become a viable force in shaping and authorizing alternative readings of founding-era texts.

"THE WHITE FLAG OF FREEDOM" IN THE "DIM AND SHADOWY DISTANCE"

In Frederick Douglass's response to *Dred Scott*, he, too, encouraged the people to read the Constitution as a shining document for freedom, and like Lincoln, he did so with a narrative of decline that used historical distance. In May 1857, in a speech commemorating the organization of the Radical Abolition Party, Douglass noted that some believed the nation

---

[87] Theodore Parker to William H. Herndon, September 9, 1858, Theodore Parker Papers, MHS.
[88] Burt, *Lincoln's Tragic Pragmatism*, 484.

had reached a new low in the push for abolition. He himself admitted that recent events left him in the dark:

Standing, as it were, barefoot, and treading upon the sharp and flinty rocks of the present, and looking out upon the boundless sea of the future, I have sought, in my humble way, to penetrate the intervening mists and clouds, and, perchance, to descry, in the dim and shadowy distance, the white flag of freedom, the precise speck of time at which the cruel bondage of my people should end, and the long entombed millions rise from the foul grave of slavery and death. But of that time I can know nothing, and you can know nothing. All is uncertain at that point.[89]

The future, like the past, was distant and inscrutable. Confusion about the future seemed to undercut traditional teleological understandings of historical movement, but it also inspired greater faith in human initiative. In light of Taney's decision, in which "the highest authority" spoke in favor of slavery, Douglass seriously considered violent measures along with political and constitutional means.[90] Just a few months later, Douglass would accept John Brown into his house and hear about Brown's dark plans for the South. While recent developments led Douglass to consider other options, including violent ones, they also challenged his belief in those options' ultimate success. Would *Dred Scott* be the final straw to break Douglass's faith in eventual abolition? Had certain success turned to certain doom?

Even as history clouded the future, though, it left hope on the horizon. "Loud and exultingly have we been told that the slavery question is settled, and settled forever," Douglass observed. "It was settled thirty-seven years ago, when Missouri was admitted into the Union"; again in the 1830s with the gag rule; again in the 1840s with the annexation of Texas and the Mexican–American War; and again in the 1850s with the Fugitive Slave Law and the Kansas–Nebraska Act.[91] Douglass explained, "The fact is, the more the question has been settled, the more it has needed settling."[92] While offering a familiar chronicle of the proslavery empire's rise, Douglass identified how the nature of that rise revealed the empire's instability. He had learned the historical lesson that uncertainty cut both ways. If the Slave Power's continual progress introduced doubts about eventual abolition, the indeterminate nature of that progress suggested that history's direction might be altered toward abolitionist ends.

---

[89] Frederick Douglass, "The Dred Scott Decision: An Address Delivered, in Part, in New York, New York, in May 1857," in *FDP, Series One*, 3:164.
[90] Ibid., 3:167.   [91] Ibid., 166   [92] Ibid., 167.

With this understanding, Douglass plugged *Dred Scott*, "the last and most shocking of all pro-slavery devices," into his antislavery equation.[93] This equation contained multiple variables, including human initiative and Providence. The appeal to both human and divine action bore affinities with Johann Gottfried Herder's effort to align individualism and providentialism.[94] Looking to God, Douglass appealed Taney's decision to "the Supreme Court of the Almighty," and his appeal had a transformative effect: "This very attempt to blot out forever the hopes of an enslaved people may be one necessary link in the chain of events preparatory to the downfall and complete overthrow of the whole slave system."[95] Like Parker, Douglass learned to read proslavery successes as signs that freedom was in the offing; while Parker subjected Taney's decision to the march of moral sentiment, Douglass submitted it to the designs of Providence. He noted, "I am superstitious enough to believe that the finger of the Almighty may be seen bringing good out of evil."[96] Douglass's phrasing indicated a tenuous relationship between faith in progress toward a millennial state and the realization that "all is uncertain." His providentialism and millennialism did not negate indeterminate historical movement. Indeed, they inspired it, suggesting that change always remained possible, allowing Douglass to predict ultimate antislavery victory while observing continual proslavery progress. In this case, religious belief encouraged, rather than hindered, the spread of modern historical views.[97]

Douglass did not ground his prediction in Providence alone but, like other hopeful antislavery writers, tied it to the sentiments and actions of the people. The slavery debates had encouraged many participants to recognize humans as historical actors, a recognition that developed in relation to traditional beliefs about the divine as a historical force. In the United States, this recognition that human action contributed to historical movement grew out of a series of developments, including the Arminianism of American revivalism, which acknowledged humans' active role in receiving Christ's grace, and the romanticism and Transcendentalism of figures such as Parker, who envisioned new Christs. These intellectual trends fueled a growing belief that humans

---

[93] Ibid., 169.   [94] Beiser, *The German Historicist Tradition*, 131–62.
[95] Douglass, "Dred Scott Decision," 3:168, 169.   [96] Ibid., 169.
[97] Eileen Cheng has made a similar point about the historian George Bancroft. She contends that Bancroft's interest in unintended consequences followed from his providential understanding. Cheng, *Plain and Noble Garb*, 143–51.

played a determinative historical role, an idea that emerged in tandem with similar European developments.

In the United States, debates over slavery encouraged this view. For example, beginning in the late 1840s, African American abolitionist Martin Delany argued that blacks must cease looking to God for deliverance and instead secure it themselves.[98] During the same era that Karl Marx observed that "men make their own history," abolitionists such as Parker and Douglass began to emphasize the role of humans in the drive toward abolition.[99] As the sin of slavery embodied the problem of evil in the United States, antislavery writers formulated *anthropodicies* alongside theodicies.

While observing the darkness of the hour, Douglass placed his faith in the people to create a brighter future. He believed the antislavery movement had "taken a deeper, broader, and more lasting hold upon the national heart than ordinary reform movements," which rose and fell in rapid succession.[100] *Dred Scott* proved beyond all doubt the Court's subjugation to the Slave Power, but Douglass had "no fear that the National Conscience will be put to sleep by such an open, glaring, and scandalous tissue of lies."[101] While some argued that abolitionism had incited proslavery intransigence, Douglass asserted that "all measures devised and executed with a view to allay and diminish the anti-slavery agitation, have only served to increase, intensify, and embolden that agitation."[102] In this schema, the Court's attempt to settle the issue once and for all demanded that the people respond in greater measure. Trusting in that response, which had begun to issue forth, Douglass declared that "slavery is a doomed system" and that "liberty is destined to become the settled law of this Republic." He based this belief "upon the nature of the American Government, the Constitution, the tendencies of the age, and the character of the American people."[103] When he converted to a Smithian constitutional reading in the early 1850s, he had problematized the idea that one could readily uncover the framers' views. Now, Douglass joined Lincoln in uncovering an antislavery consensus that called for a popular response.

---

[98] See Kytle, *Romantic Reformers*, 159–205; and Guyatt, *Providence and the Invention of the United States*, 233–34.

[99] Karl Marx, *The Eighteenth Brumaire of Louis Napoleon*, in *Marx and Engels Collected Works*, trans. Richard Dixon et al., 50 vols. (London, 1975–2004), 11:103.

[100] Douglass, "Dred Scott Decision," 3:165.   [101] Ibid., 3:167.   [102] Ibid., 3:169.

[103] Ibid., 3:171.

Douglass centered his faith in a free future on the link between the American people and their founding past. He insisted that Taney's "tissue of lies" conflicted with the ideals of the nation's forefathers, who "have said that man's right to liberty is self-evident."[104] Though Douglass was one of the nation's most unrelenting critics, he clung to this principle. He still knew "of no soil better adapted to the growth of reform than American soil" and believed the "groundwork" prepared by the framers promised to produce a "Christian Civilization" that far surpassed the one that existed.[105] He held that "the Constitution, as well as the Declaration ... and the sentiments of the founders of the Republic, give us a platform broad enough, and strong enough, to support the most comprehensive plans for the freedom and elevation of all the people of this country, without regard to color, class, or clime."[106] Douglass bound his emancipationist faith to the nation's sacred legal texts and, as he had done with the Bible, wrested them from his opponents. In this way, his argument paralleled Parker's and Lincoln's even as it claimed a broader platform of freedom for blacks.

As at the beginning of the decade, at its end Douglass held that it was "a fit time to discuss the constitutional pretensions of slavery."[107] Now a firm antislavery constitutionalist, he argued that "the power arrayed against us is not a parchment," nor was slavery to be abolished by "changing the dead form of the Union." Douglass continued, "We have to do not with the dead, but the living, not with the past, but the living present." Douglass believed the favored pasts – both the biblical and constitutional eras – supported his drive toward freedom in the present. Like Parker and Lincoln, he did not think constitutional abolition required an amendment. The fault, he told his audience, was not in the founding fathers but in themselves, not in "the peculiar character of our Constitution ... but the wicked pride, love of power, and selfish perverseness of the American people."[108] While figures such as Taney deferred to the framers on moral questions, Douglass, like Parker, absolved the founders of guilt so as to firmly place blame on his contemporaries, including the Bostonians who stood by as federal troops marched Sims and Burns back to slavery and the Garrisonians, whose desired disunion would "shut up the system in its own congenial barbarism."[109] Douglass held firm to his belief in the progress of the spirit of liberty even as he identified moments in which his contemporaries failed to align themselves

[104] Ibid., 3:168. [105] Ibid., 3:171. [106] Ibid., 3:171–72. [107] Ibid., 3:174.
[108] Ibid., 3:172. [109] Ibid., 3:173.

"*We Have to Do Not ... with the Past, but the Living Present*" 293

with that spirit. He believed slavery's sin had become obvious, making the permissive acts of those who knew better all the more troubling. Abolition was the only means of absolution.

After throwing one punch in the direction of Garrison, Douglass readied for a second: "I have a quarrel with those who fling the Supreme Law of this land between the slave and freedom." The fight rested in a strict interpretation of the Constitution: "I must see that it is there plainly stated that one man of a certain description has a right of property in the body and soul of another man of a certain description." Citing traditional interpretive rules, Douglass explained that intent "must prevail" and "must be collected from [the Constitution's] words."[110] He reminded his audience that the Constitution did not mention *slave* or *slavery* and did not identify "we, the people" as "white." It did, however, include provisions such as the due process clause, which made slavery an "open and flagrant violation of all the objects set forth in the Constitution."[111] Douglass stressed the absence of a proslavery letter to reveal an antislavery spirit. Referencing Spooner, Goodell, and Smith, he challenged the assumption "that the WRITTEN Constitution is to be interpreted in the light of a SECRET and UNWRITTEN understanding of its framers."[112] Douglass maintained that the best interpretations focused on the text's words alone.

But as in the past, he combined a focus on the Constitution's words with an appeal to an original antislavery expectation. Taney had argued that because "the Constitution comes down to us from a slaveholding period and a slaveholding people ... we are bound to suppose that [it] recognizes colored persons of African descent ... as debarred forever from all participation in the benefit of the Constitution and the Declaration."[113] Douglass, joining respondents ranging from little-known journalists to prominent politicians, denounced this understanding as "a brazen misstatement of the facts of history" and insisted that "the testimony of the founders ... prove Judge Taney false, as false to history as he is to law."[114] Like other antislavery respondents, Douglass latched onto the historical nature of Taney's reasoning and provided historical facts, gleaned from sources such as George Washington's correspondence, to show that "all, at that time, looked for the gradual but certain abolition of slavery, and shaped the constitution with a view of this

---

[110] Ibid., 3:175.   [111] Ibid., 3:176, 177.
[112] Ibid., 3:177, emphasis in original. See Spooner, *Unconstitutionality of Slavery*, 88–89.
[113] Douglass, "Dred Scott Decision," 3:178.   [114] Ibid., 3:179–80.

grand result."[115] Douglass did not deny slavery's presence at the founding, but he emphasized the founders' abolitionist expectations. In his view, the intention gleaned from the Constitution's words rested on an understanding that the framers had written in anticipation of eventual emancipation. According to Douglass, that anticipation included an injunction to use historical change against historical stasis.

While Taney had insisted that progressive changes in sentiment toward blacks could not alter original proslavery meaning, Douglass averred the opposite: deplorable proslavery developments could not alter original antislavery meaning. Although both assertions drew attention to change and cultivated a sense of distance from the founding era, they differed in their understanding of how distance related to interpretation. Douglass joined Curtis and McLean, along with Parker and Lincoln, in describing the Constitution as a document that was created in a proslavery past but that was meant to be read anew in an antislavery future. The fact that historical contingencies had produced a proslavery context did not justify a proslavery reading. According to Douglass, Garrisonians wrongly conflated the Constitution (which "is one thing") with its administration (which is "another, and, in this instance, a very different ... thing").[116] Despite anticonstitutionalists' pretensions to historical soundness, Douglass believed they confused historical usage with historical text.

To further counter the proslavery reading, Douglass drew a comparison with the ongoing biblical debate: "The slaveholders of the South, and many of their wicked allies at the North, claim the Bible for slavery; shall we, therefore, fling the Bible away as a pro-slavery book? It would be as reasonable to do so as it would be to fling away the Constitution." Unlike Parker, Douglass had never been willing to relinquish the Bible to the proslavery defense. Parker's prior openness to setting aside both the Bible and the Constitution was based on historical evidence and the idea that moral sentiment progressed over time, but he had since laid claim to both texts, in large measure for historical reasons. Parker still recognized slavery's presence in the biblical and founding eras, but he extracted universal truths from the texts of these eras, which contained, in his view, transient proslavery teachings. Douglass adopted a similar approach. He stated that the "American people have made void our Constitution by just such traditions as Judge Taney and Mr. Garrison have been giving to the world of late .... I shall follow neither. It is not what Moses allowed for the hardness of heart, but what God requires,

---

[115] Ibid., 3:181.   [116] Ibid., 3:182.

"We Have to Do Not ... with the Past, but the Living Present" 295

[which] ought to be the rule."[117] Douglass separated out and saved the universal truths of freedom from association with the peculiar proslavery teachings that had been confused as part and parcel of the nation's sacred texts.

Douglass responded to *Dred Scott* by using a sense of historical awareness that favored freedom. Troubling developments made him uncertain about prospects for abolition, but he emphasized the unsettled nature of those developments to suggest that Providence could repurpose temporary proslavery victories for ultimate antislavery success. He saw that potential in the spread of antislavery sentiment among an American people who exhibited unique reformist tendencies. They had been blinded by pride, power, and a proslavery constitutional interpretation that conflated historical text and historical use, but Douglass possessed the interpretive tools and historical facts needed to restore the Constitution to its original antislavery form. His efforts were not meant to revive the conditions of the founding era, an era in which slavery existed, but rather to reveal the framers' expectation of abolition so that a new era might begin. After explaining that the struggle to realize those expectations rested "not with the past, but the living present," Douglass called on Americans to "live up to the Constitution, adopt its principles, imbibe its spirit and enforce its provisions."[118] Douglass expected a "counter-revolution ... on the part of the people" to overturn the "revolution in the judicial history of the country" that came through *Dred Scott*.[119] He trusted the American people to read the past with new eyes and then join in the divine work of building a brighter future.

The arguments of Douglass, Lincoln, and Parker underscored what *Dred Scott* already had made clear: the Constitution was the most important text in the interpretive debates over slavery, and historical arguments mattered most in political and public debates about constitutional interpretation. Taney's decision had expanded the realm of debate, leading obscure journalists and prominent politicians, who confidently challenged the decision on historical grounds, to peer into the past for facts. Rearticulating historical readings exposed an expanding number of Americans to conversations about the relationship between the nation's present and its founding past. These conversations did not replace traditional historical views with a robust modern historical awareness, but they did introduce a significant portion of the public to discussions that insisted on historical difference, distance, and change, thus predisposing

[117] Ibid. [118] Ibid., 3:183. [119] *Frederick Douglass' Paper*, March 27, 1857.

the public toward sensibilities often associated with modern historical thinking. Over the course of a couple of decades, the intellectual processes by which interpretive debates over slavery indicated substantive temporal dislocation had developed; these processes had moved from confined scholarly discussions about biblical times to expansive public debates about the founding era. The extent to which the debates spread historical awareness cannot be fully measured, but examining the development of the conversation shows the emergence of an intellectual environment in which participants had to confront historical distance and change as interpretive problems.

A range of arguments resulted, including static constitutional readings that ignored historical change, calling forth either a slaveholding or an antislavery era, or that summarily dispatched the founding era as unenlightened. But the most determinative reading arose among antislavery figures such as Parker, Lincoln, and Douglass, whose selective appeals to the past had greater potential to reveal historical difference and distance than those of their proslavery and antislavery contemporaries. Given the narrow nature of their appeals, these figures had less to lose in digging into the past than those who searched for a monolithic antislavery or proslavery period. Once they recovered an original expectation of abolition, they rescued the Constitution and then let the proslavery past sink into oblivion. In contrast to many contemporary interpreters, these figures read the Constitution in light of the distance that their historical readings revealed. This interpretive development indicated that an awareness of distance complicated approaches to the past but did not close it off from use. In other words, the slavery debates produced a number of historically aware interpretations of the nation's legal text.

Douglass's response to *Dred Scott* included several of the crucial components that characterized the responses of Parker and Lincoln, although each of these figures took different paths to arrive at an antislavery reading of the Constitution. At the start of the decade, Douglass wanted to banish the nation's supreme legal document to a dark past, but by 1851, he had embraced the radical antislavery constitutionalists' stress on the words of the text. However, he was not a purist in this regard. Still interested in a historical reading, Douglass replaced a contextual interpretation that discovered original proslavery intent with one that discerned original abolitionist expectations. He expanded this constitutional reading in response to *Dred Scott*. Clearing the fog created by the Slave Power's political and legal victories, Douglass provided the people with an unobstructed view of an antislavery Constitution. With faith in God, he called on the people to see the Constitution as a shining banner of freedom.

Parker took more time than Douglass to adopt a popular antislavery reading. He had appealed to the founding generation's expectation of abolition since the 1840s, but his trust in the Constitution had decreased during the 1850s. Signs of recent proslavery progress had darkened his view of the American past, at times threatening to completely sever his tie to the founding era. While the *Dred Scott* decision troubled him, he also used it to rekindle his lingering faith in that era. Like Douglass, Parker responded to the decision by stressing the Constitution's words, laying claim to its universal principles, setting aside its particular flaws, and binding together the framers' and ratifiers' antislavery intentions. In arguing that the Constitution was the act of the people at the framing, Parker endorsed the interpretation of the people in the present. With a firm belief in the progress of antislavery sentiment from one hopeful generation to the next, he pushed for a progressive popular reading of the Constitution.

Lincoln arrived late to the conversation, but he consistently promoted an antislavery interpretation once he turned his focus onto slavery. After reentering politics in response to the Kansas–Nebraska Act in 1854, he expressed a willingness to abide by the Fugitive Slave Law and to respect slavery where it existed even while crafting a historical argument that stressed a congressional right to limit slavery's spread. In the late 1850s, Lincoln remained focused on curbing slavery's expansion rather than securing its abolition, but he drew closer to Parker and Douglass in a number of ways. Like them, he challenged Taney's opinion with a bolstered historical argument. While suggesting that the *Dred Scott* decision conflicted with public sentiment (which sentiment Lincoln linked to the framers' expectations), Lincoln spent most of his time highlighting the framers' original expectations and contrasting those expectations with recent proslavery advances. He emphasized the expediency and necessity of the framers' compromise and insisted that they had proposed to abolish slavery as fast as circumstances would allow. To this assertion, he added the argument that they had used "covert language" so that when abolition did come, the Constitution would not reveal the nation's unfortunate slave past. Then, to justify a new constitutional reading, Lincoln used the fact that unexpected circumstances had emerged. Although he adopted the framers' practical approach to slavery, his narrative suggested that his contemporaries should work to bring an end to the institution.

While Douglass, Parker, and Lincoln each focused on the words of the Constitution, none of them did so at the expense of founding-era context. Rather than decry the interpretive use of historical sources, they challenged the historical arguments of Garrisonians and proslavery proponents with founding-era facts. Such facts included African American voting at ratification and the founding generation's expectation of abolition. These three figures' insistence that the framers and ratifiers anticipated eventual abolition acknowledged implicitly what Lincoln's emphasis on the necessity of the constitutional compromise explicitly granted: slavery's powerful presence at the nation's birth. In other words, arguing that the framers had been careful to avoid using certain terms in constructing the Constitution underscored the significance and the significations of the document's silences. And that was precisely Lincoln's point: through the framers' arduous efforts to keep the historical reality of slavery out of the text, they had created an ahistorical document, a document for "the ages" in Douglass's phrase.[120] When moral sentiment demanded abolition, nothing in the Constitution stood in the way.

Though Lincoln indicated his willingness to ignore slavery's past by arguing that the framers wrote the Constitution in a way that, in a postemancipation future, would obscure slavery's founding-era presence, he recognized that post-founding-era developments made a full erasure impossible. He thus contended that in spite of their own context, the founding generation had written and ratified universal truths that they expected would be realized in more egalitarian contexts constructed by their descendants. In their own distinctive ways, Lincoln, Parker, and Douglass each worked to bring about such contexts.

In the view of each of these figures, the favored founding era was not a golden age to be restored or a dark age to be damned; rather, it was a temporal moment of both limitation and promise in which the framers had crafted a document meant to outlive their own context. Lincoln, Parker, and Douglass insisted that the state of affairs in which they lived differed from the one that the framers had expected. Their view deepened the sense of temporal dislocation from the founding era created by narratives of decline. But, again, theirs were not nostalgic calls to set aside historical progress in an effort to preserve the traditions of their fathers. Rather, they made progressive calls to set aside antiquated practices by laying claim to the founders' expectations. In contrast to the

---

[120] Frederick Douglass, "The American Constitution and the Slave: An Address Delivered in Glasgow, Scotland, on March 26, 1860," in *FDP*, *Series One*, 3:348.

constitutional interpreters that dismissed change to retrieve static original meanings, these antislavery readers highlighted change to push toward the realization of original expectations. Achieving those expectations, however, would require further change.

Parker, Douglass, and Lincoln seemed to grasp the promise of contingent development. Each suggested that Taney, despite his best efforts, could not freeze time and settle an issue that history consistently unsettled. Douglass acknowledged uncertainties about the nation's historical direction but emphasized the contingent development of proslavery progress to bolster his hope in humanity's divinely directed work of abolition. Lincoln called attention to the unprecedented nature of *Dred Scott* and the unexpected proslavery context it revealed, and he suggested that those opposed to the decision should work to overturn it and create a new antislavery context. These moves indicated the indeterminate nature of historical change. Parker's ambivalence between assumed moral progress and asserted political decline also signaled uncertain historical movement, which he used to argue that *Dred Scott* could not arrest freedom's progress. Each of these figures turned contingent historical development to his advantage. Unexpected changes had strengthened the Slave Power, but the contingencies of the Slave Power's rise suggested the course of events could be manipulated toward antislavery ends. Who, though, was fit to alter history's path? Parker and Lincoln seemed to believe it was up to their white contemporaries. African American intellectuals such as Douglass had other ideas.

8

A "Modern Crispus Attucks"

On March 5, 1858, a multiracial group of Americans met in Boston's Faneuil Hall to commemorate the death of Crispus Attucks, a figure, most likely of African and Native American descent, who had been killed during the Boston Massacre exactly eighty-eight years before.[1] While the attendees met to remember a black historical actor and his role in a revolutionary event, they did so with contemporary actors and actions in mind. Meeting just a day before Taney's infamous decision turned a year old, the commemorators celebrated Attucks to protest the legal injustices leveled at Dred Scott and all black Americans. Observing the ways in which their contemporaries' investment in the Revolution had paid political dividends, the commemorators honored a black revolutionary with hopes that black contemporaries would soon be granted equal participation in American society. While historical awareness had shaped American interpretive debates over the Bible and the Constitution, that awareness was even more determinative in black efforts to win freedom and claim citizenship and its attendant rights.

Like the fugitive slave cases, *Dred Scott* trained attention on the status of African Americans and their revolutionary forebears. And, once again, black actors initiated the conversation; African American writers and orators shifted the focus of the discussion from the past and present status of slavery as an institution to the past and present situation of blacks in America. The nature of the constitutional debate militated

[1] Mitch Kachun, *First Martyr of Liberty: Crispus Attucks in American Memory* (New York, 2017), 7–28.

against this development. During the 1850s, Lincoln argued that the framers had written a Constitution that would have obscured slavery in the American past but for the contingent rise of the Slave Power. Lincoln's approach revealed an original expectation of abolition, but this interpretive focus on the framers obscured the experience of free blacks during the founding era. Furthermore, Lincoln's insistence that the framers had expected time to erase slavery from the American past could also mute the collective experience of African Americans, threatening to erase from history the individual lives of countless former slaves. All of these developments complicated black efforts to remember and use their past in seeking a more expansive place on the nineteenth-century American stage.

Theodore Parker, who believed that his African American colleagues inhabited a lower rung on the ladder of civilization, asserted that blacks lacked the spirit of moral progress and martial prowess attributed to the Anglo-Saxon race. This, Parker believed, explained slaves' failure to rise up and strike down their masters. In focusing on the fact that slaves had not violently overthrown the peculiar institution, Parker set aside evidence of black valor in slavery and freedom. Even the *Liberator*, which reported instances of slave resistance, could not pay too much attention to forceful struggle without undermining Garrison's pacifist goals. When whites did picture slave resistance, they frequently framed it as frenzied rebellion rather than ordered military effort. Euro-Americans' widespread failure to acknowledge black bravery came at a high cost for those struggling to demonstrate their patriotism and secure their place as American citizens.

Black reformers understood the high stakes of historical argumentation. Tasked with answering both those who believed blacks were too violent and those who believed they were too timid, they worked to ensure that this kind of amnesia did not go unchallenged. Long before *Dred Scott*, black writers had been marshaling historical evidence to attack slavery and racism and to chart a course toward a brighter future. Historian William C. Nell, who organized the March 5 celebration, had spent the better part of two decades chronicling the efforts of Attucks and other black soldiers. Thus, when Taney used a historical narrative to declare blacks noncitizens, Nell was poised to highlight the patriotism of historical actors such as Attucks. Inscribed with revolutionary power, black historical figures and their actions became an important interpretive site to challenge both slavery and racism. In recovering the place of blacks in the American past, Nell and his fellow commemorators hoped to carve out greater political space for their descendants in the American present and future.[2]

This hermeneutic of black bodies in motion, like the emerging antislavery biblical and constitutional readings, read past actions as inspiration for present reform. This interpretive style also bore a close relationship to black readings of the Bible. The similarity was most clear in the way these readers used the Exodus account to map a providential journey out of the dark pit of slavery and into the promised land of freedom. While many blacks found inspiration in a story about a historical people from an ancient past, this typological reading oriented them toward a future in which God would lead them out of bondage. Such an investment in historical precedent and future fulfillment characterized other aspects of black life, including freedom celebrations, where participants commemorated emancipatory moments, condemned ongoing slavery and prejudice, and anticipated future abolition and equality.[3] Like Frederick Douglass's response to *Dred Scott*, such anticipation placed faith in the dual work of Providence and people, including black actors.

Nell and other Attucks Day commemorators worked in this interpretive frame. Their historical narratives yielded the lesson that black actors could harness history to bring about more egalitarian conditions. These figures reverenced the egalitarian promises in the Declaration of Independence, largely because they viewed the Revolution as a fight for freedoms and rights in which blacks had shown bravery and assertiveness. Their focus on reading black revolutionaries such as Attucks, rather than static texts such as the Constitution, laid claim to the first Revolution in a way that signaled the need for a second revolution – and a second set of revolutionaries. While on the one hand this approach rendered irrelevant the prolonged interpretive debates over the Bible and the Constitution, on

---

[2] On the efforts of black Bostonians, including Nell, to achieve citizenship and belonging, see Stephen Kantrowitz, *More Than Freedom: Fighting for Black Citizenship in a White Republic, 1829–1889* (New York, 2012).

[3] See Eddie S. Glaude Jr., *Exodus!: Religion, Race, and Nation in Early Nineteenth-Century Black America* (Chicago, 2000), especially chapter 5. On the importance of the Exodus trope in debates over colonization and abolitionism, see David Brion Davis, *The Problem of Slavery in the Age of Emancipation* (New York, 2014), 83–104. Many blacks also focused on the historical subject of Africa, which represented an ancient place of origin and a sacred source of collective pride. A communal oral and written tradition about Africa countered the idea that blacks had neither a past nor a future. See Laurie F. Maffly-Kipp, *Setting Down the Sacred Past: African-American Race Histories* (Cambridge, MA, 2010), 16–64, 154–200.

the other hand it imbued those debates with even greater meaning by placing black lives at the center of the conversation.

Accounts focused on black agents both drew on and complicated broader developments in historical awareness. In his writings, Nell provided evidence of black intellectual, social, and economic success, which challenged Anglocentric views of history's movement. At the same time, Nell tied a romantic emphasis on human action to present reform.[4] Similar to Parker, Lincoln, and Douglass, Nell tracked both historical progress and decline, which indicated ambivalence about history's movement. But rather than outline the unexpected rise of the Slave Power, as many antislavery writers had done, he traced the contingent growth of racial prejudice. While his histories indicated that "men make their own history," they also signaled that "they do not make it under self-selected circumstances, but under circumstances existing already, given and transmitted from the past."[5] Nell aimed to make sure his contemporaries did not forget the already existing circumstances of black experience.

Nell's consideration of those circumstances taught lessons of possible change. While his attention to negative changes did not draw as much attention to historical distance as contextual constitutional readings did, his writings showed an even greater openness to contingent historical development than those constitutional interpretations displayed. This was a lesson with profound importance for black Americans: Nell's effort to identify racist beliefs and institutions historicized those beliefs and institutions, indicating that they could be amended or laid to rest. While Parker applied the lessons of historical distance to the reading of sacred texts, Nell drew attention to contingent change to encourage his contemporaries to revise social relations. The process of observing both white prejudice and black valor signaled that human actors could bring about new conditions. Nell's historical writings set the stage for him to insist that blacks had a role to play in that transformation.

By focusing on black revolutionaries in his writings, Nell signaled that their descendants carried martial abilities. That indication played on the anxieties of white southerners and also informed white northerners that they could count on African American arms in a civil conflict. Blacks

---

[4] See Stephen G. Hall, *A Faithful Account of the Race: African American Historical Writing in Nineteenth-Century America* (Chapel Hill, 2009), 94–104. See also John Ernest, *Liberation Historiography: African American Writers and the Challenge of History, 1794–1861* (Chapel Hill, 2004), 95–101, 132–54.

[5] Marx, *Eighteenth Brumaire*, in *Marx and Engels*, 11:103.

already were emulating their forebears according to some, including Wendell Phillips, who was one of the only white abolitionists to highlight black military valor. In speaking at the Attucks commemoration, he expressed his desire for "another ATTUCKS" and found one with the help of Thomas Wentworth Higginson, who had observed a "*modern Crispus Attucks*" during the attempt to rescue Anthony Burns.[6] On the surface, efforts to commemorate Attucks and find his modern equal implied a desire to recapture and relive the past, but just below the surface of these efforts rested the hope that blacks would emulate their ancestors' actions to open a new and more expansive era of freedom. The commemorators' appeals to the past did not collapse historical distance but instead indicated that the time was ripe for another period of profound historical change. They looked to the past in hopes of widening the distance between past and present.

Rather than attend to those who addressed distance in biblical and constitutional interpretation, this chapter focuses on those who aimed to capitalize on the promise of contingent change in historical argumentation. Constitutional debates had highlighted historical change and figures such as Lincoln and Parker had and would use an awareness of this change to work toward a new era of freedom. Douglass, Nell, and others took a step further in reading the actions of black historical agents and the instantiation of white racial prejudice in ways that signaled the possibility of a second revolution. Nell's research and writing carried practical purpose, intellectual promise, and revolutionary potential. His work fueled black reactions to *Dred Scott*, prompting many to use the case to renew the revolutionary spirit. These respondents crafted historical arguments to confront the racial prejudice they identified in both Taney's decision *and* Parker's speeches, and they looked to the first American Revolution to envision a second revolution in which blacks would play starring roles.

"A NARRATION OF THOSE MILITARY SERVICES"

Douglass, who continually struggled for a second revolution, both embodied and identified African American assertiveness. His autobiography, which included a narration of his transformative row with slave-breaker Edward Covey, was in some ways representative of a broader

---

[6] *Liberator*, March 12, 1858, emphases in original.

history of African American combatants.[7] In his speeches, Douglass highlighted portions of that martial history to quash racist notions about blacks' capacity for serving as soldiers and functioning as citizens. In an 1845 speech in Ireland, for example, he referred to the exploits of Madison Washington. A slave bound for New Orleans, Washington had orchestrated a rebellion aboard the ship *Creole*, killing a slave trader, sparing the rest of the crew, and securing the freedom of the slaves on board. Douglass, who later wrote a short novel about Washington, noted that when the US Congress received news of the event, it "was thrown into an uproar that *Maddison* [sic] *Washington* had in imitation of *George Washington* gained liberty."[8] In the same speech, Douglass cited the efforts of black revolutionaries and claimed for them "the first blood that gushed at Lexington, at the battle field of Worcester, and Bunker Hill."[9] In a subsequent speech, he again asserted that "it was a negro who shed the first blood, and fired the first gun" at the Battle of Bunker Hill.[10] Douglass showed how the American contradiction between freedom and slavery was embodied in black revolutionaries and their emulators, whose efforts had been buried while those of their white contemporaries were celebrated.

Nell was foremost among those resurrecting and celebrating the martial exploits of African Americans. He built on the civil rights efforts of his father's generation, which laid a black institutional foundation in Boston. William Guion Nell had been a founding member and vice president of the Massachusetts General Colored Association (MGCA), which counted David Walker among its ranks. While contending for abolition, the MGCA protested discriminatory laws and promoted self-help through religion and education. When the association merged with the NEASS in

---

[7] Frederick Douglass, *Life and Times of Frederick Douglass*, in *The Frederick Douglass Papers, Series Two: Autobiographical Writings*, ed. John W. Blassingame, John R. McKivigan, and Peter P. Hinks, 3 vols. (New Haven, 1999–2012), 3:109–13. On the importance of Douglass's fight with Covey, see Blight, *Frederick Douglass*, 65–66, 261–62.

[8] Frederick Douglass, "American Prejudice against Color: An Address Delivered in Cork, Ireland, October 23, 1845," in *FDP, Series One*, 1:60–70, quotation on 68, emphasis in original. The novella was titled *The Heroic Slave, a Heartwarming Narrative of the Adventures of Madison Washington, in Pursuit of Liberty* (Boston, 1852).

[9] Douglass, "American Prejudice," 69–70, quotation on 69.

[10] Frederick Douglass, "Slavery and America's Bastard Republicanism: An Address Delivered in Limerick, Ireland, on 10 November 1845," in *FDP, Series One*, 1:80. Douglass likely had in mind Peter Salem, who was reported to have shot and killed British Major John Pitcairn. See S[amuel] Swett, *Historical and Topographical Sketch of Bunker Hill Battle*, in *An Essay on the Life of the Honourable Major General Israel Putnam*, by David Humphreys (Boston, 1818), 247.

1833, it signaled a shift among Boston's black activists toward a more integrationist approach.[11]

The younger Nell inherited the former generation's emphasis on intellectual improvement as a means of overcoming white prejudice and achieving greater political and legal rights. In the early 1830s, he studied law under the tutelage of William Bowditch but decided not to practice due to a Garrisonian refusal to submit to the Constitution. Instead, Nell turned his attention to desegregation, training his focus on a number of Boston's public services. He also performed various tasks for the *Liberator* and, beginning in 1840, he used his relationships at Garrison's paper to confront segregation in public schools. This was an uphill battle, but after a decade and a half of struggle, Nell and his fellow reformers achieved success: in 1855, Massachusetts prohibited racial segregation in its public schools.

During the 1840s, while working to extend educational opportunities for Boston's black youth, Nell continued his own studies. Wendell Phillips, who Nell praised as "my dear benefactor," encouraged these intellectual pursuits.[12] In an April 1841 letter to Phillips, Nell stated his intent to pursue "a course of profitable reading." Admitting he was "not at all as familiar with History as [he] aught to be," he chose it as the subject of his studies, and even identified the topic of his research: "I have been unable to find out much of the History of Attucks," he wrote, citing a few brief references to the revolutionary figure. While Attucks was mentioned in some early histories of the Revolution, the amount of attention writers gave to him had decreased.[13] In an 1839 speech at which Nell was present, Reverend Jehiel C. Beman, a black abolitionist, referred to Attucks as the first to shed his blood for independence.[14] The speech may have sparked Nell's interest in the historical figure. Regardless, in his 1841 letter to Phillips, Nell voiced his determination to "continue to make inquiries that [he believed would] furnish [him] with some *interesting* facts in the Biography of Attucks."[15] This marked the beginning of Nell's work as a historian focused on Attucks and other black revolutionaries.

---

[11] On these developments, see Kantrowitz, *More Than Freedom*, 13–40.

[12] William C. Nell to Wendell Phillips, August 1839, Wendell Phillips Papers, MS Am 1953, Houghton. On their relationship, see James Brewer Stewart, "Comfortable in His Own Skin: Wendell Phillips and Racial Egalitarianism," in *Wendell Phillips*, 117–21.

[13] See Kachun, *First Martyr*, 29–45.   [14] *Liberator*, August 9, 1839.

[15] William C. Nell to Wendell Phillips, April 15, 1841, Wendell Phillips Papers, MS Am 1953, Houghton, emphasis in original. On this interchange and Nell's role in reviving Attucks as a revolutionary figure, see Kachun, *First Martyr*, 46–57.

During the next decade, Nell continued his historical research while struggling to make ends meet. In late 1847, he left the *Liberator* and its financial problems and relocated to Rochester, where he took part in a new financial endeavor: helping Frederick Douglass and Martin Delaney publish the *North Star*. While there, he published an essay in the newspaper in which he argued for black citizenship and referenced Attucks, whom he described as "the first martyr in the American Revolution."[16] In 1849, Nell left Douglass's paper and returned to Boston, where, as a Garrisonian, he felt more ideologically comfortable.

Nell's historical lessons inspired local resistance. Shortly after his return to Boston, he joined the city's other abolitionists in opposing the Fugitive Slave Law and assisting fugitive slaves. As the divide between Garrison and Douglass widened, Nell publicly sided with the former, and in 1853, he founded the Garrisonian Association and acted as president. Although Nell drew a few painful volleys from Douglass, and launched a few himself, both worked to rescue black historical actors from oblivion.[17]

In the same period that constitutional interpreters began using historical sources such as Madison's *Papers* to search out the framers' intent, Nell dug into the past to unveil the actions of black revolutionaries. His historical research expanded to include black soldiers of the Revolution and the War of 1812. He pored over written records and traveled long distances to conduct interviews. He hoped written recognition of black patriots would produce other kinds of recognition for his black contemporaries. On March 5, 1851, eighty-one years to the day since Attucks's death and just a month before the arrest of Thomas Sims, Nell marshaled his research to petition the state legislature to fund an Attucks monument. His petitions were denied, but Nell made sure black soldiers would be remembered in ink if not in stone.

A few months after his petition, Nell published *Services of Colored Americans, in the Wars of 1776 and 1812*, in which he used historical documents, histories, and interviews to chronicle African American military exploits. In his introduction, Nell paid tribute to the Quaker poet and abolitionist John Greenleaf Whittier. In 1847, when Whittier became an editor of Gamaliel Bailey's *National Era*, he published a brief "statement of facts" about black service during the Revolution and the

---

[16] *North Star*, May 5, 1848. See Kachun, *First Martyr*, 47.
[17] See Kantrowitz, *More Than Freedom*, 111–12, 152–57, 175–80; and Blight, *Frederick Douglass*, 224–25.

War of 1812.[18] Whittier had referenced black military service to answer a colonizationist's question about whether blacks merited an American home. On that occasion, Whittier lamented that black revolutionaries "have had no historian."[19] As Whittier penned these words, Nell was becoming the historian the poet had hoped to find.

Given his Garrisonian associations, Nell knew readers might question his focus on black resistance. He explained that while black successes in other fields had been noted, "circumstances have veiled from the public eye a narration of those military services which are generally conceded as passports to the honorable and lasting notice of Americans."[20] To correct the historical oversight, Nell outlined the efforts of African American soldiers, beginning with his first historical subject, Massachusetts's Attucks.

Because records often overlooked instances of black patriotism, Nell had to be creative in his use of sources. He cited an 1851 letter – written against Nell's petition to fund an Attucks monument – in which the author had argued that Attucks had been "the most conspicuous, inflammatory, and uproarious of the misguided populace." Based on that insight, Nell cleverly concluded that Attucks "had been foremost in resisting, and was first slain."[21] Black agents had long been subjects of interpretation and were often used to argue that all blacks were unfit for freedom and citizenship, but Nell managed to repurpose such readings toward egalitarian ends. He welcomed "every taunt that such correspondents have flung at Attucks and his company, as the best evidence of their merits."[22]

Nell's attention to Attucks's actions and black martial activities during and after the Revolution was more than an effort to correct the historical record; it was an interpretive political act. His reading demonstrated that if rights and respectability rested on a connection to revolutionary fighting, then blacks had as equal a claim as whites. In arguing that Attucks's assertiveness had ushered in the Revolution, which indicated the contingent nature of historical development, Nell's narrative also signaled that black action was a determinative historical force. In an aside, Nell observed that the revolutionary generation was "strongly in favor of the abolition of Slavery."[23] While Nell did make use of the antislavery appeal to original expectation, he remained focused on black action.

---

[18] William C. Nell, *Services of Colored Americans, in the Wars of 1776 and 1812* (Boston, 1851), 3.
[19] *National Era*, July 22, 1847. [20] Nell, *Services of Colored Americans*, 4. [21] Ibid., 6.
[22] Ibid., 7. [23] Ibid., 7.

Writing to Phillips in October 1852, Nell indicated his intention to share "some additional facts" in the second edition of his pamphlet.[24] Shortly before publication late that month, Parker "submitted an interesting article on ... colored soldiers buried under the ruins in New York."[25] In the article, which Nell included in the second edition, Parker noted that a recent excavation had unearthed "a large quantity of human bones." Seeming to rely on phrenology – a pseudoscience then in decline – Parker wrote that the skulls "bore the unmistakable marks of the [African] race."[26] Parker believed science supported his beliefs in racial difference, but he was using the report to combat racist notions; once again prejudicial assumptions commingled with egalitarian efforts.

Parker's report fit comfortably in Nell's narrative; it both identified the heroic actions of African American ancestors and underscored the development of racial prejudice among Anglo-American descendants. Apparently, the human remains belonged to black soldiers who had battled at Long Island in 1776. Satirizing those who promoted segregation in life and in death, Parker wrote that although "the black and the white had fought against the same enemy, under the same banner, contending for the same 'unalienable right' .... The white Saxon, exclusive and haughty ... must have his place of rest proudly apart from the grave of the African."[27] Parker mocked the revolutionaries' ugly ethnic distinction and then criticized their political progenies' descent into even darker realms, observing that while tyrannical England had emancipated their slaves, the republic of freedom had become a nation of slave-catchers. Dramatizing the scene, he wrote that "while these faithful bones were getting shovelled up and carted to the sea, there was a great Slave-hunt in New York."[28] Black revolutionaries' fight for freedom, like white framers' expectations of abolition, had been met with slavery's spread.

Almost double the length of the first, Nell's second edition received favorable reviews in antislavery newspapers, though writers focused more on past historians' collective failure to address black fighting than on

---

[24] William C. Nell to Wendell Phillips, October 5, 1852, Wendell Phillips Papers, MS Am 1953, Houghton.

[25] William C. Nell to Wendell Phillips, October 22, 1852, Wendell Phillips Papers, MS Am 1953, Houghton.

[26] William C. Nell, *Services of Colored Americans, in the Wars of 1776 and 1812*, 2nd ed. (Boston, 1852), 21.

[27] Ibid.

[28] Ibid., 22. Parker was probably referring to efforts to capture William Henry, a fugitive slave from Missouri.

Nell's laudable efforts to bring it to light. The *Pennsylvania Freeman* repeated what Whittier had observed about Nell's "overlooked" subjects, complaining that students in school did not learn about the death of Attucks and the heroics of Peter Salem, even though "these are facts that can hardly be unknown to the authors of our popular histories." Nell and his reviewers believed this historical myopia had lasting consequences: a failure to acknowledge black military efforts barred blacks and their descendants from taking their rightful place in American society. The *Freeman* warned that this injustice might produce a violent response. "Human forbearance has a limit," the paper noted. "The meek, the gentle and forgiving may be roused by continual wrong to a terrible revenge.... We may yet reap the natural fruit of their cruelty and oppression in a harvest of blood."[29] In contrast to the cool and deliberate *actions* of Nell's historical figures, this reading portrayed the prospective black response as an automatic and unthinking *reaction*. It suggested that a failure to reward martial service among one generation of blacks might result in a violent uprising among a subsequent generation.

The uprising never came. Instead – showing the kind of self-conscious approach that much of Nell's research demonstrated – black Bostonians used overdue historical recognition to petition for a militia. Following the lead of African Americans in other northern cities, in late February and early March of 1853, William J. Watkins and Robert Morris, armed with Nell's pamphlet, separately petitioned a state legislative committee for funds to establish a black militia in Boston. Watkins had taught at his abolitionist father's Academy for Negro Youth in Baltimore before moving to Boston in 1849, and Morris, who had defended Anthony Burns, was working with Nell to integrate Boston's schools. In their petitions, both Watkins and Morris used Nell's pamphlet but made different historical arguments.[30] The former focused on the spread of white prejudice, while the latter emphasized blacks' use of available rights.[31] Once again, different antislavery accounts indicated ambivalence about historical movement and the potential to bring about change. The petitions failed, but the petitioners persisted, as did Nell in his research.

---

[29] *Pennsylvania Freeman*, November 25, 1852; see also *Liberator*, December 17, 1852.
[30] William J. Watkins, *Our Rights as Men: An Address Delivered in Boston, before the Legislative Committee on the Militia, February 24, 1853* (Boston, 1853); Liberator, March 11, 1853.
[31] See Minardi, *Making Slavery History*, 153–61.

A *"Modern Crispus Attucks"* 311

"VALIANT AND CONSISTENT SOLDIERS IN FREEDOM'S ARMY"

In 1855, the same year that Massachusetts desegregated its schools, Nell published *The Colored Patriots of the American Revolution*, an expansion of his earlier work. In her introduction to Nell's work, Harriet Beecher Stowe wrote that "the colored race have been generally considered by their enemies, and sometimes even by their friends, as deficient in energy and courage."[32] This volume, Stowe concluded, would correct that opinion.[33] Nell again acknowledged Whittier's past efforts and used the names of Phillips and Stowe, but his project stood on its own. As Whittier stated in a review, it "needs no extraneous aid."[34]

Nell followed the format of his pamphlet editions in this new work, beginning with Attucks. He covered the martial efforts of African Americans from all thirteen original states and from newer states as well. He again identified the founders' antislavery sentiments, citing, for example, Samuel Adams's insistence that Surry, a slave who had been gifted to his wife Elizabeth Wells Adams, live with them as a free woman.[35] But Nell remained focused on black agents. He described their successes in nonmilitary realms as well, chronicling, for example, the life of poet Phillis Wheatley.[36] Such luminous figures were another site of interpretation. Nell wrote that these "cases of individual enterprise and genius" demonstrated "the improvements daily developed by that class, which has commonly been stigmatized as incapable of mental and social elevation."[37] Progress in America, Nell's narrative showed, was not exclusive to the Anglo-Saxon race. He demonstrated that despite growing racial prejudice, blacks rose in the nation's ranks.

While Nell narrated different developments than did Parker, their historical accounts similarly traced both historical decline and progress. In his appendix, Nell outlined decline in the form of white prejudice and progress in the form of black accomplishments. As part of that decline, he identified post-founding-era legislation that added "white" as a qualification for certain rights and activities, including naturalization, militia service, and mail delivery. For example, Nell cited an 1828 letter in

---

[32] Harriet Beecher Stowe, *Introduction* to *The Colored Patriots of the American Revolution, with Sketches of Several Distinguished Colored Persons: To Which Is Added a Brief Survey of the Condition and Prospects of Colored Americans*, by William C. Nell (Boston, 1855), 5.
[33] Ibid., 6.   [34] *National Era*, January 17, 1856.   [35] Nell, *Colored Patriots*, 96.
[36] Ibid., 64–73.   [37] Ibid., 111.

which Postmaster General John McLean, the same McLean who would dissent in *Dred Scott*, wrote that a "colored person" could not carry mail.[38] Nell concluded that although the Constitution did not recognize "distinctions of color[,] ... that instrument leaves it in the power of Congress and individual States to trample on ... the rights of colored citizens."[39] While his sad account demonstrated that the Slave Power "rules this nation," he qualified his narrative with cases of blacks challenging that rule by gaining citizenship, casting votes, receiving passports, and mastering professions.[40] He also described the organization of abolition societies and highlighted blacks' prominent place in them. While many antislavery writers narrated both the rise of the Slave Power and the spread of antislavery sentiment, Nell simultaneously outlined the spread of racial prejudice and the advances of African Americans. These accounts suggested an ambivalence in historical change, which Nell, like Parker and other antislavery writers, worked to reconcile.

Nell's account, like those of Parker and Douglass, partook of both traditional and modern historical thinking; it contained teleological elements but also indicated contingent development. Reflecting a popular view that historical movement tended toward a certain end, Nell believed in ultimate progress toward abolition and equal rights. However, he emphasized the role of human actions and showed how those actions resulted in both progress and decline, which indicated contingent change. Although Nell believed in ultimate progress, his narrative revealed uncertain historical movement. Like that of Parker and Douglass, Nell's faith in the future was fueled by the insight of history's unsettled direction. The unexpected changes of the past inspired his hope in expected future changes.

In contrast to most of the era's other historical writers, Nell focused on both blacks and whites: He demonstrated black action in the face of racism and highlighted the conspicuous role whites played in its spread. Nell's emphasis on these actors bringing about moral and social progress or decline drew attention to the contingent nature of beliefs and institutions, which could be altered and overturned. Tracing the spread of prejudice, in particular, historicized the racist scaffolding that had been used to construct and uphold the nation's discriminatory legal and political structures, thus undermining their permanence. To be sure, Nell did not detail the complicated development of racist ideas and systems but showing their advance suggested that if prejudicial frameworks had been made, they could be unmade. In Nell's work, the struggle for social

---

[38] Ibid., 312. [39] Ibid., 315. [40] Ibid., 316.

justice carried this historicizing impulse. And by integrating blacks into an erstwhile white narrative and thus challenging the belief that Anglo-Americans drove historical progress, Nell indicated that both blacks and whites had significant roles to play in ushering in an era of abolition and equal rights. Nell rejected the idea that this was the exclusive project of modern white saviors and instead stressed the actions of new black revolutionaries.

Although Nell's book recounted historical actions, his work was oriented toward the future. He cautioned, "Let it not be inferred ... that because many colored soldiers were, from the force of circumstances, assigned a subordinate position ... that their more immediate descendants are to remain satisfied with a half-way excellence."[41] Joining a range of antislavery biblical and constitutional interpreters, Nell indicated that circumstances had changed. This observation of change often included a call for people – usually white people – to bring about emancipation. Nell, however, argued that black descendants should lead out, "like Crispus Attucks," in a new "battle for equality."[42] Nell's historical excavations taught this grave truth: "the Revolution of 1776 ... aided, in honorable proportion, by colored Americans, [has] ... yet left the necessity for a second revolution."[43] Drawing power from the actions of his founding-era predecessors, Nell urged his contemporaries to create an egalitarian society.

In the process of recovering and celebrating the martial exploits of Attucks and his emulators, along with African American successes in other realms, Nell also unveiled the workings of "colorphobia."[44] This meant that rather than feasting on the fruits of their ancestors' labors, black descendants were denied a seat at the table. In other words, while demonstrating what black actors had sacrificed to win and preserve American freedom, Nell showed that their sons and daughters had been rewarded with slavery and prejudice.

There was a silver lining to this tale of failed promises and dashed hopes. Nell's work identified the assertiveness of black agents and exposed the constructed nature of prejudicial practices. The message was clear: contemporaries could overthrow those practices with a second and more inclusive revolution. Nell encouraged his black readers "to be incorporated with the mass of Americans ... and so prove valiant and consistent soldiers in Freedom's army." In contrast to other antislavery figures such as Parker, who seemed to believe whites would win the war alone, Nell

[41] Ibid., 378.   [42] Ibid., 378–79.   [43] Ibid., 380.   [44] See *North Star*, March 23, 1849.

envisioned that this revolution, as with the first, would be one in which blacks and whites fought side by side. Historical contingency could yield hopeful or hopeless readings. In 1855, Nell opted for the former: "To compare the present with the past ... we can hardly believe the evidence daily presented of the onward progress of those mighty principles then proclaimed to the American nation."[45] Darker days soon clouded this bright vision, but Nell's historical understanding lighted the way.

"THE REVOLUTION WHICH IS NOW GOING ON"

Two years later, when Taney's ruling ushered in those darker days, African Americans again responded to prejudice by pushing for greater freedom, as reported in antislavery newspapers. Some blacks made creative use of the new ruling. In June 1857, the *National Era* reported that Taney's decision "continues to be used by the colored people in a way that the Judge did not probably contemplate." The writer cited a case in which a black man who had been charged with debt successfully argued that, because he was a noncitizen, the law had no jurisdiction over him.[46] In July, the *Liberator* reported on a case in which Joseph Mitchell, a free black man from Illinois, had brought suit for damages against Charles Lamar, a white resident of Wisconsin. John McLean, who was then sitting on the US Circuit Court of Illinois, used an opening in Taney's wording to rule that Mitchell had a right to sue based on the fact that he had not descended from slaves.[47] Other northern judges also ignored Taney's decision.[48] Such cases involved a mix of individuals and a tangle of motivations, but they demonstrate some of the creative ways in which blacks navigated the new legal environment.[49] The *National Anti-Slavery Standard* also reported on blacks' continued success in achieving freedom in extralegal ways, observing that the Underground Railroad "appears to be doing good business in spite of the Fugitive Slave law and Dred Scott

---

[45] Nell, *Colored Patriots*, 381.

[46] *National Era*, June 18, 1857; see also *National Era* 9, May 7, 1857. Such reasoning did not always work. In 1860, *Douglass' Monthly* reported that Thomas Downing, a prominent African American businessman, cited *Dred Scott* in refusing to take the oath to be examined as a judgment debtor. In this case, a New York judge issued the draconian ruling "that for the present purpose he might be considered a human being and a citizen." See "The Dred Scott Decision in the New York Courts," *Douglass' Monthly* 2 (April 1860): 251.

[47] *Liberator*, July 24, 1857.   [48] *National Anti-Slavery Standard*, July 4, 1857.

[49] See Martha S. Jones, "*Hughes v. Jackson*: Race and Rights beyond *Dred Scott*," *North Carolina Law Review* 91, no. 5 (2013): 1757–84.

decision."⁵⁰ These developments and actions echoed Nell's historical findings about black ingenuity and assertiveness and again signaled unexpected historical developments.

Antislavery newspapers followed Nell's pattern of highlighting African American creativity and action, while also reporting setbacks and persistent prejudice. In the summer and fall of 1857, the *Standard* cited instances in which free blacks had been fired from their jobs and denied passports on the basis of Taney's decision.⁵¹ It also noted that *Dred Scott* had destroyed hopes that Solomon Northrup, a free black man who had been kidnapped and sold into slavery, and who had achieved some fame through his memoir, *Twelve Years a Slave* (1853), could sue his kidnappers.⁵²

Some black commentators read the *Dred Scott* decision in Garrisonian fashion, viewing it as a legal artifact rather than a binding law. This included Mary Ann Shadd Cary of Delaware, who had migrated to Canada after the passage of the Fugitive Slave Law. She began publishing the *Provincial Freeman* in 1853, which made her the first female publisher in Canada and the first African American female publisher in North America. With little tying her to the United States, Cary did not hesitate in condemning its prolonged liaison with slavery. In March 1857, she published a letter from her Philadelphia correspondent. The African American correspondent argued that Taney's "decision is precisely in keeping with the pro-slavery usages ... of this government." While noting that some believed it would "work ultimately to the advantage of those aimed to be ostracized," the correspondent saw "but a faint prospect of a very great change for the better," at least "as long as this abominable decision and pro-slavery constitution remains."⁵³ The *Freeman*, which also reported that a group of Philadelphia blacks had recently condemned the Constitution, hoped that those blacks who still assented to the document would "look at facts instead of everlastingly theorizing."⁵⁴

Black abolitionist Robert Purvis was also tired of the constitutional theorizers. He found "nothing new" in *Dred Scott*. In the Philadelphia meeting referred to in the *Freeman*, he issued the following resolution: the attempt to "prove that there is no support given to Slavery in the

---

⁵⁰ *National Anti-Slavery Standard*, July 11, 1857.
⁵¹ *National Anti-Slavery Standard*, August 29, 1857; *National Anti-Slavery Standard* 18, October 31, 1857.
⁵² *National Anti-Slavery Standard*, July 4, 1857.
⁵³ *Provincial Freeman*, March 28, 1857.   ⁵⁴ *Provincial Freeman*, April 18, 1857.

Constitution ... is to argue against reason and common sense, to ignore history and shut our eyes against palpable facts." While it may "suit white men ... to please themselves with such theories, it ill becomes a man of color ... to indulge in any such idle phantasies," he continued. Salem orator Charles Lenox Remond offered a slightly brighter view of "times past ... when the patriotic services of colored men ... were fresh in the minds of the people," but he also saw that "the power to oppress us lurked all the time in the Constitution." Now fully developed, that power robbed Remond of the pride he once had in the fact that "the first blood shed in the American Revolution ... was that of a colored man."[55] Less than a month later, when Purvis issued a resolution at the AASS meeting in New York City, he described the antislavery reading as a "new-fangled doctrine." In a narrative that was more like Phillips's than Parker's or Douglass's, Purvis traced apparent proslavery continuity and criticized perceived antislavery innovation. He asked his black colleagues, "Are we to clank the chains that have been made for us, and praise the men who did the deed?" No, he answered: "the Constitution is fitting and befitting those who made it." Looking toward the government's overthrow, Purvis rejoiced in "the revolution which is now going on."[56] Proslavery continuity, as much as proslavery progress, justified a revolution, and the perceived spread of antislavery sentiment indicated it was already underway.

Black responses to Taney's decision continued to track proslavery progress as well as highlight African American bravery. In June 1858, the *Liberator* reported that a group of African Americans in New Bedford, Massachusetts, had issued a set of resolutions in response to *Dred Scott*. The group had observed an increase in legal "acts of hostility and malignity towards the colored peopled in this country" even though "the colored people of this country have proved themselves worthy of the confidence and respect of their countrymen," including through their "daring bravery" in the Revolution. They resolved that Taney's decision was "a palpably vain, arrogant assumption, unsustained by history, justice, reason or common sense." This collection of "colored citizens" further resolved to "neither recognize nor respect any laws for slavery, whether from Moses, Paul, or Taney." They declared, "We spurn and trample them all under our feet as in violation of the laws of God and the rights of men." Believing that the revered Mosaic and Apostolic pasts did not answer the needs of the present crisis, the group held out hope for

[55] *Liberator*, April 10, 1857.   [56] *Liberator*, May 22, 1857.

a constitutional solution, resolving to "begin and continue to petition and memorialize Congress until our grievances are heard and redressed." They called on "all *lovers of liberty* to join in waging a war of annihilation against every vestige of oppression under which we are now suffering."[57] Once again, many believed that the moment called for revolution.

Despite criticism from figures such as Purvis, some African Americans joined Douglass in contributing to popular constitutionalisms in the wake of the *Dred Scott* decision. In March 1857, the *New York Evening Post* printed a letter from George T. Downing, a prominent black hotel owner living in Newport, Rhode Island, who began work to desegregate local schools in that same year. He wrote, "Though a colored man ... I am 'a natural born citizen.'" Just as some had emphasized that the three supposed proslavery clauses in the Constitution did not include the word "slavery," Downing observed that the three constitutional uses of "citizen" made no mention of race. He thus argued that the privileges and immunities clause applied to blacks as well as whites. Downing brought together a range of historical facts to support his reading, noting, for example, that Paul Cuffe, a person of African descent, had become a Massachusetts citizen in 1778, and contending that the phrase "other *free* citizens" in the New Jersey Plan referred to free blacks. Downing further referenced the distinction Madison had made between free and enslaved blacks in *The Federalist* and insisted that interpreters "must bear in mind that at the time all parties looked to the early decrease of slavery." Like Lincoln, Douglass, and Parker, Downing used historical facts and original expectations to reveal an antislavery Constitution and to present Taney's decision as evidence of decline from the founding era. Downing did not seek to abolish the historical distance his reading revealed but instead used it to call for change, supporting a constitutional approach while also invoking "the spirit of 1776."[58] In the wake of *Dred Scott*, African Americans advanced both anti- and pro-constitutional readings, and proponents of both appealed to revolutionary sentiment.

Both blacks and whites combined antislavery readings of the Constitution with a hermeneutic of black revolutionary action. In March, the *Cleveland Leader* published a letter US Congressman Joshua R. Giddings wrote to Taney. The Ohio representative emphasized the decision's temporal implications; he believed it threatened to turn America's democracy into an oligarchy "unsuited to the age in which we

---

[57] *Liberator*, July 9, 1858, emphasis in original.
[58] *New York Evening Post*, March 20, 1857, emphasis in original.

live." Like many other respondents, Giddings focused on an "examination of historical facts," arguing that "the enquiry into the" framers' views was "more properly a matter of history than of law." Taking advantage of the interpretive focus on history, Giddings recovered black bravery: "One of the martyrs sacrificed in the cause of liberty on the memorable fifth of March, 1770, was a black man. Black men entered the continental army at its first formation. They fought as bravely, they died as freely as white men, and at the time the Declaration ... was proclaimed, colored men who had 'descended from African slaves' were serving in the troops of every colony."[59] The letters of Downing and Giddings contrasted the role of blacks in the Revolution with the status of blacks after *Dred Scott*: Scott's helplessness stood in stark contrast to Attucks's assertiveness. With Nell, Giddings believed blacks' fight for independence granted them citizenship in the nation that their fight had made possible.

Some writers specifically cited Nell's history in drawing attention to African American revolutionaries and in arguing that blacks merited citizenship. One newspaper writer used "Mr. Nell's excellent work," to show that blacks did their share of fighting in the Revolution and contended that "there was, it is probable, not a man in the nation, at that time, who supposed the right of coloured people to citizenship would ever be disputed." The writer posited that popular sentiment had changed regarding African Americans, observing that the descendants of the British soldier who killed Joseph Warren and those of the American traitor Benedict Arnold were more welcome in the United States than the descendants of Attucks or Salem.[60] Nell's work helped in the antislavery effort to highlight black action and American retrogression.

Like *Dred Scott*, antislavery writers' historical arguments were as much about present concerns as past deeds. But rather than recover static meanings for contemporary use, they read historical actions in ways that invited change. In drawing a link between African American revolutionaries and their descendants, and in identifying how the former's legal standing had been ripped from the latter, these respondents indicated a need for another revolution. And the implication was that the descendants were up to the task.

---

[59] *Cleveland Leader*, March 24, 1857. The letter was republished in the *Liberator*, April 3, 1857. See also *Liberator*, September 18, 1857.
[60] *National Anti-Slavery Standard*, April 4, 1857.

"THE TIME IS COMING WHEN THIS BATTLE IS TO BE FOUGHT"

Nell's historical research placed him in a unique position to respond to Taney. His written commemorations provided a solid foundation on which to establish Crispus Attucks Day, on occassion that gave Attucks memorialists the chance to meet Taney on historical grounds. Their historical efforts to illuminate the revolutionary era had less to do with reclaiming a sacred text than with channeling revolutionary sentiment. African American respondents to *Dred Scott* aimed at more than slavery's abolition; they also desired to revolutionize social relations between blacks and whites. In the wake of the decision, they not only criticized Taney's narrow historical vision but also challenged the limited historical understanding of white allies such as Parker. Nell and his black colleagues insisted that along with deserving citizenship and its attendant rights, blacks had a role to play in leading the nation into a new era. As Margot Minardi observes, "At no moment in the acceleration toward the Civil War were the roles of black men as actors and as narrators in history more perfectly or more powerfully intertwined than at the first" Crispus Attucks Day.[61] On that occasion, Attucks commemorators interpreted the actions of black revolutionaries in a way that endorsed the actions of new ones.

Nell had begun to organize the event celebrating Attucks before Taney issued his decision. In a late 1856 letter to his friend Jeremiah Burke Sanderson, a black abolitionist with ties to both Garrison and Douglass, Nell mentioned a "proposed 5th of March meeting ... to commemorate the Boston Massacre – Crispus Attucks et al."[62] Nell had inserted black patriotism and valor into the national narrative and now aimed to add a commemoration of black deeds to the national calendar. In February 1857, he informed Sanderson that he had "been reluctantly compelled to defer the Attucks ... commemoration."[63] Perhaps due to a lack of funds, which Nell wrote about to friends on occasion, the celebration would have to wait. Taney's decision, which came a day after the planned date of commemoration, gave Nell's project even greater

---

[61] Minardi, *Making Slavery History*, 162.
[62] William C. Nell to Jeremiah Burke Sanderson, December 17, 1856, in *William Cooper Nell: Nineteenth-Century African American Abolitionist, Historian, Integrationist: Selected Writings from 1832–1874*, ed. Dorothy Porter Wesley and Constance Porter Uzelac (Baltimore, 2002), 462 (hereafter cited as *William Cooper Nell*).
[63] William C. Nell to Jeremiah Burke Sanderson, February 18, 1857, in *William Cooper Nell*, 466.

purpose. In August, he wrote to Phillips, "I am perfecting my plans for the 5th of March." Prospective attendees, he continued, "think that the Dred Scott decision has invested the whole with a significance that should be made contributory to the rising antislavery sentiment."[64] Nell, who believed the Court's decision fanned the flames of abolitionism, now conceptualized the Attucks celebration as an event with blazing potential.

Nell's vision of ultimate progress did not leave him blind to the negative effects of Taney's "hunt against colored Americans." In an article under that heading, published days after writing to Phillips, Nell showed that state governments from Maine to Iowa had used the *Dred Scott* decision to rob free blacks of their rights to vote, obtain business licenses, and sue in court. Clearly, he concluded, "King Slavery is on the throne."[65] Nell's account also suggested that the increasingly sparse representation of black fighting in the Revolution had mirrored the spread of racial prejudice. Samuel Swett's early history, along with early engravings, depicted Peter Salem's role at the Battle of Bunker Hill, but more recent portrayals erased him from the scene.[66] Similarly, while John Adams and other early statesmen had recognized Attucks, Paul Revere's engraving, which omitted Attucks, had shaped the national view of the Boston Massacre. Another illustration, in the late J. F. Schroeder's serial on Washington, then in publication, "wholly omitted" Attucks.[67] Not every account erased black valor: Nell credited Edward Everett, who had recognized Salem's efforts in a June speech, and Henry Q. Smith, who had published John Bufford's 1856 lithograph, which assigned "Attucks his true and leading position."[68] Nell's *Colored Americans* had also featured a frontispiece with an engraving of Attucks, though one that depicted him more as an innocent martyr than an aggressive revolutionary.[69] Such efforts offered a correction, but misrepresentations persisted; Taney had built his decision on such omissions. But Nell forcefully contradicted the chief justice. In recovering the actions of black revolutionaries and the praise of their white counterparts – "facts written on the page of impartial history" – Nell argued that "colored American citizens have rights that all mankind are bound to respect."[70]

---

[64] William C. Nell to Wendell Phillips, August 24, 1857, in *William Cooper Nell*, 489.
[65] *Liberator*, August 28, 1857.   [66] Swett, *Historical and Topographical Sketch*, 247.
[67] *Liberator*, August 28, 1857; *Towanda (PA) Bradford Reporter*, August 12, 1858.
[68] *Liberator*, August 28, 1857.
[69] Nell's *Colored Patriots* also included an engraving of Peter Salem. See Minardi, *Making Slavery History*, 44–56, 138–45; and Kachun, *First Martyr*, 52–54.
[70] Nell, *Colored Patriots*, 494.

Nell continued to remind audiences of these facts through both the spoken and the written word, including a large broadside announcing the March celebration.⁷¹ The broadside informed readers that in 1783, William Cooper, Boston's town clerk, had recorded the decision to discontinue the celebration of the Fifth of March in favor of the Fourth of July.⁷² Now, in 1858, another William Cooper determined that in light of the recent "annihilation of citizenship of Colored Americans," it was time to again commemorate the Boston Massacre and Attucks, whom the broadside represented in word and image. Stating that "the names which others neglect should only be the more sacredly our care," the broadside invited readers to "come protest against the 'Dred Scott Decision.'"⁷³

On March 5, participants and protestors filed into Faneuil Hall, where "a large number of interesting relics and mementoes of the olden time" greeted them, including documents; objects; a "venerable" octogenarian, "Father Vassall"; and even a centenarian, "Grandmother Boston." In the presence of the past, Nell spoke of Attucks, his blood spilt on Boston's streets, and his body's placement in Faneuil Hall, where it rested while awaiting burial. Nell dramatized changes since that time, noting that any white man who travels to the South and "speak[s] in defence of the principles for which Washington fought ... makes himself liable to Lynch law." Despite troubling developments, Nell reaffirmed, "God is on the side of freedom; and if her votaries will be faithful, the day is not far distant when victory will perch upon her banners."⁷⁴ As with Parker and Douglass, Nell placed faith in both the divine and the human, and his understanding of the past gave him hope for the future.

John Stewart Rock, an African American dentist and doctor, spoke next. Like Nell, he highlighted black bravery and white prejudice. Directing his comments at Parker, who had a place on the platform with Rock, Garrison, Phillips, and other abolitionists, Rock challenged assumptions of black feebleness. Only a week before, Parker had offered an anecdote in which an escaped slave, torn from his wife and children, shrank at the chance to kill his captors. Parker suggested that even the nonresistant Garrison would have eagerly swung the axe to win freedom.

---

⁷¹ See *Liberator*, February 26, 1858; and William C. Nell, *Boston Massacre, March 5th, 1770: The Day Which History Selects as the Dawn of the American Revolution. Commemorative Festival, at Faneuil Hall* [...] (Boston, 1858), broadside.

⁷² On this development, especially as it related to remembering Attucks, see Kachun, *First Martyr*, 17–20, 30–31, 35.

⁷³ Nell, *Boston Massacre*, broadside.   ⁷⁴ *Liberator*, March 12, 1858.

Failing to acknowledge instances of slave insurrection at home and abroad, Parker asserted that "the African is the most docile and pliant of all the races of men," and thus concluded that "the stroke of an axe would have settled the matter long ago. But the black man would not strike."[75] Parker's romantic racial theory and his effort to convince whites of their moral responsibility to crush slavery led him to overlook important martial moments from the African American past, and Rock would not let this oversight pass unremarked.

Rock held that prejudice like Parker's had robbed the Revolution of its most fundamental meaning. Speaking for his black contemporaries, he lamented that "our fathers fought nobly for freedom, but they were not victorious. They fought for liberty, but they got slavery." While identifying past injustice and negative changes, Rock focused on present possibilities. He believed the black sons would be more successful than their fathers. He stated, "Sooner or later, the clashing of arms will be heard in this country, and the black man's services will be needed: 150,000 freemen capable of bearing arms ... and three quarters of a million slaves, wild with enthusiasm caused by the dawn of the glorious opportunity of being able to strike a genuine blow for freedom, will be a power which white men will be 'bound to respect.'"[76] In countering Taney's most notorious assertion, Rock made explicit what Nell had implied: blacks were capable of fighting – again – for freedom, and anxiously awaited the opportunity.

Rock did not overlook the limitations introduced by slavery. "It would not be surprising if the brutal treatment which we have received for the past two centuries should have crushed our spirits," he stated. Like Nell, Rock felt he needed to highlight the ways in which slavery constrained blacks. While some of Rock's contemporaries, including Lincoln, had lamented that slavery had not been erased from the American past, figures such as Rock knew that forgetting the peculiar institution's horrors would doom the process of bringing about an egalitarian society. So, Rock reminded his audience that circumstances had shaped and continued to shape black opportunities. Rock emphasized that context did not produce an inevitable outcome; it was "not the case," that slavery had destroyed the will of blacks. But "considering the circumstances," it made sense for blacks to ask whites "not only to cease to oppress us, but to give us that encouragement which our talents and industry may merit."[77]

Rock's historical accounting, like Nell's, taught profound lessons for the present moment. Remembering black revolutionaries attested to the

---

[75] Parker, *Present Aspect of Slavery*, 5, 7.   [76] *Liberator*, March 12, 1858.   [77] Ibid.

martial abilities of their descendants. Identifying slaves' endurance testified of African American will. And laying bare the unrelenting facts of slavery and prejudice contextualized the need for elevating and uplifting black Americans, a process that required economic assistance and educational opportunities. Like Nell, Rock indicated the need for black and white actors to bring about new circumstances.

After "a company of colored vocalists" sang "Freedom's Battle," a song provided by poet Frances E. Watkins, the cousin to William J. Watkins, Parker rose to address the audience. Answering Rock, he qualified his remarks about black timidity, explaining that he had spoken "of the past, not of the future." (Parker seems to have not read the copy of *Colored Patriots* Nell had gifted him.)[78] Despite Parker's persistent ignorance about martial activities of black historical actors, he shared an anecdote very different from the one that had incited Rock's response. Parker spoke of three fugitive slaves in Nebraska who had overpowered eight slave catchers and escaped to Canada. An embarrassed and somewhat repentant Parker stated, "No white skin ... could have been more valiant." But he viewed this case as unique. He hoped "the day [would] come when these exceptional instances of valor [would] be brought forward as proof that valor is likewise instantial to the African race." Parker did not share Rock's deep understanding of constraining circumstances on this point. He hoped the banner resting on the table before them, which John Hancock gave to the first black regiment of Massachusetts, would "prove not only a memento to the past, but a prophecy likewise for the future." Parker had at least some faith that the black man would "do his part" when the time came. While the least certain of black martial prowess among the speakers, he was perhaps the most involved in plans for black action. That very day he met with John Brown and members of the Secret Six.[79]

Following the Attucks Glee Club's performance of "Colored American Heroes of 1776," Phillips rose to the rostrum. He upheld the Boston Massacre as the Revolution's initiating event, stating that it "made the

---

[78] Parker's copies of *Services of Colored Americans* and *Colored Patriots* are housed in the special collections of the Boston Public Library.

[79] Reynolds, *John Brown*, 258. On Parker and other whites' racist views and on the interaction between Parker and Rock, see Teed, *A Revolutionary Conscience*, 204–11; and Kantrowitz, *More Than Freedom*, 239–43. On Parker's involvement with John Brown, see Dean Grodzins, "Why Theodore Parker Backed John Brown: The Political and Social Roots of Support for Abolitionist Violence," in *Terrible Swift Sword: The Legacy of John Brown*, ed. Peggy A. Russo and Paul Finkelman (Athens, GA, 2005), 3–22.

Revolution something beside talk." Phillips and his cocommemorators believed the prolonged constitutional debates had run their course; it was time for action. Thus, emulating the actions of revolutionaries, rather than interpreting the writings of the framers or discerning the intentions of the ratifiers, mattered most. Phillips indicated that the Revolution had been initiated by the people, proposing that revolution "always begins with the populace, never with the leaders." Observing that the black race "is on trial," he also took issue with Parker's characterizations and joined Rock in emphasizing circumstance and contingency.[80] History taught that all races had been slaves at different times and, Phillips argued, "the only race in history that ever took the sword into their hands, and cut their chains, is the black race of St. Domingo."[81] Slaves, free blacks, and abolitionists had appealed to the Haitian Revolution for decades.[82] Phillips also highlighted examples closer to home. Noting Nell's work, Phillips instructed blacks in attendance to "never forget the part [their] race took in" the American Revolution. The relationship between past and present actors was, in Phillips's view, reciprocal: remembering Attucks would inspire African Americans to "show ... valor in the field, valor in life." Phillips noted that Attucks deserved a monument, but he wanted more than an Attucks in stone – he wanted "another ATTUCKS" in flesh, and he believed he had found one.[83]

Lewis Hayden, an escaped slave and abolitionist, was Phillips's candidate. He not only helped rescue Shadrach Minkins but also played a prominent role in the attempted rescues of Thomas Sims and Anthony Burns. Transcendentalist Thomas Higginson, who had himself followed Hayden into the courthouse where Burns was being held, was the first to describe Hayden as "the modern Crispus Attucks," and Phillips agreed with the designation.

---

[80] On Phillips's racial egalitarianism, see James Brewer Stewart, "Comfortable in His Own Skin: Wendell Phillips and Racial Egalitarianism," in *Wendell Phillips*, 111–32.

[81] *Liberator*, March 12, 1858. In 1860, Phillips published a book on Toussaint Louverture and the Haitian Revolution. Black writers, including historian William Wells Brown, had spoken and written on the subject previously. Wendell Phillips, *The St. Domingo Insurrection: Toussaint L'Ouverture, the John Brown of St. Domingo* (New York, 1860); William Wells Brown, *St. Domingo: Its Revolutions and Its Patriots: A Lecture* (Boston, 1855). See Hall, *Faithful Account of the Race*, 105–22.

[82] See Sinha, *The Slave's Cause*, 177–78, 245–47, 281, 454–55; see also Davis, *Problem of Slavery in the Age of Emancipation*, 77–82.

[83] *Liberator*, March 12, 1858. This speech shows Phillips's move toward accepting violence as a means of emancipation. See Dean Grodzins, "Wendell Phillips, the Rule of Law, and Antislavery Violence," in *Wendell Phillips*, 89–110.

In concluding his address, Phillips quoted a letter that Higginson, the most eager of the Secret Six, had written in lieu of attending the event. As much as any of his contemporary reformers, Higginson articulated a martial heroism that demanded attacking slavery with force.[84] In his letter, he observed that some had the impression "that the same courage and daring [did] not exist among [blacks] in modern times," and he countered this assumption by recalling the role blacks had played in the above rescue attempts. In light of these instances of African American bravery, Higginson wrote, "We need not go back to the old revolutionary time for examples." In reference to the attempted Burns rescue, in particular, he asserted that it was a black man – not a white one – that was the first rescuer to set foot in the courthouse. There, Higginson had exchanged blows with policemen side by side with Hayden. Earning a bloody chin in the encounter, Higginson gained a new respect for his fellow abolitionist. In his report, Higginson boldly described Hayden as *the modern Crispus Attucks*" and wrote, "*When he stands there again, may there be more of us to follow him.*"[85] In using Attucks's name, Higginson – and Phillips – drew a parallel between the actions of past and present revolutionaries but focused attention on the new, the second, revolution.

Speaking next, Garrison reaffirmed his belief in moral suasion but then argued that if the revolutionaries were justified in their fight for independence, "those who are enslaved in our country to-day would be also justified." Like the other speakers, he believed the black man would "in due time strike for his liberty." (Later, he would come to view the Civil War as a justified battle for freedom.)[86] While on the subject of the Revolution, Garrison summarized and challenged Taney's argument "that when the Declaration ... was published to the world, no white man dreamed of regarding slavery with aversion." Using Nell's work, which held great "historical value," he cited resolutions from 1776 and 1777 to reveal the antislavery sentiment of the era. As many others had stated, Taney stood "convicted of grossly falsifying history." Garrison's appeal to founding-era antislavery sentiment was not meant to redeem the Constitution he had damned, but rather to rescue the abolitionists' favored document, the Declaration, from a proslavery context. Before concluding, Garrison invited his audience to pledge, "by all the sacred memories of the past," including the "blood of ATTUCKS," the "death of WARREN," and the "still higher and better examples of ancient apostles

---

[84] See Kytle, *Romantic Reformers*, 206–52.
[85] *Liberator*, March 12, 1858, emphasis in original. [86] See Mayer, *All on Fire*, 518–85.

and martyrs," that "we will not lay down our arms until liberty is proclaimed through all the land, to all the inhabitants."[87] In doing so, he quoted the same Levitical proclamation that graced Philadelphia's Liberty Bell.[88] The nonresistant Garrison continued to appeal to both the Bible and the Declaration, but now in a call that implied violent revolution.

African American abolitionist Charles Remond, the celebration's final speaker, displayed none of Parker's uncertainty or Garrison's ambivalence about black fighting. He believed black resistance already had sparked a new revolution. Remond narrated the Christiana incident of 1851, when the former slave William Parker led four fugitives in a violent struggle against Maryland slaveholder Edward Gorsuch, who had entered Pennsylvania to reclaim his slaves. Gorsuch was killed in the fight. Remond declared that Parker and his cocombatants had emulated Attucks in initiating a revolution, this time for black freedom. Echoing Rock's earlier remarks, he observed, "The patriotism of the colored man of '76 has been repaid by the most base ingratitude, on the part of the white people of this country.... Hence, the day has gone by for me to refer to those acts in any other sense than as showing the identity of the colored race with the human family."[89]

Remond's narrative suggested that white action had advanced slavery and racism, leaving the need for black actors to set aside the Revolution of 1776 and lead a new revolution. He insisted, "The Anti-Slavery cause ... will progress just as rapidly as the colored people shall will it." In tying historical progress to black agency, Remond contradicted popular accounts of historical progress, including Theodore Parker's vision, which placed the work of progress in white hands. Remond's and Parker's opposing accounts reflected the era's broader faith in progress and, by grounding progress in human action, also indicated that development was contingent. Progress came with struggle and, as Remond predicted, "The time is coming when this battle is to be fought."[90]

Each of the speakers at the Attucks commemoration responded to Taney's historical argument with a basic historical fact: blacks had fought during the Revolution. That fighting, some of the speakers argued, should have secured citizenship for them and their descendants. This was not articulated as a constitutional argument – if there was a sacred text to reclaim, it was the Declaration. The major site of interpretation was,

---

[87] *Liberator*, March 12, 1858, emphasis in original.   [88] Lev. 25:10.
[89] *Liberator*, March 12, 1858.   [90] Ibid.

instead, black historical actors and their brave deeds, which anticipated the actions of their descendants. The thrust of the commemorative orations revolved around new revolutionaries securing the Declaration's egalitarian principles. Even Nell, the historian, spoke of a past revolution in terms of the need for another.

Each of the speakers had different ideas about revolution and the role of African Americans as new revolutionaries, but those understandings trended toward Remond's view that blacks would figure prominently in the battle for emancipation and equal rights "in spite of slavery and negrophobia" and "in spite of the American Constitution."[91] By highlighting recent cases of black initiative, the speakers carried forward Nell's work of showing that African Americans possessed the needed skill and strength to lead in a new revolution. As Rock explained, slavery and prejudice had created new limiting contexts, but with the support of white friends, black assertiveness and action could and would change these circumstances. If past actions of whites had shaped the present, present actions of blacks would shape the future.

Nell's writings demonstrated not only that black revolutionaries had shown valor on the battlefield but also that African American lawyers, doctors, poets, and other professionals had achieved success despite the incursions of the slave institution and the spread of racism. In tracing the instantiation of white prejudice, his work indicated that historical actions had created constraining conditions for blacks. That effort helped historicize racism; it made it clear that racism, in its myriad forms, was the work of humans and as such humans could work to overcome it. Indeed, in reading the actions of black agents, Nell demonstrated that various kinds of historical actions – including but not limited to martial activity – challenged the constraining conditions that slavery and racial discrimination had created. His narrative implied that by removing limitations, new actions could create new contexts. More specifically, Nell showed that African Americans possessed the needed initiative, skill, and strength to lead out in the war for emancipation and equal rights. *Dred Scott* had dealt a blow to their cause, but Nell and others responded with an emboldened call for black actors to bring about revolutionary change. That was the focus of the Attucks celebration, in which commemorators shifted their attention from the revolutionaries of '76 to modern black revolutionaries.

[91] Ibid.

As with the biblical and constitutional debates, Nell's work as a historian drew attention to the relationship between past and present. Like Parker, Lincoln, and Douglass, he identified negative change since the founding era, specifically in the spread of racial prejudice via new legislation and policies. In this way, Nell's work indicated historical distance. However, he was not working to brush aside post-founding-era chaff so as to recover original antislavery grain. In demonstrating what black agents had sacrificed to both win and preserve American freedom, and in showing that their descendants had been rewarded with slavery and prejudice, Nell and other African American respondents to *Dred Scott* had no desire to restore the status quo of the revolutionary era. Instead, they aimed to initiate a new and more inclusive revolution.

Rather than appeal to original expectations to read the Constitution, the Attucks commemorators interpreted black actions to envision historical change. This position had less to do with historical distance, which was assumed in some sense, than with the contingent developments that made said distance apparent. Rather than use distance to provide progressive readings of sacred texts, these commemorators drew insight from historical contingency to map a progressive course of action. An appreciation for the nature of historical development and the role of human initiative in history inspired Nell and his black and white colleagues to forecast that new Attuckses would abolish slavery, overturn *Dred Scott*, and revolutionize social relations in the United States.

Conclusion

By the late 1850s, an assumption of historical distance and an awareness of historical change were integral to antebellum interpretive debates, whether these debates revolved around sacred texts or the actions of heroic black figures. These hermeneutics were bound up with each other. The most forceful reading of black agents came as a direct response to *Dred Scott*. Although America's explosive constitutional conflict seemed a world apart from the genteel biblical debates of earlier decades, these two interpretive developments engaged the same central conceptual riddle (what to do with history) and grappled with the same ethical dilemma (what to do with slavery). In the process, the interpretive debates over slavery deepened America's confrontation with history.

Slavery drew interpreters' attention to historical awareness, but not always in clear or consistent ways. In the first decade of the nineteenth century, a number of America's biblical scholars departed from the traditional reading of the Bible as an always contemporary text and instead interpreted it as an unavoidably historical text. However, when they confronted the incendiary issue of slavery, many of these scholars reverted to a traditional interpretation; they ignored the distance their readings revealed and insisted on the relevance of Paul's directive to return the fugitive to his master.

In succeeding decades, the proclivity to collapse time persisted in biblical and constitutional interpretation even as the debate over slavery promoted readings of these texts that spread a sense of historical distance. While some set distance aside, a number of abolitionists pointed to it to damn once sacred texts as obsolete. In either accentuating or dismissing the texts' relevance to American slavery, a wide array of writers and speakers began to take note of the ways in which human experience was temporally divided up: some adopted the position that historical awareness was essential to correct interpretation, and some doggedly insisted it was not, but whether they rejected or embraced it, all had to deal with a realization that the past was more distant than it had seemed. In using historical arguments either to preserve the sacred texts and sanction slavery or to abolish both the texts and the institution, interpreters highlighted the temporal gap separating nineteenth-century Americans from their most favored pasts. In short, the debate over slavery gave rise to an awareness of temporal distance from periods with seemingly timeless appeal.

In between approaches that aimed to either preserve or abolish both slavery and the sacred texts, a middle path emerged that preserved the texts and attacked slavery. In the 1830s, religious thinkers such as William Channing and Francis Wayland conceded slavery's legal presence in the biblical past, but they posited that the apostles had prudently sowed the seeds of slavery's destruction. In the 1840s, legal thinkers such as William Goodell and Lysander Spooner similarly averred that the founding fathers had crafted the Constitution with the expectation of slavery's institutional demise. In the 1850s, even Theodore Parker and Frederick Douglass, who granted slavery's presence at the founding and proved willing to cast aside the Constitution if necessary, maintained that the Constitution could and should be adapted to meet the framers' antislavery expectations. Abraham Lincoln also argued that the framers had recognized they were crafting a historically situated text, thus implicitly authorizing attentive nineteenth-century Americans to think historically when interpreting the Constitution. While others ignored historical distance or set it aside, these figures used that distance to position the Constitution against slavery. In a culture that obsessively looked to the founding era for its cues, they believed the founding fathers had anticipated significant historical change and had expected that change to influence future readings of their work.

This development was far from straightforward. In some respects, the slavery debates augmented a preexisting longing for the past. Lamenting the spread of abolitionism or condemning the rise of the Slave Power could function to further idealize the biblical and founding eras as favored pasts that offered timeless (proslavery or antislavery) truths. In positing that the biblical and revolutionary eras contained original meanings that negative historical developments had obscured, some writers argued that historical distance could and should be overcome. These contextual interpretations and historical narratives cultivated but also restricted a sense of historical distance. Even when writers characterized progress as the fruits of the Revolution, their narratives sacralized the founding era and blunted a sense of real change. This golden age sensibility tended to conflate distinct historical eras and ignore change in ways characteristic of traditional hermeneutics. In other words, the fractured nature of these increasingly political debates ensured that earlier modes of thought persisted at the very time that more modern understandings began to emerge. While the slavery debates encouraged interpretive approaches that revealed historical distance, they also induced attempts to collapse time and recover the favored biblical and founding eras.

And yet, many interpreters sought only to rescue specific biblical and founding-era ideas. The Transcendentalist disentanglement of religious truth from biblical text provided an intellectual framework for this sifting process. When historical insight undermined efforts to describe the Abrahamic, Mosaic, and Christian dispensations as epochs of freedom, Channing, Wayland, and other readers restricted their focus to the antislavery principles of Christ and his apostles. Some, including Parker, laid stress on certain biblical words and phrases, such as Christ's injunction to treat others as one would want to be treated. Similarly, rather than describe the founding era as timeless, many antislavery interpreters upheld specific people, documents, or phrases from the period as exceptional. Constitutional readers such as Lincoln narrowed their gaze from the sentiment of the Western audience and the American ratifiers to the expectations of the founders and framers. Some, including Goodell and Spooner, appealed to the words of the Constitution alone, while others, such as Garrison, used an even smaller lens to claim a single phrase from a brief declaration of rights: "all men are created equal." Clear words held more straightforward significations than the intricate creations of complicated historical people.

In a period when slavery had cultivated even greater interest in already favored pasts, it became impossible to lay claim to a word or phrase without debating the context from which that word and phrase emerged. And as historical explication showed the favored pasts to be less appealing, narrow historical claims implied a broad dismissal of the biblical and founding eras. The struggle to rescue portions of the Bible and the Constitution drew greater attention to historical distance than efforts to either fully claim these texts and their pasts or render them entirely obsolete. The sifting process of recovering universal ideas from the sands of time singularly demonstrated that the biblical and founding eras were foreign countries. Once interpreters separated out timeless gems from the historical chaff, these historical periods remained favored, and their correspondent texts sacred, only in a newly restricted sense.

Unlike their early modern forebears, slavery's critics did not want to renew biblical times nor return to the founding era – periods that sanctioned slavery – but instead desired to fulfill the promises and expectations of those eras. While lamenting slavery's continued existence (which could nullify the distance between past and present), antislavery narrators also insisted that the proper circumstances had arrived to realize the progressive hopes and promises of past periods (which indicated that qualitative differences did, in fact, divide past from present). While antislavery sentiment had been exceptional and proslavery sentiment commonplace in the revolutionary past, they claimed that proslavery sentiment was anachronistic and that antislavery sentiment was characteristic in the nineteenth-century present. In short, the sin of slavery had become a distinctive marker of modernity, setting off the present from all past eras.

All of this had profound implications for biblical and constitutional interpretive debates; never before had historical change carried with it the insight and the imperative that Americans must read sacred texts in view of historical distance. In the case of the Bible, this understanding paved the way for alternatives to the literalist hermeneutic that had dominated biblical interpretation in the United States. This development was even more determinative in constitutional interpretation, in which a sense of distance supported the influential reading that the framers had molded the Constitution to adapt to change. This approach secured the Constitution's continued usefulness in a nation where contingent changes had unsettled notions of the nation's inevitable progress.

While antebellum thinkers acknowledged historical distance and change in inconsistent, imprecise, and idiosyncratic ways, their interpretive debates over slavery made these historical realities difficult to ignore. And as these debates historicized the Bible and the Constitution (texts with the greatest purchase on temporal transcendence in antebellum America) and their pasts (epochs with seemingly timeless appeal for antebellum Americans), it carried a far-reaching implication: if *these* texts and pasts could be historicized, *everything* could be historicized. No past or text, then, no matter how sacred, useful, or familiar, stood above and outside of time.

In November 1859, Theodore Parker was still optimistic about American progress toward abolition. Having fallen ill with tuberculosis, he traveled to Europe in hopes the trip would restore his health. While abroad, he heard news of John Brown's failed raid at Harpers Ferry, including false reports that Francis Jackson Meriam had died. Writing from Rome to Meriam's mother, Eliza, Parker praised her son for his role in "one of the *noblest and most heroic enterprizes of this Age*. – or of any Age." The age of the American Revolution was no exception. Citing Eliza's revolutionary ancestry, Parker wrote that her "son has *fallen a martyr in a cause not less holy and much more philanthropic*." Parker also compared Francis Jackson Meriam to Christ in noting that he bore "a Crown of thorns ... but also a Crown of glory."[1] Parker saw Meriam and Brown as new Christs.[2] Most damned Brown as a fanatic, but Thomas Wentworth Higginson, Theodore Parker, Henry David Thoreau, Ralph Waldo Emerson, and others aligned him with Christianity's founder and exalted him above revolutionary figures such as George Washington.[3] These comparisons carried hope in hard-won progress; Parker predicted that figures like Brown, whom he referred to as the exceptional "spectacle" of the age, would become the rule.[4] "This is only the beginning," Parker wrote Eliza. "Nine experiments will seem to fail: the tenth with succeed."[5] In light of contingent antislavery setbacks, Parker and others still kept faith in the prospect that human actions could bring about new conditions.

A few days later, Parker repeated his prediction in a widely disseminated letter to Eliza's father, Francis Jackson, a fellow Boston abolitionist and Vigilance Committee member. Parker asserted that slaves had a natural right to kill their oppressors and freemen had a natural duty to assist them. Predicting that other insurrections would follow Brown's, he believed "negroes will take their defence into their own hands." Parker retained racist prejudice in observing "*a limit even to the negro's forbearance*," but he insisted that an American "San Domingo is not a great way off."[6] After all, "America offers more than any other country to excite the slave to love of Liberty." He anticipated that "one day, it will be thought not less heroic of a negro to fight for his personal liberty, than for a white man to fight for political independence."[7] Parker retained his racialist

---

[1] Theodore Parker to Eliza F. Eddy, November 19, 1859, Theodore Parker Papers, MHS, emphasis in original.
[2] See, for example, Theodore Parker, Journal, December 2, 1859, *Life and Correspondence*, 2:388.
[3] See Reynolds, *John Brown*, 343–47, 368–69, and 406–15.
[4] Theodore Parker to Joseph Lyman, January 13, 1860, Theodore Parker Papers, MHS.
[5] Parker to Eddy, November 19, 1859.
[6] Theodore Parker to Francis Jackson, November 24, 1859, in *Life and Correspondence*, 2:174, emphasis in original.
[7] Ibid., 2:175.

views, but he had moved closer to other abolitionists in envisioning that blacks would play a more central role in securing abolition.

Parker came to expect a civil war for freedom, waged by both black and white actors. In a December 1859 letter to Edward Desor, Parker expressed his expectation that whites and blacks would join together in "a civil war," which "seem[ed] at no great distance," and acknowledged that a victory would demand the support of certain individuals rather than a certain race of men.[8] In another December letter, Parker noted that the imminent war would require leaders like Brown, "men with *fists*," instead of "miserable scholars ... lawyers, ministers, doctors."[9] The blood of both black and white soldiers, not the studied interpretations of legal and religious minds, would bring abolition. Parker wrote to Desor, "All national constitutions are writ on the parchment of a drum-head, and published with the roar of cannon!"[10]

A few months before, in September, Parker wrote a letter from Switzerland, which the *Liberator* republished in late October, days after Brown's raid. In the letter, Parker noted that "better times are coming ... *good men* and *women* are *making* better times – and even bad men help the work ... Thus the Fugitive Slave Bill turns out an Anti-Slavery measure, moving the North as nothing before had done; so does the Kansas-Nebraska Bill; so the Dred Scott Decision."[11] Parker would soon add Harpers Ferry to the list. His views were still teleological and providential, but it was precisely his belief in the ultimate progress of freedom that inspired his attention to divergences, setbacks, and reversals. His firm conviction in a clear *telos* nurtured his openness to human-driven historical contingencies, which marked both proslavery and antislavery failures and successes.

Before the Civil War further complicated Americans' expectations about the nation's direction, the slavery debates challenged beliefs in history's inevitable forward movement. As Parker repurposed the nation's sins and setbacks to fit within his vision of a drive toward universal freedom, he did so with a chastened faith. He wrote from Switzerland, "It is curious that progress is never in a straight line, for any length of time; there are windings and windings, and curvings backward, but still the

---

[8] Theodore Parker to Edward Desor, December 1859, in *Life and Correspondence*, 2:388.
[9] Theodore Parker to John Flint, December 31, 1859, in *Life and Correspondence*, 2:399, emphasis in original.
[10] Parker to Desor, December 1859, 2:389.
[11] *Liberator*, October 21, 1859, emphasis in original.

general course is *on* and *up*."[12] Progress, Parker had learned, came with contingencies, including violence and death. He died on May 10, 1860, in Florence, Italy. It was up to his contemporaries, both black and white, to make better times.

Frederick Douglass was one of those contemporaries, in part because he understood the tortured path of progress better than most. In an August 1859 editorial, he provided his own clear-eyed statement on changes related to slavery: "The friends of Emancipation in the United States have often cheered their spirits by dwelling upon the evidence of the progress of anti-slavery sentiments in the country.... Their objects, aims, and ends may be postponed, but never entirely defeated; and however unpromising the visible prospect, however dark the cloud, they see the complacent image of divinity, leading them on to ultimate victory."[13] While Douglass still tended toward a stubborn belief that abolitionists would triumph in the end, his was a hard-won hope in progress that persevered in the darkest of times.

Douglass found abundant evidence of slavery's continued advances in the speech Alexander H. Stephens gave the prior month. In his address, the retiring proslavery congressman tracked national and southern progress and tied future national success to accepting the "present constitution" as correctly interpreted in *Dred Scott*.[14] While figures such as Douglass tied moral progress to antislavery sentiment, Stephens made the opposite assertion. He tied moral progress to proslavery sentiment: "There are [now] more thinking men at the North ... who look on our system of slavery as right, socially, morally, and politically, than there were even at the South, thirty years ago. The leading public men of the South [including Jefferson and Madison] were almost all against" slavery.[15] Stephens made it clear that he did not want to recover the founding era, a period in which many southerners anticipated slavery's eventual demise. Though for very different reasons, neither northern abolitionists nor proslavery southerners wanted to return to the favored American past, an era that the slavery debates had made distant.

A sense of distance had emerged through a deeper understanding of the past, but also through a realization of what had changed since the founding era. Douglass found Stephens to be "more honest than the Dred

---

[12] Ibid, emphasis in original.
[13] "Progress of Slavery," *Douglass' Monthly* 2 (August 1859): 114.
[14] "Farewell Speech of Hon. A. H. Stephens," in *Alexander H. Stephens, in Public and Private*, ed. Henry Cleveland (Philadelphia, 1866), 645.
[15] Ibid., 648.

Scott decision... and truer to history than our Garrisonian Abolitionists," even while in doing so Stephens had torn off the mask to reveal "the cool and thoughtful conclusions of the leading minds of the slaveholding States." Douglass, like Lincoln, believed the development of proslavery thought made it indisputable that "slavery had made great progress, and has riveted itself more firmly in the Southern mind and heart, since the founding of the American Government. The whole moral atmosphere of the South has undergone a decided change for the worse." Even though the southern founders had "regarded [slavery] as a transient system," southerners "now ... regard it as permanent. Once they held it to be local; now, national. Once they defended it on grounds of expediency; now, on grounds of absolute right."[16] Had the world turned upside down? Had the transient become the permanent?

Although slavery's progress was real enough, it became a kind of mirage when viewed through the lenses of Douglass's populism and providentialism. He wrote, "Let but the right of speech be once established in the slave States ... and we shall see where slavery will stand in the judgment of the Southern people."[17] Douglass had faith in the judgment of the people – even some southerners – and the judgment of God, a combinatory force that made the sin of slavery clear despite the observations of Stephens and his ilk. Douglass's religious understanding and his belief in human action – especially in blacks and white northerners – supported the idea that if the transient had become permanent, it could and would become transient once more. Douglass worked toward emancipation with the weapon of his pen even as he awaited others to attack with bullet and sword.

Douglass received news of Brown's raid while in Philadelphia, and with the news came the threat of being arrested as an alleged conspirator. He soon made his way to Canada, where he penned an editorial defending Brown for having "imitated the heroes of Lexington, Concord, and Bunker Hill." Like Parker, Douglass aligned the actions of the raiders with those of the revolutionaries. He referenced Brown's belief in the Declaration and the Bible, sacred texts that had inspired Brown to perform "heroic deeds." Although Douglass deemed his own era as "too gross ... to appreciate" Brown's actions, he prophesied that "the future will write his epitaph upon the hearts of a people freed from slavery, because he struck the first effectual blow." According to Douglass, Brown was a being for the ages who had "initiated a new mode of carrying

[16] "Progress of Slavery," 114.   [17] Ibid.

on the crusade of freedom." More clearly than ever before, the formerly enslaved Douglass understood that the "system of brute force" had to "be met with its own weapons."[18]

While Douglass grew more certain of the need for slavery's violent end, he continued to see value in political and constitutional means. In November, he set sail for Liverpool to wait out the aftermath of Harper's Ferry. While in the British Isles, Douglass continued to promote the cause of political and constitutional abolition, an effort which involved answering Garrisonian critics. British Garrisonian George Thompson, for example, had attacked Douglass's interpretation of the Constitution in a speech Thompson gave in Glasgow in February 1860. About a month later, Douglass responded with a speech in which he once again advanced the antislavery ideas he had learned from Smith, Spooner, and Goodell.

In his response, Douglass instructed his British audience that the American Constitution needed to be interpreted based on its words alone, not in light of the framers' intentions. Knowing that constitutional interpretation had, in fact, come to revolve around historical questions, Douglass insisted that "it is not whether slavery existed ... at the time of the adoption of the Constitution; it is not whether slaveholders took part in framing the Constitution; it is not whether those slaveholders, in their hearts, intended to secure certain advantages in that instrument for slavery."[19] And yet, even though Douglass insisted that historical context should not dictate interpretation, he still used historical information to support his strict reading of constitutional clauses. He could not help but again note that the founding generation "regarded slavery as an expiring and doomed system."[20] Founding-era expectations still mattered to him, and he rescued those expectations even as he bid farewell to the framers, who "are already gone from us. They were for a generation," he stated, "but the Constitution is for the ages."[21] And in his age, Douglass argued, the Constitution could be read as an antislavery document.

Toward the conclusion of his speech, Douglass expressed his hope that the American people would turn the Constitution into an abolition text. He explained, "If there is once a will in the people of America to abolish slavery, there is no word, no syllable in the Constitution to forbid the

---

[18] "Capt. John Brown Not Insane," *Douglass' Monthly* 2 (November 1859): 161.
[19] Frederick Douglass, "The Constitution of the United States: Is It Pro-Slavery or Antislavery?" in *Frederick Douglass: Selected Speeches and Writings*, ed. Philip S. Foner, abridged and adapted by Yuval Taylor (Chicago, 1999), 380.
[20] Ibid., 384.   [21] Ibid., 382.

result."[22] The deceased framers had bequeathed to their political descendants a text that could be turned to new purposes. Douglass continued, "If the South has made the Constitution bend to the purposes of slavery, let the North now make that instrument bend to the cause of freedom and justice."[23] Douglass believed that "the freeman of the North" had "power in their own hands" and could "make the American Government just what they think fit."[24]

Douglass's belief in the power of the American people was tied to his hope in the Republican Party, but that hope was balanced with skepticism. When Douglass returned to the United States in April, he cautiously supported Lincoln before and after his election as president. And although Douglass welcomed southern secession and the onset of war, which he framed as a holy war for emancipation, the uncertainty that had hampered him in the 1850s continued to check his faith in historical movement toward a glorious denouement. News of Union victories and defeats, along with Lincoln's halting approach to emancipation and black enlistment and his persistent support of colonization, generated feelings of optimism, doubt, and anger.[25] If Douglass's heightened emotional state reflected the wartime environment, it also bespoke a new investment in the nation. In his 1862 Fourth of July speech – delivered soon after Lincoln had signed into law the congressional prohibition of slavery in all current and future territories – Douglass spoke of the founding fathers and the founding era in new terms: as *ours* rather than *yours*. He could more fully claim the Fourth in light of new conditions that seemed to make it possible, more than ever before, for him and his contemporaries to fulfill original promises.[26]

When Lincoln's promised Emancipation Proclamation came on New Year's Day in 1863, it dictated that "all persons held as slaves within said designated States, and parts of States, are, and henceforward shall be free." Furthermore, the president said nothing of colonization and provided for the enlistment of black soldiers.[27] For these reasons, the Proclamation banished much of Douglass's remaining doubt about the fulfillment of founding-era promises. Although Douglass and Lincoln did not agree on many important issues, including equal pay for black

---

[22] Ibid., 388.   [23] Ibid., 389.   [24] Ibid., 390.
[25] On Douglass's tortured faith in progress during these years, see Blight, *Frederick Douglass*, 310–84.
[26] See ibid., 368.
[27] Abraham Lincoln, "Emancipation Proclamation," in *CWAL*, 6:29–30.

soldiers, Lincoln was moving in Douglass's direction in significant ways.[28] As Douglass's biographer put it, "by the end of that terrible year of 1863, Lincoln and Douglass virtually spoke from the same script."[29] And much of that script was a Constitution amended by time.

On November 19, 1863, on a battlefield that bore the blood of around fifty thousand men, Abraham Lincoln made the Constitution a more inclusive text. At Gettysburg, writes Garry Wills, Lincoln "altered the document from within, by appeal from its letter to the spirit, subtly changing the recalcitrant stuff of that legal compromise, bringing it to its own indictment." Wills explained, "By implicitly doing this, he performed one of the most daring acts of open-air sleight-of-hand ever witnessed by the unsuspecting."[30] In this moment, Lincoln remade the Constitution into an egalitarian creed. The constitutional reading that Lincoln voiced to his audience at Gettysburg approached the interpretation that Parker had advanced in the last years of his life.[31] Like Parker, Lincoln read the Constitution, a text marked by time, in light of the timeless promises contained in the Declaration. And now Lincoln joined figures such as Douglass in the belief that a new context demanded that Americans work to realize those promises.

Lincoln's speech, however, was less the work of a master magician performing a new trick than that of an earnest artisan perfecting his trade. In under three hundred words, he encapsulated the constitutional reading he had promoted since 1854. Given his high office, the state of the nation, and the occasion, Lincoln simplified the narrative. His opening phrase captured the antislavery insistence that Americans must read the Constitution in light of the Declaration's egalitarian promises: "Four score and seven years ago our fathers brought forth on this continent, a new nation, conceived in Liberty, and dedicated to the proposition that all men are created equal."[32] Lincoln's trick was eliding the fact that the

---

[28] On Lincoln's embrace of certain antislavery principles in these years, see Eric Foner, *The Fiery Trial: Abraham Lincoln and American Slavery* (New York, 2010). See also Neely, *Lincoln and the Triumph*, 121–25.

[29] Blight, *Frederick Douglass*, 415.

[30] Garry Wills, *Lincoln at Gettysburg: The Words That Remade America* (New York, 1992), 38. George P. Fletcher similarly posits that Lincoln's Gettysburg Address served as a preamble to the nation's more egalitarian "second constitution." George P. Fletcher, *Our Secret Constitution: How Lincoln Redefined American Democracy* (New York, 2001), 2.

[31] See Wills, *Lincoln at Gettysburg*, 90–120.

[32] Abraham Lincoln, "Address Delivered at the Dedication of the Cemetery at Gettysburg," in *CWAL*, 7:23.

nation had been conceived in sin. He believed the founders had set the stage for someone such as himself to perform the trick among their descendants. Slavery's spread had made this deceit impossible in the 1850s, but the war had created new conditions and new opportunities. Months after the Emancipation Proclamation began the effort to eradicate slavery from the American present, Lincoln omitted slavery from the American past. At Gettysburg, he seemed to make the original proslavery compact disappear and reappear as an antislavery Constitution.

Putting the cancerous Constitution under the knife made it easier for Lincoln to tie together past and present. In observing that "now we are engaged in a great civil war, testing whether that nation, or any nation so conceived and so dedicated, can long endure," Lincoln implied that the war's outcome was uncertain, an idea the prolonged conflict forced many more Americans to consider.[33] Deaths and setbacks upset both northern and southern expectations about the war, but they also called into question the founding generation's experiment. Lincoln could not predict the nation's future, but he could attempt to make meaning of the current chaos; he could give the actions of the dead and the lives of the bereaved significance by placing them within a founding-era frame.

Lincoln's rhetoric tied the founders' cause to the work of those who had fought and died at Gettysburg: "It is for us the living, rather, to be dedicated here to the unfinished work which they who fought here have thus far so nobly advanced." Though he was referring to the soldiers of the current war, Lincoln might as well have been speaking of America's departed founders and their initial efforts to form a government. His reference to the "honored dead" had a double meaning: "It is rather for us to be here dedicated to the great task remaining before us – that from these honored dead we take increased devotion to that cause for which they gave the last full measure of devotion – that we here highly resolve that these dead shall not have died in vain – that this nation, under God, shall have a new birth of freedom."[34] Rhetorically, Lincoln tied the actions of men who had bled and died just months before to the words of the long-since-departed founding generation, those who Douglass had said were "already gone from us."

Lincoln was not trying to recover a moment in time or make a passing reference to "an interesting memorial of the dead past."[35] Rather, he was issuing an emphatic plea to use the nation's unexpected circumstances to bring about the ideals the founders had written down but could never

[33] Ibid.   [34] Ibid.   [35] Lincoln, "Speech at Springfield, Illinois, June 26, 1857," 2:407.

realize – a commission to effectuate "a new birth of freedom." Lincoln's famous last phrase – "government of the people, by the people, for the people" – carried an inclusive tone and a trust in the people's will.[36] When Lincoln's address is viewed in this light, it does not appear that he was swindling his audience; he did not covertly replace their old constitution with a new one. Instead, he connected the framers' emancipatory expectations with the soldiers' deaths at Gettysburg and the American people's will. In a context the framers had not anticipated, he legitimated a constitutional reading that would realize the abolitionist desires he ascribed to their descendants.

The new perspectives granted by historical distance and the new circumstances brought about by historical changes set the scene for Lincoln's efforts to finally lay American slavery to rest alongside the American dead. Although he believed the framers had anticipated that a different set of circumstances would result in slavery's abolition, the fact that they had expected abolition at all gave him the founding-era support he needed to pursue a course of emancipation. During the final months of the war, Lincoln urged Congress to pass a formal amendment to buttress his informal emendations, and to make permanent what was described as a transient war measure. In light of the belief that the framers had been prudent in protecting slavery where it already existed, Lincoln now felt justified in using an expedient proclamation to begin the process of abolishing slavery wherever it existed. In the light of historical distance and in the face of unexpected historical circumstances, Lincoln insisted on both informal and formal constitutional changes. Turning backward to the founding past provided him with vision to lead the nation forward into the future.

As Lincoln's appeal to the founding era indicates, historical awareness did not preclude but instead encouraged the continued use of favored pasts and sacred texts. In other words, the individuals who were most intent on using change and distance to maintain or revise religious,

---

[36] Lincoln, "Address Delivered at the Dedication of the Cemetery at Gettysburg," 7:23. Lincoln's words echoed Parker's 1850 speech in which he discussed "the American idea" as demanding "a democracy, that is, a government of all the people, by all the people, for all the people." Theodore Parker, "A Speech at the New England Anti-Slavery Society Convention in Boston," in *Speeches*, 3:41. Some argue that Lincoln drew on Webster for this point, while others contend that both Webster and Parker inspired Lincoln. See A. E. Elmore, *Lincoln's Gettysburg Address: Echoes of the Bible and Book of Common Prayer* (Carbondale, IL, 2009), 122–26. On Lincoln's move toward a more democratic ethos, see Neely, *Lincoln and the Triumph*, 46–64.

political, sectional, and national identities still looked to the past. And although many of them worked to expand the circle of freedom, they aimed to redraw the lines carefully. For example, a significant number of white antislavery proponents, including Lincoln, did not believe blacks merited the full benefits of citizenship. While such individuals and groups used a new historical understanding to pursue emancipation, old white prejudices constrained their view of black experiences in the past and, consequently, limited their vision of black freedom in the present.

Lincoln's suggestion that slavery's abolition could erase its presence from the American past disregarded the lived experiences of millions of enslaved blacks, just as Parker's erstwhile belief that whites alone could do the real work of abolition ignored a deep history of black resistance and military action. Lincoln's reference to the "honored dead" at Gettysburg recalled white founders but not black revolutionaries. This kind of historical neglect constrained black progress before and after the Civil War. Even antislavery proponents such as Lincoln and Parker were infected with this blindness, which meant that most white Americans could not begin to imagine the kind of work needed in the postemancipation era. This kind of oversight still plagues us as Americans.

Remedies to this historical blindness come in the form of new historical narratives as well as present actions. Nell's historical research reminded whites of black suffering and actions in the past, which carried at least two messages: first, white prejudices haunted America; and second, black contemporaries stood ready to do their part to exorcise racism. When the interpretive battles surrounding the Bible and the Constitution failed to resolve the slavery crisis and civil war broke out, this hermeneutic of black actors inspired African American service.

Nell's historical research may have indirectly helped change the president's mind about the enlistment of black men. *Colored Patriots* had inspired Boston bibliophile George Livermore to research and write about the role of black soldiers in the Revolution. Livermore finished his book – *An Historical Research Respecting the Opinions of the Founders of the Republic on Negroes as Slaves, Citizens, and as Soldiers* – in August of 1862. Later that month, Charles Sumner gave Lincoln a copy, which appears to have informed Lincoln's thinking on the matter, including his provision for black enlistment in the Emancipation Proclamation.[37] Once again, founding-era precedent pointed the way forward.

---

[37] See Henry Louis Gates, Jr., ed., *Lincoln on Race & Slavery* (Princeton, NJ, 2009), xxxix–xl.

Conclusion 343

Blacks who chose to enlist in the Union Army confirmed the message of Nell's work: black bravery in the fight for freedom. Although many white northerners remained skeptical of black service, others believed the regiments would "inaugurate a wonderful change in regard to the much despised black race."[38] Black soldiers continued to face inequalities, just as they had in the Revolution, but once again, they proved their military prowess and evidenced their rightful claim to citizenship and its attendant privileges.[39] George Hepworth, a first lieutenant in a black regiment, concluded that "the negroes are far more fit to be free than many people who enjoy that inestimable privilege."[40] Even before the Thirteenth and Fourteenth Amendments officially superseded *Dred Scott*, black soldiers had undone Taney's ruling. As the *Liberator* put it, "the necessities of the country had reversed the Dred Scott decision."[41] The martial culture of the conflict undermined notions of white superiority and black inferiority, and even as the war raged African American writers signaled black heroism.[42] These developments seemed to indicate that times had changed and that the American republic was finally changing with them.

And yet, the war and its aftermath confirmed what Nell and other abolitionists already had learned: progress was uncertain, contingent, and dependent on human action. Black military service was not all that was needed to win and secure social progress. After the war, narratives of white reconciliation overwhelmed accounts of black merit, draining the new amendments of their power.[43] Some commentators heralded the end of slavery, but blacks remained saddled with the wages of white prejudice.[44] In the century's final decades, African American historians continued to challenge prejudice by publishing narratives of black suffering and heroism.[45] During the same period, black writers troubled the era's assumptions of linear progress by pointing

---

[38] Ezra Palmer Dunnels, Journal, February 17, 1863, BA.
[39] Kantrowitz, *More Than Freedom*, 282–305.
[40] George H. Hepworth, *The Whip, Hoe, and Sword; or, the Gulf-Department in '63* (Boston, 1864), 140.
[41] *Liberator*, February 20, 1863.
[42] Lisa A. Long, *Rehabilitating Bodies: Health, History, and the American Civil War* (Philadelphia, 2004), 113–45.
[43] David W. Blight, *Race and Reunion: The Civil War in American Memory* (Cambridge, MA, 2001).
[44] See Kantrowitz, *More Than Freedom*, 309–424.
[45] Long, *Rehabilitating Bodies*, 210–37.

to the continuities between preemancipation and postemancipation realities. These connections had important implications for historical awareness.[46] New conditions had produced familiar limitations and the need to again search the past for a way forward.

---

[46] Gregory Laski, *Untimely Democracy: The Politics of Progress after Slavery* (New York, 2018).

Epilogue

At the start of the Civil War, many Americans expected a quick and decisive conflict, but years of battle soon taught them that historical movement was not so easily charted. This was a lesson already learned by Frederick Douglass, Theodore Parker, and many others who had engaged in interpretive debates over slavery. Those debates had spread a sense historical distance, change, and contingency. In turn, these and other readers incorporated that sense into their readings of the Bible and the Constitution, and though the heat of the debates threatened to consume these texts, they survived as sacred, albeit sacred in a new way.

Many of the individuals who engaged in the debates had concluded that the nation's sacred texts were written to be adapted to new circumstances. In an article published a few months before the start of the war, Henry Whitney Bellows, the longtime editor of New York's *Christian Inquirer*, explained that "it would be an egregious mistake to expect of this general instrument [the Constitution] … a provision for every individual case, a remedy for every civil wrong or injustice, or an embodiment of all the various legal and equitable wisdom which had accumulated throughout past ages."[1] Instead, the Constitution offered general, adaptable guidelines for different circumstances. Over a decade earlier, as the debate over slavery in the territories had started to rage, Bellows authored an editorial in which he seemed willing to dispatch the Constitution. However, instead he used a sense of historical distance and progress to urge his contemporaries to end slavery through a constitutional amendment.[2] Thirteen years later, on the cusp of the Civil War, he again used historical distance to

---

[1] *Christian Inquirer*, January 26, 1861. [2] See pages 184–85 herein.

argue that the Constitution was a document that could be informally molded to match the needs of the times.

Bellows applied the same reasoning to the Bible, which was the focus of his 1861 editorial. Arguing that "the Bible is our Spiritual Constitution," the Unitarian editor encouraged his readers to uncover the Bible's "general principles" rather than seeking "a provision for every case." Since the scriptures left "the settlement of special cases, and the condemnation of the many ingenious methods of sin, to an enlightened conscious," the words of the prophets did not include specific provisions against slavery and polygamy, which had been practiced by even "the patriarchs." (In his 1848 editorial, Bellows had cited the patriarchs' polygamous practices to undercut proslavery arguments from precedent.) The fact that some in the nineteenth century justified the presence of anachronistic practices "by the examples of two thousand or four thousand years ago among a half barbaric people" made it all the more important to draw attention to the "very plain and obvious principles" that the sacred writers had established. Such principles made clear – at least to an "enlightened conscience" – the sinfulness of such practices. If the prophets had specified only the sins of their age instead of laying down "general principles," "a new age would certainly have revealed new depravities," causing the Bible to lose its relevance.[3] Many antislavery writers, influenced by the debates over slavery, used a sense of historical distance and moral progress to advance constitutional and biblical readings attentive to change. These texts remained timeless, and sacred, precisely because of their capacity to adapt to new conditions, including those of mid-nineteenth-century America.

In April 1861, the month and year that initiated the Civil War, a writer for the *North American Review* also addressed the adaptability of a sacred text. Reminding readers that the framers had crafted the Constitution in the midst of political turmoil, the reviewer noted, "To this aim we owe the survivance of our Constitution to the present time, and its adaptation to the needs of a free people for an indefinite future. Its framers, planning primarily to meet the then existing exigency, would not build a ship of state, which would surely have foundered in the next gale. They constructed a raft, which should bend and yield ... and by its loose couplings and elastic movement divide and dissipate the force of any sudden shock." Somewhat like Bellows's observations about the sacred writers' words, this reviewer granted that although the framers had not made provisions

---

[3] *Christian Inquirer*, January 26, 1861.

for every possible contingency that time might introduce, their Constitution "was the very structure suited to defy time."⁴ While offering this appraisal, the writer worried that the current war, if not harnessed by caution, might prove too much even for the Constitution.

Rather than encourage readers to use the Constitution to bring about slavery's end, the reviewer urged them to allow the spirit of Christianity to gradually ameliorate the institution's harshness. Christian sentiment, in this writer's estimation, had already mitigated many of southern slavery's ills. And while stating that "the ultimate emancipation of the enslaved is the only end which Christian philanthropy can hold in view," the writer noted that "formal emancipation, so far from being the initial step, will probably be the last."⁵ Citing the oft-used New Testament example of the enslaved Onesimus, whom Paul somehow made a "beloved brother" while "leaving the external relation unchanged," the writer suggested that the gospel would slowly and gradually bring freedom to blacks.⁶ Much like Daniel Webster and Moses Stuart in 1850, the reviewer tied the New Testament past to the present, argued that abolitionists had failed to move the needle of emancipation, and insisted that "our Union, so far as it can be preserved, or if it can be restored, is of incalculable value in its bearing on the future of slavery." While taking a very different pulse of the people than Parker or Douglass had, the writer similarly held that legal "enactments that express the preponderant sentiment of the nation will of necessity be engrossed on the statute-book."⁷

Such an enactment was in the offing, though the writer could not have known it at the time. The reviewer suggested that it was precisely because the Constitution had proven so adaptable that Americans must be careful in assuming that it could bend to meet every crisis or that it could be used to quickly bring about slavery's end. However, while this author and many of his contemporaries, including Lincoln, did not see it in 1861, the Constitution would defy time by bending during the shock of a civil conflict to bring about slavery's end. This development depended, in part at least, on a sense of historical distance, which had taught some Americans that though created in time, the Constitution could be informally molded and formally amended through time.

In revising our understanding of antebellum historical consciousness, this narrative invites a reconsideration of the relationship between the Civil

---

⁴ "Slavery, Its Origin and Its Remedy," *North American Review* 92 (April 1861): 493.
⁵ Ibid., 503.   ⁶ Ibid., 504.   ⁷ Ibid., 506.

War and American thought. Some historians argue that the war brought about a complete intellectual transformation, replacing individualism with institutionalism, supplanting science with religion, and sweeping "away almost the whole intellectual culture of the North."[8] Such narratives have too often obscured our view of antebellum developments. To the extent that the war confirmed and advanced these developments, it also covered up their antebellum roots. To be sure, the momentous nature of the prolonged conflict spurred intellectual change, but it also accelerated and deepened many prior developments. Recent work on the Civil War has shown that conceptual continuities, including a persistent providentialism, endured alongside conceptual changes.[9] To an extent, the war heightened religious views often understood as premodern even as it fueled more materialistic understandings of historical change.

While the Civil War and Reconstruction complicated American engagement with the past, those events did not produce a uniform historical consciousness. Antebellum interpretive debates over slavery gave rise to a greater sense of historical distance among many Americans, but historical awareness in the United States has remained stratified and uneven since that era. The discussions covered in previous chapters about sacred texts and historical change took place in the distinct intellectual and political environments of the mid-nineteenth century, but dialogue about these same sacred texts and their relationship to history continue in our own unique intellectual and political environments. As in the antebellum past, the fractured nature of our political culture has generated a wide range of historical understandings. Americans still approach the same favored pasts in ways that either ignore historical distance or use that distance to set aside or reinterpret sacred texts. In other words, we continue to confront the past and to read the Constitution and the Bible in spite of – or in light of – historical awareness.

In 2012, when American legal scholar Louis Seidman urged his contemporaries to give up on the Constitution, respondents were divided.[10] Some acknowledged the ways in which the time separating the founding

---

[8] Louis Menand, *The Metaphysical Club: A Story of Ideas in America* (New York, 2001), x. See also George M. Fredrickson, *The Inner Civil War: Northern Intellectuals and the Crisis of the Union* (New York, 1965); and David Goldfield, *America Aflame: How the Civil War Created a Nation* (New York, 2011).

[9] See Cheryl A. Wells, *Civil War Time: Temporality and Identity in America, 1861–1865* (Athens, GA, 2005); Drew Gilpin Faust, *This Republic of Suffering: Death and the American Civil War* (New York, 2008); George C. Rable, *God's Almost Chosen Peoples: A Religious History of the American Civil War* (Chapel Hill, 2010); and Sean A. Scott, *A Visitation of God: Northern Civilians Interpret the Civil War* (New York, 2011).

[10] "Is It Time to Scrap the Constitution?" *New York Times*, January 3, 2013.

past from our present complicates constitutional adherence. Although law professor James Hathaway believed Seidman had gone "too far," he suggested that "we should pause to consider that no other developed democracy clings to as old a constitution."[11] Other legal scholars accounted for historical distance in a different way. They argued that the framers had accounted for historical change in crafting the Constitution. For example, Laurence H. Tribe, sounding much like the writer for the *North American Review*, wrote that "the rickety old structure has served us well over the centuries" by initiating a "living conversation about our relationship with government."[12] Meanwhile, Jason Mazzone seemed to channel other antebellum interpreters, including those who claimed founding-era intentions of abolition in their calls for formal emendation. He observed that "the framers wisely recognized that the articles they adopted might in the future prove undesirable, and so they made ample provision for change."[13] These appeals clearly parallel those used by antebellum interpreters in the slavery debates, even though differences exist.

Present-day appeals often assume certain kinds of historical thinking that were only just beginning to emerge in antebellum America. As in the past, some interpreters of sacred texts and some who appeal to favored pasts still seem unaware of, or easily set aside, understandings of historical distance, context, and change. In our intellectual culture, these kinds of interpretations and appeals draw cries of "ahistorical" and garner explicit discussion about awareness of historical distance, context, and change. Antebellum interpretive debates set the stage for this culture but did not often take place on that stage. In antebellum America, using too much historical context and distance to approach sacred texts and pasts – or not deferring to traditional views of the same – was seen as dangerous. Now, however, the failure to take historical context and distance into account causes alarm. While historical thinking remains stratified, especially in conversations about the Bible and the Constitution, Americans today are more likely than their antebellum predecessors to engage in or be confronted by conversations revolving around ahistorical and historical thinking.

Within this distinct intellectual environment, some of the legal thinkers who share Seidman's contempt for the type of constitutional veneration

---

[11] James Hathaway, letter to the editor, *New York Times*, January 3, 2013.
[12] Laurence H. Tribe, letter to the editor, *New York Times*, January 3, 2013.
[13] Jason Mazzone, letter to the editor, *New York Times*, January 3, 2013.

that has dominated in recent decades argue for readings that center on founding-era aspirations rather than original meanings. Sotirios A. Barber and James E. Fleming, for example, have followed Ronald Dworkin in articulating a philosophical, moral, and aspirational approach to the Constitution.[14] Abstract moral principles, rather than specific historical facts, shape readings in this register, but both Barber and Fleming contend that their approach has founding-era origins. Fleming argues that a moral reading is "most faithful to the Constitution's commitments," describing "fidelity as *honoring* our aspirational principles ... rather than as *following* our historical practices and concrete original meanings."[15] In this scheme, historical information, "most notably, original meaning, post-adoption history, and precedent," are submitted as possible "sources of constitutional interpretation."[16] Barber argues that the Constitution should be understood as a means of bringing about a greater good, an idea he traces back to Madison. He thus encourages veneration, not of the Constitution but of founding-era aspirations, and he ascribes this approach to Lincoln.[17] These aspirationalist readings parallel antebellum interpreters' appeals to original expectations, and even more than these appeals, the aspirationalist readings internalize a sense of historical distance and exhibit an openness to historical change.

Barber has good reason to point to Lincoln, as Lincoln, along with a number of antislavery writers, also articulated aspirational approaches to the Constitution. Significant differences separate twenty-first-century aspirationalists from their nineteenth-century predecessors, including the weight the predecessors often gave to history, original intent, and the text's words. However, in both past and present, constitutional aspirationalists insist that interpretation should account for historical change. And while current aspirationalists are often less inhibited in the ways that they use historical change, their readings depend on the historical awareness that their antebellum predecessors nurtured.

Similarly, many of those who rely on the Bible as a guide to modern life have also found ways to use historical awareness in their interpretations. This includes Casey Barton, a minister in the Evangelical Covenant Church, who uses historical distance to advance what he describes as

---

[14] Sotirios A. Barber and James E. Fleming, *Constitutional Interpretation: The Basic Questions* (New York, 2007).

[15] James E. Fleming, *Fidelity to Our Imperfect Constitution: For Moral Readings and against Originalisms* (New York, 2015), 3, 20, emphasis in original.

[16] Ibid., 20. [17] Sotirios A. Barber, *Constitutional Failure* (Lawrence, KN, 2014).

a temporal biblical reading. In his recent book *Preaching through Time*, Barton critiques conventional readings that imagine biblical passages as "periscopes of information in need of distillation into timeless packets ready to bridge the distance between the page and the congregation." Rather than read it in a spatial register that collapses historical distance, Barton places the Bible in a temporal frame, interpreting it "as the historical accounting of God's eventful drama in and through time."[18] Barton's reasoning is built from a Christian eschatology that subsumes past, present, and future into a unified whole, a traditional view that flattens historical differences. However, because he has internalized the idea that changes distinguish historical periods from each other, Barton discourages readings that attempt to bridge the distance between ancient text and modern people. Instead, he makes innovative use of that distance to "create a new moment of understanding and participation in the present moment."[19]

Barton aims to achieve this through a dramatic style of sermonizing that brings "moments in time together *anachronistically*."[20] He explains, "While the bridge approach seeks to traverse an imposed road between text then and knowledge or experience now, anachronism seeks to bring out inherent connections between moments in time in a dynamic and mimetic way. Continuity in the overarching drama is ... preserved as past and future are brought into the horizon of the present."[21] Barton does not work to recover an original meaning and pull it through time for present use. Instead, he seeks to foster his listeners' participation in the sacred drama by creating interactions between different periods of time through both "contemporizing" biblical pasts and "biblicizing" the American present.[22] Barton's deliberate and innovative use of anachronism, like Barber's and Fleming's new aspirational interpretations, is only possible in an intellectual culture that assumes historical distance. This culture has antebellum foundations.

This book encourages a greater awareness of the ways in which we use and abuse the American past. This requires attention to both historical changes and continuities. Even though the historical consciousness that imbues discussions about sacred texts and favored pasts began to emerge in the antebellum debates, today's discussions about these same topics are not simply new versions of the earlier debates.

---

[18] Casey C. Barton, *Preaching through Time: Anachronism as a Way Forward for Preaching* (Eugene, OR, 2017), 5.
[19] Ibid., 10.   [20] Ibid., 2, emphasis in original   [21] Ibid., 121–22.   [22] Ibid., 163–93.

In his second inaugural address, President Barack Obama articulated an aspirational approach to the founding era that made use of historical distance. He asserted, "We have always understood that when times change, so must we; that fidelity to our founding principles requires new responses to new challenges." Reciting the phrase "all men are created equal," Obama implored Americans to help "bridge the meaning of those words with the realities of our time."[23] Obama's "bridge" is not a structure meant to connect past and present, but rather a rhetorical device intended to align original aspirations with contemporary concerns. The historical awareness that informs this approach does not ignore historical distance but uses it to draw new meaning from old words. Seeking meaning in a sacred text from a favored but distant past, this approach aims to apply that meaning in the new contexts created by historical change.

And yet, this historically aware approach has its limitations. Throughout America's history, the choice to focus on founders and founding texts has obscured historical developments that impinge on present realities. The writings of a long list of black Americans stretching back to Nell and beyond demonstrate, both implicitly and explicitly, how each new generation of Americans has yet to fully confront the facts of slavery and racial prejudice in our past and, consequently, in our present. This ahistorical side effect of searching for aspirational principles has long contaminated the nation – at times unintentionally and at times intentionally.

James Baldwin trenchantly diagnosed this problem again and again in his writings. In his essay "The Price of the Ticket," he noted the repeated instruction he received in church to do his "first works over." Baldwin explained how to accomplish this: "go back to where you start, or as far back as you can, examine all of it, travel your road again and tell the truth about it. Sing or shout or testify or keep it to yourself: but *know whence you came.*" Baldwin suggested that "this is precisely what the generality of white Americans cannot afford to do," in light of what they will find when they examine all of their history.[24] As he explained in "Many Thousands Gone," they tend to "alchemize all bitter truths into an innocuous but piquant confection" instead of performing the costly

---

[23] Barack Obama, "Obama's Second Inaugural Speech," *New York Times*, January 21, 2013.
[24] "Other Essays: The Price of the Ticket," in *James Baldwin*, 841, emphasis in original.

work of confronting the past.[25] White Americans have often told their history – and memorialized both the history and the telling – in ways that spotlight apparent white progress at the expense of all else that rests in the shadows. The labor of going over their first works comes at an emotional and material price, but it is a price that cannot begin to approach what having failed to do their "first works over" has cost black Americans. "The record is there for all to read," Baldwin wrote in "The White Man's Guilt." He continued, "One wishes that Americans, white Americans, would read, for their own sakes, the record, and stop defending themselves against it. Only then will they be enabled to change their lives."[26] Baldwin acutely recognized and consistently emphasized that backward is the only way forward; only when white Americans thoroughly examine their own history will the nation be able to heal.

In the last few years, journalist Ta-Nehisi Coates and historian Eddie Glaude Jr. have added their voices to the critique of both the history Americans have told and the histories they have failed to tell and own. They argue that the prejudices that fuel white supremacy are inextricably bound up with the aspirations associated with the American ideal. Seen from this perspective, restorative calls to "Make America Great Again" – and perhaps even some aspirationalist appeals to the founders and the founding era – appear symptomatic of an endemic blindness to the pervasiveness of racism in America's past and present. As Glaude puts it, "When we *disremember* an event, an egregious moment in the past, we shape how we live in the present."[27]

What we remember and disremember attunes us to hear or mishear phrases such as "Black Lives Matter." Coates describes disremembering as a crucial component to upholding the great white dream. "The forgetting is habit," he writes. "They have forgotten the scale of theft that enriched them in slavery, the terror that allowed them, for a century, to pilfer the vote; the segregationist policy that gave them their suburbs. They have forgotten, because to remember would tumble them out of the beautiful Dream and force them to live down here with us, down here in the world."[28] This disremembering, this forgetting of black lives and their experiences in slavery and prejudice, is

---

[25] "Notes of a Native Son: Many Thousands Gone," in *James Baldwin*, 24.
[26] "Other Essays: The White Man's Guilt," 722.
[27] Eddie S. Glaude Jr., *Democracy in Black: How Race Still Enslaves the American Soul* (New York, 2016), 46, emphasis in original.
[28] Ta-Nehisi Coates, *Between the World and Me* (New York, 2015), 143.

another American tradition with antebellum roots. So, too, is the effort to correct this failure.

In the same period that some Americans used historical distance to advance progressive interpretations of the Constitution, black intellectuals such as Nell highlighted historical contingences to chart a path of historical change. By demonstrating that human action had created unjust constraints, they reminded their contemporaries that human action could also bring change and usher in more egalitarian contexts. As Americans became aware of historical distance from their favored pasts, Nell and his colleagues worked not to return to those erstwhile pristine periods or even to recover the permanent promises of transient eras, but instead to show that the past still haunted the present in obvious and oblique ways. This is one historical lesson that white Americans have yet to learn. Baldwin, sounding another ominous note in this repeating chord, wrote that "the fact that they have not yet been able to do this – to face their history, to change their lives – hideously menaces this country."[29]

If we are to move forward as a nation, Americans must remember more fully and completely not only black heroes but also – and especially – the contingent nature of black suffering and freedom. This requires us to recognize how the past does and does not relate to our present. As Coates writes, "Enslavement was not destined to end, and it is wrong to claim our present circumstance – no matter how improved – as the redemption for the lives of people who never asked for the posthumous, untouchable glory of dying for their children."[30] Some efforts to link forebears' actions with present concerns are misguided. And yet, the forebears' actions do have afterlives that extend into the present. As Coates noted, rather than simply acknowledge "the bad old days" in which plantation slavery thrived, we are better served by investigating the ways in which our ancestors' choices have had an "ongoing effect in the present." In doing so, we will realize the myriad ways in which "the long war against the black body" continues. Such an understanding challenges the notion, voiced by modern Taneys, that egalitarian sentiment has gone too far. As Coates writes, to move forward we must first turn "away from the brightly rendered version of [our] country" and turn "toward something murkier and unknown."[31]

Although a vast temporal gulf separates us from our antebellum predecessors, like them, we must confront the dead in new ways. We need to

---

[29] "Other Essays: The White Man's Guilt," 722.
[30] Coates, *Between the World and Me*, 70.   [31] Ibid., 98.

understand that the American past is historically distant even as we also realize, as Lincoln implied, that the "doings of that day" have "reference to the present" and are not only "an interesting memorial of the dead past."[32] In other words, we can only move toward something approaching the aspirations we so often locate in our founding era by confronting the fact that "the past is never dead" and, in fact, is "not even past."[33]

We must come to recognize, in Baldwin's own timeless words, that history "does not refer merely, or even principally, to the past." Instead, Baldwin asserted that "the great force of history comes from the fact that we carry it within us, are unconsciously controlled by it in many ways, and history is literally *present* in all that we do. It could scarcely be otherwise," he wrote. "It is to history that we owe our frames of reference, our identities, our aspirations." Confronting history, including its founding-era aspirations and failures, comes "with great pain and terror" because it is a "battle with that historical creation, Oneself." The confrontation comes at a price, but it also yields an inestimable new birth of freedom. In the confrontation, one recreates "oneself according to a principle more humane and more liberating: one begins the attempt to achieve a level of personal maturity and freedom which robs history of its tyrannical power, and also changes history."[34] In the antebellum era, history tyrannized some Americans, while other Americans, both black and white, worked to rob history of its tyrannical power, ushering in a new era of freedom. That confrontation, that work, remains ours.

[32] Lincoln, "Speech at Springfield, Illinois, June 26, 1857," 2:407.
[33] William Faulkner, *Requiem for a Nun* (New York, 1951; New York, 2011), 73.
[34] "Other Essays: The White Man's Guilt," 722–23, emphasis in the original.

Index

abolition. *See also* antislavery; Brown, John; Coker, Daniel; Douglass, Frederick; Free Soil Party; Garrison, William Lloyd; immediatism; Nell, William C.; Parker, Theodore; Radical Abolition Party; Spooner, Lysander
    and constitutional interpretation, xviii, 2, 26, 263
    and democracy, 171, 258
    and history, 153, 263
    and originalism, 124, 137
    and political parties, 164, 168
    and religion, xix, 17, 23, 49, 111, 334, 335
    and role of black Americans, 302, 303, 304, 312, 313, 318, 322, 325, 333
    and role of white Americans, 271, 313
    and the founding era, 26
    and the founding fathers. *See under* founding fathers
    and violence, 289, 301, 310, 326, 333, 334, 337
    arguments for, 71, 293, 310
    criticism of, 122, 147, 148–49, 165, 192, 193–94, 197, 199, 200, 204, 210, 231, 236
    evolution of, xxi, 125, 222, 312
    growth of, 145, 190, 191
    moderates, 111. *See also* Channing, William Ellery; Stuart, Moses; Wayland, Francis; Webster, Daniel
    movement, xv, 11, 13, 26, 220, 250, 254
    radical, 152–57, 176–180, 222, 253–55, 288–89, *See also* anticonstitutionism; Garrison, William Lloyd; Phillips, Wendell
    rise of, 84, 120, 152, 165, 185, 214
    through peaceful measures, 301, 336, 337
accommodation
    and founding-era texts, 169, 246
    and slavery, 111
    in the Bible, 59, 60, 77, 116, 117, 122, 123, 126, 131, 145, 202, 204
    of the founding fathers, 64, 96, 123, 149, 195, 202, 276, 281, 282
    theory of, 53, 58, 59, 63, 64, 84
Adams, John Quincy, 142, 150, 158, 187–88, 247
American Anti-Slavery Society, 115, 134, 155–57, 171, 253, 316
Andover, 55–56, 60, 62, 124, 196
antebellum America.
    and historical awareness, xxii, 5, 16, 17, 21, 22, 23, 193, 347
    antislavery spirit of, 190, 253
    as an age of freedom, 84, 204, 216, 218, 228
    as time of change in interpretation, xxii, 6, 27, 72, 86, 304, 351
    interpretation during, 13–14, 18, 20, 21
    religion in, 20, 29, 30–31
anticonstitutionalism, 157, 176, 184, 203, 206, 208, 209–10, 212, 217, 221, 228, 252, 253, 259, 281, 294, *See also* Douglass, Frederick; Garrison, William Lloyd; Higginson, Thomas Wentworth; Phillips, Wendell; Purvis, Robert

Index

antislavery. *See also* abolition
and historical distance, 261
arguments from biblical interpretation, 80, 110–17, 126, 132, 154, 216, *See also* Channing, William Ellery; Emerson, Ralph Waldo; Granger, Arthur; Parker, Theodore; Stuart, Moses; Wayland, Francis; Weld, Theodore Dwight
arguments from constitutional interpretation, 137, 154, 156, 164, 166, 176–82, 186, 189, 259–60, 293, *See also* Channing, William Ellery; Douglass, Frederick; Emerson, Ralph Waldo; Granger, Arthur; Parker, Theodore; Stuart, Moses; Wayland Francis; Weld, Theodore Dwight
criticism of arguments, 176, 230, 253
moderate constitutionalism, 193, 214, 287, *See also* Bailey, Gamaliel; Birney, James G.; Channing, William Ellery; Chase, Salmon P.; Palfrey, John G.; Seward, William
original expectations of the founding fathers, 124, 137, 155, 169, 174, 175, 179, 186, 189, 193, 206, 215, 218, 224, 226, 230, 243–46, 249, 256–57, 259–60, 272, 282, 296, 297, 299, 301, 308, 317, 350, *See also* founding fathers
original intent of the founding fathers, 193, *See also* founding fathers
radical constitutionalism, 169–71, 176, 287, 296, *See also* Douglass, Frederick; Goodell, William; Smith, Gerrit; Spooner, Lysander
sentiments in the Bible, 112, 113, 114, 118–19, 122, 126, 131, 134, 154, 197, 204, *See also* originalism:and the Bible
sentiments in the Constitution, 153, 154, 155, 164, 167, 168, 170, 175, 259, 276, 281, 288, 292, 295, 296, 297
sentiments in the Declaration of Independence, 154, 167, 175, 259, 292
sentiments of the founding era, 171, 185, 199, 202, 255–56
spirit of antebellum America, 190, 191, 253
spread of sentiment, 204, 212, 220, 221, 230, 234, 252, 255, 259, 291, 295
Articles of Confederation, 173, 237, 256

Attucks, Crispus, 300, 310
and Nell, William C., 306, 307, 308
as motivating figure, 325
monument to, 307
Austin, James T.
and biblical interpretation of slavery, 119
and conflation of past and present, 121
biographical details, 121

Bailey, Gamaliel, 164, 166, 169, 189, 224, 255, 307
and constitutional interpretation, 164–66
biographical details, 164
Baldwin, James, xiv, 352–55
importance of history to the present, xiv, 355
on confronting the past, 353, 354
on white man's guilt, 353
Balkin, Jack M., 19–20
Baptists, 124, 129, *See also* Fuller, Richard; Wayland, Francis
Barton, Casey, 350–51
Bauer, Ferdinand, 59, 81, 82, 87
Beck, Glenn, xv–xvi
Bellows, Henry Whitney, 184–85, 345–46
Bible, the. *See also* interpretation, biblical
accommodation in, 59, 60, 116, 117, 122, 123, 126, 131, 145, 202, 204
accuracy of, 29, 31–32, 33, 36, 41, 43, 44, 45, 47, 50, 51, 54, 56, 59, 70, 71, 73, 75, 76, 78, 80, 82–83, 87, 89, 92, 93–94, 97, 101, 183
and abolition, xix, xxi, 23, 49, 330, 347
and antebellum America, xx, xxi, 17
and debates on slavery, 17, 18, 270
and historical awareness, 15, 24, 350
and historical distance, xix, xxi, 346
and laws, 98, 99, 115, 271, 347
and oral tradition, 76
and originalism, 53, 70, 78, 115, 118, 119, 122, 125, 131
and slavery, xix, xx, xxi, 4, 13, 17, 23, 26, 41, 43–45, 49, 51, 53, 70, 83, 93, 110, 111, 113, 114, 116, 117, 118, 121, 122, 123, 124, 125, 129, 130, 131, 132, 135, 148, 181, 192, 196, 198, 200, 203, 262, 302, 346, 347
and the classical era, 39
and the Fugitive Slave Law, 183

Bible, the (cont.)
  antislavery sentiments in, 111, 112, 113, 114, 118–19, 122, 126, 131, 134, 154, 197, 204, *See also* originalism:and the Bible
  as a historical record, 73, 80, 84, 86, 94
  as a moral guide, xx, xxi, 46, 61, 110, 336
  as archaic, 17, 27, 54, 66, 67, 69, 70, 71, 73, 80, 82, 96, 99, 102, 126, 183, 197
  as inspiration for emancipation, 302, 326
  as myth, 80, 82, 83, 84, 85, 86–88
  as sacred, xix, xx, 9, 11, 13, 17, 22, 31, 33, 34, 42, 46, 50, 61, 65, 87, 156, 184, 222, 294
  authority of, 125
  black interpretations of, 302
  canonization of, 11
  criticism of, xix, 5, 16, 17, 24
  debates on, xix, xxi, 8, 15, 16, *See also* debates, biblical
  defense of, 51
  desacralization of, 35, 94, 269
  differences from the Constitution, xxi, 75, 149
  editions of, 61
  effects on historical awareness, 16
  exegesis of, 41, 59, 66
  historicization of, 11, 24, 38, 61, 84, 94, 109, 132
  interpretation of. *See* interpretation, biblical
  justifying slavery, 111, 114, 128, 129, 132, 181, 183, 203, 294
  parallels to founding-era texts, 162
  parallels to the Constitution, xix–xx, xxi, 3, 4, 18, 20, 25, 98, 99, 152, 346, *See also* interpretation, biblical:parallels to constitutional interpretation
  parallels to the Declaration of Independence, 127, 155
  polygamy in, 117, 122, 125
  proslavery sentiments in, 111, 125, 148, 180, 294
  relevance of, xix, xx, xxi, 3, 9, 11, 13, 17, 23, 24, 30, 31, 37, 45, 46, 52, 54, 60, 66, 67, 68, 69, 70, 73, 75, 77, 79, 86, 87, 91, 97, 99, 101, 110, 111, 116, 118, 132, 133, 197, 198, 201, 203
  sacrality of, 62, 66, 128, 179
  timeless truths of, xix, 45, 48, 51, 53, 54, 60, 65, 66, 68, 70, 71, 83, 88, 91, 93, 96, 114, 118, 122, 126, 127, 133, 197, 201, 294
biblical era, the. *See also* interpretation, biblical
  and the classical era, 55
  as archaic, 101
  as favored past, 9, 17, 196
  as sacred, 22
  historical distance of, 3, 9, 11, 13, 26, 30, 36, 37, 38, 41, 42, 45, 49, 52–54, 59, 60, 64, 66, 67, 70, 71, 73, 75, 79, 82, 85, 90, 100, 110, 111, 112, 115, 116, 117, 120, 129, 132, 133, 181, 196–98, 204
  historicization of, 108, 172
  parallels to the founding era, 10, 127, 201
  slavery in, 191, 294
Birney, James G.
  and biblical interpretation of slavery, 114–15
  and constitutional interpretation, 188–89
  biographical details, 114, 115
black Americans
  and citizenship, xiv, xv, 237, 238, 242, 243, 245, 250, 255, 256–57, 307
  and the Constitution, 256, 275, 293
  and the Declaration of Independence, 280, 293
  and the Articles of Confederation, 256
  and voting, 242, 243, 245, 275, 298
  as agents of change, 311, 314–15, 326, 327
  as heroic figures, 300, 301, 304, 305, 306, 309, 316, 318, 324, 325, 327, 329, 333, 343
  in the founding era, 242, 243, 245–46, 255, 256–57, 298
  in the Revolutionary War, 316, 318, 324, 326
  military service, 303, 305–10, 311, 313, 314, 318, 320, 322, 323, 342, 343
  neglected in the historical narrative, 305, 307, 310, 320, 321, 342, 343
  rights of, xv, 153, 229, 237, 242, 250, 311
  role in emancipation, 301, 302, 303, 304, 319
  societal views of, xv, 311
Black Lives Matter, xiv, 353
Blanchard, Jonathan

and biblical interpretation of slavery,
  134–35
biographical details, 134
Boston Vigilance Committee, 99, 209, 213
Bowditch, William I., 306
  and constitutional interpretation, 98–99,
    188–89, 201–2
  and the morality of slavery, 201–2
  biographical details, 99
Brown, John
  and abolition, 222, 267, 289
  and Harpers Ferry, 323–24, 332–34,
    336–37
  as a hero, 337
  as a leader, 334
Buchanan, James, 235
Buckminster, Joseph Stevens
  and biblical interpretation, 28, 29, 38–46,
    47, 76, 183
  and religion, 40
  and Unitarianism, 38
  biographical details, 39
  "Philemon," 41–45
Burckhardt, Jacob, 14
Burns, Anthony, 220–21, 292, 304, 310,
  324
Bushnell, Horace, 218

Calhoun, John C.
  and Congress's authority, 160
  and states' rights, 146, 150
  proslavery arguments, 148, 215
Calvin, John. *See also* Reformation, the
  beliefs on the Bible, 31
Calvinism. *See also* Edwards, Jonathan
  and biblical debates, 49
Cary, Mary Ann Shadd, 315
Cary, Samuel
  and biblical interpretation, 47–49
  and Unitarianism, 47–49
  biographical details, 47, 48
Catholicism
  continuity of, 72
  criticism of, 255
Catron, John, 235
  and constitutional interpretation, 240
Channing, William Ellery
  and biblical interpretation, 26, 48–49, 59,
    145, 330, 331
  and biblical interpretation of slavery, 111,
    112, 117–120
  and constitutional interpretation, 49,
    165–66
  and Unitarianism, 28, 48–49
  biographical details, 48, 121
  criticism of, 55–59, 119
  ordination sermon, 48–49, 50, 55–56
  Slavery, 117–19
Chase, Salmon P.
  and beliefs on slavery, 164, 166, 218, 266
Christ figures
  and role in abolition, 266, 313
  in the slavery movement, 333
  new Christs, 104, 190, 227, 266, 290, 333
Christianity. *See also* Bible, the; religion
  as a method to improve slavery, 347
Church of Jesus Christ of Latter-day Saints,
  the. *See also* Rigdon, Sidney; Smith,
  Joseph
  restoring favored past, 72
citizenship
  and black Americans, xi–xv, 307, 317,
    318
Civil War, the
  and effects on American thought, 348
  and effects on historical awareness, 348
  and the Bible, 17
  effects on interpretation, 13
classical era, the
  and the Bible, 39
  and the biblical era, 55
  as favored past, 8
  historical distance of, 8
  relation to founding era, 12
  restoration of, 23
  use in biblical interpretation, 44
Coker, Daniel
  and biblical interpretation of slavery,
    112–14
  biographical details, 112
colonial era. *See also* Puritans
  and slavery, 9
  as favored past, 8, 9
  as sacred, 23
  historical distance of, 9
colonization, 114, 154–55, 236
common law
  and historical development, 10
  effects on historical awareness, 14
  use in constitutional interpretation,
    171, 247
Commonwealth v. Aves, 241

Congregationalism, 28, 29, *See also* Evarts, Jeremiah; Morse, Jedidiah; Stuart, Moses
  and biblical interpretation, 29, 30, 68
  beliefs of, 89
Congress
  and slavery, 227
  authority of, 156, 160
  power of, 150, 160, 193, 234, 235, 239, 242, 244, 248, 252, 285, 297
Constitution, the. *See also* fugitive slave clause; interpretation, constitutional
  adapting over time, 259, 264, 275, 330, 332, 338, 345, 346, 347, 349
  amending, 49, 120, 127, 139, 142, 146, 156, 162, 165, 185, 196, 198, 211, 212, 249, 283, 286–87, 292, 345, 349, *See also* popular constitutionalism
  and ability to change, 268, 271, 341, 352
  and accommodation, 169
  and black Americans, 256, 275, 293
  and constitutional conventions, 139, 142
  and democracy, 196, 198, 201, *See also* popular constitutionalism
  and disunionism, 212
  and historical awareness, 15, 16
  and historical distance, 12, 346, 349
  and original expectations. *See* original expectations
  and originalism, 19, 86, 136, 137, 140, 144, 205–6, 231, 236–37, 238, 240, 258, 276, 296
  and religion, 208
  and the due process clause, 293
  and the founding fathers, 142
  anticonstitutionalism. *See* anticonstitutionalism
  antislavery sentiments in, 137, 153, 154, 155, 167, 168, 170, 175, 201, 259, 267, 276, 281, 288, 292, 293–94, 295, 296, 297
  archivization of, 18, 19, 160
  as a living document, 277, 349
  as a moral guide, xxi, 119, 350
  as a proslavery document, 144, 202, 204–7, 214, 228, 259, 315, 316, 327
  as an antislavery document, 164, 262, 264, 266, 269, 316–17, 337
  as archaic, 27, 67, 136, 140, 202, 203, 252, 348
  as sacred, xviii, xxi, 11, 13, 18, 23, 138, 140, 141, 154, 165, 184, 222, 230, 248, 253–54, 269, 298, 336, 346
  authority of, 137, 157
  canonization of, 10, 11
  criticism of, xvii, xviii, 2, 156, 164, 221, 251, 269, 316, 350
  debates on. *See* debates, constitutional
  desacralization of, 19, 136, 269
  differences from the Bible, xxi, 75, 149
  evolution of, 248
  framers of. *See* founding fathers
  historicization of, 11, 18, 109, 136, 138, 139, 140, 156, 163, 178, 205, 239
  imperfections of, 139, 154, 156, 163, 167, 188, 195, 206
  interpretation of. *See* interpretation, constitutional
  legality of, 122
  memorialization of, 152
  parallels to the Bible, xix–xx, xxi, 3, 4, 18, 20, 25, 98, 99, 152, *See also* interpretation, constitutional:parallels to biblical interpretation
  proslavery sentiments in, 153, 167, 168, 175, 177, 180, 181, 294
  ratification of, xv, 10, 19, 138
  rejection of. *See* anticonstitutionalism
  relationship with the Declaration of Independence, 147, 154, 167, 171, 172, 178, 199, 207, 254
  relevance of, xvii, xxi, 3, 13, 23, 26, 93, 145, 155, 156, 157, 158, 164, 202, 203, 239, 249, 250, 252, 259
  sacrality of, 136, 139, 203, 211, 243
  sacralization of, 18, 136, 139, 140, 141–42, 144, 152, 157, 158, 161, 331
  slavery in, 13, 25, 174, 188, 193, 243, 281, 293, 298, 338, 340
  territorial clause, 247, 252, 286, 312
  timeless truths of, 67, 165, 166, 188, 189, 207, 234, 248, 294, 298
Constitutional Convention, the. *See also* Constitution, the; Madison, James; *Papers*, James Madison's
  and slavery, 144
  criticism of, 165
  publication of records from, 150–52
  use in constitutional interpretation, 146, 150–52
  value of records of, 160, 161

Craft, Ellen and William, 99, 208–9, 213
Crispus Attucks Day, 300, 319–327
culture
  differences in, 5, 6, 17
Curtis, Benjamin Robbins, 241, *See also Dred Scott* decision, the:dissenting opinions
  and constitutional interpretation, 209, 242
  and the *Dred Scott* decision, 234, 245–48
  criticism of, 211–12
  defense of the Fugitive Slave Law, 209

de Wette, Wilhelm Martin Leberecht
  and biblical interpretation, 14, 57, 69, 80, 82–83, 88, 92, 93, 98, 101, 107, 198
debates, biblical, 49, 202
  and constitutional debates, 76, 166
  and historical readings, 66
  and slavery, 53, 55, 67
  between liberal and conservative, 55, 57, 59, 61, 88–101, 107–8, *See also* Congregationalism; Presbyterianism; Transcendentalism; Unitarianism
  differences from constitutional debate, 172
  effects of slavery debates on, 109, 111
  effects on historical distance, 49
  parallels to constitutional debates, 133, 137, 153, 156, 174, 241, 294, *See also under* interpretation, biblical
  proslavery arguments, 149
  topics of, 76
  use of historical distance in, 71
debates, congressional
  and James Madison, 138
  effects on historicization of the Constitution, 138
  over slavery, 146
  use of historical readings of the Constitution, 146
  use of the Declaration of Independence in, 146
debates, constitutional, 8, 16, 18, 19, 25, 31
  and biblical debates, 76, 166
  and slavery, 53, 67, 98, 138
  differences from biblical debate, 172
  effects of slavery debates on, 109, 136, 137
  focus on word usage, 130
  importance of, 199
  parallels to biblical debates, 133, 137, 153, 156, 174, 241, 294, *See also under* interpretation, constitutional
  proslavery arguments, 149
  use of historical distance in, 259
  use of history in, 58, 156
debates, slavery, 329
  and biblical debates, 53, 55, 67, 303, 329, 330, 345
  and biblical interpretation, 79, 148
  and constitutional debates, 53, 67, 98, 264, 303, 329, 330, 345, 349
  and constitutional interpretation, 79
  and historical distance, 264, 332, 348
  and the Declaration of Independence, 67
  and the Supreme Court, 236
  attempts to end, 258, 289
  causing historical awareness, 120, 127, 144, 196
  causing historical distance, 136
  causing historicization, 141, 239
  constitutionalization of, 252
  effects of Missouri Crisis on, 55
  effects on biblical debates, 109, 111
  effects on consitutional interpretation, 296
  effects on constitutional debates, 109, 136, 137
  effects on constitutional interpretation, 160, 166
  effects on interpretation, 204
  importance of constitutional interpretation in, 217
  rise of, 109, 110, 145
  role of the Constitution in, 295
Declaration of Independence, the, xv
  and accommodation, 246
  and black Americans, 280, 293
  and egalitarian promises, 302
  and influence on the Constitution, 268
  and originalism, 246, 251, 275, 280
  and proslavery original intent, 237
  and rights of black Americans, 154
  and slavery, 1–2, 238, 274
  antislavery sentiments in, 154, 167, 175, 259, 292
  appeals to during slavery debates, 67, 78
  as a living document, 277
  as archaic, 254
  as pro-abolition, 325
  as sacred, 156, 178, 224, 276

Declaration of Independence, the (cont.)
  focus on during constitutional debate, 172
  gospel principles in, 135, 154, 156, 190
  historicization of, 147, 239, 246
  parallels to the Bible, 127, 155
  principles of, 172, 175, 180, 195
  relationship with the Constitution, 147, 154, 167, 171, 172, 178, 199, 207, 254
  relevance of, 3, 239, 254, 276
  timeless truths of, 78, 127, 157, 187, 207, 224, 225, 256, 259, 276, 280
  use in congressional debates, 146
  use in constitutional interpretation, 167, 170, 172, 173, 175, 237, 256, 273, 274, 275
  values of, 26
democracy
  and abolition, 171, 258
  and constitutional interpretation, 171, 216–17, 228, 251
  and originalism, 169
  and slavery, 127, 130, 169, 220
  and the Constitution, 196, 198, 201, *See also* popular constitutionalism
desegregation
  of schools, 306, 310, 317
Dexter, Samuel
  and biblical interpretation, 28, 38
Dexter Lecturer of Biblical Criticism, 28, 38, 46, 48, 49
Dexter Professorship of Sacred Literature, 49
disunionism, 164, 176, 205, 210
  and the Constitution, 212
  criticism of, 184
Douglas, Stephen A.
  and constitutional interpretation, 274, 283–84
  and the *Dred Scott* decision, 273
  criticism of, 284, 286, 287
  debates with Abraham Lincoln, 273–74, 281–84
Douglass, Frederick
  and abolition, 21, 335, 336, 337
  and anticonstitutionalism, 205–7
  and biblical interpretation, 180–182, 216
  and constitutional interpretation, 26, 180–82, 204–7, 212–18, 263, 288–97, 299, 330, 337

  and faith, religion, 335
  and historical awareness, 26
  and Lincoln, Abraham, 339
  and popular constitutionalism, 259
  and radical antislavery constitutionalism, 213–18
  and the *Dred Scott* decision, 288, 289–90, 295, 296
  and the Fugitive Slave Law, 217
  appeals to the original expectations of the founding fathers, 206, 215, 218, 296–97
  as a symbol, 219
  biographical details, 205, 305
  Fourth of July speech 1852, 216–217
  Fourth of July speech 1862, 338
  on black soldiers, 305
  on Brown, John, 336
  on the Repulican Party, 338
  on Washington, Madison, 305
  providentialism, 336
Downing, George T.
  on the Constitution as pro-black citizenship, 317
Dred Scott decision, the, xiv, xv, 1, 233–36, 237–39, 248–50
  and constitutional interpretation, 19, 25, 262, 278, 315, 320, 335–36
  as a proslavery victory, 264
  as archaic, 255
  criticism of, 274–76, 316, 317–18
  dissenting opinions, 230, 234, 235, 241, 248, *See also* Curtis, Benjamin Robbins; McLean, John
  effects of, 21, 235–36, 264, 277, 295, 300, 320, 329, 334
  historical and legal flaws of, 265, 267
  response to, 93, 250, 288, 289–90, 295, 296, 297, 304, 316
  use of history in, 229–32
Dred Scott v. *Emerson*
  criticism of, 245

Edwards, Jonathan
  and biblical interpretation, 33–36, 38, 76
Eichhorn, Johann Gottfried
  and biblical interpretation, 28, 36, 50, 57, 58, 73, 74, 81, 82
emancipation
  and role of black Americans, 300, 301, 302

through revolution over sacred text, 302
Emancipation Proclamation, 338
Emerson, Ralph Waldo
  and antislavery arguments, 226–27
  and biblical interpretation, 72, 73–79,
    84, 90
  and constitutional interpretation, 79
  biographical details, 74, 78, 79
  criticism of, 91, 94–95
  Harvard Divinity School Address, 90–91
  Vestry Lectures, 73–78
empiricism, 37, See also Francis Bacon
equality under the law
  ideals post-Civil War, 343
  post-Civil War legislation, 311
Evarts, Jeremiah
  and biblical interpretation, 60–62
  and Congregationalism, 28
Everett, Edward
  and Unitarianism, 28

federal power
  growth of, 147
  threats of, 147
  vs states' rights, 152
Federalist Papers, the
  arguing the sacrality of the Constitution,
    139
  on slavery, 317
  relevance of, xv–xvi
  use in constitutional interpretation,
    151
Federalists
  debates with Jeffersonians, 142
founding era, the. See also founding fathers;
    original expectations
  and abolition, 26, 317, 340, 341
  and antislavery original intent, 275, 278
  and black Americans, 256–57
  and historical distance, 26, 263
  and originalism, 137, 160, 185, 189,
    223–24, 238, 240, 258
  and proslavery readings, 263
  and slavery, 12, 25
  antislavery sentiments in, 171, 185, 199,
    212, 255–56
  antislavery spirt of, 202
  appeals to founding-era texts, xv–xvi, xvii
  as archaic, 259
  as favored past, 8, 10, 12, 13, 127,
    264

as sacred, 23, 136
attempts to restore, 143, 155, 166, 168,
    231, 234, 249, 256, 260, 261, 280
attitudes towards blacks, 231
authority of texts from, 127
black Americans in, 242, 243,
    245–246, 255
connection to biblical past, 10
criticism of, 10
dismissing of, 331
historical distance of, 3, 10, 11, 12, 13,
    59, 85, 98, 120, 121, 135, 142, 149,
    153, 169, 178, 184, 186, 189, 194, 199,
    204, 211, 218, 226, 230, 231, 234, 238,
    240, 246, 248, 249, 252, 255, 256, 258,
    259, 263, 273, 278, 282–83, 284, 286,
    287–88, 294, 295, 297, 298
historicization of, 10, 12, 25, 133, 141,
    153, 172, 186, 274
ideals of, 226
influences on abolition, 342
parallels of founding-era texts to the
    Bible, 162
parallels to the biblical era, 10, 127, 201
principles, xvi, xix, 9
proslavery spirit of, 239
racism in, 231, 274
relation to classical era, 12
relevance of, 2, 10, 12
sacralization of, 161
slavery in, 169, 179, 186, 191, 193, 226,
    229, 236–37, 255, 261, 274, 282, 293,
    294, 298
texts. See Constitution, the; Declaration
    of Independence, the
texts as archaic, 4
texts as sacred, xviii, xix, 10, 161, See also
    Constitution, the; Declaration of
    Independence, the
timeless truths of, 178, 185, 187,
    189
veneration of, 330
views on slavery, 195, 215, 325
voting in, 298
founding fathers, 10, See also founding era,
    the; Jefferson, Thomas; Madison,
    James; original expectations;
    originalism
  accommodation of, 123, 149, 195, 202,
    276, 281, 282
  and abolition, 271, 308

founding fathers (cont.)
  and amending the Constitution, 142
  and antislavery original intent, 20, 178, 179, 186, 189, 193, 195, 215, 217, 224–25, 226, 228, 230, 242, 243–44, 246–48, 254–56, 258, 259–60, 261, 273, 275–77, 278–79, 280, 281, 282–83, 284, 285–87, 292, 294, 295, 296, 297, 298
  and attitudes towards slavery, 337, 340
  and constitutional interpretation, 269, 332
  and criticism of, 263
  and expressing the will of the people, 268–69
  and historical awareness, 257, 276, 282
  and historical distance, 185, 240
  and originalism, 1–2, 122, 123, 137, 142, 146, 147, 149, 150, 154–55, 158, 166, 167–69, 170, 172, 174, 175, 214–16, 224, 241, 248–50, 257, 258, 268, 283, 284, 307, 330, 332, 337, 341, 349, 350
  and proslavery original intent, 176, 210–11, 213, 238–39, 274
  and slavery, xvii, xxi, 1, 2, 27, 51, 167, 283, 287
  and states' rights, 284
  and territorial power, 285
  appeals to, 158
  as archaic, 252
  as complicated figures, xvii
  as sacred, 151, 165
  criticism of, 206, 217, 218, 254
  effects of deaths of, 19, 25, 136, 142, 152, 158–59
  effects on historical awareness, 352
  morality of, 292
  relevance of, 286, 337
  sacralization of, 161
  use of writings in constitutional interpretaion, 152
  views of the Constitution, 163
  views on abolition, xviii, 270, 330
Fourteenth Amendment, the, xiv, 343, *See also* citizenship:black Americans
framers, constitutional. *See* founding fathers
Free Soil Party, 189
  and the fugitive slave clause, 209
  criticism of, 209
freedom of speech
  and abolition, 120

freedom of the press
  and abolition, 120
Freeport Doctrine, 274
Fugitive Slave Act of 1793, the, 44, 191
fugitive slave cases, 219–20, *See also* Burns, Anthony; Craft, Ellen and Wlliam; Minkins, Shadrach; Parker, Theodore; Sims, Thomas
  effects on constitutional interpretation, 207–8, 212–13, 217
fugitive slave clause, 165–66, 181
  and antislavery arguments, 195
  and constitutional interpretation, 170, 171
  and original intent, 210
  defense of, 211
Fugitive Slave Law, the, xix, xxi, 25, 58, 334
  and the Bible, 183
  and the Slave Power, 185
  constitutionality of, 194, 200, 241
  criticism of, 194, 211–12, 217–18, 221, 227
  debate over, 93, 200, 207
  defense of, 45, 60, 194, 197, 199, 209
  effects of, 191
  effects on constitutional interpretation, 207
Fuller, Richard
  and biblical interpretation of slavery, 124–25, 127–29
  biographical details, 124
  Domestic Slavery, 127–29
Furness, William
  and biblical interpretation, 89
  and constitutional interpretation, 253–54

Gabler, Johann Philipp
  and biblical interpretation, 37
Garrison, William Lloyd
  and abolition, 21, 25, 190, 336
  and anticonstitutionalism, 221, 253
  and biblical interpretation, 153, 179–80
  and constitutional interpretation, 26, 137, 153–54, 156–57, 164, 331
  criticism of, 293
  on founding-era attitudes on slavery, 325–26
Garrisonianism. *See also* abolition, radical; Phillips, Wendell
Gettysburg Address
  and founding fathers, 340, 341

and interpretation of the Constitution, 339, 340, 341
Gienapp, Jonathan, 18
Gilhooley, Simon J., 18–19
Gilpin, Henry
and sacrality of founding era texts, 160–62
Goodell, William
and constitutional interpretation, 25, 171–73, 268, 330
biographical details, 171
Göttingen, 36, 50, 73
Graham, Sylvester
and constitutional interpretation, 195–96
grammatical–historical method, 199
Granger, Arthur
and biblical interpretation of slavery, 122–24
and constitutional interpretation of slavery, 123
biographical details, 122
Groves v. Slaughter, 236

Halle, 36, 64
Harvard, 28, 38–39, 50, 52, 53, 55, 90, 91, 168
Hayden, Lewis, 324–25
Hayne, Robert
and states' rights, 146
Herder, Gottfried Johann
and historical thinking, 37, 42, 58
hermeneutics, 329, 331, 332, *See also* Hobbes, Thomas; interpretation, biblical; Spinoza, Baruch
biblical, 31–32, 33
principles of, 231
Higginson, Thomas Wentworth
abolitionism, 253, 267
and a "modern Crispus Attucks," 304, 324, 325
and constitutional interpretation, 253
historical awareness, xvii–xviii, *See also* historical distance
and biblical interpretation, 24, 270, 350
and constitutional interpretation, 264, 265, 295, 350
and effects of the Civil War, 348
and slavery, xxii, 15, 24, 354
and the Bible, 15, 329, 351

and the Constitution, 15, 329
and the founding fathers, 257, 276, 282
caused by biblical interpretation, 71, 75, 76, 78, 85, 86, 90, 99, 107, 112, 115, 117, 118, 119, 126, 132, 133, 204
caused by constitutional interpretation, xix–xx, 99, 156, 167–68, 169, 173, 175, 177, 179, 185, 204, 226, 231–32, 244, 249, 252, 258, 260, 273, 283, 287–88, 294, 295–96, 298
caused by historical readings, 137
caused by originalism, 144, 260
caused by slavery, 111
caused by slavery debates, 21, 25, 120, 127, 136, 144, 196, 329
caused by the founding fathers' passing, 136
causes of, 14, 15, 19, 22, 24, 25, 30, 93, 95, 135, 142, 192, 232
effects of, 23, 248, 273
effects of historicization on, 27
effects of slavery debates on, 26
effects of slavery on, 13, 24
effects on constitutional interpretation, xviii–xix, 259, 276, 277, 278
evolution of, 20, 21, 22
growth of, 22, 31, 46, 60, 61, 66–68, 73, 75, 93, 114, 129, 133, 184, 185, 241, 256, 261, 279, 287–88
in antebellum America, xxii, 5, 17, 21, 22, 23, 193, 349
in modern American thought, 349
inspiring Constitutional interpretation, 352
lack of, 143–44, 145, 149, 166, 178, 211, 296
necessary for interpretation, 330
of historical distance, xxii, 2, 3, 4, 5–6, 7, 8, 11, 13–16, 18, 19, 37, 40, 41, 113
of Presbyterians, 65
historical change
and ambivalence to, 11, 26, 84–85, 113, 135, 191, 202, 218, 267, 279, 299, 303, 310, 312
as contingent, 12, 136, 242, 260, 279–80, 284, 288, 299, 303, 304, 308, 312, 326, 328, 332, 343, 354
from the founding era, 136, 142, 147, 155, 175, 186, 191, 194, 204, 212, 224, 232, 244, 260, 277, 278

historical distance, xv, xvi, xvii, xviii–xx,
    4–8, 13, *See also* historical awareness;
    morality:moral decline; morality:moral
    progress; presentism
  and ambivalence to, 312
  and biblical debates, 49, 71
  and debates on slavery, 8, 330, 345
  and effects for black Americans, 303
  and ending slavery, 341, 345, 347
  and influence on egalitarian principles,
    264
  and lack of truth, 330
  and slavery, 99, 355
  and the Bible, xix, xxi, 271, 329, 331, 332
  and the Constitution, 12, 263, 331, 332
  as a precursor to emancipation, 304
  bridging, 6, 7, 8, 13, 17, 41, 51, 54, 66,
    71, 129, 143, 166, 168, 175, 181, 186,
    210, 231, 240, 249, 257, 259, 261, 351
  effects of, 100
  historical awareness of, xviii–xix, xxii, 2,
    3, 4, 5–6, 7, 8, 11, 13–16, 18, 19, 37,
    40, 41, 113, 348, 353
  historicization of, 6, 8
  in the modern day, 351
  of favored pasts, 184, 204
  of the biblical era, 3, 9, 11, 13, 22, 26, 30,
    36, 37, 38, 41, 42, 45, 49, 52–54, 59,
    60, 64, 66, 67, 70, 71, 73, 75, 79, 82,
    85, 90, 100, 110, 111, 112, 115, 116,
    117, 120, 129, 132, 133, 181, 191,
    196–98, 204, 331
  of the colonial era, 9
  of the founding era, 3, 10, 11, 12, 13, 22,
    26, 59, 85, 98, 120, 121, 135, 142, 149,
    153, 169, 178, 184, 186, 189, 191, 194,
    199, 204, 211, 218, 226, 230, 231, 234,
    238, 240, 246, 248, 249, 252, 255, 256,
    258, 259, 273, 278, 282–83, 284, 286,
    287–88, 294, 295, 297, 298, 331
  of the founding fathers, 185, 240
  use in biblical interpretation, 42, 46, 49,
    55, 67, 70, 80, 93, 100–1, 107, 128,
    262, 329, 346, 351
  use in constitutional interpretation, 19,
    49, 190, 242, 244, 259, 260–61, 262,
    263, 265, 269, 273, 279–81, 282–83,
    288, 296, 299, 329, 330, 346, 349,
    350, 354
  use in interpretation, 23, 26, 27, 349
  use in *Scott v. Emerson*, 233
  use in Supreme Court decisions, 233, 234
historicization
  and historical awareness, 27
  and prejudice, 313
  and sacralization, 158, 163, 164, 205
  caused by James Madison's *Papers*,
    159
  caused by slavery debates, 141, 239
  causes of, 17
  effects of congressional debates on, 138
  of favored pasts, 137, 258
  of historical distance, 6, 8
  of racism, 327
  of sacred texts, 258
  of slavery, 191, 243
  of the Bible, 17, 24, 38, 61, 84, 94, 109,
    132, 332
  of the biblical era, 108, 172
  of the Constitution, 4, 136, 138, 139,
    140, 156, 163, 178, 205, 269, 332
  of the Declaration of Independence,
    147, 246
  of the founding era, 10, 12, 25, 133, 141,
    153, 172, 186, 274
  of truth, 71
  process of, 3, 4, 191
history. *See also* historical distance,
    historical awareness
  and constitutional interpretation,
    188–90
  and lack of truth, 71, 353, 354
  criticism of historical readings, 173–75
  historical readings causing historical
    awareness, 137
  use in biblical interpretation, 4, 25,
    38–46, 47–55, 62, 63–64, 65, 69,
    74–76, 82, 121, 130–31, 196–98,
    202–4, 329
  use in constitutional debates, 58, 156
  use in constitutional interpretation, xix,
    4, 25, 136, 137, 141, 145, 156, 157,
    164, 169, 170, 171, 176–77, 178–79,
    185, 193, 194–96, 199–200, 202–4,
    214–16, 228, 236–37, 240, 242, 244,
    245–46, 250, 251, 256, 258, 273–74,
    275–84, 285–86, 295, 296, 298
  use in Supreme Court decisions, 235
  use in the *Dred Scott* decision, 229–32
Hobbes, Thomas
  and biblical interpretation, 31–32, 34, 36
Hodge, Charles

and biblical interpretation, 29, 62–66, 70, 71, 94–95, 96, 130, 201
and constitutional interpretation, 200–1
biographical information, 62
criticism of, 95
Holland, David F., 66
Howard, Thomas A., 14
Hume, David
and biblical interpretation, 37

Idealism, German, 81–82, *See also* interpretation, biblical:German
immediatism, 110, 114, 115, 119, 153, 155
converts from colonization, 154
criticism of, 120, 121, 197
growth, 154
interpretation, biblical, xix, xx, xxi, xxii, 4, 5, 11, 14, 15, 18, 19, 22, 24, 346, 351, *See also* accommodation; Buckminster, Joseph Stevens; Cary, Samuel; Channing, William Ellery; de Wette, Wilhelm Martin Leberecht; Dexter, Samuel; Douglass, Frederick; Edwards, Jonathan; Eichhorn, Johann Gottfried; Gabler, Johann Philipp; Garrison, William Lloyd; hermeneutics; Hobbes, Thomas; Hodge, Charles; Hume, David; Idealism, German; Locke, John; Luther, Martin; Michaelis, Johann David; Norton, Andrews; Paine, Thomas; Parker, Theodore; Reid, Thomas; religion; Semler, Johann Salomo; Spinoza, Baruch; Stuart, Moses; Tittmann, Charles Christian; Wayland, Francis; Webster, Daniel
and grammatical analysis, 56, 58, 64
and historical distance, 55, 345
and historical readings, 4, 25, 29–31, 32–36, 37, 38–46, 47–57, 58, 59, 61, 62, 63–64, 65, 66, 69, 72, 74–76, 79, 82, 85, 86, 87, 92, 93, 100, 107, 121, 130–31, 196–98, 202–4, 329
and originalism, 42
and presentism, 45, 137
and rationalism, 81, 82, 84
and religion, 29–30
and rituals, 84
and slavery debates, 79, 148
and supernaturalism, 84, 87
and the classical era, 44
and Transcendentalism. *See* Transcendentalism
and Unitarianism. *See* Unitarianism
antislavery arguments, 51, 80, 110–17, 126, 132, 154, 216, *See also* Birney, James G.; Blanchard, Jonathan; Channing, William Ellery; Coker, Daniel; Granger, Arthur; Weld, Theodore Dwight
caused by historical awareness, 132
causing historical awareness, 24, 66–68, 71, 75, 76, 78, 85, 86, 90, 99, 107, 112, 115, 117, 118, 119, 126, 133, 204
effects of slavery on, 46, 114, 116
English, 81
European, 30, 31, 36–37, 38, 50, 53, 57, 60, 63, 73, *See also* de Wette, Wilhelm Martin Leberecht; Strauss, David Friedrich; Tittmann, Charles Christian
evolution of, 46, 53, 80, 86, 91, 112, 114, 186
German, 81, 82, 92, *See also* Bauer, Ferdinand; de Wette, Wilhelm Martin Leberecht; Eichhorn, Johann Gottfried; Fichte, Johann Gottlieb; Herder, Johann; Kant, Immanuel; Luther, Martin; Michaelis, Johann; Reimarus, Hermann; Schelling, Friedrich Wilhelm Joseph; Schleiermacher, Friedrich; Semler, Johann Salomo
grammatical–historical method, 58, 59, 60, 64
overlapping with constitutional interpretation, 182, 184, 186, 192, 253–54
parallels to constitutional interpretation, 56, 59, 67, 71, 75, 78, 85, 93, 112, 137, 144, 165, 168, 172, 173, 179, 188, 258, 274, 275, 279, 283
proslavery arguments, 100, 110, 126, 132, *See also* Fuller, Richard
rise of, 28–29, 31, 36, 38, 46, 51
use of historical distance in, 42, 46, 49, 67, 70, 80, 93, 100–1, 107, 128
interpretation, constitutional, xviii, xxii, 5, 15, 18, 19, 22, 25, 268, 337, 350, *See also* antislavery:moderate constitutionalism; antislavery:radical

constitutionalism; Bellows, Henry
Whitney; Birney, James G.; Bowditch,
William I.; Channing, William Ellery;
Curtis, Benjamin Robbins; Douglas,
Stephen A.; Douglass, Frederick;
Emerson, Ralph Waldo; Garrison,
William Lloyd; Goodell, William;
Higginson, Thomas Wentworth;
Jefferson, Thomas; Lincoln, Abraham;
Madison, James; original expectations;
originalism; Palfrey, John G.; Parker,
Theodore; Phillips, Wendell; Smith,
Gerrit; Spooner, Lysander; Stuart,
Moses; Supreme Court, the
and democracy, 171, 216–17, 228, 251
and historical distance, 345
and historical readings, xix, 4, 19, 25, 93, 136, 137, 141, 145, 156, 157, 164, 169, 170, 171, 176–77, 178–79, 185, 188–90, 193, 194–96, 199–200, 202–4, 214–16, 228, 236–37, 240, 242, 244, 245–48, 250, 251, 256, 258, 273–74, 275–84, 285–86, 295, 296, 298
and James Madison's *Papers*, 161, 163, 164–65
and original expectations, 19–20, 26, 124, *See also*, original expectations
and originalism, 42, 230, 259, *See also* originalism
and presentism, 137
and states' rights, 146, *See also* Calhoun, John C.; Hayne, Robert
and the Constitutional Convention, 146
and the fugitive slave clause, 170, 171
and the Supreme Court, 177, 186, 207
and word analysis, 293, 296, 297, 298
antislavery arguments, 93, 154, 156, 164, 166, 176–82, 186, 189, 259–60,
  See also Douglass, Frederick; Lincoln, Abraham
causing historical awareness, 99, 156, 167–68, 169, 173, 175, 177, 179, 185, 204, 226, 231–32, 244, 249, 252, 258, 260, 273, 283, 287–88, 294, 295–96, 298
criticism of historical readings, 173–75
effects of fugitive slave cases on, 207, 217
effects of historical awareness on, 259, 276, 277, 278
effects of slavery debates on, 150, 160, 166, 296

effects of the *Dred Scott* decision on, 278
effects of the Fugitive Slave Law on, 207
evolution of, 112, 152, 160, 186, 188, 207, 226, 246, 283, 295
importance in slavery debate, 217
overlapping with biblical interpretation, 182, 184, 186, 192, 253–54
parallels to biblical interpretation, 56, 59, 67, 71, 75, 78, 85, 93, 112, 137, 144, 165, 168, 172, 173, 179, 188, 258, 274, 275, 279, 283, *See also* Constitution, the:parallels to the Constitution; debates, constitutional
proslavery arguments, 58, 86, 170, 216, 278, 295
rise of, 136
slavery effects on, 216
use in congressional debates, 146
use of common law in, 171, 247
use of Constitutional Convention records in, 150–52
use of founding fathers' writings in, 152
use of historical awareness in, 295
use of historical distance in, 49, 242, 244, 259, 260–61, 263, 273, 279–81, 282–83, 288, 296, 299
use of James Madison's *Papers* in, 165, 167, 170, 176, 201, 243, 307
use of the Articles of Confederation in, 173, 237
use of the Constitutional Convention in, 152
use of the Declaration of Independence in, 167, 170, 172, 173, 175, 237, 256, 273, 274, 275
use of the Federalist Papers in, 151
who should practice, 146, 171, 201

Jefferson, Thomas
and constitutional interpretation, 139, 140, 141, 145–47
appeals to in constitutional interpretation, 155, 166, 167, 172, 196, 223, 227, 256, 280, 282, 335
criticism of, 139, 140
views on divide over slavery, 147
Jeffersonians
debates with Federalists, 142

Kansas–Nebraska Act, the, 25, 220, 223, 225, 273, 297, 334
  and the Slave Power, 185
  criticism of, 227
Kant, Immanuel
  and biblical interpretation, 81
Koselleck, Reinhart, 16

LaCapra, Dominick, 22
laws. *See also* Constitution, the
  and religion, 109, 119
  and slavery, 115, 120, 130
  and the Bible, 115
  as evolutionary, 245
  higher-law appeals, 99, 209, 221, 252, 253, 265
  in the Bible, 98, 99
  influences on, 274
  legal interpretation of the Constitution, 251
  natural, 173, 174, 175, *See also* morality
Lee, Michael J., 16
Liberty Party, 164–67, *See also* Bailey, Gamaliel; Birney, James G.; Goodell, William; Smith, Gerrit
  as a restoration of the past, 166
  criticism of, 165
  views on slavery, 167
Lincoln, Abraham
  and constitutional interpretation, 1–2, 6, 19, 26, 169, 223–26, 262, 263, 272, 273, 274–79, 281–84, 285–88, 297, 299, 301, 330, 339, 340, 341, 350
  and framers' intent, 272, 331
  and historical awareness, 26
  and racism, 280
  and slavery, 27, 336
  and the *Dred Scott* decision, 274–76
  and the Fugitive Slave Law, 297
  appeals to the original expectations of the founding fathers, 224, 272, 275, 282–84, 297, 301
  appeals to the founding fathers, 158
  biographical details, 222–23, 285
  Cooper Union Speech, 285–88
  criticism of, 283
  debates with Stephen A. Douglas, 273–74, 281–84
  Emancipation Proclamation, 338
  House Divided Speech, 277
  Peoria Speech, 223–26

Livermore, George
  on role of black soldiers in American wars, 342
living constitutionalism, 230, 248
Locke, John
  and biblical interpretation, 32, 34, 36, 37
Lovejoy, Elijah
  murder of, 120, 122, 176
Luther, Martin. *See also* Reformation, the
  and biblical interpretation, 72
  beliefs on the Bible, 31

Madison, Dolley
  publishing James Madison's work, 159, 160
Madison, James. *See also* Constitutional Convention, the; Federalist Papers, the; Madison, Dolley; *Papers*, James Madison's
  and congressional debates, 138
  and Constitutional Convention notes, 158
  and constitutional interpretation, 18, 138–41
  and originalism, 42, 159, 164, 193, 350
  and slavery, 23, 317
  appeals to, xvii, 23, 151–152, 167, 172, 193, 195, 244, 335, *See also Papers*, James Madison's
  criticism of, 139, 140
  effects of death of, 25, 137, 152, 158, 159
  memorialization of, 152, 157–58
  relevance of, xvii, 3, 23
  texts as sacred, 19
  views on divide over slavery, 147
  views on the Constitution, 18, 158
Marshall, John
  appeals to in constitutional interpretation, 151
  criticism of, 146, 150
  rulings, 145–46
Massachusetts General Colored Association (MGCA), 305
McCulloch v. *Maryland*, 147
  criticism of, 146, 150
McLean, John. *See also Dred Scott* decision, the:dissenting opinions
  and constitutional interpretation, 242, 250, 259
  and the *Dred Scott* decision, 242–45
  politics of, 241
Methodism

Methodism (cont.)
  divide over slavery, 124
Mexican–American War, the, 184
  effects of, 187
Michaelis, Johann David
  and biblical interpretation, 36, 41
Minardi, Margot, 319
Minkins, Shadrach, 213, 324
Missouri Compromise, the, 147, 149, 220, 224, 239, 244, 254
  effects of, 191
Missouri Crisis
  effects on slavery debates, 55
morality, 208, See also laws:natural
  moral decline, 116, 135, 155, 168, 175, 179, 185, 187–88, 191, 196, 202, 211, 218, 220, 222, 244, 257, 258, 259–60, 294, See also United States, the: national decline
  moral progress, 111, 112, 113, 115, 117, 118, 120, 123, 125–26, 127, 128, 131, 134–35, 168, 181, 184, 185–86, 187–88, 189, 190, 191, 195, 196, 204, 208, 211–12, 218, 230, 252, 255, 256, 276, 278, 292, 294, 298, 299, See also United States, the:national progress
  of slavery, 110–11, 112, 113, 114, 117, 120, 121, 123, 125–26, 127–29, 130, 134, 145, 149, 165–66, 197, 199, 200, 201–2, 211, 216, 224, 282, 287, 293
  of the Bible, 111
  of the Constitution, 119, 236
  of the founding era, 298
  of the founding fathers, 292
Mormonism. See Church of Jesus Christ of Latter-day Saints, the
Mott, Lucretia, 156
Morse, Jedidiah
  and biblical interpretation, 61
  and religious divide, 47

Nat Turner's rebellion, 148, 154, 236
natural law. See under law
Nell, William C.
  and black revolutionaries, 307
  and desegretation of schools, 306
  and racial prejudice, 302–4
  and the Fugitive Slave Law, 307
  biographical, 305–10
  Colored Patriots of the American Revolution, The, 311–314, 320, 342
  influence on post-war era, 342, 343
  on Attucks, Crispus, 308
  on black revolutionaries, 301, 302–4, 305, 306, 307
  on black soldiers, 308
  on colorphobia, 313
  on equality for blacks, 343
  on historical change, 312, 354
  Services of Colored Americans, in the Wars of 1776 and 1812, 307–309
New England Anti-Slavery Society (NEASS), 202, 267, 305–6
Northwest Ordinance, the, 147, 170, 193, 223, 244, 247
Norton, Andrews
  and biblical interpretation, 29, 49–55, 56–57, 59, 70, 71, 84, 91–95, 96
  and the Fugitive Slave Law, 211–12
  criticism of, 97
  Discourse on the Latest form of Infidelity, 91–93

Obama, Barack
  on aspirationalism, 352
Onesimus, 41, 43, 44, 118, 129, 131, 181, 198, 203, 347
original expectations, 19–20, 124
  of the founding fathers, 19–20, 26, 124, 137, 155, 169, 174, 175, 179, 186, 189, 193, 206, 210, 215, 218, 224, 226, 230, 234, 241–46, 249, 254, 256–60, 272, 275, 282–84, 296, 297, 299, 301, 308, 317, 350
originalism, xv, 19–20, 21, 25, 26
  and abolition, xviii, 124, 137
  and constitutional interpretation, 42, 259, 350
  and democracy, 169
  and founding fathers, 123, 154–55, 258, See under founding fathers
  and James Madison, 159, 164
  and James Madison's *Papers*, 230
  and states' rights, 239
  and the Bible, 42, 56, 70, 78, 115, 118, 119, 122, 125, 131
  and the Constitution, 19, 86, 136, 137, 140, 144, 201, 205–6, 231, 236–37, 238, 240, 258, 276, 296
  and the Declaration of Independence, 237, 246, 251, 275, 280

and the founding era, 137, 160, 185, 189,
    212, 223–24, 238, 240, 258, 275,
    278
and the fugitive slave clause, 210
and the Slave Power, 168
criticism of, 170, 173, 174, 202, 227
effects on historical awareness, 144
original intent of the founding fathers, 1–2
rise of, xvi, 53, 162
use in constitutional interpretation, 230
Oshatz, Molly, 17, 110, 197

Paine, Thomas
    and biblical interpretation, 37, 179
Palfrey, John G., 9, 53
    and constitutional interpretation,
        168–169
    biographical details, 168
Papers, James Madison's, 164–65, 189, *See also* Madison, James
    and anticonstitutionalism, 176
    and original expectations, 169, 189
    and originalism, 230
    canonization of, 161
    causing historicization, 159
    criticism of, 174
    publication of, 25, 157, 158–61, 162
    sacralization of, 161
    use in constitutional interpretation, 19,
        25, 160–161, 163, 165, 167, 170, 176,
        201, 206, 240, 243, 244, 307
    use in Supreme Court decisions, 163
    value of, 159
Parker, Theodore, 101–8
    and abolition, 332, 333, 342
    and anticonstitutionalism, 212
    and antislavery arguments, 218–19, 227
    and biblical interpretation, 21, 25, 69–71,
        72, 73, 80–88, 93, 95–101, 183, 185,
        202–4, 294
    and constitutional interpretation, 21, 25,
        26, 71, 86, 185, 187–91, 194–95,
        202–4, 262, 274, 276, 294, 297, 299,
        330, 339
    and financial support of Brown, John, 267
    and fugitive slaves, 208–9
    and historical awareness, 26
    and historical distance, 190
    and moral progress, 220–21
    and slavery debates, 70, 99
    and slavery in the Bible, 331

and the *Dred Scott* decision, 297
and the popular approach to the
    interpretation of the Constitution,
    264–72
and the uprising of slaves, 334
and views on blacks, 301, 323
appeals to the original expectations of the
    founding fathers, 269–72
biographical details, 81, 83, 187, 209
connecting law and religion, 109
criticism of, 187, 199, 210
*Discourse of Matters Pertaining to
    Religion*, 101, 104–108, 183
*Discourse on the Transient and the
    Permanent in Christianity*, 101–4
on Brown, John, 333
on prejudice, 309
on role of violence in abolition, 334
on the transient and the permanent in
    religion, 101–107
Previous Question, The, 95–97
"Relation of the Bible to the Soul,"
    97–101, 109
Review of *Das Leben Jesu*, 85–88
"Some Thoughts on the Free Soil Party,"
    189–91
"Speech at the New England Anti-Slavery
    Society Convention," 202–3
past, the. *See also* historical awareness;
    historical distance; history
    and historical distance, 184
    as archaic, 4, 5
    attempts to restore, xvi, xxii, 5, 23, 26,
        72, 98, 133, 143, 155, 166, 168
    claiming principles from, 4
    connection with present, 3, 11, 121, 272,
        348, 352, 353, 355
    differences from the present, 5
    effects on the present, xv, 354
    favored pasts, 3, 8, 330, 331, 332,
        342, 351
    relevance of, 8
    use in interpretation, 27, 39
    values of, 26
Phillips, Mark Salber, 6
Phillips, Wendell
    and anticonstitutionalism, 253
    and constitutional interpretation,
        176–79
    biographical details, 121, 176
    on black revolutionaries, 323–24

polygamy
    in the Bible, 117, 122, 125
    parallels to slavery, 117, 121, 125, 130, 184
popular constitutionalism, 169, 202, 251, 258, 259, 268, 272, 295, 297, *See also* Spooner, Lysander
    and the Supreme Court, 177
    effects of, 274
    rise of, 93, 163, 206, 290–91
    spread of, 186
popular sovereignty, 274, 283, 284
    rise of, 290–91
postmodernism, 86
Prager, Dennis, xx–xxi
prejudice, 343
    and egalitarian efforts, 266, 309, 311, 313, 327
    and stereotypes, 322
    and the role of white Americans in its spread, 312
    as a precursor to change, 304, 312
    historicization, 303
    in the military, 309
    post Civil War, 323, 343
    role in slavery, 303, 342
    spread of, 312
Presbyterianism, 29, *See also* Graham, Sylvester; Granger, Arthur; Hodge, Charles
    and biblical interpretation, 29, 30, 65, 68
    and historical awareness, 65
    divide of, 122, 129, 134
presentism. *See also* historical distance
    and biblical interpretation, 137
    and constitutional interpretation, 137
    criticism of, 64, 238, 257–58
    shortcomings of, xvii, xviii, 43, 48, 52, 58, 59, 98
    use in biblical interpretation, 45
Prigg v. Pennsylvania, 191, 236
    use of James Madison's *Papers* in, 163
Princeton, 62
proslavery arguments
    arguments from constitutional interpretation, 278, 295
    criticism of, 208, 259
    effects on constitutional interpretation, 216
    growth of sentiment, 193, 275, 289
    sentiments in the Bible, 180, 294
    sentiments in the Constitution, 177, 180, 181, 259, 294
    spirit of the founding era, 239
    victories, 194, 204, 216, 220, 256, 277, 278, 295, 297
Protestantism. *See also* colonial era, the; Puritans; Reformation, the; religion
    beliefs of, 110
    position on slavery, 121
providentialism, 302, 321, 334, 336, 348
Puritans, 9, *See also* colonial era
    beliefs of, 23
    effects on American history, 9
    restoring favored past, 72
Purvis, Robert
    and anticonstitutionalism, 253
    on slavery in the Constitution, 315

racism, 342, 353, 354
    and the Supreme Court, 240
    growth of, 257
    in American society, xiv
    in antebellum America, 280
    in the founding era, 231, 274
    in the past and present, 352
Radical Abolition Party, 222, 288, *See also* Douglass, Frederick
rationalism, 81, 82, 84
Reformation, the, 31, *See also* Calvin, John; Luther, Martin
    results of, 72
Reid, Thomas
    and biblical interpretation, 37–38
religion. *See also* Baptists; Bible, the; Catholicism; Congregationalism; debates, biblical; interpretation, biblical; Methodism; Presbyterianism; Protestantism; Puritans; Unitarianism
    and abolition, 17, 321, 333
    and biblical interpretation, 29–30
    and law, 109, 119
    and the Constitution, 208
    and truth, 98, 100, 101, 106
    conservative, 60, 63, *See also* biblical debates; Calvinism
    divide between liberal and conservative, 47, 49, 55, 57, *See also* debates, biblical; Morse, Jedidiah
    divide over slavery, 115, 124
    effects on historical awareness, 14–15, 16
    evolution of, 95, 96

God's role in slavery, 148, 149, 192,
    200–1, 218, 220, 227, 287, 290, 295
  gospel principles in the Declaration of
    Independence, 156, 190
  in antebellum America, 20, 21, 29,
    30–31
  liberal, 109, 117, *See also* debates,
    biblical; Transcendentalism;
    Unitarianism
Remond, Charles
  on black Americans' role in a second
    revolution, 326
Republican Party, 223, *See also* antislavery;
    Lincoln, Abraham
  and antislavery, 164
  beliefs of, 277, 287
  criticism of, 251
  stances of, 250
Republicanism
  effects on historical awareness, 14
Revolutionary War, the. *See also* founding
    era, the
  as American turning point, 9, 11
Rigdon, Sidney
  and historical distance, 67
Roane, Spencer
  and criticism of John Marshall, 146
  and states' rights, 146
Rock, John Stewart
  on black bravery and white prejudice,
    321–323

sacralization
  and historicization, 11, 17, 136, 156, 157,
    158, 163, 164, 205
sacred texts, 3, 4, 332, *See also* Bible, the;
    Constitution, the
  and desacralization, 269
  and slavery, 13
  as obsolete, 329
  debates surrounding, 329
  interpretation of, 8, 348
  relevance of, 8
Seidman, Louis Michael, xvii, 348–49
Schelling, Friedrich Wilhelm Joseph, 81
Scott v. Emerson, 233–35
Scott v. Sandford, 236, *See also Dred Scott*
    decision, the
Scott, Dred. *See also Dred Scott* decision,
    the; *Scott v. Sandford*
  biographical details, 232

second revolution, 316, 318, 325, 326,
    327, 328
  needed for emancipation, 302, 304, 313
  role of blacks, 328
Semler, Johann Salomo
  and biblical interpretation, 36–37, 58
Shalev, Eran, 17
Sims, Thomas, 213–14, 292, 307, 324
Slave Power, the
  and its demise, 266
  and originalism, 168
  and President James Buchanan, 235
  and Roger B. Taney, 235
  and the Fugitive Slave Law, 185
  and the Kansas–Nebraska Act, 185
  and the Supreme Court, 291
  as anachronistic, 85, 119, 169
  criticism of, 166, 168, 218, 219, 230,
    273
  effects of, 173, 275, 296
  efforts to destroy, 164
  growth of, 11, 185, 194, 202, 265
  influence of, 301
  influences on, 266
  progress of, 289
  rise of, 25, 26, 137, 169, 173, 175, 179,
    190, 191, 212, 230, 258, 263, 299,
    330
slavery. *See also* abolition; antislavery; black
    Americans; Fugitive Slave Law, the;
    interpretation, biblical; interpretation,
    constitutional; Kansas–Nebraska Act,
    the
  and biblical debates, 17, 18, 21, 22, 26,
    31, 53, 332
  and biblical interpretation, 51, 148, 329,
    See also interpretation, biblical
  and citizenship, 236
  and Congress, 227
  and congressional debates, 146
  and constitutional debates, 21, 22, 26, 53,
    138, 332
  and constitutional interpretation, 51
  and democracy, 127, 130, 169, 220
  and historical awareness, xxii, 24, 354
  and historical distance, 99
  and interpretation, 13, 329
  and laws, 130
  and morality, 113
  and retrogression in the south, 268
  and rights of slaves, 333

Index

slavery (cont.)
  and sacred texts, 22, 345
  and states' rights, 146–47, 149, 155, 164, 167, 215, 233, 239, 243, 247, 274, 283, 284, *See also* Freeport Doctrine
  and the Bible, 125
  and the Declaration of Independence, 238, 274
  and the founding fathers, xxi, 2, 51, 167, 283, 287
  and the importance of remembering it, 322
  and the Liberty Party, 167
  as anachronistic, 113, 115, 116, 118, 124, 127, 165, 185, 190–91, 204, 225, 243, 256, 282
  as archaic, 99, 126, 187, 191, 243, 252
  causing historical awareness, 13, 111, 354
  causing religious divides, 115, 124, 129
  constitutionality of, 151, 173, 184, 186, 209, 224, 225, 229, 235, 241, 274
  contemporary views, 352
  criticism of proslavery arguments, 135, 171
  debates on, xv, xvi, xviii, xxii, 2, 6, 8, 11, 15, 16, 17, 18, 21, 22, 25, 26
  effects of spread of, 226
  effects on biblical interpretation, 46, 114, 116
  effects on constitutional interpretation, 216
  effects on historical awareness, 15, 16, 24, 25, 26
  effects on interpretation, 23, 24, 25
  effects on present-day America, xiv
  founding-era views on, 195
  founding fathers and, xvii
  God's role in, 148, 149, 192, 200–1, 218–19, 220, 227, 287, 290, 295
  growth of, 164, 169, 195, 243
  historicization of, 191, 243
  in colonial era, 9
  in the Bible, xix, xx, xxi, 4, 13, 17, 23, 26, 41, 43–45, 49, 51, 53, 70, 83, 93, 110, 111, 113, 114, 116, 117, 118, 121, 122, 123, 124, 125, 129, 130, 131, 132, 135, 148, 181, 191, 192, 196, 198, 200, 203, 331
  in the biblical era, 294
  in the Constitution, 13, 25, 174, 188, 193, 243, 281, 293, 298
  in the Constitutional Convention, 144
  in the founding era, 12, 25, 169, 179, 186, 191, 193, 226, 229, 236–37, 255, 261, 274, 282, 293, 294, 298
  justified by the Bible, 114, 128, 129, 132, 181, 183, 203, 294
  legality of, xv, xviii, 115, 120, 144, 149, 172, 173, 177, 192, 287
  morality of, 2, 110–11, 112, 114, 117, 120, 121, 123, 125–26, 127–29, 130, 134, 145, 149, 165–66, 197, 199, 200, 201–2, 211, 216, 224, 282, 287, 293, 336
  nationalization of, 277
  parallels to polygamy, 117, 121, 125, 130, 184
  proslavery arguments, 147–49, *See also* Calhoun, John C.
  proslavery arguments from biblical interpretation, 100, 126, 132, *See also* Fuller, Richard
  proslavery arguments from constitutional interpretation, 170
  rights of slaves, 229, 237, 242, 274
  slave catchers, 309
  southern attitudes on, 265, 336
  spread of, 25, 137, 146, 179, 187, 192, 193, 202, 220, 228, 282, 285, 297, 309, 328
  the Constitution as proslavery, 144–145
Smith, Gerrit
  and constitutional interpretation, 170–71
  biographical details, 170
Smith, Joseph
  and historical distance, 67
Somerset v. *Stewart*, 144, 173, 244
Spinoza, Baruch
  and biblical interpretation, 32, 34, 36
Spooner, Lysander
  and constitutional interpretation, 25, 173–75, 201, 330, 331
  and historical readings, 201
  biographical details, 173
  criticism of, 201
  Unconstitutionality of Slavery, The, 173–75
states' rights, 150, *See also* interpretation, constitutional; slavery
  and abolition, 243
  and citizenship, 245
  and originalism, 239

and slavery, 149, 155, 164, 167, 215, 233, 239, 243, 247, 274, 283, 284, *See also* Freeport Doctrine
constitutionality of, 199
vs federal power, 152
Stephens, Alexander H., 335
Story, Joseph
and authority of the Supreme Court, 146
Stowe, Harriet Beecher, 311
Strader v. Graham, 233, 236
Strauss, David Friedrich, 92, 95, 96, 97, 102
and biblical interpretation, 80, 82–88
Stuart, Moses
and biblical interpretation, 19, 29, 55–56, 57–61, 62, 70, 71, 96, 183, 196–98, 204
and biblical interpretation of slavery, 111, 181, 183, 196–99, 201, 204
and Congregationalism, 28, 55
and constitutional interpretation, 58, 198–200, 204
biographical details, 55, 196
Conscience and the Constitution, 196–200
criticism of, 56–57, 202
supernaturalism, 68, 84, 87
Supreme Court, the. *See also* Dred Scott decision, the; Marshall, John; *McCulloch v. Maryland*; *Somerset v. Stewart*; Taney, Roger B.
and constitutional interpretation, 145, 146, 177, 186, 207
and fugitive slave cases, 191, *See also* *Prigg v. Pennsylvania*
and popular constitutionalism, 177
and proslavery decisions, 236, *See also* Curtis, Benjamin Robbins
and racism, 240
and the Slave Power, 291
as solver of slavery crisis, 228
authority of, 146, 177, 186, 207, 274, *See also* Story, Joseph; Webster, Daniel
criticism of, 146, 221, 250
effects of decisions, 143
fugitive slave cases, 185
justices. *See also* Catron, John; Curtis, Benjamin Robbins; Marshall, John; McLean, John; Story, Joseph; Taney, Roger B.
power of, 145–46, 207, 253
role of, 236
use of historical change in decisions, 233, 234

Taney, Roger B. *See also Dred Scott* decision, the
and constitutional interpretation, 25, 236–41, 259
and proslavery court decisions, 236
and *Strader v. Graham*, 233
and the *Dred Scott* decision, 93, 229–32, 235, 237–39, 248
and the Slave Power, 235
as Supreme Court justice, 21
biographical details, 236
criticism of, 235, 250, 251, 253, 255, 257–58, 259, 275, 282, 292, 293, 297, 299
support for, 273
views on slavery, 236
Tea Party movement
and originalism, xv
territories. *See* Congress:power of
Thoreau, Henry David
and the Bible, 183–84
and the Constitution, 183–84
and higher law, 221
Tittmann, Charles Christian
and biblical interpretation, 63–64
Transcendentalism, 272, *See also* Emerson, Ralph Waldo; Francis, Convers; Furness, William; Parker, Theodore; Thoreau, Henry David
and biblical interpretation, 24, 69, 71, 72–73, 77–79, 88–90, 100, 331
and Brown, John, 333
and German biblical interpretation, 73
and Unitarianism, 211
beliefs of, 73, 77, 81, 88–90, 92, 101
criticism of, 91, 94–95, 128
restoring favored past, 72
Trump, Donald
Make America Great Again, xvi, 353
Turner, James, 16

Unitarianism, 28, 29, *See also* Bellows, Henry Whitney; Cary, Samuel; Channing, William Ellery; Everett, Edward; Furness, William; Norton, Andrews; Parker, Theodore; rationalism
and biblical interpretation, 29, 30, 46, 48, 49, 56, 57, 59, 63, 68, 72, 88–90
and Transcendentalism, 211

Unitarianism (cont.)
  beliefs of, 47, 77, 88–90
  criticism of, 82, 101
  division of, 88
  rise of, 46
United States, the. *See also* dissolution;
    disunionism
  divide of, 193, 194, 235, 258
  national decline, 175, 189, 201, 209,
    259–60, 279–80, 286, 287, 288,
    See also morality:moral decline
  national progress, 143, 146, 163, 165,
    168, 209, 217, 225, 232, 277, 279–80,
    286, *See also* morality:moral progress

Van Dyke, Nicholas
  and constitutional interpretation, 149–50
  and states' rights, 147
voting
  and black Americans, 242, 243, 245,
    275, 298
  in the founding era, 298

War of 1812, the, 145
Washington, Madison
  and Douglass, Frederick, 305
Wayland, Francis
  and biblical interpretation, 26, 330, 331
  and biblical interpretation of slavery,
    121–22, 125–27
  criticism of, 122
  Domestic Slavery, 125–27
  relationship with coreligionists, 124
Webster, Daniel
  and authority of the Supreme Court,
    146
  and biblical interpretation, 192–93
  and constitutional interpretation,
    192–94
  and the Fugitive Slave Law, 193
  criticism of, 184, 194–96, 203
  Seventh of March Speech, 192–94
Weld, Theodore Dwight, 134, 219
  and biblical interpretation of slavery, 111,
    114, 115–117
  and constitutional interpretation of
    slavery, 115
  biographical details, 115
Whig Party. *See also* Palfrey, John G.
  and antislavery, 168
Whittier, John Greenleaf
  on black military service, 307–8,
    310, 311
Wills, Gary
  on Lincoln, Abraham and the
    Constitution, 339

CPSIA information can be obtained
at www.ICGtesting.com
Printed in the USA
LVHW050310090523
746485LV00001B/40